THE
MEMOIRS
OF
MRS LEESON.

IN THREE VOLUMES.

EDITED & INTRODUCED BY
MARY LYONS.

THE LILLIPUT PRESS, DUBLIN.
1995.

First published in 1995 by
THE LILLIPUT PRESS LTD
4 Rosemount Terrace, Arbour Hill,
Dublin 7, Ireland.

A CIP record for this
title is available from
The British Library.

ISBN 1 874675 52 X

Cover design by Jarlath Hayes
Set in 11 on 14 Elegant Garamond by
moi, *mermaid*TURBULENCE
Printed in England by
Hartnolls ltd

Contents

Abbreviations	VI
Introduction	VII
VOLUME I.	1
VOLUME II.	77
VOLUME III.	141
Table of Identification	253
Select Bibliography	268
Acknowledgments	272
Index of Place-names	273
Index of Persons	276

Benn, *History of Belfast*	Benn, George, *A History of Belfast*, 2 vols (London 1877–88)
British Library, *Gen. Cat*	*British Library General Catalogue of Printed Books*
Buck Whaley's memoirs	*Buck Whaley's memoirs including his journey to Jerusalem, writted by himself in 1797. Edited, with introduction and notes, by Sir Edward Sullivan* (London 1906)
Complete Peerage	Cokayne, George Edward & Gibbs, the Hon. Vicary, *The Complete Peerage of England, Scotland, Ireland, Great Britain, and the United Kingdom*, 12 vols (London 1910–54)
DNB	*Dictionary of National Biography*
Encyc. Brit.	*Encyclopaedia Britannica*
ESTC	*Eighteenth Century Short-Title Catalogue*
Exshaw	Exshaw, John, and successor publishers, *The English Registry ... or, a Collection of Lists ... fitted to be bound up with Watson's Almanack*
The Gorgeous Mask	Dickson, David (ed.), *The Gorgeous Mask: Dublin 1700–1850*
Gilliland's *Dramatic Mirror*	Gilliland, Thomas, *The Dramatic Mirror; Containing the History of the Stage*
Henry, Brian, *Dublin Hanged*	Henry, Brian, *Dublin Hanged. Crime, Law Enforcement and Punishment in late eighteenth-century Dublin.*
H of C Journal	Ireland—House of Commons, *Commons Journals of Ireland 1613–1800*
Landed Gentry	Burke, Sir John Bernard, *A Genealogical and Heraldic History of the Landed Gentry of Great Britain and Ireland* (9th edn)
Lewis, *Topography*	Lewis, S., *A Topographical Dictionary of Ireland*
O'Higgins, *Trials*	O'Higgins, Paul, *A Bibliography of Irish State Trials and other Legal Proceedings*
Rowan, Archibald Hamilton	*A brief investigation of the Sufferings sufferings of John, Anne, and Mary Neal*
TCD Alumni	*Alumni Dublinensis ...*
T.J.Walsh, *Opera in Dublin*	Walsh, Thomas Joseph, *Opera in Dublin, 1705–1797; the social scene*
Todd	Todd, Janet, *A Dictionary of British and American Women Writers, 1660–1800*
Watson's	Watson, John, and successor publishers, *The Gentleman's and Citizen's Almanack*
Wilson's	Wilson, Peter, and successor publishers, *Wilson's Dublin directory ... containing list of the names, occupations, and places of abode, of the merchants and eminent traders of the city of Dublin*

Introduction

Successful prostitutes plying their trade in the top end of the market rarely published memoirs. Confidentiality and discretion were always a standard part of the package offered to their clients. Ladies in that line of work came and went unseen. Their wives, fiancées and female relatives might have made educated guesses as to where they had been, but nothing would ever have been susceptible to proof, and no mistress or kept woman would ever have intruded on her lover's family life. Stylishly indiscreet behaviour was acceptable as a form of self-advertisement, so long as names, or, at any rate, most names, remained unnamed.

Late in 1794, and during the early months of 1795, gossip of a distinctly worrying nature was circulating in Dublin as Margaret Leeson prepared her memoirs for publication. Many of her ex-clients would have been worried and perplexed. Some might even have felt betrayed. Wives who had retained control of their own property, and fiancées whose fortune was an integral part of their attraction, might see a husband or a suitor in a new and rather startling light. Personal peculiarities were likely to be paraded in print. The text would probably contain a lot of interesting, amusing, and extremely unfortunate anecdotes. Then the ex-clients might have paused. Surely something like this was unnecessary. Mrs Leeson had run an elegant establishment in Pitt Street. She numbered two Lords Lieutenant among her clients. Her diamonds, her dresses, her servants, her girls and her carriages had been the talk of the town. Above all, she had been a beauty. A wealthy and beautiful demi-mondaine like Margaret Leeson would hardly be prepared to behave like a cheap blackmailer.

Memoirs: Genre and Motivation

Writers who publish their autobiographies rarely do so because they have been suckled on the milk of human kindness. Frequently they are driven by an urge to set the record straight, to avenge themselves, and to expose the villains who have made their lives a living hell. The sheer adversity and unpleasantness that often makes these lives such compelling copy is generally associated with poverty. Letitia Pilkington's *Memoirs* are an early and fairly typical example.[1] Her father was a well-to-do Dublin physician. She had an easy and reasonably pleasant childhood, but she made a foolish marriage to an impoverished clergyman, Mathew Pilkington. He was effectively a reverend gold-digger, and once he realized that his wife was unlikely to inherit from either parent, he took steps to ensure that he would be able to divorce her and remarry. Mistresses were flaunted, the children maltreated. Letitia, who was at best something of an innocent, was caught with a man in her bedroom. The Reverend Pilkington did not succeed in divorcing his wife, but he made it impossible for her to remain in Dublin.

In London Letitia got by initially as a cross between a novelty turn and a mascot for the men who frequented White's, but that wasn't enough to give her a secure living. There were too many people ready to prey on a displaced woman in her position. There were grasping, thieving landladies, and few friends on whom she could rely. Samuel Richardson and Colley Cibber both stood by her, and it is quite likely that Cibber in particular encouraged her to publish her autobiography. She had a good story, and there were also anecdotes about Jonathan Swift (she and her husband had been regular dinner guests at the Deanery). She was determined to tell her story, and so much the better if it brought her in some hard cash. Teresa Constantia Phillips's autobiography, which covered similar territory, was also published in 1749,[2] and Mary de la Riviere Manley's *roman-à-clef, Atlantis*,[3] had shocked both literary circles in London, and the smart set at Court. Whatever about Mrs Manly, both Mrs Pilkington and Mrs Phillips wrote not only to expose, but also because they needed the money.

There was nothing menacing about an author like Mrs Pilkington. She wrote because she had to, and because her life was literally her last saleable asset. Some of the anecdotes concerning Swift were distressing,[4] and did represent a breach of privilege, but her capacity to damage persons other than her husband, like James Worsdale—the painter who had used her as an unpaid ghost-writer[5]—and her London landladies,[6] was strictly limited. However, by the end of the eighteenth century, a certain degree of menace had crept into the genre as a whole, not because there had been any single set of memoirs that caused widespread public scandal, but rather because of the implications of certain changes in the book trade relating to popular literature. This new sense of menace stemmed from the popularity of two of Samuel Richardson's novels, *Pamela* and *Clarissa*. A growing demand for sensationalism went hand in hand with a growth in the market for pulp fiction,[7] and by 1775 an unpleasantly explicit fictionalized account of a courtezan's life had been published.[8] John Cleland's *Fanny Hill* had become something of an erotic standard,[9] and by the end of the century there was also a rapidly increasing market for lurid, sensationalistic, and often fairly sexually explicit Gothic novels and novellas.[10]

Given Margaret Leeson's profession, and the growing market for explicit narrative, her ex-clients' fears might easily have been justified. In any event, a number of fairly explicit references to both prostitutes and clients involved in the Dublin vice trade had already been published in satirical poems from the 1770s, like *Abstracts from the companion to the grave*[11] and *Dublin: a satirical essay*.[12] Nor was Mrs Leeson alone in threatening to unleash potentially explosive memoirs on the Dublin market in the mid 1790s. Buck Whaley had fled to the Isle of Man, a disgraced bankrupt, in 1794.[13] Shortly after announcing of the forthcoming publication of his *Memoirs* he was able to commission the building of a large house for himself and his mistress just outside Douglas, and to buy himself a seat in the Irish House of Commons.[14] Published in 1906 his *Memoirs* would have ruffled few feathers, and would hardly have justified the most minimal of pay-offs. He may well have been involved in an elaborate game of bluff, in which the circulation, or probable circulation, of Mrs Leeson's text played a major role.

Margaret Leeson, on the other hand, was anything but a cheap blackmailer. Indeed, she would have taken extreme exception to that particular adjective. She had taken enormous pride in the furnishing of her house at Pitt Street,[15] the garden she constructed behind her Wood Street brothel,[16] and the lavish nature of the masquerades and parties in both of those establishments.[17] She was neither mean nor grasping, but by the time she began work on her *Memoirs*, she was poor and had lost her looks. Her orderly and well-planned retirement had turned into a fiasco. The last three years of her life were spent floundering in an ocean of debt when, prior to her retirement, she had always found money and credit easy to come by, and thrift had never been part of her *modus operandi*.

Some time after the death of Lady Arabella Denny in March 1792,[18] Mrs Leeson decided that she had had enough, that her clients and acquaintances were an utter shower, and that it was time to begin living a sober and godly life. Accordingly, she sold the house in Pitt Street, and moved to a house which she had commissioned in Blackrock, just off the Rock Road.[19] This new house was furnished with the proceeds of the Pitt Street sale.[20] However, her planning was fatally flawed. She assumed that she would be able to realize the money represented by her impressive collection of IOUs, without understanding the nature of her hold over her debtors. As long as she was managing the brothel, there was some chance that debtors would pay up. Prostitutes in late eighteenth-century Dublin had both formal and informal means of exchanging information on poor credit risks. Mrs Leeson had herself taken legal action against recalcitrant debtors,[21] and was one of the ladies present at what was effectively a prostitutes' AGM in 1776.[22] Retirement and this form of loose mutual benefit association need not have been incompatible were it not for the fact that she had also decided to reform, and to eschew both her former life-style, and her former colleagues in the Trade.

Things went from bad to worse. Late in 1794, or early in 1795, she was taken up by bailiffs, and lodged in a spunging-house, a private debtors' prison, run by one of her former lovers, Captain Benjamin Mathews, in Angel Court.[23] Her companion, Betsy Edmonds, and her mound of useless IOUs went with her to Angel Court. While there, she employed professional debt collectors in an attempt to recoup some of her losses. She believed that she had been cheated by these men, and in one instance[24] her suspicions appear to have been well founded. Even though she and Mrs Edmonds were well treated by Captain Mathews and his wife, the time spent in his spunging-house took its toll.[25] Mrs Leeson's appearance deteriorated to the extent that one of her former lovers, the Mr Purcell with whom she had holidayed in Killarney in the summer of 1789, was initially unable to recognize her.[26] Mrs Edmonds, whose health appears to have been frail, died in Angel Court.[27] Even the house in Blackrock, a central part of the retirement plan, became a casualty. It was leased to a lawyer, Charles Fleetwood, for a fraction of its real value as rented property.[28] With a few honourable exceptions, like Miss Love, Mr Purcell, and the Falveys,[29] most of her friends colleagues and associates melted away. After her release from Angel Court, the Falveys took cheap lodgings for her in Clarendon Street,[30] and she moved from these to even cheaper lodgings in the Temple

Bar end of Fownes Street, where she died in March 1797.[31] It was all a far cry from the glory days of Pitt Street.

Some Dublin businessmen helped her as best they could. She had been on friendly terms with the radical printer, Amyas Griffith, who drifted in and out of bankruptcy on a regular basis.[32] She socialized with another printer, Bartholomew Corcoran,[33] and a third printer, William Watson, was one of the few people who attended her funeral in St James's churchyard.[34] It is likely that the person to whom she sent the manuscript of the first two volumes of her *Memoirs* prior to publication was Christopher Lewis—perhaps related to Richard Lewis who advertised his services on a regular basis during the 1770s as a free-lance editor.[35] It is likely that these men would have actively encouraged her to write and publish her *Memoirs*, and despite her own assertions that the entire print-run of the first two volumes was sold merely by using *Watson's Almanack* and *Wilson's Directory* as mailing-lists,[36] it is likely that informal assistance in marketing the text might also have come from that quarter. She managed to finish the third volume of memoirs just before her death. It is clear from the text of this volume, that a fourth, and even more outrageous sequel was planned.[37]

The Vice Trade and its Social Context

In dealing with the vice trade in late eighteenth-century Dublin, it is important to remember that the working conditions and social status of individual prostitutes were closely linked to those of their clients. The market was broad, catering for almost all tastes and incomes, but the divisions between the various categories were fairly specific. Poor men would not have been able to afford women like Katherine Netterville, while wealthy men would probably not have retained the services of common street-walkers. The market ranged between these two extremes, with an important gap at the top end of its middle ground, in that there do not appear to have been any 'flash houses' operating along lines similar to those of either of Mrs Leeson's establishments in Wood Street and Pitt Street.

A fairly trenchant piece appeared in the *Dublin Evening Post*, on 14 September 1797, calling for measures to regulate prostitution in Dublin.[38] Although the author, probably John Magee, proprietor of the newspaper, was writing about the trade in general, his main target was the street walker. The *Post* had offices in College Green,[39] where the problem posed by these women was particularly severe. They solicited openly in daylight. Their behaviour was lewd and obscene. They were the means by which giddy unthinking youth was 'decoyed into debaucheries, and not infrequently into the robbery of their parents, masters, employers, or the public.'[40] But Magee's determination was to regulate rather than to suppress. What he really wanted was an end to the continuous din under his office windows, and a brothel district similar to that administered by Papal officials in Rome, where the brothels and the health of the women working in the vice trade was closely monitored. His College Green street-walkers may have been cheap, but they did pose an appalling public health threat. A similar picture of the lower end of the market is given in *Dublin: a satirical essay, in five books*. After a comprehensive catalogue of the type of rake one might expect to meet sauntering in Stephen's Green, the author then turns to the archetypical consumer, an apprentice working late, who

> Envy's the rake his sinful joys begun,
> And pants for liberty to be undone.[41]

The most he will be able to afford is the prostitute who lies shivering in a garret by day, and is given a strong slug of gin before being packed off by her bloated bawd to ply her trade. Even such clothes as she wore would have been hired from the bawd. The author's detailed description of women like these decked out in what little finery they had is positively chilling – a set of images even Hogarth might have baulked at drawing:

> Pale, thro' nocturnal riot and disease,
> In borrow'd charms the wretches try to please;
> With outward fin'ry and perfumes begin,
> To hide the stench and nastiness within;
> First on their meagre cheeks the crimson's laid,
> Then on their necks are pastes and washes spread,
> Where azure veins branch from the pencil's aid;
> Their rotten gums with purchas'd teeth adorn,
> And promise all the fragrance of the morn;
> Already feel the putrid hand of death,
> And add to their cadav'rous stench of breath;
> The pencil or a mouse's tail supplies
> The fine turn'd brows that ornament their eyes;
> Their lank long breasts pant am'rous to and fro,
> White-washed above and plump'd with clouts below ...
> Such are the nymphs who point to pleasure's way,
> Infest our streets and lead our youth astray:[42]

If a person of quality wanted to avail himself of the services of this type

of woman, like John Fitzgibbon he would probably have used an interme-
diary to make the initial contact, and would have made sure that she was
brought either to a discreet tradesman's entrance or the back-garden gate.[43]

Street-walkers always constituted the bottom rung of the ladder, and
women who worked in poor-class brothels associated with inns or flop-
houses would have served a very similar clientele. However, prior to Peg's
three ventures in brothel-keeping, exclusivity of possession (albeit tempo-
rary exclusivity) was really the hallmark of quality. A successful prostitute
was a courtezan or a kept woman rather than the manager of a flash house.
Peg's earliest rival, Katherine Netterville, seems to have been fairly typical
in this respect. Her obituary in the *Dublin Evening Post* on 17 May 1787
describes her in the following terms:

She figured for a long time in the *bon ton* – and absolutely made the fashion. It
was her practice to confine her favours to *one*, or in other words to select a tempo-
rary husband. In this state she lived with several gentlemen in a stile of fashionable
elegance – but before her death her circumstances were so narrowed, as to leave
her but little above indigence.[44]

At the zenith of her career, Mrs Netterville could afford to snap her fin-
gers at anyone else in the profession. Although she might not have been lit-
erate,[45] she had presence, style, and a touch of class. In *An heroic epistle,
from Kitty Cut-a-Dash to Oroonoko*, published in Dublin in 1778, she was
both the main subject of the satire, and its supposititious narrator.[46] Portray-
ing her as a superior temporary wife, the anonymous author provided a
form of justification in the following lines:

> With cleanliness and neatness have I try'd
> To seem, each new-born day, a new-made bride;
> Clean sheets, well air'd, were every night thy lot,
> Perfumed with Lavender and Bergamot;
> My caps nocturnal, Flanders lace display'd,
> My shifts were of the finest Holland made;
> The curtains were adorn'd with hov'ring loves,
> The gods at banquet, or in myrtle groves,
> Or with the nymphs retir'd to close alcoves.[47]

By contrast, her trade rival in the poem, Mrs Anne Judge, was depicted
as a slattern wench, whose client left her fee on the hall table,[48] whose cook
was greasy and stank of cabbage broth,[49] and who kept a revoltingly dirty
chamber pot in her front parlour.[50] Judge was also accused of promiscuity.[116]
Allowing for hyperbole and exaggeration, it is clear from this text that Mrs

Netterville would have seen herself as a woman providing a *de luxe* service. While quality might have been assured, the main drawback in keeping a lady like Netterville was her sheer extravagance,[51] and the fact that it was a continuous rather than a once-off commitment. An alternative, where the same high standards of cleanliness and presentation were maintained, but where there was no constant commitment to maintaining coaches, paying rent, and purchasing expensive presents was clearly preferable. Kitty Netterville was not the last of Dublin's classy kept women. Peg's biography of Margaret Porter indicates that Porter had a very similar *modus operandi*, and that she was probably successful enough to have acquired the Duke of Leinster as a keeper by 1796.[52] But there can be little doubt that the focus of the quality trade had shifted by the early 1780s, largely, one suspects, because of the success of Peg's Wood Street brothel. Although it could be argued that sole traders like Netterville and Porter were exceptions, it is clear that establishments like Moll Hall's brothel in Johnson's Court, and the Pitt Street house were handling this type of trade in bulk by the late 1780s.

Oddly enough, Netterville is not a major character in Mrs Leeson's *Memoirs*, and does not feature in the sequence of biographies of prostitutes given in the third volume. The main coverage given to her is confined to incidents which probably occurred in the 1760s, like the row over Lambert,[53] and an account of an excursion to the Curragh which occurred before John Lawless went to America.[54] Her last appearance in the text is as one of the ladies taking tea in Pitt Street when the Duke of Rutland arrived. That in itself is an indication of decline: an admission that Peg had triumphed. It was not indigence in Broadstone,[55] as poor dependants would not have been on display in Pitt Street, but it was an indication that she was no longer the leader of the pack.

The middle ground of the market is less easy to define. It ranged from brothels in Ross Lane serving the legal profession,[56] to madams like Mrs Brooks in Trinity Street and women like Biddy Orde in Great Britain Street.[57] It's quite clear from Peg's account of the evacuation of the house in Trinity Street when fire broke out that she did not consider this to have been a well-run establishment. Miss Russell, one of Brooks's girls, and her client were naked. By inference, this was a piece of slovenly practice that would not have been tolerated in Pitt Street. Brooks did manage to recover from the financial disaster of the fire, and to retire with enough to support her through old age.[58] Bridget Orde, whose brothel in Great Britain Street would have been a house of convenience for patrons frequenting the New Rotunda Gardens, was dealt with in less flattering terms. Hers was a rags to comparative riches story. Her father, John West, kept a lodging house in Cook Street where she served as a cross between a valet and a skivvy.[59] She was seduced by a Mr Fetherstone when she was fourteen, and lived with him for three years as his kept woman. She then had sexual dealings with the Duke of Rutland, and managed with her parting present from Fetherstone to purchase a house in Queen Street. This was the base from which she operated as a procuress. Two of her lovers, a Mr Graham and a Mr Orde, who had property in the West Indies, helped her get set up in Great Britain Street, and by 1796 she was living with Orde in a larger house on the same street, running a successful, if somewhat downmarket, brothel. Mrs Brooks or Mrs Orde may well have succeeded where Margaret Leeson failed, simply because overheads would have been less of a problem in a more modest establishment, and because the flow of money into a less fashionable house would not have been such as to lull the madam into a false sense of financial security.

The price of market dominance was constant stylish publicity. Not only potential clients, but also the populace of Dublin at large had to be kept aware of the presence and style of a major brothel keeper. It wasn't enough to exist: one had to be seen to exist as flamboyantly as possible. If a client bought wine for Mrs Leeson, he bought her champagne. It wasn't that she particularly liked champagne, but it was the most expensive wine available, and she felt that her clients would probably value the experience in proportion to its price tag.[60] She and her girls had to be exquisitely turned out. Being the first woman in Dublin to wear a bell-hoop was as much an advertising statement as it was a fashion statement.[61] Drapers anxious to sell fabric would have promoted the trend. Respectable matrons and their daughters would have imitated her without any qualms. Men looking at other women wearing bell-hoops would have been reminded of the fact that Peggy was back in town, ready and willing to trade. Girls working in her establishments also had to look the part. This might occasionally involve an element of risk in terms of outlay, as was the case with Kitty Gore,[62] but it was an unavoidable expense, in that the image of the establishment had to be maintained. The same might be said of Peg's retaining of Isaacs, the dulcimer player,[63] or her constant presence in the Theatre Royal, surrounded by her girls, sitting in the best seats that the house could offer.[64] It all added to the potency of product image in a market where direct advertising would have been out of the question, like the ruby-faced coachman, the suite of servants, and the sheer opulence of Pitt Street.[65]

Her one attempt to sneak into *Wilson's Directory* disguised as a school-mistress ended in failure.[66] She then turned failure into a stylish joke by reapplying, on the grounds that her brothel was a school dedicated to teaching students the mysteries of nature. M'Crea did not relent, and Peg never got her *Directory* entry. However, one suspects that Peg's friends and clients would have extracted the maximum amount of amusement possible from the entire episode, reading M'Crea's letters and possibly even helping Peg frame her justification in suitably pedagogic language. Her attendance at the Hughes benefit masquerade dressed as Artemis, goddess of chastity, would have been a joke in a similar vein to the baiting of M'Crea, but she was also conscious of the need to be seen at popular public entertainments. She was at Ranelagh Gardens in January 1785, for the first balloon ascent of her old antagonist, Richard Crosbie, and made sure that she was seen shaking hands with him immediately before the actual ascent. She also attended the Mugglin Festival at Dalkey,[68] was on the quayside to see off Buck Whaley when he departed for Jerusalem,[69] and went to John Magee's La Bra Pleasura pig-racing and freak show at Fiat Hill in Blackrock.[70] The sum total of all this activity was an occasional mention in one or other of the Dublin newspapers, or a more extended notice for herself or the establishment in a piece of satire: little enough, but better than nothing.

Text and Apparatus

Mrs Leeson's *Memoirs* were published in three volumes, between 1795 and 1797, and the third volume was reissued as a half-price remainder, with a new title-page and additional prefatory matter in 1798. Only one copy of the *Memoirs* is known to survive, that held in the Joly Collection of the National Library of Ireland. The 1798 reissue of volume three is also part of this Collection. No copy of the poem *A Guide to Joy*, written in praise of the Pitt Street brothel by Mrs H. of Drumcondra, and offered to purchasers of all three volumes of the *Memoirs*[71] is known to have survived. In terms of identification, both the reissue of volume three, and the 1797 volume three held by the National Library are extremely important. When the third volume was reissued, no attempt was made to reprint either of the other two, but their contents were abridged, and included in a long preface. Some names given only in part in the text as published in 1795, are given in full in this preface. The 1797 edition of volume three is even more important, in that a significant number of the names in part given in this text were given in somewhat fuller form in a series of annotations in a contemporary or near contemporary hand.

Problems posed by the mechanics of editing the *Memoirs* relate primarily to matters of presentation, but also to the way in which the third volume was written and published. The first two volumes were quite clearly worked over by an editor prior to publication in 1795. Whether or not this work was mainly done by Christopher Lewis,[72] the effect is such that there is a considerable disparity in style between the text published in 1795, and the third volume posthumously published in 1797. The first two volumes have all the conventional subdivisions of book within volume, and chapter within book. Volume three, which contains much more interesting material than either of the first two volumes, is written almost as a single block of prose. It has relatively few paragraphs, and only one major textual subdivision, the Eccentricities, a series of stories and anecdotes interposed by Mrs Leeson between the narrative concerning the end of her active career as a madam, and the vicissitudes of her retirement. Although the writing in this volume is powerful and elegant, the appearance of the prose was both unwieldy and unwelcoming to the eye. That said, its sheer quality is such that I wished to tamper as little as possible with its original integrity. Accordingly, I have imposed the chapter as the least intrusive of artificial subdivisions. This has broken the monumental quality of the text as printed in 1797, without interfering with the thrust or the style of the author's narration. Had Mrs Leeson been in a position to have seen this text through the press herself, it is likely that further subdivisions might have been imposed, but even without additional paragraphing, the text still reads well. Apart from the capitularization of the third volume, no other alterations have been made to the basic text. Volume two has a certain disjointed quality to it, and would have been tightened as a narrative with the exclusion of the letters. However, it is clear that the author intended to include the first section of correspondence, and that she was easily persuaded into providing more of her ex-lover's letters to form an appendix.[73] As such, the letters are part and parcel of the way in which she chose to tell her own story, and, as she herself would have argued, they do cast considerable light on the characters of Lawless, Gorman, and Cunninghame.

The second presentation problem concerned the names in part, and whether or not to footnote the text of the *Memoirs*. As Mrs Leeson herself provided footnotes of her own, direct annotation would have necessitated a system of parallel footnotes at certain points in the text. This seemed to be an unduly cumbersome solution. I also found myself unhappy with a solution to the problem of the names in part involving the insertion of the missing elements of the name in the text, enclosed in square brackets. This type of insertion implies a uniform degree of certainty, which would be inappropriate where the identification was at best tentative, as in the case of Mrs H., the fat Sappho of Drumcondra.[74] Mrs Leeson describes this lady as one of the Prince Regent's earliest mistresses, living by the 1790s in retirement in Drumcondra, holding literary soirées, and occasionally writing and attempting to perform her own poetry. She is unidentifiable from any of the standard biographies of George IV. No collection of her work appears to have been published during her time in Dublin, and no advertisements seem to have survived for her one public reading in the Exhibition Rooms in South William Street. All we know from Mrs Leeson's text is that she visited Mrs H. on the evening of the robbery and assault,[75] and that the lady was probably not among those present at Mrs Leeson's own funeral. Late eighteenth-century burial registers are no longer extant for the Parish of Drumcondra although a tombstone in the churchyard records the death of a Mrs Robert Hill in December of 1796. An identification cannot be based on this type of evidence. Accordingly, it seemed best to provide a separate Table of Identification, dealing with names in part, surnames given with addresses and occupations, and titles as and when they occurred in the text, with appropriate references following the actual identification. Reproduction of names in part in the text of the *Memoirs* has been kept as close as possible to the setting of the original. This was not difficult, as the number of dashes and long dashes bore no direct relationship to the number of letters omitted from any of these names. Single dashes have been retained wherever they occurred, and the long dash has been standardized.

There were also problems concerning verification that apply specifically to the biographical sections of volume three. No other writer would have had Margaret Leeson's fairly specific interest in the other members of her profession. None of the ladies whose lives form the subject matter of these cameos appear to have written their memoirs, or to have acquired newspaper coverage in the *Freeman's Journal* or the *Evening Post*. Nor were they of any interest to Sir Jonah Barrington, John O'Keeffe or Michael Kelly.[76] However, it is unlikely that her account of the lives of women with whom she worked, or who were her rivals in trade would have contained serious inaccuracies, given that she planned to write a fourth volume of memoirs.

Inaccuracy of that sort would have damaged both her credibility and her potential market for any sequel.

Political Bias

Margaret Leeson was first and foremost a businesswoman. She might have occasionally have indulged herself in a grand gesture, like telling the Earl of Westmorland to take his custom elsewhere, or letting the Prince Regent know precisely what she thought of his airs and graces,[77] but this type of reaction on her part seems to have been the result of a whim, or a dislike taken on the spur of the moment. She wrote her *Memoirs* in an attempt to provide herself with an income on which to live, and with a possible secondary agenda of shaming some of her debtors into settling their account with her. In as much as she had political leanings, she appears to have been what would now be described as liberal with a lower case 'l', but even in this she was not consistent. That she thought highly of the radical printer Amyas Griffith, who may or may not have been one of her clients, is clear from the text of her *Memoirs*.[78] It is also clear that she respected John Magee, proprietor of the *Dublin Evening Post*, the main opposition newspaper in Dublin.[79] However, she was extremely fond of the Duke of Rutland,[80] and also listed Francis Higgins, the proprietor who turned the *Freeman's Journal* into a Castle Print, among her friends.[81] Radicalism was no guarantee of her friendship. Miles Duignan, better known as Citizen Duignan, was a man whom she hated and despised, not because of his politics, but because he had disrupted the lying-in-state of her friend and colleague Moll Hall, to distrain on her goods and chattels.[82]

There was only one area where she might have been described as having any discernible bias. Margaret Leeson was a Catholic. She liked and admired Henrietta Battier, the campaigning journalist and satirist, who attacked John Fitzgibbon, Lord Chancellor of Ireland and Earl of Clare, in *The Gibbonade*.[83] Fitzgibbon was committed to opposing any further repeal of penal legislation directed against Roman Catholics. His opposition to reform led to rioting in Dublin in 1793 and 1794.[84] Mrs Battier also wrote against the rise of the Orange Order and Orangism in Dublin.[85] But it is far more likely that Mrs Leeson's admiration for this courageous satirist was nothing more than the response of one witty and outspoken author to another.

NOTES

1 *DNB* entry for Letitia Pilkington, and also *Memoirs of Mrs Letitia Pilkington, ... written by herself.* ..., 2v. Dublin printed: and London reprinted, 1749, hereafter Pilkington, *Memoirs*. A third volume of Mrs Pilkington's *Memoirs* was published in 1750. The text of that volume used is that found in Iris Barry's edition of all three volumes, *Memoirs of Mrs Letitia Pilkington* (London 1928), hereafter Pilkington (ed. Barry) *Memoirs*.

2 Mrs Manley's *The new Atlantis*, a satirical and effectively libellous novel attacking both Tory and Whig politicians, was published in 1709, its sequel, *The adventures Rivella, or the history of the author of Atlantis*, in 1714.

3 Teresa Constantia Phillips, *An apology for the conduct of Mrs T.C. Phillips, more particularly that part of it which relates to her marriage with an eminent Dutch merchant.*, 3vols (London 1748–9).

4 Pilkington, *Memoirs*, Vol. I, p.65 and Pilkington (ed. Barry), *Memoirs*, Vol. III, pp416–21.

5 Pilkington, *Memoirs*, Vol. I, pp249 *et passim*.

6 Pilkington, *Memoirs*, Vol. II, pp142–3 (Mrs Smith of Fleet Street) and pp193–220 (Mrs Trifoli of Duke Street).

7 James Raven, *British fiction 1750–1770 a chronological check-list of prose fiction printed in Britain and Ireland* (Newark 1987).

8 *Memoirs of a demi rep of fashion; or the private history of Miss Amelia Gunnersbury.* ... 2vols (London 1775). A Dublin edition was published in 1776 (*ESTC*).

9 Two editions of *Memoirs of a woman of pleasure*, the original title of the novel now known as *Fanny Hill*, were published in London in 1749. Abridged versions of the text were published in 1750, 1755, and 1784. A French translation, *Nouvelle traduction de Woman of pleasur ou fille de joye de m. Cleland contenant les memoirs de Mlle Fanny* was published in 1770, and two different French abridged versions of the text appeared in 1776, both with false London imprints (*ESTC*).

10 Montague Summers, *A Gothic Bibliography* (London 1941).

11 *Abstracts from the companion to the grave; or, every man his own undertaker* (Dublin 1778).

12 *Dublin: a satirical essay in five books. By a young author* (Dublin 1788).

13 *Buck Whaley's memoirs*, ppxxi–ii.

14 *Ibid.*, ppxxii–iii.

15 See below, Leeson, *Memoirs*, p.143.

16 *Ibid.*, p.87

17 *Ibid.*, pp94ff, 145ff.

18 *Ibid.*, p.224, and for Lady Arabella Denny's obituary, the *Dublin Evening Post*, the 20 March 1792, p.[3]C.

19 See below, Leeson, *Memoirs*, p.229.

20 *Ibid.*, p.229.

21 *Ibid.*, p.221, and also the *Dublin Evening Post*, 18 October 1788. p.[3]A, a

report of a case brought by Mrs Leeson at the Tholsel Court before the Recorder against 'a gentleman for the recovery of a trifling debt'.

22 *Freeman's Journal*, 17 October 1776, p.96C.

23 See below, Leeson, *Memoirs*, p.233.

24 *Ibid.*, p.238, and also the Table of Identification.

25 See below, Leeson, *Memoirs*, pp233–40.

26 *Ibid.*, p.236.

27 *Ibid.*, p.239.

28 *Ibid.*, p.203.

29 *Ibid.*, pp236–8, 240–1, 257.

30 *Ibid.*, p.241.

31 *Ibid.*, pp250–1.

32 *Ibid.*, see Table of Identification, note for p.145.

33 *Ibid.*, p.167, 198.

34 *Ibid.*, p.251.

35 *Ibid.*, pp134–5, and also the Table of Identification.

36 See below, Leeson, *Memoirs*, p.243.

37 *Ibid.*, p.246.

38 *Dublin Evening Post*, 14 September 1797, p.[2]A.

39 41 College Green

40 *Dublin Evening Post*, 14 September 1797, p.[2]A.

41 *Dublin: a satirical essay, in five books. By a young author*, p.49.

42 *Ibid.*, p.50.

43 Henrietta Battier, *The Gibbonade: or, political reviewer. First number. The second edition* (Dublin 1794), p.26 'Accommodating B[oyd] will yet procure/ Some Cyprian myrtle, at the garden-door,/Of His great patron, and obsequious wait/For further authors at the stable gate.'

44 *Dublin Evening Post*, 17 May 1787, p.[3]B.

45 *Dublin Evening Post*, 24 December 1779, p.[1]C, THE HUMBLE PETITION OF THE SISTERHOOD, a free-trade squib, with suppositious authors Sally Hayes, Anne Judge, Peg Plunket and P. Austin, was supposedly also endorsed by Mrs Netterville – 'KITTY CUT-A-DASH X her mark, *late of Grafton-street*', as though she was illiterate. The author of the squib may, however, have been tilting at the author of *An heroic epistle*.

46 *An heroic epistle from, Kitty Cut-a-Dash to Oronooko. The second edition* (Dublin 1778).

47 *Ibid.*, p.3.

48 *Ibid.*, p.18. 'You had ascended, ere I cross'd the way,/And on the board four weighty guineas lay:/The shining present could I help but grudge,/When, 'pon my honour, one were much for J[udge]!'

49 *Ibid.*, p.21, Juno about to do battle with Venus, Mrs Netterville's champion, in the guise of Mrs Judge's cook – 'And now she entered at the parlour door;/One hand a shovel, one a dishclout bore,/With cabbage broth surcharg'd, which instant sped/A missive weapon at fair Venus' head.'

50 *Ibid.*, p.23. '... a jordan, of a size uncommon,/More fit for giantess than honest woman,/A reservoir, heb-domidal, I see,/With ordure thick replete and chamber-lie'.

51 *Ibid.*, p.18. 'And in that choice of culls she was not nice;/But seiz'd on whomsoever she could set,/The Proverb says, "all fish come to her net".'

52 See below, Leeson, *Memoirs*, pp50–2, 63ff.

53 *Ibid.*, p.182.

54 *Ibid.*, pp63ff.

55 *Ibid.*, pp50–2.

56 *Ibid.*, p.143. Mrs Netterville died at Broadstone, a virtual pauper. *Dublin Evening Post*, 17 May 1787, p.[3]B.

57 *Abstracts from the companion to the grave; or, every man his own undertaker; ...*, Dublin 1778, p.29. 'All Abbesses and Nuns in Town/From Cutadash to Vestals down,/Who in their Temple at Ross-lane/Are sacred to the Legal Train.'

58 See below, Leeson, *Memoirs*, pp145–7, 165–6.

59 *Ibid.*, pp146–7.

60 *Ibid.*, p.165.

61 *Ibid.*, p.62.

62 *Ibid.*, p.87.

63 *Ibid.*, pp132–4.

64 *Ibid.*, p.113.

65 *Ibid.*, pp.144–5.

66 *Ibid.*, p.143.

67 *Ibid.*, pp173–4.

68 *Dublin Evening Post*, 4 September 1788, p.[3]C, under the headline 'Dalky Excursion'. The Mugglin Festival, held in late August or early September, involved the mock coronation of the Mugglin King of Dalky.

69 'Whalley's Embarcation', from *Both sides of the gutter*, Dublin 1790, quoted by Sir Edward Sullivan in his introduction to *Buck Whaley's memoirs*, ppxxxi–v. Verse IX reads, 'And now behold upon the strand,/This cargo for the Holy Land,/Bears, lap-dogs, monkeys, Frenchmen—/Bear-leaders and dependents poor./Black Mark loung'd in the crew,/He'd nothing else to do:/Peg Plunket on her horse/Was surely there of course.'

70 See Sir Jonah Barrington, *Personal sketches*, Vol. I, pp405–6.

71 See below, Leeson, *Memoirs*, p.170.

72 *Ibid.*, pp134–5.

73 *Ibid.*, pp134ff.

74 *Ibid.*, pp169–70, and see also Table of Identification.

75 See below, Leeson, *Memoirs*, p.248.

76 Sir Jonah Barrington, *Personal sketches*, 3 vols (London 1827–32), John O'Keeffe, *Recollections of the life of John O'Keeffe, written by himself*, 2 vols (London 1826), and Michael Kelly, *Reminiscences of M.K. of the King's Theatre* (London 1826).

77   See below, Leeson, *Memoirs*, pp151–2, 84.

78   *Ibid.*, p.201, 210–11.

79   *Ibid.*, p.148, 169, 239.

80   *Ibid.*, pp144–5.

81   *Ibid.*, p.239.

82   *Ibid.*, p.171.

83   For a full listing of Henrietta Battier's *Gibbonades*, see the Select Bibliography.

84   See *DNB* entry for John Fitzgibbon, Lord Chancellor of Ireland and Earl of Clare.

85   Mrs Battier's response to John Giffard's *Orange a political rhapsody* (Dublin 1798), was *The lemon, a poem by Pat. Pindar* [*i.e.* Henrietta Battier]; *in answer to a scandalous libel, entitled The orange* (Dublin 1798). Mrs Battier's antipathy to John Giffard and his brand of strident Orangism would have been well known. It is likely that she may have a hand in the composition of the anti-Giffard verse satire, 'The Dog in Office', published by the *Dublin Evening Post*, on 17 April 1794, p.[3]A. However, it should also be noted that *The lemon*, though indubitably by Mrs Battier, might have been an attack on Robert Fowler, Archdeacon of Dublin, who can be identified as a possible author of *Orange: a political rhapsody, cf. The lemon*, pp4, 19–20.

MEMOIRS

OF

MRS. MARGARET LEESON.

WRITTEN BY HERSELF;

AND

INTERSPERSED WITH SEVERAL INTERESTING AND
AMUSING ANECDOTES,

OF SOME OF THE MOST STRIKING

CHARACTERS

OF

GREAT-BRITAIN AND IRELAND.

VOL. I.

REASON *preſcribes ſtrict Laws for giddy Youth*
But the warm temper leaps o'er cold Decree ;
And when once paſt the bounds that ſhould reſtrain,
Rambles at large, tho' conſcious it ſhould not.
Yet, let not Cenſure, with it's brow auſtere,
Too heavy fall upon the erring Fair.
He is a choice Divine, who practices
that which he teaches others.——'Tis by far
more eaſy to tell Twenty what to do,
Than be the One of Twenty who will do it.

DUBLIN:

PRINTED FOR THE AUTHORESS,
AND SOLD BY THE PRINCIPAL BOOKSELLERS.

M,DCC,XCV.

Book One

CHAPTER ONE

'Tis not in Empires and in States alone
That Power *enslaves th' attendants on a Throne;*
In Families *too oft we see its sway,*
Where petty Tyrants *will their Pow'r display.*
Intoxicated with a sudden rise,
They haughtily dissolve the dearest ties,
Wives, Children, Brothers, Sisters, all must bow,
To the imperious bending of the brow.
Kind Nature's tend'rest feelings, stifled all,
Tho' ruin follows, still they will enthrall,
To satiate an arbitrary pride
And vent a spleen, Justice and Truth decide.

MANY WERE, doubtless, the opinions of the public, when the appearance of this work was first announced; and most of them will possibly be found groundless. The Voluptuary perhaps expected to find here constant food for his inordinate desires, and fresh excitements to his passions – The Prudish were fearful that my memoirs would be totally *unfit to be read* by any female of delicacy – The Gay thought they might contain nothing but musty morals, grave declamation, dolorous lamentations and puling penitence – The solemn Pedant, was sure a woman's writings must be so void of erudition as to be unworthy the notice of the Literati – The prudent Parent declared they should be kept out of sisters' nieces' and daughters' sight, lest they should prove infectious – Whilst the antiquated Maidens, frequenters of the Tea and Card-tables, hinted they might take a peep *in private*, for they were sure my Book must offer some *nice tit bits*, and *delicious morsels* of scandal.

I dare presume to say that each of these conjectures will appear unsubstantial. Whilst I am careful not to pen a single line or use a single expression that can excite a blush on the most refined and delicate cheek; I shall yet endeavour to dimple it into a smile. Moral sentences have now lost their desired effect. Whilst Vice and Folly are best attacked by Ridicule, I shall not be any wise sparing of it, and I promise that my gravity shall not be so great as to set my readers asleep. As to my stile and diction – why – I must e'en leave them to the mercy of the Critics; only observing that my frequent conversations with some of the most learned and scientific of the College, must have rendered it above contempt.

A Female, so much acquainted with men and manners as myself, and so often the subject of public and private conversation, cannot sit down to fill the ever open-ears, and feed the ever-gaping mouth of Curiosity without some reflections. If she intends to be candid, she must necessarily expose some characters to Censure – but then their own conduct has drawn it upon them, and she stands acquitted at the Bar of Justice. She must portray her own faults and condemn her own errors – but if thereby she cautions others against falling into the like, she extends a public benefit. The Mariner is really indebted to the publisher of the Chart which points out the rocks, shoals and sands on which others have been wrecked; as thereby he may steer his vessel clear of them all, and attain the desired harbour of peace and safety. These considerations, joined to a wish of preventing sundry falsehoods being propagated (perhaps published) concerning me, were the motives of setting forth the truth; and from it I shall not swerve one tittle.

CHASTITY I WILLINGLY acknowledge is one of the characteristic virtues of the female sex. But I may be allowed to ask – Is it the only one? Can the presence of that one, render all the others of no avail? Or can the absence of it, make a woman totally incapable of possessing one single

good quality? How many females do we daily see, who on the mere reten-
tion of chastity, think themselves allowable in the constant exercise of every
vice. One woman may indulge in frequent inebriation, she may ruin her
husband, neglect, beggar, and set an evil example to all her children – but
she arrogates to herself the character of a *virtuous woman* – truly, because
she is chaste. A second female is a propagator of scandal, sets families
together by the ears, destroys domestic peace, and breaks the nearest and
dearest connexions – but all this is but a trifle – She is chaste, and the most
reputable and most pious will visit this virtuous woman. A third cheats at
cards, robs her unsuspecting and dearest friends of their health and time by
her midnight routes, and of their money by her frauds, – yet as she may be
chaste, she is a virtuous woman, and the wife of the parson of the parish
will take her by the arm and appear with her in public.

But, after all, it is more than possible that most females of the above-
mentioned classes, may be only chaste by chance, and may be totally igno-
rant whether they are so, or not – What! some modern Lucretia may cry
out, What! do I not know whether I am chaste or not? I answer, no! –
Have you ever been tried? Have you resisted importunity and opportunity
with a man you loved (for there can be no merit in resisting one you dis-
liked) and resisted from principle? If you have, I will allow you a just claim
to that appellation, but on no other terms – but enough of these reflections
for the present – let me commence my narration.

I drew my first breath at Killough, in the county of Westmeath, where
my father Matthew Plunket possessed a handsome property near Corbet's-
town. My mother was Miss A. O'Reilly, of a family related to that of my
father, and also of the Earl of Cavan. The fruits of their marriage were
twenty-two children, of whom eight only survived, three brothers, four sis-
ters and myself, who all received the best education the county could
afford. Whilst I was yet young, my eldest sister was married to Mr Smith of
Kinnegad, who then established a Malt-house and Brewery at Tullamore,
in the King's County; and my next eldest, married Mr Beatty, who kept a
China shop in Arran-street, Dublin. The family then consisted of only my
father and mother, three brothers and as many sisters; and living in an ele-
gant stile, with every amusement of music, dancing, and rural diversions;
happy in a close intimacy with the two sons and daughter of Mrs Darcy, of
Corbet's-town (our nearest neighbour) life glided on in the paths of inno-
cence and content.

But alas! a period was soon put to those Halcyon days, and sorrow, anxiety and death approached our door. My dear mother was attacked with a spotted fever, which carried her to the grave. At the first approach of this fatal disorder, my father, anxious for the lives of his children, sent us away from the infection, one of my sisters went to Mrs Smith at Tullamore, another to Mrs Beatty in Dublin, myself to an uncle in the county of Cavan, and my two dear youngest brothers were dispersed in the neighbourhood. My dear, worthy and tender eldest brother, preferring his duty to his safety, remained at home to attend his dying mother; but he caught the disorder, and died on the tenth day – Ah fatal death! the dire cause of all my wanderings, and the source of all my misfortunes.

After some months we all returned to our sorrowing father, our tears ceased to follow; we again lived in elegance, and a short-lived content; for my father was so desolate with the loss of his old partner, and his dearly loved eldest son; and so affected with the rheumatism, that finding himself unable to manage his affairs, he gave up the whole to his then eldest son, Christopher, on condition of his securing to his brother and sisters, the provisions that my father's paternal care had provided for each.

From that disastrous moment, what a change! the house having lost its mild and indulgent ruler by my father's surrender of his power, fell under the direction of one, who intoxicated with his newly acquired authority, knew not how to exercise it. Extravagant in the pursuit of his own pleasures, and penurious to the most innocent of those of his brother and sisters, he grudged them a shilling whilst he squandered pounds. The rein of parental control being taken from his neck, he became like an head-strong wild colt. And in short, sunk into an harsh, unfeeling cruel tyrant. My eldest unmarried sister, unable to bear his constant ill usage, besought her father's permission to go to Dublin, and reside a-while with her sister Beatty. The old gentleman whose greatest happiness consisted in procuring that of others consented, and she left a scene of discontent, oppression and misery. My brother Christopher thus lost one object, whereon to vent his tyrannic waspishness and over-bearing temper, but as the total sum of those ill qualities remained the same, he continued to exercise them on those who were left behind; so that each of us came in for a proportionably greater share than before.

It is highly probable that the ill usage we all received from Christopher, did not arise merely from the natural, unrestrained badness of his temper; but sprung also from another source. He had been constantly so indulgent to his own irregularities that the honest income of the house, but barely sufficed for the expences they drew upon him. His vices had made him extravagant, and his extravagance had rendered his receipts inadequate to his idle disbursements. When the property was made over to him, he was charged with certain provisions for his brother and sisters. The first was indeed, too young to become an immediate claimant, but he knew the girls were at, or nearly approaching to that period when a settlement in life might be required. When their marriage should take place, their portions must be paid, and this he studied to avoid; he having doubtless sunk deep into their property. He therefore artfully resolved to set his face against any proposal of that kind; and with a malignant cunning redouble his ill-treatment, in hopes it might drive them to a desperation, which might bring them to take steps, that might warrant his refusal of their property, that it might all center in himself. At least his conduct demonstrated plainly that such a motive might be justly ascribed to him – of this we had soon a very striking instance.

Whilst my eldest unmarried sister resided in Dublin (whither his ill usage had driven her) her accomplishments and person were too striking to be over-looked by several youths of equal, nay, superior rank. She had many admirers, amongst whom was a Mr Brady, a citizen of fair character in trade, and in an affluent situation. As my sister had permitted Mr Brady to make his proposals to my father, they came down to the country for that purpose. From every enquiry and examination, my father and all his neighbouring friends thought the match highly eligible; but Mr Christopher could not be prevailed on by any means to give his consent; which, as he stood in the light of a Guardian, was necessary for the payment of her fortune. Mr Brady quickly suspected the cause of his refusal was his wish to retain the property; and therefore to remove that obstacle, told him that her portion was no object to him; he wanted only an amiable woman for his wife, such as his heart approved, and with whom he might live happy and contented; he therefore would relinquish every pecuniary demand, and requested his consent to their union on those terms.

Mr Christopher doubtless was inwardly rejoiced at a proposal that met his wishes: But he was too cunning to make his satisfaction apparent. Had he done so he would have stood unmasked to the public: he therefore persisted in his refusal, declared he had very strong objections to the match, and he would never sanction it by his approbation. His father and they might settle the matter how they pleased, but for himself, he washed his hands of the business.

My sister, justly irritated at her brother's conduct, took the opportunity of speaking to him with greater spirit and asperity than she had ever done before. She declared that from the cruel and tyrannical treatment she had experienced from him since her mother's death, and her father's surrender of his affairs in consequence of his illness, she was resolved rather to earn her support by her own industry, nay even by servitude, than remain any longer subjected to his savage behaviour, and therefore his reign over her was at an end. At the same time she cautioned him that if he did not change his conduct, her sisters would soon be of her mind, let the consequences be what them may. They were daily advancing to maturity, would, from ill usage, imbibe a proper spirit, and neither would, nor ought to endure a twentieth part of what she had suffered. So saying, happy in her father's consent, and taught by Mr Brady to disregard that of her brother, the nuptials took place, and now the happy couple returned the next day to Dublin, taking me with them, to my great satisfaction; as I knew my brother Christopher too well to entertain even a distant hope, that he would be in the least amended by the spirited rebuke my sister had given him.

Whilst I was in Dublin, my time passed in pleasing scenes of delight; a constant round of company and amusements occupied the three months I staid there, which appeared to me but as so many days. At the end of that period I received a summons to return home. I was forced to obey, but I leave the reader to judge with what reluctance. I called to mind my past ill usage, which I foresaw was about to be renewed. I contrasted that with the tranquillity in which I had passed my time in town; and the result was a great and manifest depression of my spirits.

But I had another cause for my dejection, beside those above-mentioned. Young as I then was, I had attracted the notice of a gentleman who was frequently at Mr Brady's, his person was quite unexceptionable, and I began to feel emotions in my youthful breast, to which I had been hitherto a total stranger. I was to leave behind me him who had engaged much of my attention, and the very idea was distressing. However, soon after Mr O'Reilly (for that was his name) sent down proposals for me to my father; but they were rejected by prudent Mr Christopher, whose chief argument was that I was too young by five years at least, to enter into such an engagement; though to say the truth, in my own mind, I was of a contrary opinion, and thought myself old enough to be married – few girls of fifteen think otherwise! – However here ended this affair, the gentleman did not renew the attack, and as the wound I had received had not penetrated very deep, absence and a little time so compleatly healed it, that it did not leave even a scar behind, and I soon forgot him.

But such is the frame of the female mind, that when it has once received an impression, though that it may be effaced, it becomes more susceptible of another. So it was with me. Whilst I was in Dublin, Mr O'Reilly was not the only person who had beheld me with a favourable eye. Mr L—y, an amiable young gentleman of an independent fortune of four hundred pounds a year, had entertained an affection for me. He did not think writing would be so effectual to obtain his wishes, as a personal application; therefore, soon after the former lover had received his final dismission, he followed me into the country, and applied to my father. His character and fortune were favourable motives in the old gentleman's sight, but not so in the jaundiced eye of my brother Christopher, who had a thousand objections, and seemed determined neither to let me be happy or make any other person so, and brought my father over to his sentiments. My lover staid at my father's above a fortnight, and as he conceived a great and just dislike to my elder, he constantly attached himself to my younger brother, Garret, who was of a very opposite character. With him he frequently went on hunting and shooting parties; and in the latter I frequently joined. My presence was a spur of emulation to them, my lover wishing to please me and prove himself a good marks-man; and my brother desirous of shewing his superior skill.

Although I would have willingly consented to an union with this gentleman (who was really amiable, and had made considerable progress in my favour) yet there I was disappointed; my brother had artfully brought my father into his scheme of positive refusal; and Mr L—y, finding it useless to make farther application, took his last leave, and I heard of him no more.

The effects of Christopher's tyrannic temper manifested themselves daily. It was natural to wish for every temporary relief from the sufferings we underwent, and therefore we gladly accepted every invitation of neighbouring friends to pass a few days with them. My brother indeed, as if unwilling to lose any opportunity of exercising his cruelty, constantly refused every effort of the worthy Darcy's and Fetherstons of Dardistown, to get me and my sister with them. They therefore, addressed their invitations to my father, who never denied, and always sent us comfortably and genteely to the parties to which we were asked. But alas! we frequently paid dear for our pleasures on our return; for Christopher would seize every pretence to quarrel with us when we came back, and frequently horse-whipped and beat us in a most savage manner, so that our bodies were often covered with wheals and bruises; and I have been for days together confined to my bed from the exertions of his barbarity.

This treatment, constantly repeated, joined to the disappointment of every proposition of marriage, and the mocks, jeers and sarcasms cast upon me by my brother on that account, made me very low-spirited, I had no comfort in life but what arose from the melancholy, mutual condolements of my sister, and the tenderness of my good father: of that I could enjoy but little, as his age and infirmities generally confined him to his room, if not to his bed; and Christopher took care to keep us almost always employed. In this state of uneasiness, suffering, and discontent, I was lingering on; and my poor sister whose spirits were not so animated as mine, daily wasting away, when I happily got an invitation from my sister Smith, to spend some time in Tullamore with her. I eagerly embraced the opportunity of a temporary relief from ill usage; and, having obtained permission, went to her. To this even, my tyrant Christopher was not then averse. Perhaps, he thought the time I should be from home would be something saved in the expence of my maintenance, little as it was; and here the passion of avarice (which was daily increasing in him) counteracted his passion for cruelty, and he suffered one of his constant victims to be a while out of his reach.

CHAPTER TWO

HAVING NATURALLY a good flow of spirits, I was ever very lively when not under the immediate pressure of ill-treatment, or the dread of its approach. I therefore gave way to cheerfulness, and enjoyed much pleasure in Tullamore. The change of scene, and variety of company, speedily restored me from the languor into which I had fallen. Our frequent walking parties were delightful, and some of the military in the garrison constantly mixing with us, and shewing a politeness for which they are generally remarked, encreased the pleasure of our promenades. I had not been long in Tullamore, when a proposal for me was made to my brother-in-law,

Smith. The inamorato was not an object calculated either to flatter my pride, or engage my attention. He was a grocer, of a disgusting person, being ill made, hard-featured, with the countenance of a baboon, shabbily dressed, and to complete my dislike, wore a wig. This circumstance alone would have been sufficient to confirm a thorough dislike; for as I had been accustomed to view the smart, well powdered toupees of the officers, I could not separate the ideas of clownishness and a wig, however incongruous they might appear to others. But what gave my admirer merit in his own eyes, and emboldened him to a proposal for me, was that he was rich. But that was no charm to me when connected with so many ill qualities. It was in vain that my friends constantly extolled his goodness of heart, his great humanity, and his mild and gentle disposition: All this might be true, but he was a grocer, he was ugly, and – he wore a wig – insuperable objections.

But, to say the truth, I had another ground for my refusal of the perriwigged grocer – namely, a dawning attachment to another, and, in my youthful and giddy mind a preferable object. There lived in Tullamore, near to my brother, a Mrs Shannon, whose husband had been dead but a few months. With her dwelt a young man, who having served his time with her husband, now managed and conducted her business. He was really of a most engaging person and winning address, and from my first coming to town, had shewed me every possible mark of attention and respect, which, whilst it attracted my notice, did not escape the observation of the widow. She had sat him down as her own, and it seems only waited till decency would permit her to make him master of the business and of herself. She began to find that in proportion as his attention to me increased, it diminished with respect to her. She watched our looks with the eyes of jealousy; and being experienced in the silent language of Love, soon construed their real meaning. I also soon found how she was affected, and my pride was agreeably flattered at the preference that was so visibly given to me. In her person, she had indeed some pretensions to beauty, but I had greatly the advantage over her, in two capital points, namely, youth and vivacity. I enjoyed my conquest, and could not avoid secretly rejoicing at my triumph over her, and felt the greater pleasure in proportion to her apparent uneasiness. This attached me still more to my lover; and in spite of all Mrs Shannon's vigilance, we found frequent opportunities of conversing together in private. Whilst matters were thus depending, Mr Smith had conveyed the proposals of the grocer to my father. They had been duly considered in every point of view, and his formal consent was returned; with the proviso indeed, that I would give mine, and cordially agree to the match. Upon this reply my persecution, as I called it, was redoubled; but my aversion hourly augmented. My uneasiness at the constant solicitations of Mr Smith, and Mrs Shannon; my vexation at the unceasing application of the grocer; my dread of my brother's ill usage when I should return to Killough, which I doubted not would be soon, in consequence of my obstinate refusal; together with the affection I had conceived for Mrs Shannon's man of business, so wrought all together on my mind, and threw me into such a perturbation, that I thought I could avoid all these evils by no better means than by acceding to my lover's proposal, of going off to Mullingar, and there being married.

Having come to this determination, and acquainted my inamorato with my resolves, we were not long before we began to put them into practice. He, therefore, procured horses, and as soon as it grew dusk, we mounted and set off, accompanied by a friend of his. We never alighted till we came to Kilbeggan, where we stopped, only to take a slight refreshment of wine and cake, and bait the horses.

But alas! we had not taken our measures so secretly, but we were soon missed. Mrs Shannon's piercing eyes had discovered what my brother-in-law had not once perceived. She, with little less rage than that of tygress robbed of her whelps, ran to Mr Smith, acquainted him with her well founded conjecture, and urged him to a pursuit before the fatal knot should be tied, that would rob her for ever of the completion of what she had been so long endeavouring to accomplish. Strongly pressed by her, incited by the clamours of the grocer, his friend, and earnestly wishing to save me from what he thought an inadequate match, Mr Smith, attended by two friends, sat out after us; and we had not been a quarter of an hour in the Inn, at Kilbeggan, when our pursuers came to the door, and with pistols in their hands, broke into the room where we were. I was thrown into the greatest consternation, and utterly unable to reply to the reproaches of my brother-in-law, who insisted on my instant return, offering to tie my hands, and threatening to shoot me if I shewed the least reluctance. My lover had made his escape out of the back-window immediately on Mr Smith's entrance, and I was instantly brought like a condemned criminal, to the place from whence I came.

What short-sighted mortals we are! How frequently do we run into the very evils, we wish to shun, by the very steps we take to avoid them! My dread of returning to the control of an harsh unfeeling brother, had been my principal motive for the inconsiderate step I had taken; and that elopement hastened what I so much dreaded; for I was sent home to Killough the next morning. Indeed, Mr Smith had the generosity not to inform my father, or brother of my misconduct, and I thereby escaped any censure on that account. At my return home, I experienced a renewal of my brother's barbarity, the bitterness of which was aggrevated by contrasting it with the comfort I enjoyed from home. My poor sister made a dreadful recital of what she had undergone in my absence. Her gentle spirit was entirely broken, a settled gloom hung upon her, she had become quite emaciated, and she soon after took to her bed and died, an absolute victim to her brother's cruelty and the unassisting weakness of my poor father, who severely lamented her death.

My brother Garret and myself then remained the sole victims of Christopher's tyranny; and indeed we severely felt it. My father, confined to his bed, saw little of it, and we were loth to grieve him by a recital of our misery. If I was invited out by any neighbour, and pressed to stay to supper, Christopher would order the doors be locked sooner than usual; and on my return, I have been frequently suffered to remain for a full hour in the midst of snow or rain, till benumbed with cold, before Mr Christopher would deign to let me be admitted within the door; and then not infrequently, he would banish the cold by warming me with his horse-whip. At length, one Sunday I had gone to prayers, when I returned he asked me how I had dared to take the horse on which I rode. I answered, that I had my father's permission; with no other provocation, he beat me with his horse-whip so vehemently that the sleeves of my riding-habit, could not be got off my swelled arms till they were slit open: and I kept my bed ten days from the bruises I had received.

The measure of my sufferings was now filled to the brim, I resolved to endure no more. As soon as I was able to crawl from my bed, went to that of my father, and with a flood of tears, told him my sorrowful condition; that let what would betide, I would live no longer under the same roof with a savage, who forgot every tie of nature and humanity, and with whom my youth, my sex, and the near relation in which I stood to him, could be no pleas for decent and humane treatment. I added, that if I were forced to continue, I felt I should soon follow my unhappy sister; and therefore, I earnestly besought him to send me to my sister in Dublin, where I could dwell with comfort, and avoid a fate that must be grievous to him, and which otherwise must inevitably fall upon me.

My father was shocked so much at my relation, that in consideration of his grief and infirmities, I really repented I had said so much – but my poor heart was so full of grief, that it would have burst had I not given it vent. He wept bitterly, and consented I should go to my sister; but desired I would stay till he could procure some money for me, of which at present he had no command, since he had given the property over to Christopher.

My father kept his word, and taking the first opportunity of his son's absence, got as much money from the tenants as enabled me not only to bear my expences to Dublin, but left some in my pocket, and I arrived at my sister's house, which I regarded as a safe haven after a dreadful storm.

In my absence, my brother having no one on whom he could wreak his habitual malice, but his younger brother Garret, he frequently beat him with great severity. This the young lad bore with patience for some time; till at length, the strokes became too frequent to be borne; and though but a stripling, and several years younger than his persecutor, he resolved to pluck up a spirit; and the next blow he got from Christopher he hazarded a return. A conflict ensued, the contest was severe, long, and for a while doubtful. But Garret, deriving strength and courage from resentment, gave his elder brother such a drubbing, that he never after ventured another combat, but suffered him to live in peace. Of this I was informed by a letter from the victorious combatant, which at the same time acquainted me that my father's increasing infirmities made him desirous to see me; and that I might return in safety, for Christopher had not only given his word that he would treat me kindly; but that he himself would be my protector and defender against his brother's oppression, if he should break his word.

Tenderly loving my father, pleased with this assurance, and eager to embrace my brother Garret, I hastened home; and never did Andromeda behold her deliverer Perseus; nor the wife of Hector, see her husband return victorious from a well-fought field, with greater joy than I viewed, my young hero, Garret; and for three whole months, peace and tranquillity inhabited our dwelling.

I here would apologize to my readers for dwelling so long on the evil qualities of my brother Christopher; were it not that I conceive it somewhat necessary to lay before them events, which they have too much sameness to be amusing, are yet necessary, if not for an entire excuse at least for some *alleviation of censure* on my subsequent conduct in life. It must be obvious to every one that my wanderings, and every occurrence that may appear blamable in me, were originally owing to his behaviour. Had I been treated with the same humanity and tenderness that other girls of like condition experienced, my youth had glided pleasantly along. I might have been honourably married, and settled in life; might have made some deserving man happy, and received from him mutual content. Had slid into the vale of years without reproach, and have adorned, not debased a respectable name and family. But what was the alternative? My rising prospects rendered gloomy – every suitable proposal rejected – my temper soured, my resentments roused, and my spirits agitated by ill-treatment. Frequently driven to desperation by savage cruelty, and reckless what became of me. Every relaxation of my misery, was beheld in such a pleasurable light, that my mind, like a bow too long and too harshly bent, was no sooner loosed than it sprang wider than its pitch, and became almost masterless. My inexperienced youth, left without any friendly guidance, to ramble wild, and fall a prey to the artifices of designing men: every door shut against a return from errors, caused by unrestrained passions, roused by nature, heated by flattery, and kept alive by gratification – reflect on this, ye stern inquisitors for virtue! and then condemn as truth and justice bids – but to return to the last narrative I shall give respecting my brother Christopher.

For three months after I came back from Dublin, as I have said, we lived in tranquillity – happy had it been for me, had it continued. But the Æthiop cannot change his hue, nor the Leopard his spots. My wretched brother, tired with the long restraint over his inherent barbarity, let it break forth with redoubled fury. The family of Dardistown, continuing their attention to me, sought every opportunity of being in my company – one while, they would come and spend a day at Killough – that is, when Christopher was from home – and at other times, they would have me with them. They gave a ball to a few select friends, and I was invited. As it continued till it was too late – or rather too early for my return home, Mrs Fetherston insisted on my taking a bed with her. The next morning before I went home, she dispatched a servant to my father, to acquaint him that she had kept me, and to request he would not be displeased at my stay. Secure then, as I thought myself from any anger, I went home; but alas! I had no sooner entered the door, than my brother Christopher fell on me with his horse-whip, and beat me so cruelly that I vomited blood, and kept my bed near three months with the bruises he had given me: being several times at the point of death, and nothing but my youth and the natural strength of my constitution could have brought me through it.

Whilst this abominable exercise was going on, my shrieks and cries reached the ears of my poor father, who, as soon as a servant could help him on with his cloaths, came down to my assistance; though he was so much debilitated by the rheumatism, that he could scarce feed himself without help. When he appeared, my brother left off beating me, rather from his arm being tired from the length and excess of his exertions, than from any awe at the presence of his infirm parent. He could do nothing more than scold my inhuman tyrant, which he did in the strongest terms he could utter. He ordered me to be put to bed, and then was carried, shedding a torrent of tears, to his own.

This last proof of the unconquerable cruelty of Christopher, confirmed me in the opinion that no peace could be obtained for me, in that house. Whilst I was confined by my ill usage, my dear father would frequently cause himself to be brought to my room, where he would mingle his tears with mine, sympathize with my sufferings, and console me with the assurance, that as soon as I was able to be removed I should go to Dublin. For however grievous to him the parting with his dear child must be, he could not bear to expose me any longer to ill usage, which he was too weak and powerless to prevent. This promise acted as a cordial to me, and contributed greatly to my recovery; but I was too impatient to wait for its being perfectly compleated, and my father having procured some money from the tenants, as soon as I was able to sit upright in a carriage (which, as I said before, was not till the end of three months) I bade adieu to my sorrowing father, and sat out once more for Dublin. My brother and sister Smith, had quitted Tullamore, and occupied the house and carried on the business of the China-shop, in Arran-street, with my sister Beatty; and beside their natural affection, the knowledge I had acquired of the China trade whilst I had been in Dublin twice before, rendered me a welcome guest. I was received in the most cordial manner. They lamented the miseries I had suffered, deplored the weak and emaciated condition in which I came to town, and assured me of every comfort in their power to bestow to render my life happy. They most religiously kept their word, until I forfeited their esteem by my own imprudence.

CHAPTER THREE

If Love the Virgin's heart invade
How, like a Moth the simple Maid
Still plays around the flame.
If soon she be not made a Wife
Her honour's sing'd, and then, for life,
She's — what I dare not name.

GAY

MY LIFE, since the death of my dear mother, had hitherto been an alternative of pain and pleasure; the one constantly rendering the other the more poignant. At home, continually exposed to the harshest of treatment; abroad, soothed with every amusement that the sisters with whom I had occasionally resided, or my friends could procure. In my father's house — alas! his no more! — I was sunk in despondency, and my mind, wedded to sorrow and despair, could find no opportunity for laudable exertion. At the dwellings of others, I gave loose to pleasure, and banished every thought but of diversions that might recompense me for the evil hours I had spent at Killough. Thus I had neither time nor inclination for improvement, or laying a solid foundation for happiness, by an increase of useful knowledge. Hence my natural genius was cramped, and my heart became filled only with frivolity. The attachments I had shewn to some of my admirers, were quite transient: and if I yielded a moment to any desire for marriage, it was more than from a wish, thereby to get rid of oppression than from any love of either of the men. Nay the mortification I received from being disappointed, rather sprung from my defeated hopes on that ground, than from having my affections crossed, therefore, they lasted no longer than whilst their immediate impressions continued. But alas! I was soon to experience love as a passion, and to yield to its fascinating power.

For some time after I came to Dublin, my body was weak, my health very precarious, and my spirits heavily oppressed. Pleasures seemed to have lost their exhilerating effect, and I experienced a kind of lethargy of the mind. In short, I fell into a state, the most destructive to virtue that possibly can be. It is when the heart is replete with sorrow and languor, that is most susceptible of love. In the midst of a round of amusements, each equally engaging, and a train of admirers the giddy female gives neither a preference, and has not leisure to attach herself to either. But when softened, and inactive, the tender passions find easy admission, and the comforter, and consoler soon becomes the favoured lover – such was my case.

My brother-in-law had a very intimate friend, a Mr Dardis. He beheld my languid state with a sympathetic eye of compassion. He frequently conversed with me, and all his study seemed to be to console and comfort me. His mind appeared humane and generous. His address was soft and pathetic, though rather distant and reserved.

Not warm as a Lover, but cool as a Friend.

I felt a kind of new-born delight in his conversation. Whilst it lasted my sorrows seemed lulled into a calm, and my mind soothed into content. I forgot my past grief in the satisfaction of his soothings, and thought the hour lost in which he was not present. His visits became more frequent, his attachment to me more visible and pointed, he appeared more affable and gay, and I more cheerful. Still he only spoke the language of friendship; and under that form I had no reserve, I entertained no suspicion. The pains he had taken to bring me back from despondency demanded, I thought, at least my gratitude. His pains were not lost, I recovered my spirits, and my looks testified a complete return of health. This was visible to all my friends, who attributed it to every cause but that which was the real one. He now was seldom absent, he doubtless observed a change in my heart, before I perceived it myself; and when I did, I was unwilling to believe it. I beheld him as a true friend, and such a one is a real treasure, a comfort in sorrow, and a refuge in distress. He redoubled his assiduities. He, at length, spoke the language of love, and I listened to it with pleasure. His proposals were honourable; but we agreed, that at that time the state of his affairs and my own situation rendered the accomplishment of our wishes, by a marriage, totally impracticable; therefore, we determined to wait the favourable opportunity, which we hoped a little time would produce. This point being settled, we mutually acknowledged our love, and solemnly engaged ourselves to each other. I looked upon him as my future husband, and as such permitted his visits by night as well as day, that we might give vent to the effusion of our passion unobserved by others.

Every interview gave birth to the following; for some time he totally forebore from any freedom that could alarm virtue, or arouse suspicion. Lulled into security by this apparently honourable reserve, I apprehended nothing. Our expressions of affection gradually became more fervent; our confidence in each other, more confirmed; our dalliances less confined; our passions more inflamed; I felt a tumult in my blood, which I scarce wished to restrain, at length – to use the language of Lothario.

> Hot with the Tuscan grape, and high in blood,
> Haply he stole unheeded to my chamber.
> He found the soft, believing love-sick maid
> Loose, unattir'd, young, tender, full of wishes.
> Fierceness and Pride, the guardians of her honour,
> Were all asleep – and none but Love was waking;
> He snatch'd the glorious, golden opportunity,
> And with prevailing youthful ardor press'd her.

Here then was my first failing – the first indeed, but the fatal foundation of all that followed. Learn hence my young female readers, cautiously to guard against the first approaches of vice – learn to keep firm the barriers of virtue, and know that if the smallest breach is made in the mounds of Chastity, vice rushes in like a torrent.

> At length the morn, and cool reflection came.

I saw the greatness of my fault, I saw my seducer had triumphed, yet how could I call him seducer, when I met the seduction half way; and whatever compunction I then felt at my offence, I could not hate the offender. I saw that I had been imprudent, yet the flatterer, Hope was at hand, that that imprudence might be amended by his marrying me, which I did not doubt but his honour would prompt him to do. Yet what reliance could I justly have on his honour, when I had weakly given up my own. This indeed, Mr Dardis continued to promise, as soon as circumstances would permit; and this assurance reconciled my mind to repetitions of our guilty joys, and lulled both conscience and remorse asleep.

I then wrote to my father for money, which my mind foreboded would be the last I should ever receive from him. But it was difficult for him to procure me any, as his son had warned all the tenants not to pay any more rents to my father, and they could not be persuaded to act contrary to the orders they had received. However, my indulgent parent, ignorant of the false step I had taken, and which had really made me unworthy of his attention, resolved to leave no effort untried to serve me. An uncle of mine had come up to Dublin, to fetch one of his daughters home, who had boarded in the nunnery in Channel-row; and when I was in doubt from the long delay, whether my father could comply with my request, he sent me a draught upon that uncle for forty pounds, which was accepted and paid. I received the money with a kind of compunction, as it made me reflect on the old gentleman's paternal fondness, and how little I deserved it. However, as by the receipt of such a considerable sum I thought myself as rich as a queen, and that I should never want money any more; and as I was not of a temper to give gloomy ideas any long habitation in my breast, when I could entertain others more lively and agreeable, my repentance and compunction were of no long duration.

My spirits continued to be lively, Mr Dardis constantly repeated his visits, both public and private. He did not drop his assurances of his honourable intentions, and gave me incessant marks of his esteem, and unabated love; nay he seemed (as Shakespeare says)

> *As if increase of appetite had grown*
> *By what it fed on.*

Thus we went on, enjoying the pernicious sweets of an illicit amour, and priding ourselves in the prudent secrecy with which it was carried on, until, at length an event ensued that mocked our secrecy, and threatened to divulge it to the world; to expose me to the resentment of my family; and plunge me into disgrace. In short, I found myself in a state that could not be long hidden, but would soon produce a living witness of my indiscretion.

This tell-tale circumstance ensuing, roused me at once from the lethargy into which guilty pleasure, and false security had plunged me. I beheld in a moment all the horror of my situation. I saw myself on the eve of shame, reproach and detestation, and knew not how to ward off either. I appreciated the value of the world's estimation and an unspotted character, when I was about to loose both; and had only one single twig to break my fall adown the dark abyss, into which I was sinking; and that was by Mr Dardis fulfilling his promise. I took the first opportunity that offered to acquaint him, in a flood of tears, with my condition; the impossibility of concealing it for many days longer from the eyes of my sister and the family, and the ruin that the discovery must inevitably draw upon me. He appeared deeply struck with this event, which had not both him and I been

greatly infatuated, we must have forseen would naturally be the conse-
quence of our conduct.

Mr Dardis agreed to the necessity of guarding against censure; but at the
same time, he very forcibly urged that the making his intentions known to
my family, especially to my brutish brother, would enduce them to desire
an immediate compliance, which would thereby be rendered unattainable
by the opposition that his relations would give to the completion of his
wishes. To marry me in private might indeed, silence any scruples of con-
science, but would not stop the clamours of the world; and a public mar-
riage would deprive him of the countenance of his friends, and of all the
hopes of the benefits of succeeding to his family fortune: and of even his
present income; which would involve us both in poverty and distress. The
best method he saw in our present circumstances, was, that I should leave
my sister's house and go to genteel lodgings, which he would provide for
me, where I should want for nothing, and when I had lain in, it would be
perhaps in his power to make good his engagements to me, which he
wished as cordially as I did, and would do the moment he was able. It was
true indeed, that my sudden departure, and the uncertainty where I was
might cause some conjectures, but then they could not amount to any cer-
tainties, and whenever I should emerge into the world again my character
would be secure.

Although I was not altogether satisfied with this plan, yet, as I could not
offer any better I acquiesed [sic] in it. He then took apartments for me in
Clarendon-street, at the house of a Mrs Butler. The lodgings were genteel
and convenient, but in the most improper house to which chance could
have directed him; for although the mistress of it had a very respectable
appearance, she was one of the impure ones, and therefore, not a fit habita-
tion for the recovery of character; but this I did not know till after I had left
her.

Here I was, for the first time in my life, absent from all my relations, and
from every friend and former acquaintance. It is true, I enjoyed as much as
I desired of Mr Dardis's company, in which I was somewhat cheerful; but
when alone I was oppressed with anxiety, and could neither look back
without remorse, nor forward without apprehension of what might follow.
My mind was continually tormented with the thoughts of what my sisters,
and especially my poor father must feel at my sudden elopement. It was
possible they might not divine the real circumstance, but they could figure
none to themselves but what must be to my disadvantage. In this state of

mind I intreated my lover, to make every inquiry into what they thought, and what they said of me. He did so, and in about fortnight brought me the following intelligence.

My whole family was in the greatest possible consternation about me; as my clothes were left behind, they imagined that in some fit of discontent, though they knew not for what, I had put an end to my life in some manner or other; my brother and sister had gone down the North-wall, to make some enquiries about me, and in sorrowful expectation of seeing my body either floating on the water, or driven ashore. My brother Smith, then recollected that the driver of the coach, in which I had left his house, as on a visit, drove with his left hand. After searching all the coach-stands, he found this man, who informed him that he had sat me down at such an house in Clarendon-street. My two brothers-in-law then went to a public-house, the very next door to that in which I lodged, and in answer to their inquiries, heard that the house in which I was, was a very improper one. Distracted at this news, they gave me up as an abandoned woman, and went away without condescending, or indeed wishing to see me.

Of this circumstance I was ignorant for some time, but the news that Mr Dardis brought me of the uneasiness my absence had caused, filled me with the deepest concern. He compassionated my anxiety, and advised me to write word to my sister, where I was, that she might no longer continue in her fears for my personal safety. I eagerly followed his advice, and wrote to my sister Brady, to request she would call on me the next day. She did not fail, but conscious of my situation and willing to hide it, when she came I enveloped myself in my cloak, that my increase of bulk might not be apparent. Her visit was long, and the time was chiefly spent in interrogatories, of the manner and motives of my elopement, and in my returning such answers as seemed the most proper either to excuse, or palliate my conduct. The result of our conversation was her offer of receiving me into her house (as she assured me that in which I was, would destroy my character if I staid longer in it), and my promise to dine with her next day.

When Mr Dardis came at night, anxious to know the event of our interview, I told him all that had passed, and my intention of going to Mrs Brady. This did not meet his approbation. He very forcibly represented to me, that it would be totally impossible to conceal my condition, if I went to reside with my sister; nay, if even I staid in Dublin, now my family knew where I was. He urged the absolute necessity of a retreat, at least till I had lain in. He offered to take me to England, but my dread of the sea, and my imagination that I should be drowned if I ventured upon it, prevented my compliance with that plan. He next proposed that I should go to some country place; I consented, and he went immediately to take a place in the Drogheda stage. The next morning he went and put me into the coach; but how great was my surprise, when I found sitting there a near relation of my own, a Mrs Drumgoold, of Drogheda, who having been in Dublin on some business was returning home. She was as much struck at seeing me, as I was at beholding her. I was so depressed that I could scarce make any rational answer to her civilities, but sat a few moments revolving in my mind what falsehoods I should invent to conceal the truth. At length I told her that I was going to Drogheda to receive some money for my brother Smith. This assertion passed current, as she could not know any thing to the contrary. But it involved me in another embarrassment, she had very politely obliged me to accept her invitation of staying in her house whilst my business demanded my presence in Drogheda. But this promise I did not intend to keep, as it would not only discover the falsehood of my assertion, respecting my coming to that town, but would also betray the condition which I was most interested to hide. O sacred Truth! what does one single deviation from thee, cost us to support! how many falsehoods must be uttered to screen the first?

Whilst I remained in the coach my mind was employed in framing some plan of evading my promise to Mrs Drumgoold, and getting farther from Drogheda. When the coach stopped at the Inn, I said I would make some enquiries after the persons I wanted, and would be with her in half an hour. Instead of which, as soon as she was gone home I procured a man and horse to take me to Dunleer, a small town about seven miles farther off, and galloped away directly; but to stop all enquiries whither I was gone, and all pursuit, I requested the Inn-keeper, at Drogheda, to say to any person Mrs Drumgoold might send for me; that I had walked out of his house, just after the coach came in, and that he knew nothing more about me.

It was late when I arrived at Dunleer, and as I was totally a stranger in the town, I staid that night at the Inn. After a very slight refreshment I retired to bed. I say to bed, for rest was a stranger to me, and sleep never once visited my weeping eyes. Being left alone in the silent hours of darkness, I had leisure to consider the horrors of my situation. I became a prey to reflection, and lay self-condemned without the alleviation of a single excuse for my conduct. Oh! could we but foresee in the moments of the

23

gratification of our passions, the hours of bitter remorse they must necessarily produce, we would surely stop in career, and avoid the heart-rending pangs that follow guilt.

I arose in the morning without feeling myself in the least refreshed, but the necessity of coming to some resolution roused me to exertion. I enquired of the chambermaid, about the disposition of the inhabitants of the town and neighbourhood, and being satisfied from her answers that I might remain unknown; by the assistance of the waiter I procured lodging and board in the house of a decent farmer, at half-a-guinea a week. I found my new dwelling perfectly retired, and the people, especially the farmer's wife, attentive and agreeable. There I passed my time in innocence, though I cannot say in content, for reflection would frequently obtrude, and represent to me a father grieving for his loss, sisters lamenting my lapse from virtue, which they could not but suppose was the case; friends condemning me; and all of them enraged at my conduct. In this state religion alone could dart a ray of comfort; and I felt no pleasure but in the strict attention to my duties in the neighbouring chapel. Alas! that these emotions were but for the season. Had I even then persevered in the right path, I might not have only avoided evils which followed, but have attoned for my wanderings in a wrong one.

At length, in this cottage, where I remained totally unknown, I was delivered of a fine girl, with which as soon as I was perfectly recovered, I sat out for Dublin, at the earnest request of Mr Dardis. He met me at the Inn on my arrival, where he seemed transported with joy at seeing me, and testified the greatest fondness for the little innocent. The next day he hired a fresh nurse, and having discharged the one I had hitherto employed and brought to town, he took me to a very agreeable lodging he had procured; where, forgetting all the resolutions I had made in Dublin, we lived together as before.

There are certain temptations which are only to be resisted by flying from them. When sensuality attacks the human heart, there is no time for contending; a speedy flight alone can secure the victory: we may profitably bear up under the losses and crosses of this life, with a laudable firmness of resolution, and come off conquerors; but we must not even capitulate with allurements of sense, and the poet says,

The woman who deliberates is lost.

CHAPTER FOUR

To erring youth there's some compassion due,
But whilst with rigour, you their faults pursue,
What's their misfortune is a crime in you.
SOUTHERN

ALTHOUGH HAPPY and delighted with the company, and continued
tenderness of my undoer, and charmed with the opening sweetness of my
child, I yet, was far from possessing a tranquillity of mind. The thoughts of
my father and relations would check any pleasure I could embrace; and
damp my spirits even in the midst of gaity. My eyes would frequently swim
with tears, and sighs burst unbidden from my perturbed bosom. My lover
perceived my uneasiness, which he was so far from condemning or think-
ing in the least unreasonable, that he even urged me to seek a reconcilia-
tion with my friends. This was my anxious wish, but how to effect it was
the task. Shame kept me some time from making any effort; but at length I
resolved to make the attempt.

The first necessary preliminary was to frame some plausible excuse for
my long absence, which was indeed, very difficult to do. We had frequent
consultations on this head, when at length, he suggested one. This was to
tell my sister Smith (to whom he advised me first to address myself) that I
had been on a visit to my cousin Drumgoold, at Drogheda. This idea took
my fancy, and I resolved to put it into execution the next day.

Though there is nothing more common than deception, yet there is
nothing more hard to carry on successfully. The most trifling circum-
stances frequently are sufficient to detect it; and in this case I might have
easily imagined, that on the least suspicion of the truth, a line from my sis-
ter to Mrs Drumgoold, would have demonstrated my falsehood. Indeed,
there was no occasion for any application to my cousin, for she had been
beforehand; and highly affronted with my breach of promise at Drogheda,
she had soon after written a letter to me, full of reproaches, for my rude-

ness and ill behaviour. This epistle was directed to me at Mr Smith's, where Mrs Drumgoold conceived I was. The letter lay there for some time, but on my continuing absent, my sister opened it, and thereby discovered the route I had taken, though she knew not how far it had extended; and my incivility to my cousin at Drogheda.

Ignorant then of what had passed, and priding myself on the speciousness of the excuse I had ready to give, I went with some degree of confidence to Mrs Smith; but alas! I was not admitted so far as the parlour, she immediately called me a vile wretch, bade me begone, and pushing me violently from the door, shut it in my face.

Had a thunder-bolt fallen on me, I think I should scarce have been more confounded. I stood for a while in a state of astonishment, uncertain what to do, or where to go. The disappointment of my hopes and expectations, however unjustly formed, struck me in the most forcible manner. However, in some minutes I recovered myself; and before I would totally abandon all thoughts of a reconciliation, I resolved to make a trial of my other sister. To Mrs Brady, therefore, I instantly bent my course; but to my farther distress, from her I experienced, not merely a similar, but a more severe repulse.

Becoming more desperate by this second repulse, and resolved to leave no effort unessayed, I went to another relation Mr H— P—, in High-street, but I was destined that day to a succession of rebukes, each rising above the other; I was driven from him with scorn and contempt, and he even threatened to beat me for having (as he said,) the impudence to come to his house, and scandalize it by my appearance.

I returned home agitated with a thousand contending passions and my breast torn, with rage, shame, sorrow, distress and repentance. I still remained in the lodgings Mr Dardis had provided, but took a firm resolution to see him no more. Ah! had I wisely taken and kept that resolution some months before, I had not then been a prey to anxiety and remorse. I wept and lamented day and night, and had not one moment's peace of mind. I thought it in vain to try my sisters again. But I had yet a father, a tender, indulgent, offended father, my duty as well as my distresses urged me to write to him. With a trembling hand, and an aching heart, I penned my letter. I despaired of a reply, as I knew myself to be unworthy of his least regard – I owned, with the prodigal son, that 'I had sinned against Heaven and before him, and was no more worthy to be called his child.' – But tenderness and affection, had not abandoned the dear old man's heart, he wrote to me, and directed me to return to Killough, in the stage. I hesitated not a moment to obey his welcome summons, and I quitted the lodgings Mr Dardis had taken for me and returned home, flattering myself that I should find an asylum in my father's house. But alas! he had no longer the command of it; when I arrived my brother Christopher, constant in evil, and born for my destruction, refused me admittance. I sat down on the step of the door weeping, till my dear father spoke to me from the window, whence he told me he had no power left him more than I saw; but he would write to my sisters to receive and board and lodge me. I acquainted him how they had treated me, and that it would be vain to apply to them. At length, my father prevailed on his son Christopher to let me in, which he did; but it was only to provide a man and horse to take me to Kinnegad; whence he ordered me to go back to Dublin, in the stage-coach, and gave me a solitary guinea. I then took a last leave of my father and my brother Garret. The dear parent wept bitterly, embraced me, blessed me – and I saw him no more – this parting scene was too distressing to be remembered without emotion, even at this distance of time.

I staid that night at Kinnegad, and the next morning entered the stage-coach (for which I had nothing to pay) and arrived in the evening, with my guinea in my pocket, which, with my cloaths and a few trinkets, was the whole fund on which a young girl with a child, had to build her future maintenance through life. And as I was determined to return no more to Mr Dardis, I took a small lodging at five shillings a week, where I remained quite retired, and perfectly secluded from the world.

Book Two

Where shall the fallen meet with Pity?
Where find the kindly hand to raise them up?
Not among sisters. *They will cast ye off.*
And, lest the fame of their good families
Be tainted by your failing, *foolishly*
Will force ye to embrace that train of life
Which taints it more, to gain the very food
Which they deny ye — And thus drive you on
Far in the path of Vice, *through* shew of Virtue.

CHAPMAN

MY WEAKNESS and indiscretions had thus brought me, at almost the outset of life, to what was literally a state of solitary misery. I had no support but what I derived from the sale of my cloaths, which went article by article to satisfy the cravings of nature, till I was reduced nearly to nakedness and starving. I had now sufficient leisure to contemplate my folly, and descant on my misdeeds. I had humbled myself even to the Dust. I again went to my sister Smith, who had a large family of children, and implored her with tears to take me once more into her house, when I would make her's and her childrens' cloaths, and never offend or disoblige her in any respect. Alas! she was obdurate, and refused me in the most peremptory manner. I applied in the same manner to my sister Brady, with equal ill success. She was unlimited in her upbraidings, violent in her abuse, and she declared if a morsel of bread would save me from death and destruction, she would refuse it to me. Harsh and hard dealing sisters! it is you, who by rejecting a penitent offender, and shutting the door against a return to virtue, drove me on the rocks, which for a long time wrecked my peace of mind. I returned to my little lonely habitation, with a soul embittered with the treatment I had received, and a body almost worn down with anguish and poverty. I remained there till I had nothing but what covered me, not one second article wherewith to change what I wore, and for eight days had lived only on one pound of hung beef and a few potatoes; using the water in which they were boiled, as the only diluter of my wretched scanty meals.

Thus having arrived to the verge of perishing through real want, feeling anxiety of mind, and the keen pangs of hunger, and destitute of every asylum in Dublin, it occurred to my thoughts, that as, whilst I lived at my father's house, I had been frequently serviceable to the tenants and their wives; I had no doubt, if I could get down amongst them, their gratitude and hospitality, would afford me shelter in one or other of their cabins, and give me at least potatoes and butter-milk; which I should then esteem as most comfortable food. Full of this idea, I resolved to set out that very night. My landlady kindly lent me her cloak, to cover the wretched remains of my wardrobe, which were clean and tight, though mean and much worn. Proceeding up Strand-street, towards Smith-field, two gentlemen (named Strange and Droope) met me, and looking on me as an innocent, ignorant country girl, took me by the hand and invited me to come in with them, to drink tea and go to the play. I was frighted at this address, ran from them, and took shelter in the shop of Mr Moore, a jeweller, on the Inn's-quay. I had been formerly intimate with this family when I was in prosperity, and before my unhappy lapse from virtue. Luckily that lapse had not come to their knowledge, any more than my present situation. I was cordially received by Mrs Moore, and pressed to stay to tea, which I did; and prompted by hunger, eat till I was really ashamed to eat any more. After tea I took my leave and proceeded to Smith-field, but to my great vexation found all the places in the stage, both within and without were engaged.

Disappointed in my design of going to the country, I had no alternative but to return to my lodging. I walked very slow, pensive, and revolving in my mind how I could procure another meal, for what I had eaten at Mrs Moore's seemed rather to have excited than satisfied my appetite. The enemy of mankind is said to be ever ready to instill temptations to vice, and to seize the most favourable opportunity for his insinuations. So alas! I found it in the present moment. I, who had resisted every incitement to evil, whilst any the most homely and penurious means of life remained, became desperate when every resource seemed to be cut off. I reflected on my conduct, respecting the two gentlemen who met me in Strand-street. I could not help condemning myself for my shyness. They appeared to be gentlemen, I said to myself, and surely would not have done me any harm. I wish I had not refused their kind invitation. At least I should have gotten a comfortable meal, which was what I much wanted, and to which I had been long an entire stranger. None of my relations will give me one, why then should I reject it from another. It is not probable that I shall meet them again, but if I should, I will not be the fool I was.

Thus I argued with myself, and was fully occupied with these thoughts as I walked, when passing by the door at which I first saw them, I beheld the very identical persons alighting from a coach. They seemed pleased at meeting with me again, and pressed me to go into the house, which, after some slight hesitation I did. When we entered I saw a little gentleman writing at a table in a corner of the room; he joined us and tea was ordered. Though I had already drank tea on the Inn's-quay, I was not sorry to partake of it again; but here, as before I was ashamed to eat my fill. The little gentleman (Thomas Caulfield, Esq; a near relation of Lord Charlemont,) took more particular notice of me than the others. I was asked a multitude of questions, to which (as I had already suffered by falsehoods) I answered with ingenious truth. When tea was over, Mr Caulfield asked my name and where I lodged. I told him, and he begged permission to see me home, probably with a design to know if what I had said was truth, I consented, and we took leave of the other gentlemen.

As we walked together, he slipped two guineas into my bosom, and told me if I would give up the idea of going to the country, where, from what I had said, I must be certain I had no chance of being well received; and if it should appear that I told him nothing but truth, he would settle me comfortably and conveniently, would be my protector, and I should never want. There are many virtues, which when carried beyond their due bounds degenerate into vices, one of these is *Gratitude*. This operated powerfully in my breast. This gentleman had relieved my wants when they were become extreme. I was in possession of more money of my own than I had seen for many months; my hunger was not yet appeased, but through him I had the means of satisfying it, which I was impatient to do. The miseries I had undergone were present to my mind, and he had promised he would screen me from their future approach. All these thoughts rushed at once into my mind, awakened my sincerest acknowledgments, and I esteemed it but a grateful return to promise all he requested. He saw me to the door of my lodging, and being thereby assured of the truth of what I had told him, and where he might find me, he very respectfully took his leave and wished me good night.

I entered my room in a very different disposition from that with which I had quitted it a few hours before. Then, all was distress, doubt and uncertainty. Now, my mind was tranquil and I looked foreward with hope. I had nothing to expect from my relations and former friends but desertion, reproach and want. From Mr Caulfield, my days to come presented protection, endearments and plenty. The contrast was great, and I must embrace the one or the other. I was blind to the sacrifice I was about to make, I did not consider that I was taking a second and similar step to that which had caused all my distress: and that I was about to plunge deeper in vice, which would render my return still more difficult, even if it could be accomplished – which alas! it never was.

As soon as I was seated I sent my landlady to purchase eatables for supper; and never in my life did I eat one so welcome and so sweet, nor perhaps ever in such a quantity: and having fully satisfied the cravings of hunger, I slept with the greatest tranquillity.

The next evening, Mr Caulfield came to see me; but his appearance in laced cloaths, and the sudden change in my way of living gave my landlady some alarm: she said her house was not suited for the reception of a fine gentleman, and therefore desired I would get another lodging. As money was not wanting, this was no difficult task. Mr Caulfield soon procured one, where I lived in a genteel stile, unnoticed and unsuspected; where he visited me whenever he thought proper, and we became daily more pleased with each other.

Here let me anticipate the exclamations of many of my female readers. They will doubtless say, 'we pitied your first transgression; you might plead youth, inexperience, and affection, but here you had no excuse. You weakly yielded to the temptation of a stranger, a casual acquaintance. You say you were on the point of starving, and rejected by all your friends and relations, but you should have sought to restore your connection with them, by the prudence and chastity of your future life, and thereby proved the sincerity of your repentance. You should have gone to service, you should have really died for want, rather than have procured sustenance at such a price as you have paid for it. Nay, when you had got the two guineas from the gentleman, and he had left you at your door, you should have pursued your intended plan of going down to the tenantry about your father's house, and have lived on potatoes and butter milk, begged from them; and have piously taken all your sufferings as just punishment for your offences – but, fie upon you! you listened to the first temptation, you did not strive either to resist it, or to fly from it, and therefore deserve no pity.'

All this is easily said, all this may be true. But pray permit me to ask in my turn – were *you* ever on the point of starving? Did *you* ever experience real want, and part with every article of any value to procure a scanty meal? Did *you* ever live for many days on a single pound of salt meat, and have only the water in which a few potatoes were boiled for your beverage? For not till I had endured all this misery, and felt the severe pangs of hunger, did I err again: Perhaps you utter your censures in a decent, comfortable room, after a plentiful meal, and surrounded by your relations and friends. Therefore, we may well say,

He jests at scars who never felt a wound.

And perhaps you are not *quite sure* you would have *really died for want!* ere you had fallen like me. How could I have gone to service? Bred up as I had been, for what service was I fit? Who would have taken a servant without a character? and who had I to give me one? Neither had I cloaths fit to make even a tolerable decent appearance. My harsh sisters indeed, might have saved me from ruin, but that their *outrageous virtue* disdained. Had they pitied and forgiven my first fault, in all human probability I had not committed a second; but instead of holding out an hand to raise me up and support me; instead of alluring me back to the paths of Virtue, by gentleness and compassion, they plunged me into sorrow and distress; and by rendering me wretched and desperate, hurled me down the descent of Vice. Hence *they,* not *me* must be chiefly condemned. Nay I will affirm, from the evidences of observation and experience, that the real cause of the multitude of unhappy women, is the harshness of their own sex; who, thinking to elevate their own real, or pretended virtue, by condemning the failures of others, shut the door against repentance and amendment; and thereby compel thousands to continue in error, because their characters being blasted, they have no means of support from any industry they may be willing to fly for bread. For, the maxim is true that

> *none stand so firm as those who have once slipped, and are*
> *enabled to regain their footing, by the Christian Humanity*
> *of such of their own sex as posses, and exercise it.*

But, to return to my narrative. Mr Caulfield's attention to me daily increased. He frequently invited and entertained me at his house in Abbey-street, where he extensively carried on the business of a wine merchant, and I passed my time smoothly, intoxicated with pleasures that banished all reflection, till I was brought to bed of a son, which seemed to augment my lover's satisfaction. He had often told me he never intended to marry, as he feared he should never have a child. But soon after my lying-in, as if thereby his fears on that head seemed to be dissipated, he listened to the advice of his relations (amongst whom he counted the Earl of Charlemont) and his friends, and paid his addresses to a Miss Hawkesworth, to whom he was shortly after married.

This event for a while gave me most poignant sorrow, and as my temper was become somewhat violent, I was greatly provoked at his abandoning me. Silly are those women, and highly infatuated, who can imagine that connexions, which are sanctioned neither by the laws of God or man, can be permanent, longer than it suits the convenience of the thus connected parties. No, they must, necessarily must, have a period: And the certainty of this is the cause why most women in that line strive to realize as much as they can, whilst the connexion subsists, not knowing how shortly it may terminate.

However, Mr Caulfield behaved honourably in regard to me, he assured me my boy should never want, nor I neither, whilst I conducted myself with propriety; and accordingly gave us both an adequate annuity.

CHAPTER TWO

Pure from the Rock springs forth the Virgin Stream,
And gently glides untainted and serene.
Its limpid surface gladdens all around,
'Till, rolling down the mount, it meets a mass
Of stagnant waters in some muddy pool.
Then, if no kindly hand raises a bank
To turn it from Corruption, whilst its flood,
Is yet but slightly ting'd with waves impure,
It mingles with the foulness, and contracts
Each noxious quality the slime imparts;
O'erflows the brink, and, gath'ring as it spreads
The poisons it encounters, never more
Is pleasing to the taste, or wholesome drink.

THOUGH LEFT BY MY LOVER, I was not destitute, his generosity had afforded me means of every necessary comfort. But as I wanted his company, I found a void in my mind. To fill up which, I contracted an acquaintance with a certain Lady of fashion, who introduced me to some of the most elegant Demi-Reps in town. Knowing I was passionately found of music, she invited me to an entertainment she gave at a Tavern, in Smock-alley, which was accompanied by an enchanting concert. I soon became so attached to this lady, that we were scarce ever asunder, and my hours stole away without care, without attention, without reflection. As stinging thoughts would sometimes intervene uninvited, I banished them as soon as they intruded, and sought in a whirl of company and dissipation, for that calm I could not find in my own breast when I was alone.

Mr Caulfield hearing of my new acquaintance, called on me to warn me against her. He told me he entirely disapproved of this lady, that she was a very improper companion for me. That there were as many women ruined by their *female* as their *male* connexions, and ended with forbidding me to see her.

I found the society of this lady very agreeable, and I continued my inti-

34

macy with her, which so exasperated Mr Caulfield, that he withdrew my annuity though he continued that of my son, till he died of an inward complaint: when I again became destitute. Although I entirely owed my loss of independence to this lady, I was still fond of her, and refused to break off with her. My mind indeed, became again tortured by disappointment and anxiety, so that I could not find peace at home, and therefore fled to my old remedy of being constantly abroad. But a life of dissipation cannot be maintained without some funds. My constant companion said she would find soon a remedy for that defect; and a gentleman of the name of Jackson, was introduced to me, whose company and conversation were very agreeable. After a few weeks acquaintance, Mr Jackson begged my permission to bring with him a very particular friend, to which I consented. This was a Mr Lawless, a near relation of the Countess of Clonmel, who will be the subject of many pages of these memoirs. As both these gentlemen were equally assiduous in their attentions and endeavours to please, I was much divided to which of them I should give the preference. They had many amiable qualities, but those alone would not suffice; they neither of them was wealthy; and as money was absolutely necessary (especially in that line of life which I had unfortunately embraced) I devoted a considerable part of my time to an English gentleman, of the name of Leeson, who, as my wealthy friend, made up in the article of cash the deficiency therein of my other two friends.

Whether it was that Mr Leeson, wishing to have me entirely to himself, suspected that in my present lodging, I had too frequent opportunities of seeing my former acquaintance, he proposed to take apartments for me more elegant, and more convenient, and where he thought, perhaps, he should be more the master. As I had always a taste for shew and splendor, I had no objections to a removal; but when he intreated me to drop at once all the connexions I had formed, both female as well male, to reject all their visits, and confine myself solely to his society, I could not help thinking his proposal, ill-natured, selfish and tyrannical; yet, reflecting that he was to bear the sole expence of, not only every necessary, but of every comfort, convenience, and even luxury of life, I was to enjoy: that he declared his passion for me was solid, and unchanging, and that his character and disposition were honourable; I thought I owed a compliance with his wishes, and consented with much seeming complacancy [*sic*], well-judging I could so far sometimes elude his vigilance as to see an old acquaintance. Ah! wretched lot of human nature! how constantly doth one evil quality draw others into its train! to my former errors, I now added *avarice* and *deceit,* and sought excuses for them in my own mind.

My condescension increased Mr Leeson's fondness for me, but that very fondness led him to suspicions and jealousies, that created uneasiness to us both; and he even dismissed my former mantua-maker, lest she should bring letters or messages from any of my old acquaintances, and introduced one of his own chusing. He had incessantly in his mind the ideas of Mr Jackson, and Mr Lawless. He sometimes beheld them passing by the door; and was sure it was on my account. At other times, he thought they were aiming at some stratagems to see me, and his mind was so agitated that at last, he resolved to take me out of Dublin, far from the reach of admirers. Accordingly we went to an excellent house, and beautiful demesne, he possessed in the county of Kildare; where we lived in perfect tranquillity and content. He, being freed from jealousy became placid in his temper, and every day more agreeable. And I, being thus weaned from other objects, placed my chief satisfaction in striving to please him.

At length, a business of the greatest consequence demanded his presence in Dublin. His mind then began to be again agitated. As his business would necessarily oblige him to a residence for a considerable time, he could not entertain the idea of leaving me behind in the country; and as he well knew the city afforded numberless temptations and allurements to pleasure, which frequently seduce the innocent, much more one who had already tasted of the Circean cup, he trembled to expose me again to them. However, something must be determined, and he thought to provide against the worst. He took a neatly furnished house, at the skirt of town, on Ranelagh-road (now within a door of the Circular-road,) where he kept a very vigilant eye over me, and suffered no visitors but such as he introduced himself; and with none even of them did he suffer me to remain alone, for a single minute.

In this manner we lived for a whole year, with the greatest good humour; and he was so pleased with my reserve, that he testified his esteem by every possible means, and declared his entire approbation of my conduct. He even became so thoroughly attached to me, that he proposed to make me his wife; and, as such a change would induce an alteration in his mode of living, he would look out for another house, which should be entirely furnished to my mode and fancy.

This procedure in Mr Leeson, was certainly very kind and good natured, and fully demonstrative of his regard: but however, I might have carried myself outwardly, a recluse and retired way of life was not agreeable to me. I thought it hard to be thus totally deprived of all society with my former intimates; and nothing but a fixed attention to my interest, could have enabled me to endure it. However, to speak candidly, I was not so absolutely reserved as Mr Leeson thought me. Stolen pleasures are generally held to be very sweet, and in spite of his vigilance, I sometimes enjoyed them to compensate for the external constraint I was forced to assume. I sometimes gave admission to my old friend Mr Lawless, through the parlour window; and sometimes also to Mr Jackson, when I was sure that Mr Leeson dined out, and was not to come home before a certain hour, against which time my lovers were removed, and all things ready for the quiet reception of my deceived keeper. Nay, I had gained his own servant so well in my interest, that whilst any other friend was with me, he would keep watch at the parlour window, lest his master should return unexpectedly and surprise us.

Mr Leeson, being, by my cautious conduct, fully satisfied that he was the sole *God of my Idolatry,* and was perfectly secure of my affections, left town for some time, to superintend some improvements he was making at his country seat.

Prior to his setting out for the country, he had taken an house for me in Park-street, which was but just built; and having had it fitted up in an elegant manner, he pressed me to go and reside in it before he departed, that I might be introduced to some of his relations, who might frequently give me their company before we were married. This did not suit the mode of living I intended to follow in his absence, I therefore, after paying him my thanks for his kindness and attention, told him I feared the newness and dampness of the house would give me cold, of which I was remarkably susceptible, on which account, I would rather stay where I was till his return, by which time the house would be sufficiently dry and aired. Such was his tenderness, that I had only to speak my wishes for him to acquiesce. He consented, although (knowing that I was remarkably fond of milk) he had taken a field, at ten pounds an acre yearly, and put two cows into it. He also, gave me an unlimited Bill of Credit on a friend of his, who was a merchant, for any money I might want in his absence; and, then taking an affectionate leave of me, he departed for the country.

Mr Leeson had scarcely got down to his seat, but suspicions arose again in his mind. He fancied that I might have some private reasons, for staying in the house where I was; and therefore, though he admitted my excuse for not going to Park-street, he wrote to his friend the merchant, to get me another place of residence, and remove me from Ranelagh-road. His friend instantly complied with his instructions, and I yielded without the least hesitation. For the house in which he had taken lodgings for me, was kept by a very particular friend, to whom I could safely confide all my secrets, having by presents of considerable value, and proper doceurs, gained her over entirely to my interest. Besides, the very merchant was deeply interested for me; and indeed, I had myself recommended him to Mr Leeson, as a person to whom he might consign my supplies, and though rather suspicious in every thing else, he very unsuspiciously acceded to the proposal.

I was quite contented in my new lodging, the people were devoted to me, my merchant ready to screen every thing that I wished not to come to Mr Leeson's knowledge; I could act just as I pleased, and I occasionally received the visits of Jackson and Lawless, particularly the latter, who was the greatest object of my affection.

After some time, Mr Leeson wrote to acquaint me that his affairs would detain him still a month longer in the country. This news gave me great pleasure, as I thought I could have my swing all that time – however, before the month was out he came, when he was least expected. I shall relate this at full, as it affords a striking instance, how easily men who think themselves the most cunning and secure may be completely duped.

As I thought myself in the greatest security, I sometimes went and staid for a few days at the lodgings of Mr Lawless, my particular favourite. I was there, when one morning, between five and six o'clock, Mr Leeson came to town and rapped at the door of my lodging. The people of the house were alarmed, and from the description I had given they immediately guessed who it was. As they knew I was from home, they readily concluded it would be improper to let him within the doors. They therefore denied that any such person as myself dwelt there, they bade him begone, and scolded him heartily for disturbing a family at such an undue hour. Mr Leeson was enraged at being, as he thought, deceived by his friend the merchant, in telling him, he had taken a lodging for me in that house; and flew directly to him to upbraid him for his falsehood, and to know where I really was. The merchant arose and received him, assured him I lodged there, and asked if he signified his name to those who spoke to him from the window. He said he had, but instead of admitting him they only abused him. The merchant guessing how matters were, was much pleased that Leeson had not been let into the house, and told him that what had passed was a proof of his attention, and the care of the people of the house, not to suffer any visitor to see me in Mr Leeson's absence; and as they had never yet seen him, he ought rather to applaud than to condemn their conduct; adding that if he would stay till he was dressed he would accompany him to me. This entirely calmed my gentleman's mind, he apologized to the merchant for his misconstruction; and waited with patience, till his friend was ready, which he delayed as long as he could, without giving any room for suspicion.

In the mean time, the merchant dispatched a note to me, in which he briefly related what had passed, conjured me to get home directly, and to be ready to receive them, and give the people of the house their cue. The moment I received this news, I got a coach, drove to my lodgings, changed my cloaths, put on a morning cap, and when Mr Leeson and the merchant arrived, I was seated very calmly in the summer-house, attentively reading a book.

When I perceived them coming up the walk, my heart began to beat at my consciousness of the deception, and that if in any wise detected it would be my ruin. But I had better fortune than I deserved. Mr Leeson seemed quite happy at meeting me, received the apology of the good people of the house, with great satisfaction, and, even thanked them for their conduct; and remained quite confident at my virtue and attachment. Thanks to my friend the merchant, and those with whom I lodged.

CHAPTER THREE

What gudgeons are we men,
Ev'ry woman's easy prey?
Tho' we have felt the hook, again
We bite and they betray.

GAY

The pleasure surely is as great,
In being cheated, *as to* cheat.

HUDIBRAS

The man that's robb'd not knowing what he loses,
Tell him not of it, he's not robb'd at all.
I found not Cassio's kisses on her lips.
SHAKESPEARE

AT THIS PERIOD of my narrative, I doubt not but most of my readers will exclaim against me, and ask what excuse I can now offer for my conduct – I will candidly answer – NONE – I confess it was absolutely *inexcusable*. Yet, although I own it can have no palliation in the eyes of the world; though I confess I cannot plead ill usage to drive me, want or poverty to urge me, temptation to excite me, or love to allure me to what I was doing, yet, I was not without some reasons that appeared plausible, at least in my own eyes, for my excesses.

There were sundry notions that I had imbibed from the arguments of some of my companions, and from my own reflections, which had great weight with me; especially as they coincided with my inclinations, and quieted some scruples that from time to time, would obtrude themselves in my mind.

I, at that time, was fully persuaded that Polygamy was not wrong in its own nature, but merely as it was a great difference between what was *evil in itself,* and what was *evil by human prohibition,* which I think they called *malum in se* and *malum prohibitum*: that there were many customs sanctioned by law far worse in their effects than a Polygamy, which the law forbids. If the law forbids a plurality of *wives,* it might be understood that it equally forbids a plurality of *husbands,* but the express letter of the law, as I am told, does not condemn a plurality of *husbands.* Some indeed, may urge, that as I had no husband this reasoning would not apply. But I looked upon marriage merely as an human institution, calculated chiefly to fix the legitimation of children, and oblige their parents to breed them up and provide for them; to ascertain the descent of property; and also to bind two persons together, even after they might be disgusted with, and heartily tired of each other. Nay, it was pointed out to me, that though the Church of Rome, to which I belonged, exalted marriage into a *sacrament,* yet at the same time it strongly recommended, and in many cases obliged its professors to a *single life.* Now, I concluded that if marriage was what I thought it, and that there was no express law against a plurality of husbands, there could be none against a plurality of gallants; and that I, as yet single, should commit much less sin in admitting them than if I were married. I have long since seen the fallacy of those arguments, but at that time, they were deemed of considerable force; and by them I excused my conduct to myself.

I have hitherto introduced some occasional reflections for the consideration of my *female* readers, and will now beg leave to offer one to those of the *other sex.*

My conduct, with respect to Mr Leeson, will fully shew, that neither pleasure, content, affluence nor gratitude, can bind a woman of a loose turn of mind, and changeable disposition, to the man who has formed an illicit connexion with her. That he can have no confidence in an affection, however strong it may appear, that is not founded on Delicacy and Virtue. That her chief concern is how to raise pecuniary advantages from his infatuated fondness, and blind attachment to her; and will even prodigal the superfluities of his misguided bounty on another man who may be more agreeable in her eyes. That she will exercise her cunning to deceive him, and hide her infidelities from his knowledge; and when she has deceived, will laugh at his credulity. And – that a man who keeps a woman, experiences every possible *inconvenience* of marriage, without reaping any one of its *advantages.* Mr Leeson was sufficient wealthy and handsome, and I ought to have been contented with him, but I liked Mr Lawless better; yet, whilst I esteemed him most, I entertained his friend Jackson. And great as his love seemed to be, when he found he had not wealth sufficient to satiate my desires, and the continual demands of Caprice, Luxury, and Extravagance, his delicacy did not make him object to my living with Mr Leeson, who could supply his deficiencies. He was of a different opinion with *Othello,* who said

> —*I'd rather be a toad,*
> *And live upon the vapours of a dunghill,*
> *Than keep a corner in the thing I love,*
> *For other's uses.*

Though I had escaped so well, and avoided detection of my ramble to Mr Lawless's lodgings, at this time, yet my good fortune did not long continue. Mr Leeson, after living with me with great content, for some time, and enjoying with singular pleasure every amusement I proposed, he had another call to the country. But whether he entertained any suspicions of his friend, the merchant's, partiality to me; or was resolved before he married me to have still farther proofs of my fidelity; he engaged an Englishman, named Van Nost, to watch my steps. Which indeed, he did to some purpose; for being lulled into security, by my past escapes, the very next day after Mr Leeson had gone into the country, this new spy beheld Mr Lawless, and Mr Jackson, enter my lodgings with a band of music. He heard the concert, saw the entertainment go in, and did not see them depart. He made a strict enquiry through the neighbourhood, and when he had collected news enough to fill his budget, he wrote the whole account very circumstantially to Mr Leeson.

What were the feelings of Mr Leeson, when he received the detail of my faithlessness (too circumstantial to be denied, and too well authenticated to be doubted) may be imagined, from the consequence. He wrote immediately to the merchant to stop paying me any more money from that day; and the same post brought another letter to me; in which, after sufficiently upbraiding me with my faithless, and abandoned conduct, he declared – he had done with me for ever.

In many of our punishments Providence gives striking proofs of a just retaliation. When I received this letter, I was sitting in the same summerhouse, in which, but a few weeks before, I sat and hugged myself in the success of the deceit I had practised on Mr Leeson. The moment I cast my eyes on the letter, and before I knew any thing farther than that I was cast off and abandoned, this circumstance darted into my mind. Wretch that I am! (I cried) not content with the love and esteem of a worthy man, I basely deceived him. Here in this very spot, I beguiled his eyes, and made him believe my attachment to him was sincere. He weakly condemned himself for having entertained any suspicions of me. Now he has found his suspicions were too well founded. My treachery is manifest, and he has abandoned me for ever: and here, where I committed the fault, I justly receive an account of the punishment I so truly deserve. When my sobs and tears would give me leave, I read the whole letter and was distracted. I now saw myself without any means of support, I called to mind the misery, sorrow, poverty and distress I had already undergone, and saw them all about to be renewed. I sincerely regretted my ingratitude to Mr Leeson. Yet, fond, amiable, and generous as he had been to me, I candidly confess I was more distressed with the loss of his purse than his person.

I was sitting in this distracted state, which was verging to a stupid inattention to all things around me, when Mr Lawless entered. He was shocked to see me in that condition, and with every tender and soothing endearment, roused me from my anxiety, and enquired the cause of my distress. The fatal letter was yet in my hand, and I had only to reach it to him, to make him acquainted with my sorrowful situation. When he had read it, he besought me to raise my spirits, and banish my apprehensions of want, for that whilst he possessed a shilling I should partake of it. He added, that luckily he had it now more in his power to provide for me than heretofore, for but a few days had passed since his eldest brother had died, and though he inherited no real estate from him, yet, he had bequeathed to him his whole personal property, which would enable him to support expences that hitherto he had been unable to afford.

From the first time I saw Mr Lawless, he had been the foremost in my esteem. I really loved him, and during every connexion I had formed, I never failed to give him every proof he could desire. Therefore, it is not wonderful that I yielded to pleasing sensations at finding him still attached to me as strongly as ever; and that he had the power as well as the inclination, to quiet my fears of falling into poverty. Great as my trouble was, I was soon lulled into a calm. We entered the house, and there made the necessary arrangements for our future life. I promised sincerely he should have the sole possession of my heart and my person; and he, on his part, assured me of a like return. I inwardly rejoiced that I should have an opportunity of quitting that kind of life, to which I had submitted during Mr Leeson's reign, and live in uninterrupted felicity with the man of my heart.

We presently returned to Dublin, where we passed five years and a half together, during which time no wife was ever more fond, virtuous and faithful than I was to him; and to give him his due, no man ever treated his wife for the first three years, with more attention than Mr Lawless shewed to me. In those five years I bore him five children, each of which appeared as a new link of a chain to secure our mutual affections; and my care of them filled up every vacant hour of time. Happy period – happy should I have been had its duration been extended through life. But alas! I was destined to meet content only as gleams of sun-shine in a showry day, which merely serve to darken the gloom, when they are over-cast and hidden from our eyes.

For three years, Mr Lawless never partook of any public or private amusement without my participation. His love daily increased, even to an height that sometimes proved disagreeable, and indeed, was the only impediment to our mutual felicity. If I was seen, or spoken to by any of my former acquaintance, female as well as male, he was uneasy and became peevish. If, at the play, I even accepted an orange, or returned a salute from any gentleman he immediately insisted on our return home, though the performance was not half over. This was frequently very disagreeable to me. Conscious to myself of my strict fidelity to him, I thought myself greatly injured by his suspicions; and as my temper was naturally warm, and my passions highly irritable, I was not always placid upon those occasions; and we had sometimes high altercations.

CHAPTER FOUR

> *I commit many faults, but* NONE *to* THEE.
> *Indifference would never suit my fate.*
> *My passions are unruly; and, sometimes*
> *Break loose on my best friend: But then you should*
> *Consider them as the* effects *of* Love.
> *As the* effects! *— nay, they are* love *itself.*
> *For* love *itself is all the passions,*
> *At least to me: whether it be desire,*
> *Or hope, or fear, or anger, or revenge,*
> *In all its diff'rent motions — still is* Love.
> SOUTHERN'S *Fate of Capua*

HITHERTO we had lived in happiness, because we had lived with confidence in each other. Mr Lawless's late conduct, had shewn that the seeds of Doubt were still in his breast, and my heat of temper, perhaps took the wrong way to eradicate them. I should have considered that his desire of preventing any relapse into promiscuous amours, sprang from his affection. I should have behaved with double reserve; and not have met his solicitude with haughtiness and wranglings, which tended more to confirm than dispel — even unjust suspicions.

About the beginning of the fourth year, Mr Lawless began to dine out, and to go to public amusements without me. This more and more soured my temper, rendered me still more irritable, and though still fond and faithful, yet, at intervals, I admitted that fiend Jealousy, to take possession of my mind. Priding myself on my strict fidelity to him, I thought every moment of his absence was occasioned by his attachment to other females and a fresh insult to me. Hence I redoubled my invectives, and my passions often rose even to termagancy. I did not reflect that I was proceeding in the same path, that I had condemned him for treading; and that whilst I knew *my* jealousy sprang from Love, I ought to have been assured, that *his* doubts and suspicions arose from the same motive.

Mr Lawless then began to keep very late hours. This irritated me so much, that dressing myself very plain that I might not be noticed, I have frequently sallied into the street, attended by my maid-servant, and a watchman, and trudging on foot through rain, mud and dirt (for I would not put him to the expence of coach or chair hire) would visit every tavern, gaming-house, and place of pleasurable reception in search of my wandering Strephon. I often stood listening through key-holes, and under parlour windows, to try if I could hear his voice, till I have been covered with mire, drenched with the rain, or almost petrified with cold. Yet, all that, I endured with pleasure if I could but find him, which sometimes I did, but more often failed in my attempt. At those times, after a fruitless search I have returned home, with a mind tortured with what I thought a proof of his infidelity; or with apprehensions lest any mischief had befallen him. Yet, the sight and caresses of my children would give me some consolation, till I retired to my bed, when my disquietitudes returned with double force, and I passed without sleep till six in the morning; which became his usual hour of returning home. Then our animosities were renewed, and became more frequent; and in the place of former delicacy and endearments, nothing was heard but mutual revilings, and upbraidings, which drove tranquillity from the house.

O jealousy! wild and insatiate fiend! let every female guard against its first approaches, for she knows not to what horrid lengths it may carry her. Well did the poet, Dryden, say of it.

> *False in thy glass all objects are,*
> *Some sit too nigh, and some too far.*
> *Thou art a fire of endless night,*
> *A Fire that burns, yet gives no light.*
> *The torments of the damn'd we find*
> *Alone in thee*
> *O Jealousy!*
> *Thou Tyrant, Tyrant Jealousy!*
> *Thou Tyrant of the mind.*

Happy are those breasts which never entertain it; or whose prudence, mildness and equanimity can avert the cause, if cause there is, and not by passion, strife, and outrage, provoke a repetition of injury, and a continuance in the practice of it. I am the more urged to give this cordial, this salutary advice, since I experienced to what horrid extravagancies jealousy in a turbulent mind, may hurry the wretched victim: and even at this distance of time, I shudder at the recollection of what I shall now relate.

Sometimes when I have found it impossible to drown my grief in sleep, I have risen from my bed, and throwing up the sash, would hang out of the window till his return. There are never wanting a set of officious women, who, out of pretended friendship, will plant thorns in the mind of a suspicious and jealous woman, by bringing her tales of her husband's or lover's infidelity. One of this kind had been with me, and seeming to pity me, had related her certain assurance that Mr Lawless passed some of his nights with other females. This intelligence made me more eager to continue my nocturnal searches, in hopes of detecting him, and that night I hunted everywhere, but in vain. I returned in a rage, distracted with what I had heard, and the idea that perhaps at that very instant, he might be revelling in the arms of one of his favourites. I took a firm resolution of murdering him at his return, and then putting an end to myself. I kept a keen razor in my hand, and watched at the window for his coming. The hours I waited there steeled my heart, gave edge to my resentment, and fixed my determination. At length, I beheld him coming up the street, and frantic with rage, I ran to meet him on the stairs and execute my bloody purpose. Here let me adore the mercy of the Almighty, which saved his life and prevented me from the crime. In my hurry, I left the razor in the window, and was weaponless when I met him; and as a farther prevention, he returned in a better humour than usual, took me in his arms, apologised for his late return, and told me the house in which he had staid so long. My rage cooled instantly, my ardent love resumed its place, and I became calm. When in bed, where I could not sleep, I easily conceived, that, if he had really been where he told me, I had no cause for alarm or complaint; but still my jealousy, that had not been conquered, but only lulled for the moment, suggested, that he deceived me: then my resolution of revenge returned, and I resolved still to execute my design, if I found that he had told me false. I feared that if I sent to enquire if he had been at the house he said, the master of it might probably be in the plot, and send word that he had. Alas! my own contrivances in respect to Mr Leeson, had taught me to suspect perfidy in him. I therefore acted with more cunning; and when I arose I sent my servant in Mr Lawless's name, to desire they would look for a shirt breast-pin, which he had dropt there last night. They replied they had not seen it, but kept the servant whilst a strict and careful search was made in the rooms in which he had been. I was then satisfied that he had told me nothing but truth; for had he not been there they would not have sought for the pin. Then I rejoiced that I had not perpetrated what I had so iniquitously resolved, and for some time, as I became more placid, we lived with more tranquillity.

About this time Captain Mathews returned from America. Before I had known either Mr Jackson, Mr Lawless, or Mr Leeson, I had been acquainted with this gentleman: he had shewn great attention to me, and visited me very often. He was young and agreeable, and had a pretty fortune. As he was in the army, his regiment was ordered to America, and at that time I really regretted his departure. He had been some years abroad, and when he returned to Dublin, was desirous of renewing the connexion. He had made enquiries after me, but the private and retired way of life I led having made me little known, his search was fruitless for some time. At length, as he was sitting in the window at Daly's Coffee-house, he saw me pass by in a coach. He directly recognised me, and immediately followed the carriage, till he saw me alight from it, at my own little habitation, in Wood-street, which small as it was I prefered to the castle of Dublin, as it had been the scene of many happy hours.

When Captain Mathews had been informed of my retired mode of life, that calumny could not fasten its cankered tooth on my character, nor malice taint my fidelity to Mr Lawless, he thought it highly improper to come to me openly: but he found means to get a letter delivered to me, in which he requested me to give him a meeting, as he had a very handsome present for me. This I refused. He then sent a diamond ring – which I returned. This diamond ring was brought back to me, accompanied with another of equal brilliancy; both were rejected. Another effort was made. As, perhaps, he suspected I had looked upon his presents as too trivial for my acceptance, he now sent the rings again with a packet of bank notes: all these were refused. For at that time, his whole estate would have appeared insufficient to induce me to infidelity, to the man I so sincerely loved. At length, the Captain proposed marriage, but even that I refused. I prefered the society of Mr Lawless to any other connexion, although it might be sanctioned by law; and the company of my little children, for whom, if compelled by necessity, I would have sought to gain a support by my labour, rather than have married the first peer of the realm – and with this last refusal ended the fruitless proposals of Captain Mathews, and he desisted from any farther attempt.

Still the altercations between me and Mr Lawless, continued, and my jealousy and reproaching temper, embittered both our lives for about a year longer. Our time during that space was chiefly occupied, with doubts and satisfactions, quarrels and reconciliations. At length, as Mr Lawless's fortune was solely personal, and as he was never a man of economy, a capital derangement, or rather dissipation of his finances ensued; especially as his father, supposing he was married to me (which indeed, he never was) very much disapproved of his conduct. This added to his peevishness and petulence; and whenever I thought calmly, I attributed the greatest part of his disagreeable behaviour and irregularities, to his unsettled state of mind, on the melancholy prospect his affairs presented continually to him. Yet to the last, he shewed his strong affection for me, though very often in a manner that the most virtuous of wives could not have relished. His jealousy and diffidence increased daily. If when going out on family business, any man saluted or even spoke to me, he was alarmed at it, and would on our return not only scold, but frequently proceeded to blows; and would put me to my oath, that I had no connexion with the person who had paid me any mark of common civility; nor any kind of knowledge, that exceeded the strictest bounds of civility. But why need I complain of his conduct, when, as if we acted by sympathy, my doubts, suspicions, and jealousies of him went on in an even pace with those of his concerning me. If at any time we entertained a few friends, and he out of good manners would call on any female at table to take a glass of wine with him, it so far irritated me, that I could not eat a morsel more, and it rendered me disagreeable to the company for the whole evening after.

One particular anecdote of my turbulence and ill behaviour, I cannot avoid relating, as it may be a lesson to some of my female readers to avoid a similar conduct, by shewing its absurdity, and that it constantly fails of obtaining the end it proposes.

A gentleman had made a dinner party for Mr Lawless and me: There was a lady in company, to whom I thought he paid too particular an attention, at which I was so much galled, that it was with the utmost difficulty I could prevail upon myself to behave with tolerable decorum, for the remainder of the day. At length, the company broke up, and I was glad I had an opportunity to give vent to my spleen and discontent. As soon as we had got into a coach to return home, I began to scold and upbraid Mr Lawless. I seized his gloves, and threw them out of the carriage window – which were soon followed by my muff, his hat, and whatever I could lay my hands on. When we got home, where we might make as much noise as we pleased, we became vociferous in our contention, till we were both nearly tired. I refused to go to bed, he insisted I should, which I still refused. He then cut the strings of my cloaths, and threw me into bed. I twisted from him and got under it; he, greatly enraged at my obstinacy, pulled me out, and in the struggle hurt me so much, that he was obliged to send for Surgeon Cleghorn, who found me so bad that he was forced to fetch in Dr Cullum. By their united care, I at length recovered, with the loss of my child, of which I was above four months gone. Fatal effects of jealousy, rage and contention! I lost the things I had thrown out of the coach; had raised my spirits into a temporary madness; had, by my obstinacy drawn on myself ill usage; subjected myself to a long and dangerous illness, had incurred the expences of medical advice, and all the consequent charges of a sick bed; and to crown all, had been the death of the child I carried – and what was the mighty cause of all this train of calamities – because Mr Lawless behaved with politeness to a lady in company, in another gentleman's house. Reflect on this, ye Females of turbulent tempers. See what ye gain by being, what is too frequently your boast, *women of spirit;* and though your cases may not be exactly similar with what I have related; yet, from as trifling causes do your passions rise. Think that *mildness* is the true distinguishing characteristic of woman; and that a rage, and what is called *spirit* – which is the child of Pride and Folly – degrades the sex below its real dignity, nay, it defeats its own purpose; for reproaches and revilings tend more to disgust a man, than to establish or recal his love.

We now lived an unhappy life, yet, in the midst of all I continued true and faithful to him. His money was all gone, and for some months we subsisted on the sale of our watches, rings, cloaths, and ornaments. After them followed most of our household furniture. To complete our misery, our children died one by one, a little time after each other, excepting one only, who itself a few months after sickened. This darling boy was then at his nurse's, at the upper end of Bride-street. He was attended regularly by Dr Cleghorn, and I saw him twice a day; till at length, the Dr called on me, and recommended me to prepare for the worst, for he had no hopes of his life. I ran like a distracted woman to take a last farewel of my only surviving, yet, dying darling; but on my entrance into the nurse's house, found he had just departed. I snatched up the infant's scarce cold body in my arms, and wrapping the tail of my gown around it, ran screaming through the street, to my own house, and presented the child to Mr Lawless. He was much shocked at the sight, and was greatly affected at seeing the last of our five children snatched from us. I was indeed, carrying another, but the birth of that was uncertain, and at best but a distant comfort. Alas! I did not then behold the hand of Providence, which foreknowing the calamities that were soon to follow, wisely and mercifully took my children from me, 'ere they lighted upon us. Besides, these illegitimate children gave me pleasure, and were taken from me to punish me; and it seemed like the sentence that Nathan pronounced against King David, 'How be it, because by this deed (the unlawful begetting them) thou has given great occasion for the enemies of the Lord to blaspheme, the child also that is born unto thee shall surely die.'

Before I relate the unfortunate conclusion of my connexion with Mr Lawless, I beg leave to mention a very singular adventure that happened, some time before the death of my children, and whilst our prosperity was yet present.

Mr Lawless, thinking to give me a pleasurable jaunt, proposed that we should go to the Curragh races; a celebrated lady, then known by the appellation of *Kitty Cut-a-dash,* was to go also; she then lived with a Mr James Cavendish, who was particularly fond of the turf. We two went in the coach of a gentleman, who was drawn by four excellent bay geldings, that had been given to him by a certain Lord, for some services he had done for his Lordship. The gentlemen were to ride their horses. We all got to the course, and having feasted our eyes with all that was to be seen, went to Burchell's, at the Nineteen-mile House, for some refreshments; but we found the house so full, that there was not even a room to dine in, much less beds for us. Burchell and his wife, who knew and was very fond of me, offered to lay a cloth for us in their bed-room, and to procure a pallet in the same room, for the accommodation of us two females. To this I readily agreed, but Miss Kitty objected, as she had her Jemmy with her, whilst my swain was absent. In this dilemma, Mr Cavendish met with two gentlemen of his acquaintance, who had one of the parlours. We agreed to dine there, and proceed to Kildare to sleep. We dined, were very merry, drank our Champaigne, and time slipped away insensibly, till ten o'clock, when Mr Cavendish, Lord Boyne, and a Mr Trotter, came in the coach with us, and their servants rode their horses. The night was very dark, and one of the grooms, who boasted that he knew every foot of the road, offered to be our guide, and went before us on a grey horse, that he might be better seen by our coachman. We had proceeded about two miles on the sod, when our guide mistaking the way, led us against a ditch. Our horses being mettlesome and high fed, made no stop, but leaped and brought the coach clear over undamaged. We screeched and begged to be let out, but in vain, for the coachman, as self-conceited as our guide, said he would soon gain the road, and wheeled about, but in turning, ran the pole against the bank of the ditch, when it snapped in two. The gentlemen wanted us to stay in the coach till day-light, saying we could sleep very comfortably therein. To this I firmly objected, and then it was agreed we should ride to Kildare on the horses. There were but three, so Kitty rode, on the bare rump behind Mr Cavendish, I sat before Lord Boyne, and guided the horse, whilst he kept himself fast by holding me round the waste [sic]; and Mr Trotter led the van on the grey horse. The servants were all left to take care of the coach.

We then set out again for Kildare. We travelled in this manner, backwards and forwards for above three hours; and never did I suffer more than I did that night, being almost perished with cold, and almost ready to drop from the horse. Kitty indeed, was not in the same situation, she got warmed by the frequent falls she had; and I believe nothing kept me alive but my laughing at her, for she clung so fast to her Jemmy, that whenever she slipped off, she dragged him down with her.

At last she spied a light, that seemed to proceed from a cabin, about two miles distance. We made towards it, Mr Trotter on his grey, leading the way; when on a sudden, we lost sight of our guide, he having got into a sand-pit, where he and his poney, kept dancing amongst the stones at the bottom, to which they had fallen, for a full quarter of an hour before they could get out. He shouting out to us to keep where we were. Had I not seen him fall, I should have been directly on top of him, and Lord Boyne, and our horse on me; and then in all probability, my memoirs would have finished here, as there must have been an end of *Margaret*.

Mr Trotter now, with constant efforts had succeeded in getting himself and his horse out of the sand-pit. He still persisted in making for the light, and at length, we reached it without any more accidents, than two or three more falls of Kitty; who did not seem to mind them much, as she had Mr Cavendish with her, of whom at that time she was very fond. I had not a like consolation, for as soon as Mr Lawless had packed me off, he went

51

somewhere else, and did not come to join us as he had promised.

When we got to the cabin we roused the people, and by a handsome reward, procured a man to conduct us to Kildare, which he very properly did, and we reached the town at about three in the morning. As it was so late, nobody was up in the town but some bucks, some gentlemen gamblers, who were fleecing each other. Not a bed to be got, all the taverns full, and every private house engaged. What was then to be done? we could not sleep on horse-back in the streets all night. The reader has had many proofs, that my temper was not of the most placid kind; and I began to vent my discontent on Kitty. A strong altercation began, I reproached her with preventing us from staying at Burchell's, where we might have avoided all the inconveniencies we had undergone: and she in her turn, upbraided me that I would not remain in the carriage, where we might have been warm and comfortable, and might have enjoyed some sleep. I urged, that I was deterred from staying in the coach, that I might not be exposed to attempts which one of the gentlemen had hinted as we drove along; for this was in my virtuous days, as I called them; and though I strongly believed, that Mr Lawless staying behind was owing to some pre-concerted infidelity, yet, at that time, nothing could have tempted me to have returned the compliment.

Whilst we were thus jarring, our gentlemen had been searching the town over for beds, but not one could be got. However, Farrell the piper, who they found playing in one of the taverns, had given them the key of his lodging, which he offered for our acceptance. We hastened to it; but of all the wretched habitations I had ever seen, this was by far the worst. The curtains were of ten different colours, and the bed most miserable. However, necessity urged, and we lay down in our cloaths for about three hours, and then got our breakfasts from the tavern.

By the time our hairs were dressed, the coach was got mended and brought to Kildare. We returned to the Curragh; but I was so distracted with jealousy, at the disappointment of not seeing Mr Lawless, that after staying one heat, nothing could induce me to wait for a second. I would go to town in spite of all the intreaties of Kitty, who was forced to come and leave her Jemmy behind, sore against her will.

I had contracted an acquaintance with a Mrs Johnston, who lived in Fownes's-street, and was kept by a relation of my first love, Mr Dardis; when the carriage came into Dame-street, I got out, took my leave of Kitty, and walked down to Mrs Johnston's house. I gave a single rap at the door, and as soon as it was opened, I pushed in without saying a word, and opened the parlour door, without giving the least notice. There I found Mr Lawless sitting tete-a-tete, and drinking Champaigne with Mrs Johnston. We all three stood as petrified. My jealousy was wound up to so high a pitch, that I screamed, trembled, and was quite beside myself. I snatched up the decanter, and was about to dash it in her face, when Mr Lawless seized and held my hands, and prevented me from murder; which had I thrown the double-flint glass decanter in her face, must have ensued. She was so astonished at the sight of me, that she sat motionless in her chair, and never offered to defend herself, to stir, or even to utter a single word. Lawless took me home, and in time appeased me. But I had my revenge of Mrs Johnston, for I immediately sent for the gentleman who maintained her, related the circumstance, and also many other proofs of her infidelity, which had come to my knowledge, and which she could not deny. And he immediately forsook her, and would never see or support her more.

But to return to my narrative from whence I have digressed.

The finances of Mr Lawless being not only exhausted, but also whatever could be raised from our superfluities, and even some of our necessaries, he began seriously to revolve in his mind what means could be found for future support. His friends advised him to quit the kingdom, as his father was resolved, not to give him any farther subsistence in Ireland, which he refused in the most peremptory manner, but at last consented to give him a draft on Messrs Smith and Ramage, merchants in New-York, to be paid to him only, on his arrival there; the old gentleman being persuaded if he gave him any money here, it would be shared with me, as it most certainly would have been.

This determination was like a clap of thunder, it struck me almost senseless; although there was no prospect of subsistence, I was distracted at the thoughts of his going to America. He argued with me, justly, that his continuing here would, only serve to plunge us both into greater distress, without even a probability of extricating ourselves from it. On the other hand, I exerted every art of persuasion to induce him to stay with me, and endeavour to find out some means of support, but his pride would not suffer him to listen to me. He now became the most kind and tender man he could possibly be, which still more endeared him to me, and rendered me still more reluctant to agree to our separation. Oft would he cry, whilst the tears trickled down his cheeks – Oh! my dear Margaret! If I am obliged to go abroad, will you still bear me in your remembrance? will you cherish

53

and love, for my sake, the babe you carry, if it comes to maturity, as it is the sole one that will be left of our all. I have replied properly, and asked why he would think of leaving me?

I long thought he would never accede to his father's proposal; but alas! he had determined, though he would not acquaint me of his resolution: As he well knew he could not bear the pangs of a formal parting (and so he told his friends) he secretly engaged a passage in an American vessel, and got his cloaths and baggage privately on board. The night before he departed, he came to me and said he was to go the next morning a few miles from town; he again asked, if I would remember him, and love the expected infant. He would not go to bed, but at one in the morning, said he must sleep that night at his lodgings, where his uncle was to call upon him early, to go out of town together, and give him some money: this satisfied me, I had no doubts, and suffered him to go. He came twice or thrice back to my room before he quitted the house, pressed me affectionately to his bosom, and blessed me with uncommon earnestness. At that time, I took no notice of these particulars, though they frequently occurred afterwards to my mind.

The next morning arrived; a morning that will be ever remembered with anxiety, whilst recollection lasts or sensibility remains. The most particular friend of Mr Lawless came to visit me, and presented me with a letter from him. As soon as I had the letter in my hand, I was seized with an unusual fluttering of my heart. With a trembling hand I broke the seal, and with a moistened eye, read the words,

My darling Peggy
I sail this morning to America—

I could read no more. The paper fell from my hands, my sight grew dizzy, I fell lifeless from my chair, and continued in fits for several hours. At length, a flood of tears came to my relief, but came to affix the seal of certainty on my misfortune. I then strove to read the remainder of this fatal letter, and the retracing of his dear lines, seemed my only, though melancholy comfort. It continued in these words.

I could not bring myself to tell you, my love! I was going to leave you. Do not be angry then with your dear Lawless, when real affection, and a disposition not to give you pain, was the cause that made him thus abruptly break from those bonds, by which he would joyfully for ever be united to you. Yet, rest in peace and be certain of hearing from me by every opportunity; and, as you love me, my dear Peggy! take care of our baby, child – Adieu! and may every blessing of Heaven guard you till we once more meet.

From a state of fainting and almost insensibility, these lines roused me to fury. Words cannot express the tortures of mind. I tore my hair, I beat my breasts, rent my cloaths, and became outrageously and raving mad – until nature, nearly exhausted by these violent passions, sunk spiritless and stupid, and the whole frame of my nerves were palsied. In this state I continued near a week, incapable to answer any question with propriety. My friends, alarmed at my condition, brought in two physicians (Doctors Cullum and Cleghorn,) who ordered me instantly to quit Wood-street, to breathe a purer air than that close part of the town afforded. I was then moved to Ranelagh-road, almost powerless, being obliged to be carried in arms to the coach, and out of it up stairs to my new lodgings. I was every day carried into the garden, where I remained for two hours a-day, propped up by pillows; as my debility was too great to sit unsupported. Here, labouring under extreme weakness of body and distress of mind, I remained till by the change of air, and the consolatory conversation of my friends, I grew something better; and gradually, but slowly, recovered strength and spirits enough to be delivered of a fine girl, who was dearer to me than all the children I had borne, as it was the last pledge of my dear Lawless, and his image was minutely traced on the countenance of the new-born innocent.

CHAPTER FIVE

Each substance of a grief hath twenty shadows
Which shew like grief itself, but are not so:
For sorrow's eye, glazed with blinding tears,
Divides one thing entire, to many objects
Like Perspectives, *which, rightly gaz'd upon*
Shew nothing but confusion; ey'd awry
Distinguish form – so, I
Looking awry on his departure
Find shapes of grief, more than himself to wail
Which look'd on as it is, is nought but shadows
Of what it is not – weep not

For more than his departure; more's not seen
Or if it be, 'tis with false sorrow's eye
Which, for things true, weep things imaginary.
SHAKESPEARE'S *Richard II*

FOR SOME TIME AFTER Mr Lawless had sailed for America, my grief, though violent, was yet methodical. In my melancholy, sickly state, I had leisure to exert my fancy, and to combine in one accumulated sum the divers articles, for each of which I ought to grieve. First, his absence deprived me of the main comfort of my life; yet, it was not the sole cause of uneasiness. I figured to myself the consequences of his absence, both to himself and to me. In regard to himself, I imagined he would be more easily consoled than I should be, as he had many more new objects of consolation than I had. He had a comfortable subsistence; the means of mine were drained. He had incessantly a variety of new objects surrounding him to give him pleasure, and banish me from his mind; I was confined to constant sameness, and every thing around me only presented what brought him momentally to my recollection. He would doubtless, be caught with the charms of females he might see, and enter into connexions with them. The very idea of which was a poinard to my heart; whereas I was sickly, and emaciated; and it might have been said of me as of the unhappy Jane Shore.

Now sunk with grief, and pining in despair,
Her waining form no longer can excite
Envy in woman, or desire in man.
She never views the sun but thro' her tears
And wakes to weep the live long night away.

In the next place, I was sunk in poverty, could scarce afford the comforts necessary for my sick situation, and my lying-in, with the most scanty hand, and had no prospect before my eyes, by which my circumstances might be amended. However just at this period, a Miss Fleetwood, who was under the protection of Lord Cl—m called on me, and wanted to take my house in Wood-street. As I was well acquainted with her, I immediately concluded the bargain; and what she paid me was highly welcome, as it provided a sufficient maintenance for myself and child, under my sickness and adversity. I remained some months in my country lodgings, till I was so far recovered as to be able to go out. My friends advised me now to turn my views to the brighter side of my affairs, and to banish as much as I could all gloomy ideas, as whilst my thoughts were incessantly bent on subjects of melancholy, I could not expect any re-establishment of my health. My physicians also told me that unless I would exert myself a consumption would inevitably come on, and then I should be accessary to my own destruction.

This advice was so frequently inculcated by all around me, that I found the absolute necessity of following it; and also of increasing my finances. When I went to the country, I had let my little house to Miss Sally Hayes (for whom I had a very strong friendship) at half-a-guinea a week, which was my sole support, in my illness and lying-in. And that was the first lodging she ever occupied after she had left her father's house, with Mr P—. When I let my house to Miss Fleetwood, it was on condition that Miss Hayes should still have her own apartment, and after she had quitted it, Sally still remained there. When I found myself able to remove I sent my child to nurse, and returned to Wood-street, where we lived together, in constant expectations of hearing from Mr Lawless. Month after month came, but yet not a line from him. Whatever outward appearance of cheerfulness I assumed, I was inwardly greatly disquieted. I conceived he must have been dead, or what was still more grievous to me that he was ungenerous, ungrateful, and had forgotten me.

As I had been so many years in a situation so very recluse, and had so long been absent from every place of public amusement, I was in a great measure a new face. My friends congratulated me on my return to the world, and I had presently a very numerous train of admirers, each emulous to gain my good opinion, and striving who should pay the greatest attention to me. This flattered my vanity, I sat with them, partook of their treats, went with them to public places, and frequently accepted their presents – yet, this was all they could obtain from me, as I was resolved to keep faithful to Lawless, till he should return from America, or I could receive certain news he was dead. For faithless as he was to me, I still had so much affection for him, that I could not reconcile to myself the admitting any other person to my bed.

Amongst the number of those who laid close siege to me, and did not quit their attacks on my firm resistance, as several did, was the very same Captain Mathews, my old friend, I have already mentioned. He teazed me morning, noon and night, to be again taken into my favour, and be the representative of Mr Lawless. He was soon convinced, that the strong attachment I had entertained, put it out of the power of even interest, to alter my good opinion, or make me unfaithful. But the difficulty of gaining me, made Captain Mathews still more eager to obtain my esteem. I went so far in indulgence to the love-sick swain, as to accompany him to a country entertainment, that was both expensive and elegant; but I took that opportunity to convince him of the folly and inutility of making any farther addresses to me, as I was most resolutely determined not to accept of any man, till I had heard from, or of Mr Lawless. Captain Mathews, then offered to take me to any part of America, where I could expect to find Lawless, upon my promise that if he was unable to support me, or unwilling to receive me, that I would then accept his offer and attach myself to him.

His proposal was, indeed, very generous, and fully demonstrative of his sincere regard for me, but I rejected it. I well knew Mr Lawless had it not in his power to afford me a subsistence, and thought it would be cruel in me to give him the pain (as I yet flattered myself he would feel) at seeing me in the arms of another. Besides, as I could not find he had written to any of his own relations, any more than to me, I yet imagined I should receive some letter from him, in which he would explain his conduct towards me and acquaint me with the real state of his affairs. And, indeed, had Mr Lawless given me such information of himself, and even told me that he would return to me as soon as ever it was in his power, I would have waited, however long, for so joyful an event; and have endeavoured to support myself, by honest industry, had it been even by plain-work, or washing small linen, during the interval. But alas! it was otherwise decreed, I was fated to taste the bitter cup of misery, and plunge in a whirl of those pleasures, which bring remorse and sorrow in their train.

Book Three

CHAPTER ONE

I've often heard
Two things averr'd,
By my dear Grand-Mama;
To be as sure,
As light is pure,
Or knavery in Law.
He who will prove,
Once false in Love,
Will make all truth a scoff;
And every woman that has — you know what
Will never leave it off.

FIELDING

FULL EIGHTEEN MONTHS had passed and yet no letter: still I lived in daily expectation, when one morning Mr C— (the gentleman who had brought me the letter from Lawless, when he sailed from Dublin) came to enquire if I had heard from his friend. I told him if I had I should certainly have come to acquaint him with it, as I knew their intimate friendship. He then begged I would not be uneasy at his acquainting me with what he had heard. This is a very common, but a very absurd way of prefacing dis-agreeable news, as the very request excites an alarm; and if the news must be affecting, how foolish to expect that trifling precaution will prevent dis-quiet. However, I promised I would not be uneasy; although at that moment very much so, from the expectation of hearing I knew not what. Mr C— then told me Mr Lawless's uncle, and his brother, had each got a letter from him; on hearing which, he had been to them to make an enquiry if there was not one for him, or me – but there was none. Notwithstanding the preparation for this displeasing intelligence, and my saying I would not be affected by any thing I could hear, my heart sunk in me at this proof of his neglect. My pride was mortified, and my self-love greatly hurt, and my resentment roused. What! (cried I suddenly exclaim-ing), cruel, base, deceitful, ungenerous man! Have I so long kept myself faithful to thee for this return! Have I, for this, lived in obscurity, and refused the ample and generous offers of several gentlemen, to be thus neglected? No, I will no longer entertain any affection for thee! From this moment I will tear thee from my heart! From this hour I hate, I loathe, I detest thee; and I swear I will yield myself to the first agreeable and prof-itable offer that is made to me.

Though I had formed this resolution in respect to another connexion, I did not immediately put it into execution: So numerous were my admirers, that I was bewildered in my choice, and hesitated where to fix. I then regretted that I had refused Captain Mathews, as I might have lived with him in a genteel stile, he having then an income, on which, by proper management, we might have been comfortably supported; but he was gone to England, and out of my reach. The principal of my admirers, who was a *single* man (for my whole life through, I never was fond of those who were *married*) was an amiable young gentleman, who had been very sedulously after me, whilst taking his degrees for the Church, in the College. He renewed his acquaintance with me, and I gave him more encouragement than before. He came to see me every morning, and when I permitted, would send in supper and wine, and stay some hours with me. I was pleased with his perseverance, and made him hope that in a short time I would meet his wishes.

But the ill usage of Lawless, had changed me to what I never was before. In short, I was become a compleat *Coquet*. I entertained every one who fluttered about me, I received every present that was offered, accepted of every entertainment that was made for me; gave them all hopes, yet yielded to none. I was disgusted with the man of my heart, therefore gave my heart to none. I looked upon all men as my lawful prey, and wished to punish the crimes of one on the whole sex; to get all I could from each, and grant nothing in return. I applied to myself the words of *Millwood,* who I sought to imitate in every thing but her cruelty.

> *Women, by whom ye are, the source of joy,*
> *With cruel arts ye labour to destroy;*
> *A thousand ways our ruin ye pursue*
> *Yet blame in us those arts first taught by you.*
> *O may from hence each violated maid,*
> *By cruel, barb'rous faithless man betray'd;*
> *When robb'd of innocence and virgin fame,*
> *From their destruction raise a nobler name;*
> *To right her sex's wrongs devote her mind*
> *And future* Millwoods *prove, to plague mankind.*
> GEORGE BARNWELL

Yet notwithstanding I had began a kind of course of coquetry, my natural turn was not adapted to continue long in it. Though I perfectly reconciled my conduct towards men, under the colour of just retaliation, my passions were not totally extinguished by the long time I had waited for the return of Mr Lawless. Mr L—, my young clergyman, was amiable both in person and manners. I made him, at length, a promise of yielding, and even fixed the evening when he was to come to my house. Yet, that very day, I appointed to sup with a gentleman at the Rose and Bottle, in Dame-street. I went, the supper was elegant, and the pleasure was enhanced by a band of music, of which I was ever very fond, and which I always insisted on having, to enliven our repast, when I agreed to sup with any gentleman. The evening had nearly concluded with every possible hillarity, when a chairman came and brought me a letter, which he was to deliver to me only. I went down to him in the hall, I found it was from Mr L—, who requested me to come home as he was then waiting for me, and had sent his own chair, lest I could not conveniently procure one at that hour. I then recollected my promise to him; and, somewhat warmed and elevated with Champaigne I had drank, I stepped into the chair without the least hesitation, without either cloak or hat, both of which I had left above in the room where I had supped; as I knew if I went or sent up for them they would not have been given to me; and my company would have prevented my going to my first engagement with Mr L—, I therefore went home as I was, and left my company to think what they pleased, and console themselves for my sudden departure as well as, or how they pleased.

When I came home I found the agreeable Mr L—, waiting for me with great anxiety, fearful lest I would not come, and happy at my appearance. Champaigne is a wine I never loved, but only it was dear, and I liked to put those who treated me to as much expence as I could. What I had drank had so exhilerated my spirits, that I threw off all reserve, forgot all my resolutions, and – admitted him to a bed, that no man but Lawless had entered with me for many years. When I awakened in the morning, I was as perfectly tranquil, and thought as little about it, as any modest widow when she takes her second husband; but the servants all the next day, cried 'their old master was forgotten.'

From that day Mr L— lived with me, and supported me in the most abundant manner. I soon proved with child, of which he was not a little proud, and for several months we continued a very agreeable life. At length, he had occasion to go into the country to see his friends, and left me a sum of money, fully sufficient for all expences till his return. But alas! I could not wait for that. Having gone so far in the road of Variety, I could not be confined to one man. Gratitude indeed, ought to have made me as faithful to Mr L—, as I had ever been to Mr Lawless; but *Love,* the sole bond of fidelity was wanting. I had began to slide down the steep declivity of Vice, whereon those who venture seldom stop till they reach the bottom. I had contracted an acquaintance with a Mr Cashel, he was young, gay, handsome, and an undoubted gentleman, but he had no money. As I had admitted his visits for some time, I entertained a liking for him, and soon took him to supply the place and absence of Mr L—. Learn, ye *keepers!* – how much ye deceive yourselves, when ye imagine ye can engage a woman to yourselves alone. No, be ye certain there can be no sure and permanent connexion between the two sexes, unless Virtue is the cement; of this the following event will be a most convincing proof; if any proof can be wanting to confirm a truth, that lies open to every person's reason and reflection.

When Mr L— returned, he had lodgings of his own, and he came to me as usual. He had sent in supper and wine, as he was accustomed to do. As Mr Cashel was then in my house, I was greatly perplexed how I should act between the man who generously supported me, and him who had not a single guinea to give me: But affection at that time prevailed with me more than interest. I concealed him whom I admired, whilst I let in him who admired me. As I was then very big with child, I pretended indisposition; and made that my excuse for intreating Mr L— not to sleep with me that night. With the utmost gentleness and good-nature he acquiesced with my desire, totally unsuspicious of my real motive; and departed, leaving Mr Cashel master of the field. The next night, Mr L— met me at the theatre. Here the same infatuation possessed me, and hurried me to act a part which was not only absurd, but exposed me to great uneasiness. Conscious that I could impose upon him as I pleased, I told him that my present condition would render it very improper for a time to come, to admit him to my bed, to which I could not agree till after my lying-in, I therefore, strongly recommended him to fill up that chasm with some other woman. For some time he hesitated, but at length he seemed as half consenting to my proposal. I then asked him, what he thought of Miss *Netterville* (alias *Kitty Cut-a-dash,*) he said he should like her very well, and I promised to gain her consent.

What inconsistant creatures are women, when under the influence of their passions! Here, although it was my interest to keep well with Mr L—, who was my sole support; yet, my passion for my other Spark, who was almost pennyless, prompted me giddily to estrange him from me, and even to turn a procuress for his pleasure. I vainly imagined it would be only looked upon by him as a temporary amusement. That I could still maintain my ascendency over him; and could recal him when I pleased. Foolish, deceitful, deceived woman!

Having thus broke the ice, I congratulated myself on my cleverness, and invited Kitty home with us to supper. I took her aside and told her Mr L— had not slept with me since his return to town; that I was fonder of Cashel than of him, and would advise her to take Mr L— off of my hands, and to receive him for a time. Adding that he was very generous, and she would find her account in this connexion. To this she readily agreed, as she never piqued herself on constancy to any one, and we fixed that we would sup with her the next night, and I would leave him with her. Accordingly we went the next evening, to her house in Grafton-street, where after we had supped elegantly, I took my leave of them and came home alone.

CHAPTER TWO

This purse will tell you that I thank you.
Is ev'ry thing in order? – put on your best looks,
as well as cloaths;
Gold, that does ev'ry thing, shall make you smile:
Carry an invitation in your face,
To ev'ry one you see, no matter who,
Naught shall appear
Within these walls but plenty, mirth and love.
No matter what the fools of form shall say,
Let them believe us mad, we'll pity them,
And their dull want of knowing how to love.

SOUTHERN

STILL MORE INCONSISTENCIES! I had no sooner turned my back on the couple I had put together, but my old companion, Jealousy, came to visit me. I revolved in my mind the agreeable hours I had passed with Mr L—, all his good and amiable qualities recurred to my remembrance: I saw they were then all lost to me. They were transferred to another, and I myself had negociated the transfer. I could have cut out my own tongue for having desired him to visit her. But the die was thrown, there was no remedy and I must abide by the cast. These thoughts so rankled in my mind, that when I came home I did not find Mr Cashel (for whose sake I had committed this folly) half so agreeable as he had hitherto appeared to be, and I was not in the best of humour even to him, nor could I conquer my jealousy for some time.

In the mean while Kitty acquired an ascendency over Mr L—, little less than fascination; of which his pocket soon found the effects. She was tenfold more expensive to him than I had been. She was insatiable in her wants, and made him bring her presents from every shop, wherein he could establish any credit; which his being a clergyman, made it more easy for him to obtain, than it might otherwise have been. He ran some hundreds with Mr Grogan, the mercer, for silks and sattins; with Mr Moore, the jeweller, for diamonds, and many other shops for other articles, till at length he pretty well ran himself a-ground.

When I saw this profusion of presents, I condemned myself that I had not engrossed the like: But for my inexcusable folly all these things might have been mine: I looked upon it as a robbery from me; and became ten times madder than I was, the night I had left them together. Besides, Kitty treacherously told him all my secrets that I had entrusted to her; and my attachment to Cashel, amongst the rest. This completely shut the door against his return to me, which was the more grievous to me, as I began to be in want of money, and my dear Cashel could not supply me with any.

Equally stung with envy, pride, jealousy, and resentment, I resolved to take a signal revenge on my treacherous she-friend. She then was kept by Mr Kilpatrick, who had been exceedingly generous to her. I sent for him, told him every circumstance of her faithless and abandoned conduct in respect to him; not reflecting that I was equally guilty in regard to others, and bade him give me as his author: For, like *Zanga,* I did not think my revenge was compleat, without she knew the stroke that would destroy her, came from my hand. The gentleman seemed to have his eyes opened, he thanked me for my intelligence. He broke off with her immediately, and never visited her again, but shortly after married an amiable lady, nearly related to the Earl of Belvedere.

In due time I was brought to bed of a young Miss L—. The father, though he saw me no more, yet behaved like a gentleman. He liberally paid all the expences of my lying-in, till I went abroad; and paid for the child in every respect, till she was four years old.

Miss Netterville and I, after the mutual ill offices we had done each other, broke out into an open war: We indeed, fought at a distance, and spoke all the ill we could of each other. However, at length she hired a set of ruffians, to go into the upper gallery of the play-house, and thence call out scurrilous names, and abuse me whenever I appeared in the lattices. This was so constantly repeated, that the mob made it their nightly practice to join in the clamour, till it became unnecessary for Kitty to hire people for that purpose. I had no other part to take, but to sit still and give no heed to their abuse, but pass over in silence what I could neither avoid nor remedy.

Giving myself up entirely to a round of pleasure, and admitting much company, I soon found my little house too small to entertain them. I therefore, took a large one in Drogheda-street, and Sally Hayes lived with me. I hired an handsome chariot, and we dashed away, cared for nobody, wanted for nothing, had numerous presents, frequented every public amusement, were every night at the play superbly dressed, and lived like princesses. We constantly drove to the Curragh races, in a coach and four, my servants in liveries of scarlet and gold, and Isaacs, the dulcimer player in our rear. I always took rooms for the week at Burchell's, the Nineteen-mile House, to the joy of our male, and the envy of our female acquaintance. We thus lived without care, and without thought or reflection, supposing this way of life would ever last; and that age and wrinkles would never approach us; that, as *Roe* says,

> *– Then all was jollity,*
> *Piping and minstrelsy, gay mirth and dancing;*
> *Till life flew from us like an idle dream,*
> *A shew of mummery without a meaning.*

CHAPTER THREE

> *There was a time in the gay spring of life*
> *When ev'ry note was as the mounting lark's*
> *Merry and cheerful to salute the morn:*
> *When all the day was made of melody.*
> *But it is past, that day is spent and done,*
> *And it has long been night, long night with me.*
> *I have been happier, you have known me so.*
>
> SOUTHERN

SOME SHORT TIME AFTER, the post-man came early to the door with a letter. I soon recognised Mr Lawless's hand. The letter indeed, was from him, the first I had received for the space of four years. It informed me that he was returned from America, that he had landed at Cork, and desired I would come to him there. But I was greatly changed. The time was past in which I would almost have given one of my eyes for a letter from him. Now I received it with the utmost indifference, and read it with disgust. I was irritated with his four years total silence, and therefore had not the least inclination to meet him. However, I communicated this epistle to such of my female friends as had known us both. They all argued strongly in his favour, but to them I replied, 'that his maltreatment of me, for nearly the last two years we had lived together, notwithstanding my exemplary conduct and fidelity to him; my saving and domestic way of life; my having cheerfully parted with every article of finery, so precious to most women, for the support of him and his children, and my constancy for a long time after he was gone, ere I would admit another lover; had all met with no return but ungrateful neglect; for which reasons, I could not possibly have any inducement or inclination to see him.' To be sure in this detail, however true, I quite forgot to urge the provocation I had given him by my jealousies, turbulence, and constant altercation. My eloquence was fruitless, my friends pleaded much in his behalf; especially Sally Hayes, who said the expence would be but trifling, for I had a carriage, it was only adding two horses to my own two, and four would trundle us to Cork, in a little time. She also joined another argument, that perhaps he had saved some money, which I should certainly lose if I did not meet him. This consideration was more prevalent than every other. I was arrived to the same character, which I had heard some of my learned College friends ascribe to the famous Cataline, in a Latin line, which I remember was – *Appetens alieni, profusus sui,* which they told me meant – *Covetous of the property of others, lavish of that which was his own.* The thoughts of getting Lawless's money turned the scale, and determined me to set out for Cork.

Accompanied with my little friend, Sally Hayes, we arrived in that city, quite in stile. I met Mr Lawless, but not with my wonted ardor. I thought I never beheld any object more disagreeable. Not that he was either disfigured, or deformed in his absence, as he had hazarded no wounds in battle, nor any change from want, or climate. But I did not look upon him with the same eyes as formerly; his neglect (a crime which no woman can bear) had penetrated deep into my heart. I soon let him know I was entirely my own mistress, and was accountable to no one for my conduct or actions; and as I was come to Cork, I would see every thing there that merited attention, and partake of every pleasure and amusement that city afforded.

I then went into a lodging Mr Lawless had taken for me, where Sally and I dwelt. It was on Hammond's-marsh, at the house of an old stiff Puritan; who had he known who we were, would have thought his habitation would have taken fire of itself, and have burnt down to the ground. There we lived a month, making daily excursions to Cove, Glanmire, the Rock, &c.: dressed with a flaming elegance, that dazzled every one, and remained quite unknown, till the Sunday before we left the place.

On that day, we had driven to Sunday's-well, when I sent the carriage back, and resolved to cross in the ferry-boat, and walk home. The boat had about twenty persons in it, amongst whom there happened to be a whiffling, impertinent cox-comb, such puppies as infest every public place. He had seen me in Dublin, and knew who I was. He spoke to me, but I made him no answer, as I did not know him. Piqued at my silence, he buzzed my name and that of my companion, which drew the eyes of above twenty directly upon us, and peeped under our bonnets; some said it was Peg Plunket, with Sally Hayes. Others that it was not. Mr Lawless was very prudently silent, but I really thought from the behaviour of these people, as I had been told that Cork was a lawless place, that they would have pushed our man from between us, and have carried us where they pleased. However, when we landed many of them dispersed, only a few followed us, and dogged us; but we tired their patience, and they could not trace us to our lodgings; in which we staid but two days longer and then sat out for Dublin, accompanied by Mr Lawless on horseback.

CHAPTER FOUR

If he swagger, let him not come here: no, by my faith: I must
live among my neighbours, I'll no swaggerers here: I am in good
name and fame with the best: I have not lived all this while to
have swaggering now. Shut the door I pray you.

SHAKESPEARE

— his addiction was to courses vain;
His companies unfetter'd, rude and shallow;
His hours fill'd up with riots, banquets, sports
And never noted in him any study,
Any retirement, any sequestration
From open haunts.

SHAKESPEARE

WHEN we came back to Dublin, I found Mr Lawless had not returned rich from America. However, though disappointed in my expectation of money from him, gratitude prevailed on me to admit him into my house, where we each provided for our separate expences. He had excused himself to me for his not writing, as he alledged that the war had prevented a free intercourse of letters between the two countries. I seemed to admit the excuse, though it was evident the correspondence, if partly impeded was not totally stopped: witness the letters he sent to his relations, though none to me or to his friend. My love for him no longer existed, yet, such is the frailty of woman, that I became with child; and when I was about eight months gone an event happened, that made too much noise, and was too serious in its consequences to be admitted.

At that time, Dublin was infested with a set of beings, who, however they might be deemed *gentlemen* by their birth, or connexions, yet, by their actions, deserved no other appellation than that of RUFFIANS. They were then called *Pinking-dindies,* and deriving boldness from their numbers, committed irregularities, abhorrent to humanity; and gave affronts when together, which singly they would not have had courage even to attempt. They ran drunk through the streets, knocking down whoever they met; attacked, beat, and cut the watch; and with great valour, broke open the habitations of unfortunate girls, demolished the furniture of their rooms, and treated the unhappy sufferers with a barbarity and savageness, at which, a gang of drunken coal-porters would have blushed. At the head of this infamous set was a man, who, though of a noble family, disgraced it *then* by his behaviour; and who has since made his name famous for contriving to *mount nearer to Heaven,* than he had any reason for expecting ever to arrive.

This person took it into his head, without any provocation, to use me in the same manner that others had been treated. He came one evening to my house in Drogheda-street, at the head of a numerous gang of his associates, and insisted on being admitted. On my refusal they smashed all my windows, broke the hall-door, and entered through the shattered pannels. They then demolished all the furniture of the parlours; and with drawn weapons, searched the house to find Mr Lawless, whose head they swore they would cut off, and carry away in triumph on the point of their swords; though he had not given offence to either of the party. Luckily he was absent. This shock, with the ill-treatment I received from these self-called gentlemen, at a time when my being so very big with child, would have moved compassion in the hearts of wild Indians, threw me into a fit. I lay as dead, when some of my neighbours took me out lifeless, and carried me in that state to one of their houses.

Still these ruffians continued their outrage, till the watch came. They then turned and gave battle, and many cuts and hurts were received on both sides. At length, the riot continuing, to the terror of the whole street, the then Sheriffs (two of the best and most vigilant that Dublin ever boasted,) Messrs Moncrieffe and Worthington, arrived with a party of the military, at whose approach the rioters dispersed.

When these magistrates had restored peace I was brought back, and after three weeks was delivered by Surgeon Vance, of a dead child, with one of its legs broke, in consequence of the injuries I had received from these valorous Heroes. The little girl too that I had by Mr L—, was at the time of this affray laying with her nurse in the two-pair of stairs floor, and was so frightened that she took a fit of screeching, and never recovered of her terror, but died in consequence of the fright. Thus these magnanimous warriors, actually murdered two helpless infants, bruised and mal-treated their defenceless mother, destroyed the furniture of a house, terrified a whole neighbourhood, and wounded some of the watch – for FUN. How void their hearts must be of humanity and true bravery; and how destitute of sense must be their addled brains, who can act in this manner: and whilst they act thus, and usurp the respectable name of gentlemen, can have no pretence to courage! But to return.

When the two worthy Sheriffs had seen all quiet, they departed, leaving a guard of military to protect the house. The next morning, the street was crouded with people, to look at the disorder in which the house was left. However, I got it repaired before night, at a considerable expence, and had a guard of soldiers for a whole week. I lodged examinations against seven of these savages, with their ring-leaders at the head of them, and offered large rewards for apprehending them. When Mr Balloon heard I had began a prosecution, he swore he would shoot me; and I on my part, openly declared I would keep a case of pistols in my pocket, and blow his brains out if he approached me. The minor ruffians dispersed, when they found examinations lodged, some went to the country, and others to different parts. Their Chief thought his being of a noble family, would be his protection and enable him to brazen it out: and some of the lads of the College, who were dissipated enough to be his companions, came repeatedly to my house, to intimidate me, and threaten what they would do if I treated them as I had done their friends: for they would not only demolish what was within it, but would pull down my own house itself. I answered, if they did I would build it up again, and make them pay the expence. At length, by paying high, I got Mr Balloon apprehended and lodged in New-gate, for he could not be admitted to bail, unless the medical gentlemen declared I was out of danger, which they did not do; and when I was deliv-ered of the dead child as I mentioned, Surgeon Vance, declared he was ready to depose on oath, that the child had been dead from the time I was so misused, and was actually killed from the injuries I had received. I then said, as soon as I could get abroad, I would lodge fresh examinations against the prisoner for the murder of my infant. Counsellor Wolfe, declared if I did, it would surely hang him. This spread great alarm, the Baronet, his brother, had striven to get him bailed, suggesting that a malig-nant fever raged in the gaol; and requested that if he could not be bailed he might be removed to the Sheriffs' house, but all in vain. The Sheriffs and some other respectable persons applied to me, and at their intreaty I dropped the prosecution for the murder of the child, but continued that for the breaking of my house. At length, the trial came on before Judge Henn. I had a cloud of witnesses of the riot, assault, and destruction of my prop-erty, the jury gave their verdict of guilty, and he was sentenced to be fined and confined. I then obtained a fiat for my damages. When the time of his confinement expired, and his fine to the crown was paid, he thought I had forgotten him, and would proceed no farther; but revenge is sweet. I car-ried on my suit for my damages. A second trial ensued, in which he was cast; and I had him arrested for the amount, and again put him into New-gate. Green-wax processes issued against the other rioters, which kept them out of town, but I proceeded no farther against them; as I at length, got paid all the damages the law awarded me from their Chief. Thus ended my intercourse with that gentleman. I was so far from malice when all was over, that when he was about to go up in the balloon from Ranelagh-gar-dens, as I thought no less than that he would be drowned, I heartily for-gave, and shook hands with him. But taught by this affair, I never after would have any acquaintance with Collegians, nor ever entertained one of them.

While these prosecutions were depending, when urged to drop them, I have often gave as a reason for my refusal that *revenge is sweet*. My readers must have already seen (and will in the course of these memoirs, see frequent other circumstances) that I seldom failed of not only resenting any affront or ill-treatment given here, but have taken a pleasure in avenging myself of enemies, in proportion to the degree of the offence. Hence I may be judged to have been of an implacable temper, though I really was not, according to the ideas I entertained of revenge and implacability. I was ever humane and generous, ready to pity and assist others in distress, which I have frequently done to my own injury. I have often forgiven offences, when the offending party has confessed the offence, and sued for pardon. But I ever found it hard to overlook insults that touched my pride. In the case of this riot, my injuries were great; but my pride was as much wounded as my person. The offenders took the wrong way of molifying me, and averting my resentment. Instead of apology, they employed menaces. They constantly added fresh irritations: and as I took no revenge but that which the laws of my country sanctioned, I cannot even now, think I carried it too far. *Zanga* says,

> *What is revenge but courage to call in*
> *Our honour's debts.*

It is true, some of my more grave and serious acquaintance have urged the precept, *to turn one cheek to him who has smote the other.* But this requires surely some modification, and was never designed to be *literally* obeyed. It can never mean that we should expose ourselves to fresh affronts, rather than to take vengeance by the means of magistrates and of laws, made on purpose to defend mankind against insults, by the punishment of those who commit them. It must also suppose that the injury is tolerable, or that those who suffer it, can sustain it without much loss, or much inconveniency to their families. For we cannot think, that the Author of that precept can command good, quiet, peaceable and inoffensive persons, to suffer themselves to be beaten or wounded by the wicked: to expose their lives to the hazard of losing them, or their property to be spoiled, rather than make their complaints to the magistrates. If that were to be the case, there would be an end to all civil society, in which the inoffensive cannot be preserved against the violent, but by means of the law, and the magistrates who execute them. Besides, if I could have over-looked all the miseries I had sustained, as far as regarded myself, I was bound to avenge them by the laws, out of my duty to the community at large; for as they were done from mere wantonness, had they gone unpunished, that would have served only to embolden the perpetrators, to have extended their insolence and riotous abuse to others. Therefore, I am, I think, fully justified in what I did respecting the above outrage.

Not being willing to interrupt the thread of my narrative, I purposely omited several anecdotes that occurred; as they were a kind of extraneous matter that had no immediate connexion with my adventures, with the several gentlemen I have mentioned. But as they may afford some amusement, I shall close this chapter with a few of them.

Whilst I was in my highest prosperity, I was told the celebrated Miss Catley had spoken very scurrilously of me at the house of a gentleman where I visited; I therefore, resolved to affront her openly the first time I could meet her. Some days elapsed without an opportunity, my passion had not cooled, but was rather irritated by the delay. I could no longer contain myself, but went to her lodgings. She not being at home I hastened to the play-house, thinking I should find her at rehearsal, but she was gone from thence also. About two days after, as I was driving down Fownes's-street, I saw her come out of the stage-door. I bid the postilion stop, and I called to her. She came to the carriage door, when I asked how she could presume to revile me, and speak of me in so scandalous a manner as she had done. She denied she had ever said any thing about me; adding, that whoever told me was an infamous liar, and if I believed them nobody would believe me. So saying she turned away; when, not thinking her reply in any degree satisfactory, I, filled with spite, called her a little street-walking, London ballad-singer, and told her I would have her hissed every time she came upon the stage. About an hour after, I saw her coming along Dame-street, and wanted to have another wrangle with her, as my spleen was far from being exhausted, by the few words I had said, bitter as they were. I accordingly stopped at a Mercer's shop, at the corner of Parliament-street, that I might speak to her as she passed; and again repeated my former words; She immediately caught up one of her sons that was with her, went into the shop, and fainted, or at least pretended so to do. A chair was got for her, and took her home, when she told her friend, Colonel Lascelles, I had used her so ill that she had fainted, and must have satisfaction of me. The Colonel sent for an attorney, and had her examinations drawn, in which she swore I had ordered my postilion to drive over her, and her bastards. This I solemnly declare was a falsehood, for such words never came from my lips; not did such a thought enter my mind. However, she positively swore it; and the Colonel declared he would get the bills found against me, if it cost him five hundred pounds. He was so enraged, that his dear mild lady should be offended, that he became like Cain, *he was wroth and his countenance fell*. However next morning, after the examinations was sworn, a friend I had at the Aldermanic Board, sent privately to inform me to get bail ready, or I should inevitably be taken by constables; which disgrace he wished me to avoid. I was not long getting bail for my appearance, which being given, I was to remain unmolested till the commission. During that interval, the Colonel was indefatigable in his endeavours with the grand jury, to get the bills found against me, but when it came before them, my interest proved better than his, and the Petticoat prevailed over the Sword and Gorget. Some of the gentlemen observed to the rest, that it would be a pity not to favour a woman, who, by spending considerable sums amongst the traders of this city, was of service to it, preferable to a woman who was only a bird of passage; who came here to pick up all she could from the public, and then carry it to another country; as it was well known that Catley never laid out a single farthing in Dublin that she could avoid. On this consideration, and that nothing but bare words had passed, and no assault, the bill was thrown out, to the great mortification of the Warbler and her Champion, and my no small joy and exultation.

Much about that time, intending to go [*sic*] the play, I had sent my servant to keep places in the lattice for me and Sally Hayes. When I went to the theatre, about eight o'clock, the box-keeper told me that there were three ladies in the places that I had taken. I was much surprised and could scarce believe him, telling him that no one would dare to usurp my places. However, when we came into the box, I saw three females filling the front seat, and my servant sitting behind, I asked him aloud, why he suffered those ladies to get into my places? He answered, they took them by force in spite of me. O! ho! said I, if that is the case I must see what is to be done: for I engage I will send them as smartly out, as they got in. So saying, I got to the seat behind them, and tapped one of them on the shoulder; when she turned her face I knew them to be a nobleman's daughters. But rank had no terrors for me, when what I thought my property was concerned. I requested mildly that they would let me have my places: one replied, her servant had kept the seats for her, and she would keep them. I touched her shoulder again, and speaking a little louder, said, well! if I cannot get them out by fair means I must be a little rougher. She made no answer but turned her eyes to the stage. Why ladies, said I, there is not a gentleman in the house, but by your sitting before me will think you are some girls of my acquaintance, and visit you as such. But now I think of it, I am mistaken in my conclusion, for indeed you are too ugly to be of my profession; particularly should they see you by day-light, they will be off. Indeed you won't do. Seeing they were unmoved by this sarcasm, I resolved to try other means, and thrusting one foot between two of them, I soon made room for the other, and seated myself on their hips. Though the daughters of a peer, they were also well known to be what are stiled, *Peter's children, every finger furnished with a fish-hook,* or at least with bird-lime, for whatever they could touch stuck to them. I therefore, called out to Sally Hayes, 'Don't you think it was very lucky I did not wear my diamonds to-night? and doubly so that I left my purse at home, for it would soon have been made lighter, as I have got amongst robbers. Yet, I have one comfort, a lady of my character is a gentleman's companion, but a thief is not.' – In a few minutes the ladies decamped, leaving me and Sally mistresses of the field of battle.

end of Volume I.

MEMOIRS

OF

MRS. MARGARET LEESON.

WRITTEN BY HERSELF;

AND

INTERSPERSED WITH SEVERAL INTERESTING AND
AMUSING ANECDOTES,

OF SOME OF THE MOST STRIKING

CHARACTERS

OF

GREAT-BRITAIN AND IRELAND.

VOL. II.

Then will I grant thee all thy foul's defire;
  All that may charm thine ear, and pleafe thy fight:
All that thy thought can frame or wifh require
  To fteep thy ravifh'd fenfes in delight.
The fumptuous feaft, entranc'd with mufic's found,
  Fitteft to tune the melting foul to Love:
Rich odours, breathing choiceft fweets around;
  The fragrant Bow'r, cool Fountain, fhady Grove:
Frefh Flowers, to ftrew thy Couch, and crown thy Head;
Joy fhall attend thy fteps, and Eafe fhall fmooth thy bed;
  What pleafures, vain miftaken wretch are thine!
(Virtue with fcorn reply'd)
  Draining the copious Bowl, ere thirft require;
  Feafting ere hunger to the feaft invite:
  Whofe taffelefs Joys anticipate defire
  When Luxury fupply'd with appetite.

JUDGMENT OF HERCULES.

DUBLIN:

PRINTED FOR THE AUTHORESS,

AND SOLD BY THE PRINCIPAL BOOKSELLERS.

M,DCC,XCV.

Fig. 2. p. 500.

The Theatre Royal, Smock Alley, Dublin.
Scene of a Mexican stand-off between Mrs
Leeson and Signor Carnavalli.

Book One

A thousand oaths, an ocean of his tears,
And instances as infinite of love,
Warrant me welcome. But indeed
All these are servants to deceitful man.
SHAKESPEARE

SOON AFTER MY VICTORY over the head of the Pinkin-dindies, Mr
Lawless's father died, but what he left him was scarce worth mentioning;
and having no farther expectations here, his friends advised him to go to
England. With their advice he found it necessary to comply; and requested
me to sell all the property I had in Dublin, and live with him in London
for the remainder of my life. However, I begged to be excused. I thought it
much better to stay where I was, immersed in all the pleasures of the
world, and to be entirely my own mistress, than to go with him, and pinch
upon his pittance; or to expend what I had saved in inching it out. He
went off by himself, not thoroughly satisfied with me; and I saw him
depart, with emotions far different from those with which I beheld his
going to America. My love was not then in such a state as formerly. Time,

his neglect whilst abroad; and the dissipated life I had led for some time, had blunted my sensations in respect to him.

When Mr Lawless was in London, he kept continually writing to me to urge my coming to him; but Sally Hayes and I lived in Drogheda-street, in an endless round of pleasures, or at least what seemed such to me, till my dear little girl died, in consequence of the riot I have already mentioned. The loss of her seemed the greatest affliction with which I had ever been attacked. I was really frantic for some weeks, and could receive no consolation. The house in which I lived, kept up my grief by continually presenting objects to my eyes, that by reminding me of my dear child, momentarily renewed my regret. I therefore determined to quit, not only my house, but even the kingdom itself. Hoping that a variety of new objects, and new scenes of dissipation might lessen, if not entirely put an end to my sorrow.

I wrote to Mr Lawless to London, told him my resolution, and that I should shortly be with him. Accordingly I arrived in London, and went directly to his lodgings, but was told he was out. I then drove to a Coffee-house, that I had heard he frequented, and left a note announcing my arrival, and whither I had gone; which was to an Irish lady, with whom I had been well acquainted in Dublin, and who received me in a very cordial manner. I had not been there long when Mr Lawless came. He seemed over-joyed at my arrival, appeared to be as fond as ever; and took me home to his own apartments. O Man! Man! sex of deceit! However glad Mr Lawless was at my coming, I since found that when I called first on him, he had a girl with him, which made him be denied to me till he could dispose of her; which he did directly, by taking lodgings for her in a distant part of the town. It is true, he spent both his days and nights with me, but a portion of every forenoon was dedicated to his visits to her.

I very naturally wished to see some of my Irish old acquaintance; but this he constantly opposed, under some pretence or other; well knowing that as most of them were well acquainted with his having kept this girl, for some months before my arrival; his deceit would be soon detected if they saw me. I was therefore, always denied to any of them when they called at our lodgings, for he represented them as company totally unfit for me to keep.

For some time I remained his dupe; but one forenoon, when my spark was gone on his morning tour, I went to the lady I had first seen on my coming to London, who indeed, was the only one Mr Lawless was willing I should see. She had well known his connexion with this girl, but was unwilling to tell me of it, as he had sworn her to secrecy in that point, as soon as I came. However, we went together to take a walk, and I requested she would bring me to some of my old acquaintance; assuring her that I would not let him know that it was by her I was directed to where they lived. We accordingly, visited one of them who had some more of them, with her. In the course of our conversation, one of the ladies asked what Mr Lawless had done with the girl he had kept. Another winked at her, which I observing, asked what Lawless? and what Girl? They all sat silent for some minutes, when one of them said, 'why should she be deceived?' its *your* Lawless. He keeps a Miss Sharman, he has kept her a long time, and drives her about every day in a phaeton.

I was much shocked at this intelligence. To think, that he had formed such a connexion at a time, when he was continually writing in the most affectionate terms, and urging me to come to him, hurt me greatly; in my pride at least, if not in my love, for that was nearly extinct. However, I was happy I had made that discovery in time; as without this intelligence, I might have continued to live with him amidst scenes of ill usage and distress.

I directly formed my resolution what to do. I resolved that I would put an immediate stop to all farther connexion with Lawless for ever. I took an house from one of the ladies present; then returning to the lodgings, I packed up all my trunks and boxes, and carried them to my own house, leaving my gentleman to dine by himself when he returned from his Miss Sharman, and to think what he pleased about me. Where to find me, after he came home and missed, me he could not conceive. My having taken all my baggage with me, assured him that I had quitted him, and that I was not out on any excursion. The servant knew nothing of where I had gone; and he was ignorant of the cause of my so sudden elopement. Conscious indeed, to himself of his duplicity, he conjectured I must have found it out. He then went to seek me at every house where he thought I might possibly be, saying at each, that he was sure I could not be long absent, as he knew I was so very fond of him, that doubtless he would have forty letters left for him at different Coffee-houses, before to-morrow night. But he soon found his mistake. The reign of Love was over, as was also that of Jealousy, though resentment kept its place. The day passed, but not one of his forty expected letters was left for him.

Enraged at his disappointment, he then thought that my friend whom he had sworn to secrecy had betrayed him; he flew to her, and threatened he would murder her if she did not tell him where I was; upbraiding her with her treachery to him, and calling her by every opprobrious name his malice could suggest, or passion cause him to utter. She protested she had never told me of his connexion with Miss Sharman; but, being really terrified at his threats, she confessed who gave me that information, and that I was in the house of her who gave me an account of his duplicity, which I had taken ready furnished, for a year certain. My sole motive for this step was, that having told all my friends in Dublin, that I was going to London, to spend the rest of my life with Lawless, I was really ashamed to return so soon, lest I should be laughed at, and the consequence I had so long assumed should be let down, which would have considerably wounded my pride.

Mr Lawless having gained intelligence of my residence, came the next evening to pay me a visit, when he came into the drawing-room, I went to the looking-glass, and began to settle the diamonds in my head-dress; at his entering I turned my head round, and with a look of ineffable contempt, asked him what he wanted. His reply was, 'what do you think I want? I want you, ungrateful woman! what have I done to cause you to leave me in the manner you did?' – O nothing at all, my good man (said I,) I want no altercation with you, and only desire you would go about your business. This is *my* house, and I insist on never seeing you here again. He then began to offer some apology, but I cut him short, by telling him I required none; and looking out of the window, said I should neither listen to, nor mind any thing he said, and then began to sing. He then went away almost mad, at my distant behaviour.

The next morning came a letter from him, containing a deal of fulsome nonsense, endeavouring to clear himself of his villainy. I told the bearer it required no answer. The day after, Mr Beg, an intimate of Lawless, came to me with another letter, which I took and threw on the fire, and then opened it with the poker, without reading a word, and thrust it into the flames. I told Mr Beg that I wished the fellow who sent it was in its place, till he was burnt to ashes, for enticing me to a strange country, wherein I had not a single friend. In short, he kept teazing me with letters and messages for some time; but I continued inflexible, would never forgive him, and he finding all his efforts totally in vain, desisted from the fruitless pursuit, and here ended all connexion with Mr Lawless.

CHAPTER TWO

No care, no stop! so thoughtless of expence,
As neither to know how to maintain it,
Nor cease the flow of riot. Takes no account
How things go forward, nor has any care
Of what is to continue, – will not hear,
Till strong necessity shall make to feel.
SHAKESPEARE'S *Timon of Athens*

BEFORE I LEFT DUBLIN I had paid all my debts, and besides the money and effects I brought with me to London, I had left a few hundreds in bank. This was very lucky for me, or perhaps I might have starved in a strange country, where I knew no one who would assist me, and where the English gentlemen are more cautious and less liberal and generous than those of Ireland. However, resolving to make as great a figure in one metropolis as I had done in the other, I drew all my money from Ireland, kept an elegant house, No. 4, Cleveland-row, and hired for a companion an Irish woman, who had been wife to a respectable merchant in Dublin; but having caught her in bed with his clerk, he had turned her adrift, and she had retired to London.

I now entered into a fresh round of pleasures, different indeed, from those I enjoyed in Dublin. There, not only the expence of them came from sundry pockets, but I could always lay by something handsome, but in London, I myself was forced to bear the bulk of the charges. However, as I had money I was resolved not to balk myself of any desire or amusement, whilst it lasted; totally careless of what supply I might get when it was all spent. I visited every public diversion, the theatres in winter; and in the summer I was frequently at Ranelagh, till twelve or one o'clock, and then to sup at Vauxhall, till six or seven in the morning, dancing and drinking burnt Champaigne, and sometimes even rioting. All the fine ladies and demi-reps, wondered where I got so many diamonds, and such variety of fine cloaths, especially as they thought many of themselves were much *handsomer than I was*. Some of my countrymen, to vex them the more, told them I was admired by some people of the first fashion in Ireland; and that I had realised ten thousand pounds, which I had left in a bank in Dublin. This report made me the object of envy, and well accounted for my expensive mode of living. It also made me more proud and haughty than before, and to maintain an air of superiority, highly flattering to my pride and vanity, of which the following is an evident proof, bordering even on insolence. One morning walking down the Strand, I saw a fine dashing person, attended by another, go into a shop near Temple-bar. My curiosity to know who it was led me to follow him in; where I soon found it was the Prince of Wales, and fixed my eyes full upon him till he had finished giving his orders, which were for some stripes for waistcoats. I then addressed the shop-keeper, and desired he would cut off enough to make two waistcoats of the same stripe, and pack it up very well, as I wanted to send it as a present to my shoe-maker, in Dublin. The Prince turned, and looked stedfastly at me, and then walked out of the shop.

Some few days later, I was riding to dine at Richmond, in company with one lady, and three English gentlemen. I heard a great noise of clear the way, clear the way: I looked behind and saw the Prince come, driving furiously in a very high phaeton, with the same gentleman with him, and a train of servants. The gentlemen who were with me said, Ride on one side, and make room for his Royal Highness. Not I indeed, answered I. There is room sufficient, there is one-half the road for him; and I have as much right to the other half, as he or any one else; ye are three cowards, and I shall laugh at you as long as I live for your mean servility. By this time the Prince was come a-breast of us, and as he passed he stared at me, and looked as sour as if he would have bitten my nose off. But that did not intimidate me, I galloped off, and kept up with him till he came to a gate, which opened to that part of the park wherein he lived; into which he turned, after he had given me half a dozen as crabbed looks, as ever I saw on any gentleman's countenance.

I then stopped and waited till my company came up, when they questioned me why I would not quit the middle of the road. I replied, I did not chuse it. They then asked me if I did not think it very wrong in me, to ride on by the Prince's phaeton. I said no; as I think part of the road was for my use, as well as for that of the King; and if you English are servile and timid, we Irish are not, so I beg you would drop the subject, as I assure you if the same circumstance was to occur to-morrow, I should act in the same manner; or indeed, as I thought proper.

At length, we got to Richmond, a most delightful spot indeed, where we dined, and drank as good Champaigne, as ever I tasted in Ireland, every thing exquisitely good, and served in so superb a manner, that I am sorry to say, I never saw such a tavern, in any part of my own country.

After dinner we set off for London, about nine in the evening, and as I had been somewhat tired with riding, I took a seat in the phaeton with one of the gentlemen, but the wind blew so strongly on me, that when I came home, I found myself attacked with a pungent pain in my side. Yet, I disregarded it so much that I went directly to a ball, thinking to dance it off. However, I paid dear for my indiscretion, being seized by a pleuretic fever, under which I lay above a month, and totally senseless the greatest part of the time. This was an harvest time for the woman I had taken as my companion. She had been wife to a respectable merchant, as I mentioned, and being my country-woman, I took a great liking to her and paid her particular attention. Which she returned so as to prove that those of our own country, are the worst companions you possibly have when out of it: as they are the first to deceive you. Mrs Green, to verify this maxim, and thinking I should not live to demand them, stole seven diamond pins, a gold watch, three trunks of cloaths, and many trinkets, and articles of value. When I recovered, and missed my things, I applied to a justice and had two of my servants sent to Tothill-fields Bridewell, on suspicion. I should have provided similar lodgings for my kind country-woman, but she had taken flight on my first rising out of my bed; and as I shortly after set out for Dublin, I never found her, and would not carry on any prosecution against the servants; who, if guilty, were far less so than Mrs Green, as I had placed no confidence in them.

On my recovery from this dreadful illness, I found my money nearly exhausted, and that the extent of the robbery had deprived me of the means of appearing with equal elegance, as when I dazzled the eyes of all beholders. This, and my encreasing disgust to London, made me determine to return to my own country, and accordingly I sold off my house and furniture, packed up the few valuables I had left; laid by twelve guineas to bear my charges over, and putting the rest of my money in my pocket, sallied out a shopping to purchase something handsome, as presents to my friends in Ireland, male and female, and bought away to a considerable extent. I then packed up my purchases, and bidding adieu to London, travelled to Holyhead, embarked on board the packet, and safely landed on George's-quay, rejoicing that I had again my feet on my dear native soil.

CHAPTER THREE

Odd's me, the fellow has put me into such a titteration
That I tremble from head to foot. Me! who am approached
With reverence, by Church-wardens, and the Heads of the parish.
But I'll take the scurvy Knave down, I'll have him Coruru
Nobus, *aye! and his* Roysters, *too, I'll warrant you!*

BEAUMONT and FLETCHER

SUCH HAD BEEN my inconsiderateness in my expences, that when I landed on George's-quay, I had just two shillings left in the world. This indeed, paid Wybrants's boat; but I had my trunks to clear at the Custom-house, my passage in the packet to pay, and a coach to hire. However, I thought very little about it, I had friends in Dublin, and was come to where the celebrity of my name would open the sluices of profit. I apologised to the Captain, and telling him who I was, requested he would call on me next day in Mecklenburgh-street, where I was then going; and procured a chair from College-green, to carry me there.

When I came to Mecklenburgh-street, words cannot express the joy with which Sally Hayes, and Mrs Hall received me. I desired they would pay for my chair, for I was returned to Dublin, ten pounds worse than a beggar. They with great cordiality gave me what money I wanted, and when the Captain came the next morning, I gave him two guineas for his civility in taking my word. The next business was to get my baggage from the Custom-house. I went myself, and was welcomed to Dublin, by several of the gentlemen there, who said they were happy to see me returned. One of the searchers having asked me for my keys, in order to examine my trunks, several of the officers cried, O fie, sure they would not suspect me for having any contraband goods, and they would engage that I had nothing but my own apparel. The trunks were discharged unsearched, to my great satisfaction, as indeed I trembled, lest sundry articles I had brought over, for presents, and for my own use, should have been seized, as they were liable to have been if seen.

When my things were got home and unpacked, I made myself very grand by distributing a great number of presents. To some I gave gowns, to some caps and feathers, rings and buckles to ladies, and pocket-books to gentlemen, till I had distributed my whole cargo. This procedure made it thought I had returned from London, much richer than I went, and the idea of wealth produces always a degree of respect: as people are generally more ready to pay court, and assist those they are sensible does not want it. And the real state of my finances was never suspected, nor ever known but to Sally Hayes, and Mrs Hall.

The next day I dressed and went into town, and as Sally and I walked, we made very striking figures with bell-hoops, which I had brought over, and as they were the first ever worn in Dublin, we were greatly stared at. The mercers and linen-drapers, were glad to see me, as I was a very good friend to them, as I wore my petticoats trimmed half a yard up, and always obliged gentlemen who presented me with cloaths, to buy three times as much silk, or other materials as was really necessary. Every one we met, of my acquaintance, seemed very happy at my return; and indeed, I found myself of more consequence than I thought I had been; so that I said to myself, Well, Peggy you will not long be poor.

When we returned home, I had visits from a great many gentlemen; all welcomed me home, some gave me a bank note, some sent in wine, some came out of friendship, and others out of curiosity. Some of those who would scarce look at me before, came to see how I looked since I came from London, and how far my visit to that city had improved me. In short, the concourse was great that evening, and for the most part of the night.

I continued with Mrs Hall, till I could procure an house for myself, which I soon did, in Wood-street, for the second time: not a little one as before, but one that was large and convenient; with a large waste ground behind it, which at a considerable expence, I converted into an elegant garden, where I lived very comfortable for one year, with one of my old lovers.

Just at this juncture, Mr Georgi and Signor Carnavalli, had taken the Theatre in Smock-ally, for the performance of Italian operas, two nights in the week; and as the Signor thought himself a very great man, he endeavoured to establish new rules never before introduced in Dublin. The chief of which, was to exclude on his nights every lady of my description, from admission into the theatre. He was advised not to attempt such an innovation, but he persisted in his resolution. When I heard of Carnavalli's intention, I was much displeased, and determined he should abandon his design.

On the first night he opened, I was otherwise engaged and could not go, but Mrs Hall, and Miss Townley, went. They were just seated in one of the lattices, when the Signor came up to them, and turned them out. He told them all the seats there were set, and they might go to the gallery. The two ladies, like cowards submitted, and quitted their seats. The next morning they called on me, and told me how they had been treated. I rated them soundly for their pusillanimity, and declared that if I had been there, the Italian Thing would have found it very difficult to turn me out, after I had once got in: but that I would try if he would dare to make such an attempt with me. On the ensuing night, I went with a Mrs Judge; but was rather unfortunate in my companion, who was the most cowardly female I ever saw. When we entered the box-room, the two door-keepers, Jackson and Wilton, were planted at their different posts. I got to the stairs that led up to the lattices, when Jackson followed and took me by the arm, saying, Madam, you cannot go there. I asked the reason of my being refused admittance, to where I frequently sat, when he replied, it was the orders of Mr Carnavalli, and I cannot disobey them. I struggled for some time and strove to force my way up, but he being stronger than me, took me in his arms and carried me back into the box-room, and on setting me down gave me a push. Irritated with such behaviour, I gave him a slap in the face, with my whole strength. My companion stood by all the time of our contention, with her mouth gaping, and not offering to give me the least assistance. Had Sally Hayes been with me, it would have been quite otherwise, and Jackson would have carried some marks of our resentment. But this was not the case, they detained the box ticket, for which I had paid at the door; spoiled all my cloaths, by their pulling and dragging me, and I lost one of my earrings. I stood in this manner, and sent round for Carnavalli, when he came, I asked him if it was his order I should be excluded from a place for which I had paid. He said yes, and that I should never go in whilst his operas' lasted. Very well, Sir, I answered, you'll abide by the consequences; and I'll bet you an hundred guineas I will, I then took a chair and came home, crying all the way for spite and through vexation. I had not long been at home, when four of the first noblemen in the kingdom, came to condole with me for the usage I had suffered; and said if I did not make an example of Carnavalli and his servants, I deserved every ill-treatment, such fellows could give. I was ever very prompt to take revenge for insults, and told their lordships that my resentment did not want advice to give it an edge.

This was on Wednesday night, and the following Saturday was to be the next opera night. The next morning, I went and consulted an eminent barrister, with whom I was very intimate; and pursuant to his advice, on Saturday morning I lodged examinations, and procured warrants against them for an assault, and for robbing me, by detaining the ticket for which I had paid. I sent and desired Mr Roe, the keeper of Newgate, to be with me a few minutes before six, and got four of the most desperate, ill-looking fellows of bailiffs, that Dublin could afford, to attend me. I then took a coach, and directed the catchpoles to keep in sight of the coach, and to come up when I should cry *Holloa! Boys*. Thus prepared, I drove to the theatre, and to the stage-door, as I knew that would best answer my purpose, as I should not be so soon known there. I knew Carnavalli was the first fiddle, and by the hour, must be at that time in the orchestra. When the coach was close to the stage-door, my coachman told the door-keeper, that there was a gentleman there who wanted to subscribe, and Mr Carnavalli was sent for; he came in two or three minutes, without his hat, to receive the subscription money. When he came to the coach-side, and saw I was in it he gave a start, and would have returned into the house; but at that moment, I gave the signal of *Holloa! Boys*. the bailiffs came up and took him. He began to talk, when I said, 'fellow, I have nothing to say to you. Here gentlemen! take this ruffian, and leave him in the centre of Newgate, and I shall accompany you myself.' – I called them *gentlemen*, and clever gentlemen indeed they were, for I believe each had twenty or thirty scars in his pretty face. I went with my gentlemen, and their prisoner Carnavalli, without his hat, his well powdered hair, drenched with the pour of the rain, which luckily fell at that time; and dropping his spangles as he went. When I saw him safe lodged in Newgate, we all returned to the box-door, I directed the fellows to stay without, whilst I alighted and went in. There were locks put on the lower doors, I suppose, in order to keep me out, and the moment the door-keepers saw me they ran to lock them. Jackson and Wilson, were quite ignorant of what had been done to their master, which was unknown to all but the bailiffs, the coachman and myself. I said to Jackson. O fie! won't you let me in? he answered, indeed I can't, it's my orders. I cried out, *Holloa! Boys*. my four gentlemen came up, and I told them to take these two scoundrels, and leave them where they had left their master; and be sure you conduct them through the rain, without their hats. I then turned to a great company that was in the box-room and lobby, and making a profound courtesy, said, 'Ladies and gentlemen, I am extremely sorry to deprive you of the pleasure, you may expect from this night's entertainment; but I have sent Mr Carnavalli, the first fiddle, to Newgate, and am now sending two of his domestics after him, lest he should want company or attendants:' – and away I went, leaving them all in amazement. I conducted the door-keepers to Newgate, and then went home in the highest content; and slept sweeter that night, than I had done for a considerable time before.

The next day being Sunday, there was a review of the Volunteers in the Phoenix Park, and the weather being very fine, drew a great concourse of persons of all ranks. To be sure, I went there in high stile, and as the adventure of last night, had ran through every circle, I was the great object of attention, and was particularly stared at by multitudes. I had the satisfaction to be congratulated for my spirit, by most of the gentlemen present. I replied, that I had not yet done with the fellows. Several ladies of the *sisterhood,* also accosted me with their thanks for my asserting their rights. I told them it was more than they deserved, since they were so mean spirited, as to submit to the Italian's new-fangled rules. That it was for my own sake I had proceeded as I had done, for no person merited the enjoyment of any rights, who had not the courage to assert and maintain them.

Although I had taken these steps with Carnavalli, and his door-keepers, yet, I was not contented. Their punishment was not my main object, which was to get free admission to the lattices on the opera nights; and this I was determined to obtain, even by force. The following Wednesday, was to be the next night, and I was resolved to be thoroughly prepared. I accordingly requested two gentlemen, who I knew had no aversion to what they called, *kicking up a dust,* at any time, to go with me to the opera, and support me; and promised to give them tickets. They readily assured me of their assistance; indeed, they were two of a kind of Bucks, that though they were always well drest [*sic*], had seldom a shilling in their pockets, therefore, they could never afford the opera. They thought, to be there with their swords, and fiercely cocked hats, would make them appear great and grand; and that they should be taken for somebodies.

This arrangement was settled, but I had no occasion of putting it in practice. Carnavalli and his fellows had procured bail, and were at large. And when I went to Daly's play on the Tuesday night, Mr Tresham, his box-keeper, after wishing me joy of my victory, told me that Mr Carnavalli presented me with the freedom of the house; and that Jackson and Wilton, had refused to keep the doors any longer, lest I should get them knocked on the head. I thanked Mr Tresham for his information, and said I was determined to come sometimes to the opera, but not at the expence of such a shabby fellow, as I was well able to pay for my seat; and he had made the offer of the freedom of the house, out of fear.

I then went to the opera without any riot or molestation; though I went there but seldom, and that only that I might be seen by the audience, to have triumphed over Carnavalli's new rules. As I had gained my point, I did not take any farther steps against the fellows, but let the prosecution drop; to the great satisfaction of the Italian fiddler, who was much terrified lest I should proceed: and became as abject, as before he had been insolent. But all poltrons, are tyrants, when they have an opportunity of exercising their despotism.

CHAPTER FOUR

Tho' our revels are scorn'd by the Grave and the Wise,
Yet they practise all day, what they seem to despise.
Examine mankind, from the great to the small
Each mortal's disguis'd, *the whole world is a* Ball.
Sing Tantara rara Masks *All.*

I HAVE FOR SOME CHAPTERS, forborn to make any reflections on my conduct. Indeed how could I? it would not bear reflection; and my readers will doubtless, make many in their own minds, much to my disadvantage. This, I own will be just, and I have nothing to say in my defence. I had entered so deep into a series of errors, and so plunged into the whirl-pool of dissipation, that I became ingulphed therein. My eyes were blinded, that they beheld not the evil. My ears became deaf to admonition, had even any one attempted to admonish me; which alas! none offered to do. My success in one plan, gave me courage to go on to another. My wants were all sup-plied by others, through vanity or folly; and, I was led to look upon the men who surrounded me merely as my tools, made only to minister to my expences, or contribute to my pleasure. Every one with whom I congre-gated, male or female, seemed to shut the door against *thought,* and incite me to fresh irregularities. I had my pride flattered by having attained a

91

celebrity, and an eminence in the line I had unfortunately taken. I was looked up to as a kind of pattern to the ladies of the *sisterhood;* and many men thought it an addition to their character as Bucks, choice spirits and men of fashion, to be acquainted with me; nay, divers have made it their brag, that they had spent their evening with me, who were never once admitted within my doors. My capital error was, in the entering into the course of life I led; for once when in, I had no means of getting out of it. Nor do I even now, know one single line, situated as I was, I could have embraced for support. The miseries of poverty, which I had so severely felt, were not forgotten; and their remembrance only urged me the more, to prevent falling into like circumstances, by any means within my reach. Living in splendor, enjoying every luxury of dress, table or shew, no matter from which source they were derived, made me resolve not to quit the means of gaining the end. Thus, I went on in a circle of pleasures, one commencing where another ended. As for character, I had totally disregarded it, or to speak plainer, I had acquired one character, in which I gloried; and which to me, supplied the place of any other: and I was made to cry out with *Falstaff,* 'Why 'tis my vocation. 'Tis no sin for one to labour in one's vocation.' Not but I often entertained thoughts of amendment, though I knew not the day when I should begin it, but put it off from time to time; saying, for many years, with *Prince Hal,*

> *When this loose behaviour I throw off*
> *And pay the debt I have not promised,*
> *By how much better than my word I am*
> *By so much shall I falsify men's fears:*
> *And, like bright metal on a sullen ground,*
> *My Reformation, glittering o'er my faults*
> *Shall shew more goodly, and attract more eyes,*
> *Than that which hath no foil to set it off.*
> *I'll so offend, to make offence a skill*
> *Redeeming time, when men think least I will.*

I have already related some anecdotes, shewing my temper and frame of mind, and shall before I pursue my narrative give another, to shew how far not only impunity, but success, had emboldened me to proceed to any length.

An order had been given by government, that there should be no more Masquerades, on account of some disturbances that had happened. This spirited me up to have one of my own, at my own house, to shew how much I disregarded all law or order, let the consequences be what they might. I sent and got two hundred tickets printed, and gave them away amongst my male and female acquaintance, and fixed the night for the first of May. My intention ran like wild-fire through the city. Those who had tickets applauding me for my spirit; and those who could not procure any, condemning me for my impudence, as they called it. For a fortnight before the appointed time, I had above twenty busy visitors of the latter class, trying to dissuade, or frighten me from my attempt. They told me, if I persisted my house would be pulled down about my ears, for acting contrary to the order of government, with which the whole town was acquainted, and I could not therefore, plead ignorance. However, as I had gone to a considerable expence, I was resolved to go on. I had my house laid out in a most elegant stile, and had five hundred coloured lamps, of blue, lilac and green. When the night came I got Mr Robinson, the high constable to attend, with a guard; an eminent shoe-maker (Mr Warren) and a Mr Smith, were my door-keepers. At six o'clock, the street was full from end to end, and I really began to be frightened for fear of the mob. About seven they began to be somewhat riotous, and swore they would demolish all the windows, if I and Sally Hayes, did not come out and shew ourselves immediately. I sent them word we would comply with their desires as soon as we were drest. But before we could get ready, one of the ruffians threw a large stone, and broke a pane of glass in one of the dining-room windows; then indeed, my heart began to flutter. However, I put the best face I could on the matter, and with Sally Hayes went to the upper step of the door, and shewed ourselves to the mob: who, after a few minutes, gave us a huzza, and told us to go in, for they were satisfied, and no damage should happen. But they would not let one of the company into the house, till they had shewed themselves; and then let them quietly proceed.

The company then began to flock in very fast. Sally and I wore fancy dresses. A fortune-teller, very characteristically drest, Mr Pearson, who supported it with much humour. A jockey, by Captain Hamilton. Mr Jones in a domino. Mr McNeil, a sailor. Mrs Hall, a pye-woman. Kitty Cut-a-dash, an orange-girl. Nancy Weems, a nun. Miss Townly, a flower-girl. Miss Redding, a ballad-singer. Mrs Healy, a cast-cloaths woman. Mr Gibton, a sailor. Mr Cashel, a sweep. Mr Crawford, a domino. Mr Meares, a clown. Lord St Lawrence, a whipper-in. Numbers of dominos and sailors. Lord Westport, a blind fiddler. Lord Headfort, a drummer. Lord Molesworth, a coachman, the best in England or Ireland. Mr Finlay, a gardiner. In short, I did not distinguish a tithe of them, as they did not unmask at supper.

The supper consisted of every thing the season afforded and money could purchase; it was elegantly laid out in the two-pair of stairs street-room, and with the wines, gave general satisfaction. The back-room, contained the only bed in the house (all the others being removed) and for that bed I had put myself to a great expence, the furniture being of new muslin, richly spangled. It was kept locked up, being designed for the Duke of Leinster, who, after all the preparation, never came.

After supper we all came down into the drawing-room, where a band of music struck up, and we danced till six in the morning, when the company departed. I then paid the musicians and the guard, gave them plenty of drink, and then went to sleep in the Duke's bed; and thus ended my masquerade, of which government took not the least notice.

CHAPTER FIVE

Each change and excess have thro' life been my doom
And well I can speak of its joys and its strife.
The bottle affords us a glimpse thro' the gloom,
But Love's the true sun-shine that gladdens our life.
Thus a long time I thought, but not think so no more,
For usage and time will diminish the store.

ALTHOUGH I HAD BEEN at very great expence in fitting up my house in Wood-street, yet, in about a year, I found I should be necessitated to leave it. The under-waters had so penetrated to the foundation, that I not only thought the house unwholesome to live in, but even unsafe. I therefore sought for another house, and met with one that was building in Pitt-street, but not quite finished. I liked the situation and took it, and till it was compleated, which was not till the end of two months, I removed my furniture to different places, and resided with a lady, who kindly offered me the use of her house. At length, Sally Hayes and I took possession of my new house, and for some time lived in our usual manner.

Since some time after Mr Lawless's departure for America, I had not known what love was. I used frequently to sing the song that so well expressed my disposition.

> My pride is to hold all mankind in my chain
> The conquest I prize, tho' the slaves I disdain.
> I teaze them, and vex them;
> I plague and perplex them;
> Since men try their arts our weak sex to betray,
> I'll shew them that woman's as cunning as they.

But behold! after several years of apathy and indifference, I was again entangled in the nets of Love, and became as infatuated, with my *second,* as ever I had been with my *first* Love, Lawless.

I became acquainted with a Mr Robert Gorman, I thought him the only man worth my notice, and fell in love with him to a most extravagant degree. Whether he had an equal passion for me I know not; he said he had, and I believed him. He was extremely handsome. He was almost constantly with me, and then I despised all the rest of mankind, they became odious in my eyes, which could not look with pleasure or complacency on any but my dear Bob.

His father had a country house, near Black-rock, and insisted on his son's coming to live with him; having, as I suppose, got some intelligence of his attachment to me. I was much dissatisfied; and could not sleep one night without him; he therefore, used as soon as ever his father went to bed, to slip out of the house and come to town to me, and get back again the next morning, before the old gentleman was up: soon after, I arose and drove to Booterstown, or the Rock, where we met and dined together; he then returned to his father's house, and I went home expecting him at night.

This course went on uninterruptedly for some time, till some busy devil, envious of our happiness, told old Mr Gorman, how his son had deceived him: therefore, he always staid up till he saw his son in bed, and then locking all the doors, took the keys up with him. This prevented our nightly meetings for a while; but Love, fertile in stratagems, put one into Bob's head, and enabled him to elude his father's vigilance. He went down into the kitchen; and established an ascendency over the servants, by a few bottles of wine, and some money, till they became devoted to him. It has been well observed, that there is but one road to the heart of a domestic, and whoever is generous cannot miss it. He made one of the men, after the doors were locked, stand in the area, he mounted on the man's shoulders, and so clambering over the rails got at liberty, and scampered off to me. This stratagem succeeded, night after night, for several weeks, to our mutual satisfaction. At length, whether the old gentleman suspected something, or Bob had been betrayed by somebody, is uncertain; but one night he went into his son's room, and found there was the nest, but the bird had flown. This put him into a kind of quandary. His son was out, the doors were all fast, and all the keys were in his pocket. The chamber-windows were too high for him to get out of them; but out he was, and which way he got out he could not guess. But he reflected that however Bob got out, he must come in the same way, as he was always in the house before the doors were open; and therefore, resolved to watch his coming home; this he did and espied Bob, come over the rails and drop into the area.

The mystery being thus unravelled, the old man found it would be in vain to attempt the keeping his son from me; if he remained in the kingdom; therefore, he determined to send him to the East-Indies, where he would be far enough from me. Bob, having received a severe lecture from his father, left the house, and came to me, where he kept himself secreted for three weeks. The family was distracted, and Bob's brother came to me every day to enquire after him, but he would not be seen. At length, I persuaded him to see his brother; and accordingly, he wrote that he would meet him next day at Durham's tavern, which he did, and went home with him. But the father would not see him till he consented to go abroad, as he had dissipated some hundreds of his father's property, by gambling and other means. Every thing was got ready for his departure to England in one day, and his brother was to go with him, to equip him properly there, and to see him off. When all this was settled, Bob called on me in the morning, told me he was going to England, for a little time with his brother, as he then was ignorant whither he was to be sent. He laid before me the necessity of obeying his father, in order to be restored to his good graces, as he had been very expensive to him; and depended entirely upon him for his future establishment in life: and that he would write to me from the Head, and from London.

The departure of the second man I ever loved (whatever affection I pretended to others, to hum and deceive them) was an object of grief to me. I fretted exceedingly, and kept my room for some days. Bob was faithful to his promise, and we continually corresponded, till his brother had got every thing ready for his voyage. He then wrote to intreat me to come to him, on the receipt of a letter from him by his brother; who, having received his solemn promise to go abroad, and given him a handsome sum of money, was to be in Dublin in a few days.

Short absences, it is said, fan the fire of love, whilst *long* ones put it out, so I found. The short time I had lost my darling Bob, made me only the more eager to see him again. I therefore, without the least hesitation, sat out for England, the very day after I had received the expected letter, and soon joined the man of my heart. After a short stay in London, we went to Portsmouth, where the ship lay in which he was to embark. However, it was near six months before it sailed, during which time we lived happily, and went to every public amusement.

The last fortnight was indeed very gloomy, as every day's approach to his sailing, made us anticipate our grief for our separation. He had indeed, another cause of discontent, of which I was totally ignorant; he had spent above one hundred pounds of the money, he had received to bear the charges of his voyage. Had I known his want, he should not have suffered a moment's uneasiness at it; for though I had but little money with me, I had many things of value, which I would have gladly pawned or sold for his supply. But his noble soul, scorned the very idea of being under such a compliment to a woman. He formed a plausible story in a letter to his father, and drew upon him for this deficiency. His bill was accepted and paid, and then, and not till then, did he acquaint me of his past embarrassment. Many a man would, like a mean wretch, have taken the advantage of a woman's fondness, had the opportunity offered. With many such I have met: some have actually robbed me, others have borrowed my money, and to this hour have never paid me. (*But I shall, in my next volume, lay before the public a list of all who are in debt to me, with the sum, and how long owing.*) Two or three days before Bob was to sail, he came with me to London, put me safe into the stage-coach, that was to bring me towards the Packet, and we parted with great grief and the utmost reluctance.

Book Two

CHAPTER ONE

There's not a weed so noxious on the Earth,
But holds some virtue clos'd within it's rind;
And few there are, howe'er far gone ill,
From whom some quality of use to man
May not be drawn. Heav'n only sees the Heart,
Then let us not condemn from outward shew,
But let the good *be shelter for the* bad,
Plead in it's favour and incline our thoughts
To comely Charity, towards our neighbour.

BEN JOHNSON

WHILST WE WERE AT LONDON, a Manchester gentleman paid his addresses to me. As I was then with Bob, I would not listen to him; but as Bob was on the eve of going abroad, the gentleman told me, if I would take Manchester in my way home to Dublin, he would make me a present of an handsome gig, and four very delicate ponies. I promised that I would, as I thought the gig and ponies would be very stileish. However, such was my distress on parting with Bob, that though I actually came through Manchester, I could not bear to keep my promise. Though, to confess the truth,

I had a terrible conflict between my love for Bob, and my desire for the gig and ponies; and I did not value myself a little on this capital piece of self-denial.

When I arrived in Dublin, I found all well, but Sally Hayes, who was almost inconsolable for the loss of a favourite Captain, who had been obliged to join his regiment. We being sisters in affliction, lived like widows for a while; till, like other widows, we strove to drive away the thoughts of the past, by the enjoyments of the present; and we followed the advice of Shakespeare,

> Take you some *new* infection to your heart
> And the rank poison of the *old* will die.

A Captain H—, paid his addresses to Sally; she loved him for near two years, with as much fervor as she did any of her former favourites: nay, more, for when he was ordered abroad, she took it so much to heart, that it brought on a billious complaint, which in the end, carried her to her grave: but here I anticipate.

As for myself, a very handsome young fellow of the name of Cunynghame, became very assiduous to please me. He visited me many times, before I thought proper to admit him to my favour, as he was too great and too general an admirer of the fair sex. He was expecting a commission in the sixty-seventh regiment. However, as I was totally disengaged, I thought he would make me a very agreeable dangler and attendant, as I was so much in public: for indeed, he was fit for nothing else; and therefore, I inlisted him in my train; – but I shall leave mentioning him for a time, to give place to some intermediate matter.

Hitherto, for many pages I have candidly shewn myself in my *worst* light; I now beg leave to mention some anecdotes, which I hope will place me in a more advantageous point of view; and that, however vindictive I may have appeared, when ill-used, Pity and Humanity, were no strangers to my breast. These short narratives will not be quoted exactly in the order of time; but are thrown together, that they may be seen at one glance.

When the Regiment of Black Horse, was in garrison in Dublin, one evening three troopers of that regiment came to my house, and demanded some money to drink my health. I met them in the hall, and asked if I owed them any money? They said no. Then, I think (said I,) it is very well that I can pay my debts, and not give money to strangers to drink. It is what I never did nor ever will. If any person in real distress applied to me, I would relieve them as far as in my power. On my refusal, the soldiers rushed by me, and ran up stairs, saying, they would search for a deserter. I told them there was no such person there, but they might search as far as they pleased; which they did. This was merely a pretence of the soldiers, thinking thereby to extort money from me; but when they found I would give them none they went away, after making a great bustle.

I had at that time, a lady with me in my house. I requested she would take a chair and go to the Barracks, to some of the officers of that regiment, and acquaint them with the behaviour of three of their men. This she did, and the officers directly ordered the gates to be shut, and a search made. Eleven of their men were missing out of their rooms. A guard was sent in quest of them, and they were all taken, brought hand-cuffed to the Barracks, and put into confinement.

The next morning, an officer wrote to me, that Colonel Crampton requested I would come to the Barracks at eleven o'clock; and that I would drive to the back of the Barracks, on Arbour-hill, and he would order the men round there, as it would be more private. They were indeed, ranged there before my carriage came. The Colonel then asked me if any of the men who had behaved ill at my house, were among those eleven. I immediately pointed out the three, telling him that one of them was the man who wanted to extort money from me, and had been very impudent and insolent: the other two came indeed with him, but had behaved remarkable civil. The Colonel ordered the offender back to his confinement, till a Court-martial should be held on him. In a few days, the man was tried and sentenced to receive some hundred lashes, at which I was much pleased; for, if such behaviour were to be passed over, there would be no end to it. Every day in the interval, between the sentence and the day it was to be put in execution, I had three or four letters brought me from the prisoner, interceding in his behalf. At last, the man's wife came crying to my door, and would not quit it till she saw me. I then pitied the woman, and wrote by her to the Colonel, to request he would pardon the man, as for my own part, I sincerely forgave him. The Colonel complied, and the man was released without any other punishment than the confinement he had suffered; – after this, sundry of the man's comrades came to my house to thank me; and declared if any of the regiment were to meet me on the mountains of Connaught, or the farthest part of Ireland, they would carry me on their backs to any, the most distant place to where I would chuse to go. And whenever I met any of the officers of that corps, they never failed

VOLUME II.

to thank me for my forgiveness of, and pleading for the man.

A young gay fellow, of the name of Gibbons, was particularly fond of
Sally Hayes. He gave her several valuable presents, and some bank notes;
which profusion shortly ran him a-ground, and he was without money.
This not suiting him, he resolved to have money let it come from whence it
would, and in what manner soever. He began by forging a note on his
uncle, for a thousand pounds; but it did not succeed, as the sum was too
large to be negotiated. He then forged a note on Mr Maquay, sugar-baker,
in Thomas-street, for eighty pounds. With this he came to me, and begged
I would direct him where he could get cash for it, for it was as good as the
bank, and he would give five guineas for the discount. I not knowing but
all was right, gave him a letter to an eminent citizen, saying, it would
much oblige me if he would give cash for the note, to the gentleman who
brought it, as it was a very good one, a proper discount would be given;
and if he had not all the cash in the house, that he would favour him with
what he had, and the gentleman would wait on him next morning for the
remainder. I knew the citizen would have let me have as much, without
either note or bond. However, he had but thirty guineas to spare, which he
gave Mr Gibbons, and told him he should have the rest on the morrow.

In the mean time, Sally Hayes and I were engaged to dine with two
gentlemen at a tavern in Cope-street, and were gone there. When Gibbons
returned, my servants inadvertently told him where we were, and he came
to us, though rather unwelcome, as we did not want his company, but had
omitted to give proper directions to my servants.

The citizen, although he had given thirty guineas, in consequence of
my letter, was still so cautious as to go to Mr Maquay, before he gave the
remainder. He shewed Mr Maquay no part of the note but the signature,
and asked him if that was his hand? he declared immediately it was not.
This alarmed the citizen, who, fearful he should be charged with uttering a
forgery, crumpled up the note in his hand, and sat off directly; running as
if a mad bull were after him, and never stopt till he found a gate-way,
behind the door of which, he hid for some minutes, till peeping out and
perceiving he was not pursued, he took courage to go to a magistrate and
lodge examinations against young Gibbons. Then armed with a warrant,
he got an officer and came to my house; being told where I was he fol-
lowed me, and going into another room, sent the waiter to desire to speak
to me. I went to him directly, when he asked me where the gentleman was
that I had sent to him for money that morning, for he wished to see him. I

101

told him that he might do it if he would only walk into the next room, and asked him and his friend to follow me. As soon as he entered he bawled out aloud, and bid the officer seize that man and take him off to Newgate. Off they dragged him directly without his hat; and then the citizen and his friend, went to their own room. My heart ached for the poor young fellow, thus devoted to a certain death. I followed the citizen, threw myself on my knees before him, twined my arms round him; and with a flood of tears begged mercy, and that he would not take the unfortunate young man's life. At length, I softened him, and he agreed Gibbons should be brought back, and released, if I should give him the thirty guineas he had disbursed, and pay all the charges, this I did immediately, though the young man was nothing to me, and the poor fellow was returned to us. Thus I saved an unhappy fellow creature's life; and gave him into the hands of his father and brother, who had come on my sending for them. They did not arrive till the business was affected; and if they had come sooner, it would have been to no avail, as they had neither the money to give the citizen, nor that influence over him which I had. But, Oh! Ingratitude! what was my reward? Gibbons and his father went to law with me for the money I had paid to save his neck, and some other sums I had previously lent him. But I recovered my debt, and let him fall into other hands.

I had been one day to dinner at Rathfarnham, when returning in the evening, I found an hackney coach at my door, and was informed by my servant, that the person who came in it, and was waiting for my coming home, was a young woman who she believed, had escaped from some mad-house. I was very angry that such a person was let in, but went into the parlour to see who it was. When I entered, I beheld a most beautiful young person, who appeared to be about fifteen years old, to have been elegantly bred, and to be some girl of family, though ten shillings would purchase all the cloaths on her back. When she saw me she threw herself on her knees, and wept bitterly, saying she had been so cruelly used by her parents, that she could no longer bear it. I asked who they were? when she replied, that if she were to tell me, she knew my character too well not to be certain, that I would send for and give her up to them. I answered, 'My good girl, if I thought you were a virtuous girl, most probably I should; but you appear to me, rather as one just come out of a mad-house, or an hospital, and I fear you are not good. But tell me the truth, and then I shall know how I am to act by you.' – Oh! No, said she, I am no such person, and did you know my parentage, you would not speak to me thus harshly.

And I know your family, and the story of your life, as well as you do yourself.

This it may be well supposed, made me the more eager to know who she was; and supposing that her intent was to go upon the town, I resolved to use every effort to prevent it; as I have ever done when in my power; for I never in my life was accessary or instrumental to the corruption of any girl; nor ever received in my house any one who had not already been deluded. I strongly remonstrated with this young woman, on the infamy of the way of life into which she seemed desirous of entering. That many a fine woman, who had kept their carriages, and lived in the most extravagant, luxurious, and superb stile for a few years, had fallen when the town was tired of them, into the most abject, and unpitied poverty; and died miserable, and in the want of the most common necessaries of life. This is positively a fact. I have been a witness to the distress of many such, and have always relieved them as much as I could, though some of them have been so high and proud, as to think it not worth their while to speak to me, till I got into high life. Yet, I returned good for evil; and however, I have frequently met with ungrateful returns, yet I do not regret what I have done for them – but to return.

When I had finished my harangue, to which she had listened with the profoundest attention, the poor girl replied, – It was not her desire or intention to embrace that shameful way of life, the consequences of which I had so pointedly as well as humanely depicted; what she sought, was to live with me, wash my small linen, and attend me when at home as companion, or humble friend; for her heart was almost broken with the usage which she had met. She had been locked up in a two-pair of stairs room, her food cut off and sent to her on a plate, not being admitted to table; and compelled to work till her fingers were almost eaten away. All these hardships were inflicted by an old maiden aunt, to whose care she had been committed for a few weeks. In lieu of her own cloaths, which had been taken away whilst she was in bed, and were locked up; an old white dress was given her, which had been bestowed on the maid some time before, and had an hundred darns in it. In that condition she took the first opportunity of the door being open, and ran out without any cloak, or any thing on her head; took the first coach she met and came to my house.

Here let me again animadvert on the ill-conduct of many parents, who by harsh usage often drive their children, sons as well as daughters, to desperation. Bad indeed, must be that disposition which cannot be moved by kindness; and extraordinarily good must be that temper, which is not perverted by cruelty. Besides, if harshness is even used as a method of amendment of any errors in youth, and not merely (as it too often is,) from a tyrannic inclination, it generally fails of its end. Here, in the instance before us, a young girl was driven from her home by ill-treatment; and in my ownself, I have bitterly experienced the fatal consequences of my inhuman brother's cruelty, that first exposed me to miseries, that led to the way of life I had embraced. But for him I should not have erred. Nay, had I had only a friend, who would have given me the advice that I cordially gave this unhappy girl, I might have been as virtuous a woman as she is now.

It was in vain that I pressed her to let me know who her relations were. I told her it was near eleven o'clock, and as I could not keep her any longer in my house, I must place her with one of my neighbours, and in the morning I would advertise to know her parents, and where I should take her, for she should not stay with me for any consideration on earth. Still she persisted, saying, that if her parents got her home again, they would tie her with cords, and use her still worse than before. I told her, no, I would take care of that, I would go to them, and give them such a lecture that would harrow up their souls, and induce them to use her like a queen; and if they did not, then I would receive her, and never let her go to them again.

Finding all my efforts in vain, I then altered my tune, and threatened to turn her out into the streets at that late hour, for the first ruffian she met, to drag her as he pleased. This menace had its effect, she then told me who her parents were and where they lived. This determined me how to act with her.

All the time I had been talking with her, two gentlemen had been waiting in my front parlour, who had been watching to get a second glimpse of her, as they had seen her when they first came in with me. I therefore, sent for a coach, put one of my cloaks upon her, and went into the coach with her, directing the coachman to drive to a different place to where I intended to go, in order to deceive the two gentlemen. And to make them still more sure, I locked them in the parlour, and gave the key to my servant, telling her when she thought the coach might have got some streets off, she might let the curious, disappointed gentlemen out.

When we were at some distance, I gave the proper directions to the coachman, and we drove to the house the poor girl had left: she kissing my hand, and wetting it with her tears all the way we went; and praying she might yet have it in her power, to nurse me, wash my feet, and be a comfort to me in my old age.

When we arrived at the door where she was to enter, I left her in the coach, and went in myself. I found her father, and said sufficient to him, to make him promise she should be used well, and that he would not let her crabbed aunt or any one else, say an uncivil thing to her. I said also, I would come once a week, and know from her own mouth how she was treated; and if ever she ran away again, I would let her stay with me and advertise the whole transaction, with names and places of abode. But I never heard one word of complaint again.

My two bucks that I had locked up in the parlour, having just seen this girl, and being much struck with her beauty, had told the transaction to some of their companions; and as they were always on the look out to ensnare young birds, were very urgent with me to get her to my house; and would give me any thing I should ask if I would send for her. This I constantly refused. They then requested that I would let them know who she was, and where she lived. This also I denied to do, as I never was or would be in the most distant way, instrumental in deluding any young female.

Another anecdote of this kind, and I have done for the present with this subject.

Some short time after the above adventure, a very fine dressed lady, very young, and very ugly, came to my house, and said she wanted lodgings. I told her I had none; nor indeed, did I ever chuse to let any one lodge in my house, who did not go with me into public company. For above half a year she was coming to me, and teazing me to let her live with me. She was always well dressed; and every time she came she wore a different dress. I at last asked where she lived, she said in New-street. Sure, said I, there cannot be an house in that street, fit for a woman of your appearance to live in. She replied, there was, and she had a friend who supported her there. I advised her to stick to that friend. In about a fortnight after, she came to me again, in a new garb, neat and elegant. As from her coming so often to see me, we had contracted a kind of acquaintance, I asked her to stay for tea; she complied, asking me, if, in case she should be locked out, I would give her a night's lodging. I answered, ten, if she wanted them. In the evening she went away, but returned in about an hour, and said she could not get in. That night she slept with me. The next day I was engaged to dine out of town, and to take Kelly, the dulcimer player with me. I asked my guest to go with me, to which, after some hesitation she consented. We went and passed a very agreeable day. When we came home, I told the maid to see the strange lady to bed, then to lock the door and bring me the key.

The next morning early, Kelly, the dulcimer player, came to me, and to my great surprise, told me the lady who I had taken out of town with me the day before, was a boarder in the Nunnery, where he had seen her four or five times when he had been to play there. I could scarcely believe him, but he assured me he was quite certain of the truth of what he said.

I had the lady called down to breakfast, and when that was over I took her into my own room, where she confessed the truth. I then reasoned with her, and sometimes scolded her. I wanted to know what could be her motive, to want to embrace such a way of life, as she seemed desirous of following. That she must be both very vicious, and equally villainous, to leave such a comfortable, elegant place as the Nunnery, to throw herself into a line, in which she certainly must starve, and die in a cellar without a morsel to eat, or a bed to lie upon. For indeed, you mistake the trade, which you are not framed to follow with any the most distant prospect of success. I sent her away, crying bitterly, and bid her bless God, that she had a decent support, in a virtuous place where she could want for nothing, and exhorted her to keep it as long as she could. She went away, and I saw her no more.

CHAPTER TWO

'Tis a pitiful piece, like a farce in a fair
Where show, noise and nonsense misrule,
Where tinsel paradings make Ignorance stare
Where he who acts best is the fool.

G.A. STEVENS

LIFE IS CHEQUERED, good and bad fortune alternately arise. So it is with the actions of those who do not derive them uniformly from principle, but solely from the impulse of the moment. My heart was naturally good, and thence arose the conduct I held in the above instances. But on the other hand, that natural good was frequently perverted by evil examples, by the love of pleasure, and from want of reflection. I must therefore, depict myself as I really was, and now having related some worthy actions, I shall return to some other anecdotes, not so deserving of commendation.

A noble Lord, of my own name, but to whom I had not the honour of being in the least related, expressed a great regard for me, and was one of my constant visitors. He often urged me to name what I particularly wanted, that he might make me a present of it. Knowing him to be both rich and generous, I was frequently inclined to ask for a gold watch, set with diamonds, a diamond necklace, or a pair of diamond bracelets; yet, I could never muster up courage to request any thing so valuable, lest I should be refused. At length, he so teazed me to ask something, that I hastily replied, Then my Lord, I want a good Palliass for my bed. My Lord directly said, Egad then I will fit you, I have a Frenchman, who was the greatest connoisseur in Paris, in that very article, and I will send him to take measure of your bed. Monsieur came accordingly, and having got the dimensions, about three days after, brought me in his lordship's coach, the most elegant palliass I had ever seen, made quite in the French taste. I gave the Frenchman a guinea, and slept very comfortably on it that night, and indeed ever since; having had it cleaned or new covered, whenever soiled or time had injured it in the least; and whilst I live I shall ever have a remembrance of Lord M—, about me.

Much about the same time, I had invited a smart select party to a ball and supper. The company was all met by twelve, every lad had his lass and were dancing merrily. Sally Hayes and I were setting out the supper in the dining-parlour, when a most violent rap came at the door as if it would beat it down. I ordered my man not to admit any person, for as the whole company was come, there was not room for any more. When the door was opened, in rushed Captain F—e, of the Castle, with Mr Dicky D—n, and two more sparks, with whom I was unacquainted. These bucks wanted to be of the party, and to be admitted where they were dancing. I told them it was a select party, if it were not I should be as glad of their company as of any others; but as that was not the case I begged they would depart, as the supper was ready to come up, and I wanted the room clear. The Captain returned a very rude, impertinent answer, and put out one of the candles. Sally Hayes seeing this behaviour, seized an horse-whip, with a long lash, which lay on the chimney-piece, whipped the Captain round, and round the table, which was pretty large; and then turned him and his comrades out and locked the street door. The supper was brought in, the company came down, and the night was spent in mirth, to which Captain F—'s merry go round, did not contribute a little.

The very first week of the establishment of the police guard, I had been at the play and had returned home full drest, it was turned of eleven, and I was engaged that night to sup at Mrs Hall's, in Johnson's Court, and it being a light night, I thought I could walk from Pitt-street, it being so short a distance. I went out with my footman, but had not got out of sight of my own house, when a police-man came running up to me as hard as he could trot, and asked where I was going? I answered, what's that to you where I am going? and my servant asked what assurance he had to stop his mistress. I will let you know that replied, the police-man, she and you too must come to the watch-house. I asked for what, he said I should go, – I answered, well my good fellow! Remember you will pay for this, and I advise you to be quiet. The man was peremptory, so in my way I called at my own house, and got a pair of coloured shoes, that I might not spoil those I had on. All this while I reasoned with the man, and assured him he was doing wrong. No said he, I am doing my duty. Do you know me? – he said he did not, nor did he care who I was, go I should – Well, my fine fellow, I replied, I am Peg Plunket, and this is my house, and I don't think you can have any orders to take me up. But come, let us go to the watch-house, and you shall pay dearly for your conduct. All this time, I suppose he thought to squeeze half-a-guinea or a guinea out of me, but he was mistaken: I went with him to the watch-house in Aungier-street, and asked the guard there to shew me the best apartment they had; and sent a servant to either Captain Carleton, or Captain Atkinson, to let them know where I was. The two gentlemen came directly, to my great comfort, who was not very well pleased with my curious situation, they put me in a chair and sent me home, and put the fellow who took me into the black-hole. It being Saturday night, he lay there till Monday, when I attended and made my complaint, on which he was broke. I then went home and mounted my horse for a ride, from which when I returned, I found my police gentleman on his knees at my door, begging I would get him his bread again. I pitied the poor fellow, bad as he had behaved, and wrote to Alderman Warren, and the rest of the gentlemen, thanking them for their politeness to me, and requesting they would pardon and restore the man, as I had heartily forgiven him, which they did.

CHAPTER THREE

There have been Knights, and Lords, and Gentlemen, with their
coaches; I warrant you, coach after coach, letter after letter,
gift after gift, smelling so sweetly, all musk, and so rustling,
I warrant you in silk and gold; and in such elegant terms, and
such wine and sugar of the best, and the fairest, that would have
won any woman's heart.

SHAKESPEARE

I HAVE ALREADY MENTIONED my having entertained a Mr Cunyng-hame as a dangler. He was indeed, a likely young fellow; and having obtained the commission in the sixty-seventh regiment, which he expected, became a more respectable attendant on me. His regiment coming to Dublin Barracks, he was obliged to live there; and furnishing his apartments in an elegant stile to accommodate me, requested me to come and live there with him. But to do that entirely did not suit my disposition. However, I compromised the matter with him, and used to pass four days with him, and three days at my own house, where I could see what friends I pleased.

Through my connexion with this gentleman, I became acquainted with a Lieutenant W—, of the navy. He, like many other gay sparks, frequently visited me. One day in particular, he came about one o'clock in the forenoon. I was then under the hair-dresser's hands in the dining-parlour, and sat before a very large looking-glass. My side-board was directly opposite to the glass and behind my back, but I could see distinctly all around. To my great surprise and confusion I beheld in the glass, the Lieutenant go to the side-board, and take two silver table spoons, and some tea-spoons, and put them into his coat pocket: thinking doubtless, as my back was towards him that he was not observed. I was so amazed at such an action, by a gentleman and an officer, that I really had not power to utter a word; but as he came round to the middle of the room to speak to me, I looked at him stedfastly, and my hair being finished, went with him into the other parlour. Still I could not tell him what I had seen, and in a short time he departed. I then called to Sally Hayes, told her what had happened. My gentleman had gone to sell them at a shop in College-green, where the master knew them to be mine; and having said so, the lieutenant said I had given them to sell as I wanted money. He then bought them, but not having sufficient change desired he would call again. In the mean time, notice being sent around to the shops, it came out that they were stolen. The shop-keeper then declared he would stop the officer, when he came for the change; and could not be mistaken in the man if he even did not call, as he should know him wherever he met him, being in a uniform totally different from any in Dublin, and would lodge him in Newgate. Of course, if he had I must have appeared and prosecuted him. I directly sent my compliments to the shop-keeper, and requested him not to stop the officer, for it would cost me much trouble, as I must inevitably hang him; but not receiving a satisfactory answer, I went myself to the shop-keeper; told him I had given the spoons, and would much rather drop the affair, were they even worth ten times what they were, than hang or transport any man. Indeed, had I been inclined to prosecute those who robbed me, I might have sent an hundred of them over the Atlantic long since; – here the business ended, and I saw my new acquaintance no more.

Whilst I was connected with Mr Cunynghame, Sally Hayes and I were invited to dine with a friend of hers in French-street, and we took Cunynghame with us. We passed the day very cheerfully, but there happened a great fall of snow, and when it was time to come home, there was no carriage to be got. However, as we felt no cold, being tolerably warmed with good wine, we resolved to walk home. It was pretty late, and we came on, kicking the snow before us, as if we cared for nobody. We had come down about half the length of the street, when we were met by Counsellor B—y and another; who said to Cunynghame, you have two ladies, and one is sufficient for you, you may therefore give me the other. On this a dispute arose, and they knocked each other down. The officer had neither sword nor cane, but the counsellor had a sword, which he drew, and made a push at Cunynghame, which passed a-slant through his cloth waistcoat, and slightly grazed his breast, but did no other damage. The captain being enraged, wrenched the sword out of the counsellor's hand, and broke it in two; and then, with the assistance of me and Sally Hayes, gave them both a very sufficient beating. The counsellor called the watch, and I bid Cunynghame set off for home, and leave us, as by that time we knew each other.

The watch came, and they charged us, and we them. We all stood above half an hour in the snow, scolding and abusing each other; till being heartily tired, and growing very cold, we let each off, and shook hands. Indeed, to give the little counsellor his due, he behaved in a spirited manner, and called upon me several times to obtain the captain's address, which I declined giving, as I knew a duel must have ensued.

When the year expired that kept the regiment on Dublin duty, my poor Cunynghame was obliged to go to Country Quarters, and was cantoned about Tralee and Clare Castle. This put an end to my barrack engagement. He wanted me very much to go with him; but as his finances were but middling, and nothing but interest, could have induced me to such a ramble; though he was a fine showey fellow, I had much rather remain in Dublin, where I knew every wish could be gratified. I endeavoured to weep, but the tears, disobedient to my call, refused to come into my eyes. However, I made some semblance, and he departed fully persuaded of my ardent affection. He kept up a correspondence with me all that year, from Tralee or Clare Castle. The next year he came to Cork, to embark with his regiment for the West-Indies; and I was prevailed upon to pay him a visit, for about ten days before he sailed. I heard from him from Barbadoes and St Kitt's, also from London on his return; and, about seven years since, from Tullamore, where our epistolary intercourse dropt.

Book Three

CHAPTER ONE

Another, and another still succeeds
And the last fool as welcome as the former.
ROWE

MY NEXT PARTICULAR ACQUAINTANCE was the charming Captain St Leger, and charming indeed he was, far exceeding all I ever knew. He visited me very frequently whilst he was in this kingdom. I next was acquainted with J— W—, Esq; who was then very young, and had very little money, but what he had, young as he was, he knew very well how to keep; for very trifling were my gains from him, though he was ten times more troublesome, than many gentlemen from whom I derived ten times the advantage. He would often break my windows, and pull the rails out of the kitchen stairs, whenever he could not meet with me at home. I bore with this behaviour for some time, till meeting him one night in the box-room, I asked him for money; he replied, he had none for himself; an altercation ensued, at the end of which, finding I could get no money, I gave him a severe slap on the cheek, and left him to pay his next debts of honour better; nor would I receive him ever after.

I still encreased in celebrity, and was esteemed the first woman in Ireland in my line. I was visited by nobles and gentlemen of the first rank in the kingdom; for it became quite the fashion to be acquainted with me. Miss Sally Hayes was my constant companion whilst she lived, and the woman I loved best, as she had a spirit congenial with my own. But alas! I lost her; for, as I mentioned before, she contracted some bilious complaints from vexation, at the loss of a favourite captain who went abroad, which carried her off.

Though I greatly regretted the loss of poor Sally, it did not occasion any change in my mode of life. I was ever particularly fond of music, I engaged Isaacs, the dulcimer player, at fifty guineas a year to play for me once a week; but after two years, I found that did not answer; therefore I continued to send for him when I wanted him, and take my chance of his being disengaged. Often I had him to parties at all the different outlets round Dublin, particularly at the Dargle, or the Glen of the Downs. I used to have my groom, with the dulcimer tied on his back Isaacs playing on it, and another man on the violin, to play through all the walks; and when on the road, I had a coach or a gig for them to play as we went; or sitting on the banks at the Salmon Leap, at Leixlip, at Carton, or the neighbouring demesnes.

Although in general, my life went on in a circle of amusements, yet, I sometimes met with very disagreeable adventures. At the earnest desire of Mr Henry Monck, I drest myself in his uniform, and went in it to the Rotunda. I was there accosted by an officer of the name of Hunt, with *How are you, Peg*. I thought that salutation as very unmannerly, walked on and made no reply. He still kept following me, and calling me *Peg,* and being piqued at my not vouchsafing to speak to him, he asked me aloud, how I dared to wear an uniform, and threatened to pull it off my back. Much chagrined, I left the room, and resolving to have satisfaction for the rude and unmanly affront, I wrote an account of the treatment I had received, and sent it next morning to the committee of officers. They took it into consideration, and thought it so ungentleman-like, that a court-martial was held on him, and he was dismissed from the corps. This disgrace had such an effect on Mr Hunt, that he died a few weeks after.

A little before Sally Hayes died, a set of young officers, the Captains Boyle, Hanger, Freemantle, Monck, Cradock and M'Guire, paid a visit at my house. Not finding me at home (as I was then at the barrack) they made a great riot in the street; they wanted to get in but got no admittance, they then broke every window in my drawing-room, not leaving a single pane of glass whole. Luckily it was just daylight, or Sally Hayes would not have been able to recognise them; but she knew them all and would not admit one of them. The next morning, she came to me to the barracks, and told me the whole affair, and the treatment of those Castle heroes. I sent for an attorney, and lodged examinations against them all but Captain Boyle, as he was a kind of favourite with Sally and me, which saved him from the scandal that fell upon the rest. The bills were all found, and then I had incessant visits from their friends, to beg I would not bring them to trial. I, at last, forgave them on each coming down handsomely, and paying my attorney, and all the charges.

CHAPTER TWO

Letters bear witness of their writers' minds
Display their Talents, and, shew forth their Taste
Or set their Ignorance to public view.

IT HAS FREQUENTLY BEEN SAID, that the mind and genius of persons, are better displayed in their letters than by any other means. I have already mentioned the long epistolary correspondence, I had with three gentlemen, Mr Lawless, my dear Bob Gorman, and Mr Cunynghame. Therefore to vary the scene, that I may not be constantly speaking of myself, and that my readers may themselves judge of the literary abilities of those gentlemen, and not merely from my report, I shall lay before them a few letters from each.

My adventures with Mr Lawless are well known, by what I have already related. And his neglect, with his treachery to me – the following came from London, and was written in a great Pet.

On my coming to town from the Bath, I found your letter, and must acknowledge on reflection, am not surprised at such a one from you, I now only regret I was so sincere and ingenuous with one (though I ought ere now to have known you sufficiently,) who possesses so vile a heart. I did not for some days past, think I should trouble myself, with condescending to write a single line in answer to such an epistle; however, as it is to be the last, you see I am quite agreeable to your determination. I shall only say, any thinking person in a like situation, would have been obliged to me; but *you,* ever different from your sex, must now doubtless, ever continue so. On the subject you have been pleased to write, I have only to add, I never entertained the smallest partiality for that person, neither did I see her for full three months before I left Dublin. That part of your letter alluding to regard, &c. I just think as much of, as I am confident it really merits: I am not at this time of day, to be imposed on so; and as to your behaviour on the occasion, I shall think no more on it, but that I should have been glad (if possible,) in one instance only, you could have kept your promise. As to your disposal of the other, certainly, as you may think proper, my motive for wishing for that one was, merely owing to the regard I once thought you entitled to from me, be assured not any late merit; for that, though you have had confidence enough to write and persist in the contrary, I am well and fully satisfied of. As to your resolutions and determinations, I shall not say a syllable, but leave you to your own choice entirely, as I should not wish to be a means of making any individual unhappy on my account; and as to your two last insinuations, I equally despise, as I do the assertions falsely thrown out, either by you or any lying informant: not that I think it necessary or incumbent on me, on that head, to say a word. And now Madam, though I shall not conclude in like stile you are pleased. I shall, let your residence be where it may, wish you all happiness, confident, that on my part (in reality) I have not in the least injured it. 1st September. I dare say, you may make up your mind, about any dissatisfaction you have in meeting me here, as I hope not to be in the way of being so disgustful to you. So much for your future happiness when here. Adieu, since it is the last, and must be for ever.

Meeting with a very smart answer, he wrote the following, striving to varnish over his conduct.

My dear Peggy,

This day I received your last, as to the former, I think you need not have expected an answer to. Had you given yourself a moment's reflection, I am confident you must be sensible I did not merit such a one from you, for *mine* was far from *meaning* to offend you, though I find you very wrongfully took it in that light.

I assure you it hurts me as much, as it nearly can you, your frequent reflections of an affair, that each time I hear of, makes me hateful to myself; however, after my candid declarations to you, it is not only unkind, but highly ungenerous in you, to upbraid me with what I now regret from my soul; and be assured my dear Peggy, *few* as my connexions were, that what you alledge against me, respecting that Sunday night, is the most unjust insinuation you could harbour, as I carefully avoided her, some considerable time before; after all I have said to you already on this (I cannot avoid terming it unfortunate and unlucky,) subject, yet, still I could

115

from my heart wish, you would think no more on it, as rely on it my dear Peggy, you never had more reason in your life, to think lightly of a matter of the kind, than you have of *that,* as there is nothing you should think less serious of, for every reason whatsoever; so I could wish most strenuously as you ought, you would never more think about it.

In answer to your observation of *being,* and writing treacherously to me, I shall only say, to a certainty in my own defence, what long before you knew, or had the excuse you have latterly taken the advantage of. You are in your *soul* sensible, you gave me every reason to entertain that opinion of you, from the equivocating manner in which you wrote, and answered my letters. I do not wish to particularise, I know you must, and are conscious of it, and that, I think, is *too* sufficient, not to enlarge further upon it. I should be sorry, my dear Peggy, you could suppose I wished to write any thing *merely* to hurt or distress you; my thoughts on that head, were no such intention, it was only owing to your conduct towards me, and writing in the manner you did (after the first or second letter I had,) since I saw you, and *all that,* a long time before you had the excuse you so dwelt on lately. Damn the cause of the poor excuse, I wish most heartily I had never known it. But you are doubly ungenerous in saying, I never debarred myself a moment's pleasure on your account, as that I look upon the height of ingratitude for you now to affirm, as you then had acknowledgment enough to own. I constantly gave up my time to you solely, but that, as well as every thing else, you seem to wish to forget. As to my being in Dublin, staying there or elsewhere, I am now fully convinced, can be no object to you. Dublin has ever hitherto, been a place I could not propose any real satisfaction in, this you must be satisfied of, as I am, from not only the people I had immediately to deal with, but also the busy inquisitives at large. My affairs here, since my being in this quarter, has been considerably injured by my last stay in Ireland. I once thought I had a friend, at least in my dearest Peggy, that I might confide in, but that is now over, so shall not attempt a relation of matters, that cannot touch or affect any individual whatsoever, at least where I might expect it would; and now be assured my dear Peggy, you are the last I would trouble about my affairs or disappointments.

Great as you term this place, and as it really is, yet, I do not know that I ever had less satisfaction in the most obscure, or that I ever had more anxiety, distress, or uneasiness of mind, than I just now feel. The person you mention having your intelligence from, respecting me, I cannot conceive from what view he could frame such a falsehood, as I never either knew or heard of such a person, much more what you relate: perhaps he found your weak side, and thought it would answer him some private end, I do not know any other construction to put on it; you know best now whether it was so or not, for most solemnly I can assure you, I neither knew him, or any such person as he endeavoured to make you believe I might have been connected with, which so help me God, I am not, nor any other whatsoever.

From the last letter you thought proper to write to me, I expected nothing less, than what you have now said, about the paltry stockings; but had I really been as you observe, with some dear girl, let me assure my dear Margaret, that should be no preventative, which, to the contrary of any such intention, I never entertained one single idea of the kind, since I saw you.

And now, my dear Peggy, let me with equal pleasure inform you, it is equally disagreeable to me; and I dare venture to say, much more so, to have been obliged to keep up the very disagreeable style, some time past subsisting between us; but so far from wishing to add to your mind's distress, believe me, my dear Peggy, it would on the contrary, add to my happiness considerably, to render it every ease in my power, however different you may wrongfully suppose. It concerns me not a little, your relation of your frequent fits of illness; however, it must be some consolation to you for the loss of poor dear little Sally, as you say, whenever you are afflicted in the manner you mention, you have one with you, who alleviates your pain and anxiety. Whether you mentioned that by way of causing me uneasiness, I shall not take upon me to say; but this I must say Peggy, with truth and sincerity, nothing would distress me more, than to find you stood in need of a friend and not have one. May you never want that, or any other attention, which can afford you the satisfaction you wish for, which is, and ever shall be, most fervently the wish of him, who remains with warmest esteem, my dear Peggy's, truly sincere.

J.L.

PS Wednesday 10th, the day after the Lord Mayor's great day here, which in reality is to me a mere nothing. I thank you for your last intelligence, should you hear any thing more particular, will thank you to let me know, or any thing new in your quarter from you, will be acceptable. My regards (if you please) to all friends. I hope you will not misconstrue, or be offended at any thing in this scroul.

The time now grows short, but my good people not letting me have the command of some of my money, has hurt me much, as I might by that means, have had a decent certainty by this time. Adieu my dearest Peggy, I suppose I have tired out your patience. May you however, be easy and happy, though I cannot.

Shall I hear from you immediately, and in what manner, but will wait with expectation, so say no more for the present. I think your two last seals, were by no means so neat as your cypher.

This was not his usual mode of writing. Whilst I was straining every nerve to serve him, and sending him every assistance in my power, before I went to him to London his stile was different; as may be seen by the annexed letter, the last of his that I shall quote.

My dear Peggy,
I entreat your excuse for not hearing from me long ere this, in answer to your's of the 10th, which has been occasioned only, by my absence from town, since a few days after I last wrote you; your letter has been laying ten days for me, but did not expect any, as you delayed so much longer than your usual time of answering me.

I shall not take upon me to say, how much I am obliged to you and Mrs Netterville, for both your good intentions, and most friendly dispositions to serve me;

and if either or both, can succeed, shall ever acknowledge, a true and sincere sense of obligation in return.

I assure you, I could not have the smallest objection, to the mode or manner of application, you have desired and recommended me. At the same time, should be exceedingly sorry, if Mrs Netterville, would harbour a single thought, that my declining it, proceeded from a want of either the highest respect, or most sincere regard and esteem. My only motive being, merely a matter of delicacy on such private affairs, the consequence of a third person knowing on't, might possibly turn out rather prejudicial than serviceable; therefore, have no doubt, she and you will use all your friendly exertions, in my favour and behalf. I request your prefering her my sincere acknowledgments, and best wishes.

And now, my dear Peggy, I hope in the course of ten days from this time, to be enabled, with that gratefulness I sincerely and justly owe you in return, for your friendship and good nature, to repay the different obligations I have lately experienced from your hands; and which, I hope most strennously [sic], has not been attended with any degree of inconvenience to you.

It gives me infinite satisfaction to hear you are likely to recover, what I am thoroughly sensible, is nothing more than your just right, and that you may be successful is my most ardent wish: it also affords me not a little pleasure, to find you have those different miscreants you mention, so much in dread and awe of you. May you ever have it in your power to keep such reptiles, at a distance and defiance. I wonder you have never mentioned Mrs Dixon, since I wrote you about her son; I hope she and all friends are well, to whom request you will kindly remember me, to Sally in particular, whom I am apprehensive, has very unjustly considered me in a different light from what I ever deserved; for, be assured, I entertain the same sincere esteem I ever have done for her.

Adieu, my dear Peggy, and hope immediately on receipt hereof, to have the pleasure of hearing from you, remaining with gratitude, most sincerely your's,

J. Lawless

Monday, 28th Feb. Great news confirmed this day, of Admiral Rodney's success, but that my dear Margaret, delights not you, nor woman neither. I would have been this night at the play, to see their majesties, but declined it, for this pleasure in writing you. Once more adieu, God bless you. 10 o'clock.

I thought it was better for me to agree to my good peoples' desire, than now to begin another twelve, or, I should have said, fourteen years variance with them, though it is at the same time, very hard on me at this juncture.

I now proceed to some of my dear Bob's letters; whose absence I always deplored, who was faithful to me, and never merited my resentment.

The following is the first I received from London, and is at once a testimony of our mutual affection, and the honour he always possessed.

London, Sunday 12th April, 1783.
My adorable Peggy,

I had this day, the happiness of receiving your two letters; and my love, I have been neither able to speak eat, or drink since I saw them; as the idea of your being unhappy on my account, makes me miserable, my love. With respect to your coming to see me, it would be the height of madness, as every one would conjecture you left Dublin for that purpose; it may, I believe, be possible for some to have an idea, but it must be a faint one, of the feelings of my heart, at being torn from you, but it was unavoidable. I can never express my gratitude, for your offers of extricating me; but my dearest love, I could not clear myself in Dublin, for less than seven hundred; and if that were even paid, I could never bear the idea of living in the stile I would be obliged to do, considering the manner I have existed; added to this, I should have been obliged to give you up as one of the first preliminaries: to be obliged to live there without seeing each other, would be a thousand times worse to us both, than even being separated. Besides, my life! though fortune has frowned on me for some time, she may in a little time begin to smile on me, as my darling Peggy has so often done; so that we must hope for the best, but prepare for the worst. I am to be in the East India Company's service, as that is what I am advised to in preference of the king's. I shall go to India either with the commander in chief, or with a particular friend of mine, who has been there many years. I shall go with the first introduction, so that it will be my own fault if I do not get forward; and I hope I shall always be capable of doing my duty. The army I believe you know was always my passion, and the Indies is the place of all other, that every military man is pushing for. So that I have every prospect not of subsisting as a gentleman, but of getting a fortune, which I some day or other, though remote, will hope to lay at your feet, when you have forgot that there was such a one as little Bob. My picture you shall have by the first opportunity, as I shall begin to sit for it to-morrow. I only regret, that I am not able to send you some more valuable token; but, my Peggy, I am sure will take the will for the deed. If I should be able to suggest any probable method of your seeing me before my departure, I shall let you know; but I hope you will give up thoughts of it, as the seeing me for a few days, would only revive the uneasiness that I have been the unfortunate cause of to you. If I am a gentleman I love you, or may I be branded with every infamy, says

BOB

After receiving many other letters, I went to him, as I mentioned before, but at length, we were forced to part, and he sailed. He wrote the following letter from Madeira.

Eurydice, at Sea, Wednesday 15th October, 1783.
My heavenly delight,
I had the happiness of your letter, dated Michaelmas day, on Friday last. About an hour before we sailed, I went on shore in hopes of getting a line from your pretty hand, and if I had been half an hour later, should have lost my passage; but my love prayed for me, and I saved it. I really don't know what I should have done if the ship had sailed without me, every thing I had on earth was in her but five

shillings. We have been fortunate for so far, as we have got as far in five days as other ships have been five weeks going. We have got clear out of the bay of Biscay, and are about six hundred miles from England without any accident, except the springing of a leak, which did not prove dangerous, and was soon repaired. I think myself remarkably lucky that this ship has sailed, as I must undoubtedly have been put to extremity, had I been obliged to have gone in an Indiaman; for, my love, I had but fifty pounds, leaving England, after laying in provisions for my passage. I would not let you know this before I sailed, lest you might distress yourself for me, as I know the goodness of your heart so well, that you would do any thing sooner than have me distressed. But now, my love, I hope there is no danger of that, and that I may live to make you happy. The sea has been very rough since we left Spithead, and I seize this moment, which is the only calm we have had to write to my sweet Peggy. Welcome, I need not say your letter was to me, but God knows when I shall get another; and yet, I must be content, and wait with patience. I should have began to answer your letter, my love, before this, but the sea has run so high, that it was almost impossible either to sit or stand. You see, my life, how uncertain our stay was, when once the orders arrived; for, though we did not expect to sail before Sunday at soonest, we sailed on Friday. I am happy to hear that you at last wore my picture, as you longed for it so much, it must I am sure, have been set with infinite taste and elegance, when it was your fancy. I wear your picture the whole day; and when I go to bed I have it under my head, lest the heat of my hand should disfigure your lovely face. I now come to the part of your letter, where you say it distresses you reading my letter, and saying, farewell my Bob. Judge then, my delight, what my distress must be when I reflect, that every hour (even now that I am writing to you,) takes me ten miles farther from the idol of my soul. You kissed my picture, so have I your's heavens knows every day, nay every hour, since I left you, and shall till I see you again, let that be when or where it will. Bless you, my love, and protect you, my returning to Dublin is quite out of the question, at least for some time. As to their mentioning me at home, I am perfectly easy about it. My brother I believe loves me, and I imagine the rest does so too, but I hope I shall be able to live without any of them. I can see but little variety, you may judge at present, nothing but sea and ship; the same faces every day; the climate is perceptibly warmer already, we expect to reach Madeira in a week more.

Madeira, 24th October. We arrived here the 22d, without any accident, after a rough sea; you recollect Jones, the purser of the Race Horse, at Spithead, that we dined with, and that you gave the garters to, his ship was here before us; whenever he heard I was come, he sent a boat for me and introduced me to the principal people of the town, and brought me to dine with one of the first people the day I landed. We shall leave this on Sunday, for the Cape of Good Hope, I can tell you but little about this island, as I have been but one day on shore: it consists chiefly of friars and nuns, with a number of English, Irish, and Scotch merchants; the people are very hospitable, but miserably poor. They make very pretty flowers, I wish I could send you some of them, as I think they would please you. I should attempt it, if I thought there was a likelihood of your getting them safe, but I fear that is out of the question. The Tabbinet did not arrive before I left Gosport; I desired Mrs G—, to forward it by an India ship, if it should come to her house. You recollect Brown's direction. If you love me, which I have no doubt of, you will write to me by the first opportunity: if you do not find the method of sending your letters from Dublin, enclose them to Brown, he will take care of them, and inform you how to forward them after he leaves England. Jones, and Wallace the surgeon, desire to be remembered to you affectionately. May every happiness that can attend a human being, attend you, my love! says one, who doats on you, my heavenly Peggy. The people here said I was Frenchman. I had on my painted stuff waistcoat, and a long sword: every one wear swords, so you may guess I would not be out of the fashion. In fact, it would be unsafe to walk in this place unarmed. I must conclude, my love, as the ship that carries this, sails to-morrow, and I must send it immediately. Bless you once more, and make you as happy, as I shall be wretched till we meet, says

R.J.G.

Remember me affectionately to Sally, Mrs Hall, Miss Love, &c. M'Dermott and Burroughs.

Present my compliments to Mrs Pearson. I hope to deliver her letter to her son in less than four months. I shall write to you the first land I see, and frequently on my passage. Adieu, farewell, not for ever I hope.'

He wrote next from the Cape of Good Hope, December 25, 1783; and when he got to Madras, he sent the following, which I insert for the sake of his travelling observations, which may be amusing to many of my readers.

Madras, 14th March, 1784.

My heavenly darling,

We arrived here the 9th, after a very tolerable passage, at least it was more so to me infinitely than I expected on sailing. The weather at one time intolerably hot, at another freezingly cold. I had the good fortune of being liked by the officers and passengers, which made me much more comfortable than I could possibly have been; for, with every comfort and convenience, very few of which I had, five months at sea, is very trying to one who has never before been accustomed to it: though I assure my love, I had the character of being more composed in every vicissitude, than any except the downright seamen. However, I think I have got a knowledge of the world, by spending so much time at sea, that I would not want for a great deal. You may compare being at sea, to being shut up with a number of people in a house, without having any intercourse with the rest of the world, nor any resource, but what you have had the caution to provide. I staid four days at Madeira, where I met Jones the purser, and Wallace the surgeon, that we dined with at Portsmouth, they were very civil to me, and introduced me to several people of consequence in the island. Madeira is the place that the famous wine of that name comes from. It is inhabited chiefly by Portugueze [sic], they are of a sallow complexion, very poor and very lazy; the lower class are almost black, the women I

121

think are very ordinary but sprightly, and have fine clear voices. It is a beautiful island to look at, and abounds in fruit of all kinds. The English merchants are particularly hospitable to strangers. From thence we went to the Cape of Good Hope, nothing very particular happened in our passage; we had it very cold for some time, colder infinitely than I ever felt it before. When we got on the coast of Africa, the heat was almost intolerable, directly under the sun, at one time incessant rain, the next hour broiling heat; which exhausted the most robust constitutions amongst us. I believe you know mine is not the most delicate. I have not been ill a day, my love, since you had the trouble of nursing me at Portsmouth Common. I hope I may be equally fortunate in India, the European officers complain much of the climate, but I think they want spirits only. The soldiers here to be sure, earn their bread harder than any profession whatsoever; however, it is the most honourable, and they are often rewarded for their services. The regiment which I intended to have gone into was the 36th, it has lost a number of men, though they have only been six months in the country; yet, subalterns have shared two hundred pounds in taking one fort. Before I made this digression, I had mentioned the Cape of Good Hope, it is inhabited by Dutch, but was taken in this war by the French, and the French troops remain in possession of it until the ransom is paid, which the Dutch are unwilling to pay; they are fond of the English, and treated us tolerably well. I had the good fortune of meeting two acquaintances there, that I had known formerly in Scotland, which was some little satisfaction to me, as I could dine and sleep with them occasionally. There is not such a thing as a tavern in the whole town. The Dutch are tolerably hospitable, but amazingly fond of money. I was well received, being introduced by gentlemen who had been there before, had been out to India, and were returning home. Would to Heaven, it were my fate, to be returning or going any where, where I might be blessed with a sight of you; but the fates have decreed it otherwise. I had the misfortune of loosing a friend at the Cape, he was unluckily shot in a duel; though he had my own pistols, and shot his antagonist through the belly. He was a young man, astonishingly well recommended, called to the bar, and going to practice in India: but, what distressed me most to think of, was his having a wife. I wrote you two letters from the Cape, which I hope you have received, I would have written to you as you desired on the passage, but there was no possibility of every being a moment alone on board; this, and the constant rolling of the ship, was the only thing that could possibly have deprived me of the delight of conversing with you, as writing to you is the only substitute I can have for speaking to you. I wrote you one letter, between the Cape and Madras, which I sent by a ship we met at sea, bound to France, but I fear you have not received it. The only gratification this world can afford me next to seeing you, is writing to you, or thinking of you. I shall now, my love, endeavour to give you some little idea of India, though you will perceive I have only been here five days. The natives of the country are all black, the better sort of the men wear a muslin gown, plated tight about their waists, a sash round the waist, and a large quantity of muslin, rolled about their heads: the inferior class seldom wear any thing, except what decency requires, over a particular part. Their women have little or no covering more than men, they load their toes and fingers, with a great quantity of paltry rings, and often have plates of silver round their ankles and wrists, rings through their noses and ears; and their hair, which is quite black, stuck with flowers. This, you will say, is a curious manner of ornamenting: at first, I pitied their ignorance, but saw them so perfectly well pleased with themselves, that I could not help laughing at them; they are very neatly formed, and by far the most active people I ever saw, very delicately made. They have no other idea, but being in some degree dependant on the English, and many people without large incomes, have fifty servants; indeed, it is impossible to keep the worst house, with less than ten; you may hire them at about eight shillings a month without diet; and yet, I would rather have two real English servants, than ten of them; but that is impossible, for if you have white servants, you must have blacks to attend them: every private soldier in the horse, has two blacks to take care of his horse only. The country is beautiful about Madras, but every thing intolerably dear, eight shillings for a bottle of white wine, and twelve for claret; provisions in proportion, owing to the war, which was carried so far as the skirts of the town. I have been rather unfortunate in not meeting one of the gentlemen here, to whom I was recommended, except General Burgoyne, and he is under an arrest. As I hear, that several of them are gone to Bombay, I hope that my meeting them there, will make amends for my missing them here. The horses here are very pretty, all with long tails, and amazingly sprightly. There are but few white women in India, but these few are paid the greatest respect to. There is seldom an instance of any woman tolerably handsome, coming out here that is not greatly provided for. I wonder a number of our country women, with small fortunes, do not try their luck. Could you, my love, live in India amongst blacks, I think you said, you could live any where with me; but my darling, the passage is the disagreeable part, yet, I would ask you, if I had any thing to support you, as soon as I have you shall know it. I am sure, let what will happen, you can never want; but, my love, as you value me, be careful of your constitution, as health is the only thing that can ensure happiness. I have been particularly careful of myself. I shall sail for Bombay in four days, where I hope to arrive in about a month. As I go in the Eurydice, I shall be much more comfortable than I was coming out. All the passengers left her except me, and I mess very comfortably with the Lieutenants. Captain Courtnay, who commands, is a fine dashing young fellow, very fond of me, and is an old companion of Captain Packenham's, who, I have heard you speak of. Should any thing happen at home, by which I should be able to exist, I believe I shall return home to you, my love; but that I fear is very remote, if it should happen at all. I am therefore, determined to take hold of every opportunity, where it is possible that any thing can be made. I cannot give you any information respecting myself. I hope from the number of officers that have fallen, I shall have some rank, and of course, may have an opportunity of doing something. I wish you could see the dress I am sitting in, as I am sure you would like it; a white waistcoat, with sleeves, edged with red; long breeches to my slippers, which are of white linen, bound with red; and a straw hat, the crown covered with muslin, and adorned with the feathers you gave me, which

I shall never part with, but with my life: not a dust of powder in my hair. I am I think, rather fatter than I was when I left you, from being more confined than I was accustomed to before: I am browner in my complexion, occasioned by the heat. I shall soon hope to see Mrs Dixon and Mrs Pearson's sons, as soon as I do you shall hear from me. I shall hope for a letter from you, by the first ship. Remember me to Mrs Dixon, Mrs Pearson, Mrs Hall, Sally Ashmore, Betty Love, Nancy Wimms. Don't forget me to Nelly Palliser, I hope she has met with every success, as I think she deserves it. If I omit any one, I beg you will remember me to them, as you know I don't mean it. Remember me in the warmest manner to poor Perry, John Burroughs, if he does not forget me, tell him I shall write to him when I reach Bombay. Heatly has my best wishes: I think if he leaves the thirty-second, he should come to India. Tell M'Dermott, I hope to drink some bottles with him in old England yet. For God's sake, mention me to James, my old servant, let him know I don't forget him, and hope to see him yet. I wish I could send you something from this country, as I know how welcome it would be to you, but there are so many chances against your receiving it at present, it almost discourages me from making the attempt. However, I shall try it as soon as I have found out the safest method of conveyance: the corded muslin is beautiful, how I long that you should get some of it for short dresses. Direct to me when you write, to the care of Lieutenant Pearson, Bombay, as I shall leave my direction with him in case of my removal. As I have some idea of going to Bengal, which would be much more advantageous to me.

Remember me to Fitzgerald, say every thing that your good nature will suggest of me, to those who enquire about me: I hope that none of the mechanics will lose by me, as I despise the idea. I gave an exact list of every shilling I owed, to my brother, which I have every reason to believe, he will pay as soon as he can, in case I should not return. I must now my heavenly comfort, conclude, with wishing you every satisfaction this world can afford, and offering my prayers for your safety. Adieu! Adieu!

Adieu (thou idol of my soul!) though

not for ever, I hope.

ROBT J. GORMAN

I am sorry to inform you my love, that Captain Eames, Mrs Dixon's son, was taken prisoner with General Mathews, and that they have not been heard of. They are supposed to have been poisoned, with many others; but certain it is, that they are no more. I shall make every exertion in my power, when I arrive at Bombay, to know the state of his affairs, and to represent his mother's situation in the most lively colours, in order that she may receive some relief. I beg you will remember me affectionately to her. May you be as happy as I shall be wretched, till I once again behold you: think of the distance between us, eighteen thousand miles; and then say, whether the idea of my lovely Peggy, can ever be erased from the mind of her faithful, and ever doting,

BOB

All his other letters I omit, as however delightful they were to me, they may not be so to my readers.

I now come to the third of my correspondents, whose letters were widely different from those of the others, in both style and subject. They fully demonstrate that those who are conscious of handsome persons, generally pay but little attention to the improvement of their minds; they ornament the outsides of their heads, regardless of what ought to be therein, and their epistles, like their discourse, are generally confined to superficial *small talk*; a confusion of ideas, and a polite neglect of grammar, or even spelling. But let the gentleman speak for himself.

My lovely Leeson,
I hope you'll not take it ill, for my not calling to you to-day, I assure you, my dear Leeson, it was not for the want of affection, but partly owing to a could, I got last night. I must compute it to my going out last night without a surtoot, it effects me with pains in my bones, and my limbs rather stiff. I intend to take a bath to-night, and I'll be able to see you to-morrow, if not, you may depend I will write. Nothing my dear Leeson, would have prevented me calling to-day, if it had not been for my indisposition; and I am sure, when I tell you, I have been unwell, you'll not be angry with me. But my dear Leeson, when I think of the coolness, you treated me with last night, and sending a letter to Mr Barret, without ever enquiring for me; if I had ever such an inclination to call to you, that ought to have prevented me; but I love you too much, to think such a thing, would prevent me calling to one, I love as I do you.
I am, dear Leeson, yours,
loveing and sincerely.
S.L. C—M.

My dear Leeson,
There is not a more distressed or troubled man in the world, than I am at present; and particularly so, if I thought I treated you ill; and am sure, when I tell you the reason of my absence, you will not blame me. Part of the money I got for my exchange, I lost at hazard; and to compleat my misfortunes, I saw the gentleman I lost the money to, at Tralee; he and I had some disagreeable words, but there it ended. Mr Warren and I went to the country, to see if we could rise the money I lost: fortunately we got it sooner than I expected, which was the occation of my coming Monday, instead of Tuesday. The reason of my not going to you last night, I will tell you to-night. I hope you will not imagin I have used you ill, as I assure you, on my honour, you would be the last person in the world, I would offend. There is only one sitting for my picture, and you may expect to see it to-morrow.

Out of a multitude of his other letters, from different quarters in Ireland,

THE MEMOIRS OF MRS LEESON

and from the West Indes, I shall lay two before the readers, which I have selected for the singularity of their style and contents.

Mary Borough, June 11, 1784.

Dear Leeson,

The morning I parted with you, I went to Neace, and stead there that night, the next day we marched to Kildare, and was time enough to see the Rases: in the evening, I was in company with K—h, O'R—y, and Tomy N—t, about ten o'clock I took my leave of them and went to bed; the next morning, we got up at three, and marched for Mary-borough, where we halt a day, and intend to go Rossgray to-morrow. There is no one of our party but Captain W—, T—y B—r and I, and assure you Toby, speaks very well of you, and we drink your health every day, after dinner out of tumblers, and assure you we don't forget Sally Hays.

My dear Leeson, I am sure I wile never forget your goodness to me, and if I never loved you, I am sure your good-nature and generosity most have made me love you, and I never loved you so much as I did latterly. I have not time to say any more, as I am called to dinner, only to give my best respects to Sally Hays and Nancy Wems; you will heare from me as soon as possible, untile then far wele.

I am, my dear Leeson,

your's sincerely.

S. L. C—M.

I received a very extraordinary letter from Dublin, that followed me here, and would not suppose you to be the author, had I not known your hand. As to the epithets you were so good as to annex to my name, such lyeng rascel, &c. I only laught at; as I supposed jelousy to be the cause of it. And have you mistaken me so much? Why, I defy you, the whole world, and the power of calumny, to point out one instance, when my character could be impeached, or even called in question. I would tare my heart-strings by the very root, before I would do any thing mean or low, or act contrary to a man of strict principal and honor. And you charge me with every thing bad.

Fifty pounds a night is the great mystery. Instead of venting your spite on me, you ought to revenge yourself on the person, who wanted to bring you and I at varience. I assure you Leeson, if I had a sum of money to spare, I don't know any woman more deserving of it than you; or, is there any woman on earth, should have it before you. If it is any satisfaction for you, to know I keep a woman, I do? As for my having a connection with one woman more than another, I have not by G—d, and I believe never will. therefor, you need not expect that I would be constant, to the finest woman in the universe.

If you inform me, who the woman is that you say, I wished so much money on, you will oblige me particularly; for, upon my honor, I am a stranger to her, and you may rely on it; if any woman was to get a sum of money from me, it would be you. The reason I write to you on the subject is, that you may prevent any such report. The person that propagated such a one, must be the most infamous of all assassins, to attack me in such a mean cowardly manner. And, if such report should take place, I might be injured very materially, for reason I don't chuse to mention. Upon my honour, it is as false as the perfidious wretch, that promulged it. And if I hear any more of it, I will prosecute him or her for defamation.

I am, dear Leeson,

Your's truly.

L— C—M.

Heathlawn,

Eyrecourt.

Book Four

*As in their faces, so in mind and heart,
Men differ from each — few alike.*
BEN JOHNSON

I WOULD NOW RESUME MY NARRATIVE, but for some few years there was an entire sameness in my way of life; the change of which, will be the subject of my *next volume:* The remainder of *this* will be occupied with a set of anecdotes, which have no absolute connexion with each other, though singularly amusing.

I had formed an acquaintance with Lord G—d, son of a noble Earl, he called on me one evening, in company with a noted *attorney* (who, at that time had the management of my Lord's family affairs in his hands, had since got into Parliament, and very lately paid an intrusive visit to the dominions of Neptune, whence he never returned alive.) His lordship complained he was very thirsty, and desired I would send for a pot of porter. It was brought and they both drank of it. When they were going Lord G—, threw a guinea on the table, and desired the attorney to put down another. He replied, 'Not I indeed, my Lord! I think your guinea is sufficient to pay for fifty pots of porter! What! two guineas for a pot of porter! I have not such a fortune as you have, to throw away my guineas in such a way.' – Why M—l, said my Lord, I thought you would give five guineas for sitting in that lady's company. But I suppose you have no change about you. Come, come, I'll pay one for you – which he did. His lordship went away laughing, and the man of the law scolding, muttering, and grumbling as he went along.

What a contrast between the two. The one sordid and mean, the other noble and generous. Many pleasing parties have I had with his lordship, Captain M—ws, and young D—d L—, who all frequently visited me. Young D— indeed, used generally to employ the time he was at my house, in admiring himself in my large looking-glass. He would contemplate his person with a great degree of complacency and self-approbation, then would turn round to me, cut three or four capers, and cry out, – 'Well Leeson, ar'n't I a damn'd handsome fine fellow?' – Whatever I thought, it was my business to praise him, in order to coax him out of something genteel, and therefore, my constant reply was, that there was not an handsomer man in town; nor in my opinion a finer dancer.

One of the drollest characters I ever knew, was a gentleman who lived not far from the Linen-hall. He was a mean looking ugly old fellow, and the dirtiest wretch I ever sat in company with. He was one of my danglers for a time, but had no chance of pleasing me. He teazed me to leave my house, and he would take a very elegant one for me, and settle one hundred pounds a year upon me for life. I coaxed him and fed him up with hopes till he gave me the first year's allowance in advance; and then told him I would give him a definite answer in three days. The interval seemed tedious to him, and he came to me at the expiration of it. I then told him, that he could doubtless get ladies enough, but as for me, I was too fond of a public life, to bear confinement. I thanked him for the hundred pounds he had so generously given me, to buy an horse, which I would certainly do. I would use the beast well, for his sake, and the first time I mounted it I would ride by his door, that he might see, that his present was not ill bestowed.

A little before Sally Hayes died; I was called into the parlour to a handsome young lad of about seventeen or eighteen years. We had a short conversation, but he would not tell me who he was. I went into the next room where Sally, and Mrs Hall sat, and desired one of them would go and know who and what he was. Mrs Hall went to him, but returned back no wiser than she was before. Sally then went, saying she should soon know him, if he was any body worth knowing; but she could not make him out. I then approached him, and said, Sir, I have not the pleasure of knowing you, nor can either of the ladies I sent in. I therefore must wish you a good night; and desire whenever you shall do me the favour of another visit, that you will bring some gentleman with whom I am acquainted to introduce you, for I never admit any strangers unless they are properly recommended. This seemed to displease him very much: he danced about the room, and pulling out a handful of guineas which he threw on the sopha [*sic*] (but I must observe, he threw them where he could easily pick them up again; which he did, without leaving a loose one for the servants) asking me if I did not think he was a gentleman. I answered, I could not tell whether he was or not – What, said he, does not my appearance look like one? I replied, why really, Sir, your scarlet frock, in my opinion, seems rather against you; as, I assure you when I first came into the parlour, I took you for some English *flashman,* such as the ladies in London have about them. They are commonly hair-dressers, or waiters, dressed every Sunday in just such another frock and small cloathes, as you have on now. My gentleman now became like a madman. He gave me half a score hearty curses, calling me every opprobrious name he could recollect, and picking up his guineas went away swearing he would never enter the house again. However, about two years afterwards, he thought proper to come again, and then I knew him to be a Mr B—r, of Kilkenny. Then I and Mrs Hall were his particular favourites. He shortly after came to be Lord T—s, by his father's obtaining a very ancient earldom. However, though advanced in rank, that was the only point in which he was more respectable, and we resigned his lordship, for others of more consequence.

After the death of Sally Hayes, I became acquainted with a lady on Summer-hill, of the name of *Wynne,* I believe she had been formerly of the sisterhood, but was then married to an Englishman. This Mrs Wynne was constantly applying to me to let a young lady of her acquaintance live with me: for as at that time I had no one, she thought it a pity such a large house as was mine, should be so totally disengaged. This young lady was a Miss Kitty Gore. I mentioned this circumstance to a Miss Ross for whom I had a sincere regard. She warned me against taking Miss Gore into my house; which, if I did, I would soon have occasion to repent it. I asked the reason; when Miss Ross assured me, that Kitty Gore had a most infamous character, and that she had a mother who was ten times worse, who would be constantly coming after her; and who had never lodged in any house, but had been turned out of doors, for the usage she gave her daughter.

On hearing this, I sent my answer of refusal to Mrs Wynne, relating what I had heard. Thus, properly forewarned, it was natural to think I would have persisted in my refusal, and have kept the promise I made to Miss Ross, never to let Kitty Gore into my house. But, in truth, I was always an easy fool, who suffered myself to be over-persuaded. Mrs Wynne called on me, assured me that Miss Gore's mother was quite another char-acter, and said so many fine things of the daughter, that I consented to receive her.

The next evening the mother called on me, and desired to know when her daughter, the young lady Mrs Wynne had recommended as a lodger, might come to me. I told her next night. But the next morning the old woman came again, and said her daughter had lodged two months at Mrs Burnett's, No. 22, Whitefriar-street, where she owed seven guineas, and could not get her cloaths out, till she had paid that sum. She requested me to advance the money, which I immediately did. At night the mother and daughter came; but no cloaths, no trunks, no one kind of baggage. I enquired when her cloaths would be sent; they said to-morrow – but alas! to-morrow never came, and her whole wardrobe might have been com-prized in a comb-case; and the very cloak Miss Gore had on had been bor-rowed, and the mother, when she saw her daughter housed, took it back to the person who lent it.

Well, Miss Gore was now with me; and proved such a shocking creature as to baffle all description. But, I anticipated; – as soon as the mother was gone, I asked again about her cloaths, when she owned she had not a shred more than was on her back, but what was in pawn. I desired to know the cause of her poverty; she answered, she had lived with a very great scoundrel, a surgeon, a Mr —, who had made her pledge every thing she had; that she had left him three several times, but he had found her out, and brought her back. And so (said I) I suppose he will do here. Not, replied she, if he thinks I am poor; but if he thinks I am in cash, he cer-tainly will – but I won't go with him again.

Well, child, said I, you are a likely girl, and may do very well, if you take care of yourself, and behave properly; but you can't keep my company, without making an elegant appearance. If I should take up proper things for you, will you be honest, and repay me? She swore an hundred oaths that she would, and that she would never forget my humanity, but be always grateful for my kindness. The next day, I took her to the several shops, at which I usually dealt, and let her have as much as she pleased, of every thing she wanted, to nearly the value of an hundred pounds.

Being dressed in a genteel stile, next day her mother came in the morning, to see what she could get from her. She denied she had any money (though she had then a twenty pound note,) and begged I would say the same, or else the old woman would beat her till she got all, or, at least, what she had got. At length, after much altercation, as we were tired of her company, I made her daughter give her ten pounds, with which she went off, and we were rid of her for about a fortnight.

Miss Gore had not been long with me, but I got a thorough knowledge of all her past transactions. She had lived a long time in the Four Courts Marshalsea, with her father and mother; and then, in the same place, with a gentleman who was confined for a very considerable sum, till he detected her in doing some very improper things. He caught her in another gentleman's room; and when he looked into his chest, he found the mother had made free with it for a long time. He then turned her off to look for new friends. She and her mother went into town every night, till the girl made connexions with some ladies who kept convenient houses, and lived successively with several of them; particularly with Mrs Dillon, in Fishamble-street; Mrs Sterling, in Jervis-street; Mrs Wynne, on Summer-hill; Mrs O'Brien, in Longford-street; Mrs Burnet, in White-friar's-street; and, at length, with me, to my great misfortune.

In about a fortnight after Miss Gore came to me, she paid forty pounds out of what she owed me; which money, with much more, and several genteel presents, she got from a Mr Palmer, who was very kind to her: She might have continued to receive his favours, had not her old acquaintance, the surgeon, concluded she was rich, from seeing her riding out every day with me, elegantly dressed; and on visiting her, hearing that she had cloaths sufficient to serve her for at least two years, if she bought no other. He now resolved to get what property she had into his clutches; he therefore came and requested she would come and live with him again; and to induce her to comply, trumped up a story that he had been left some money at his father's death, and would do every thing in his power for her. He told me if I would send her cloaths to his lodgings, he would pay me what she then owed me (which amounted to fifty-two pounds). Relying on his promise, I, very weakly, gave the security for my debt out of my own hands, and delivered all her cloaths to the messenger she sent for them;

taking neither note or bond from her or her friend, the surgeon.

After waiting three or four months, and no money coming, I sent to the gentleman for payment. The answer he sent me was, that he would never pay me a farthing, and that I might send for it to Mr Palmer. I then took out a writ, and arrested Miss Gore; the surgeon got bail for her, and defended the suit. After a short time, her attorney came, and offered to pay me the half; but I thought it too bad to loose twenty-six pounds, for my foolish good nature, refused, and the case came to trial.

In one point I was very deficient, and wanted law-cunning. There was a counsellor, as eminent for his talents and abilities as for his scurility and grossness of language; him I should have engaged, and then, right or wrong, I might have got my cause. But, failing in that prudential step, he was retained against me; and though I had three very respectable counsellors (one of whom returned a fee of ten guineas, and politely assured me he would do all he could for me;) yet, the gentleman against me, uttered such a volley of abusive language, as influenced the Jury against me. I had all the tradesmen, from whom I had taken up things for Miss Gore, as evidences for me; and their bills and receipts were produced, insomuch that the Judge himself said, the case was so clear, there was no occasion for any more evidence; and gave a charge to the jury accordingly; notwithstanding which they found a verdict against me; influenced more by the clever counsels' wit, satire, and abuse, than by justice. But it must be remarked, they were not a jury of honest respectable citizens; but a set of picked-up fellows, hired, like hackney coaches, for a shilling fare each, who valued neither soul nor body; and probably had not the price of a dinner, till they received their hire from Kitty Gore's honest friend and protector.

I have now continued my narrative, and the corresponding anecdotes, to the end of this volume. I shall proceed, in my *next,* to those of a later date, even down to the present period; which, I doubt not, will prove still more entertaining to the reader than the past; as many now, living characters, will be produced, and my own conduct related with the same fidelity I have hitherto done, without concealing my defects, or striving to palliate my errors. I shall also, for the sake of Justice, enumerate those, of what rank soever, who have been so ungenerous as to continue in my debt, for money truly and lawfully due; that those who have defied justice, may not escape shame.

Appendix

CHAPTER ONE

WHEN I HAD COMMITTED the foregoing sheets to the press, I requested an old friend (who was well acquainted with both books and men) to peruse them, and give his candid opinion. He took some time to consider them attentively, and communicated his thoughts in the following letter:

—Street, Dec. 12, 1794.
Madam,
I have read that part of your memoirs, with the perusal of which you favoured me, and must own I was highly pleased. You have kept strictly to your promise at your outset; and whilst you have candidly acknowledged your errors, have accompanied them with such reflections as totally prevent them from being seductive; and render them very fit to be put into the hands of young females, to serve (as you remark, yourself) as a chart by which they may avoid the rocks and sands, on which many are wrecked. Many of your adventures are amusing, some very laughable, and others excite our pity at your early sufferings. Whilst, altogether, they give an instructive view of the vices and follies of human kind.

The original letters you have interspersed are satisfactory; and, as you say, form a striking contrast of the tempers and abilities of the writers. But you have acted rather partially; you have given us more of the epistolary correspondence of the gentleman you stile your favourite BOB, than of the two others. I agree that there appears more of affection and genius in them; but the public hath little to do with the mere affection part of them, which concerns yourself alone; and if the other gentlemens' letters contain what is amusing to the reader, they merit as much attention, in one particular especially; that is, we find by your narrative they all three were travellers, and to different parts. Mr L—s to America, Mr C—, to the West Indies, and your favourite BOB to the East. Some of the itenary remarks of the latter you have given; but why not those of the others? As, you say, they corresponded with you, doubtless some of their letters contain some accounts of their voyages, that might be acceptable to the reader. The cursory observations of travellers in their private letters, which are not written with a design of publication, are often as agreeable as the remarks and descriptions of tour writers.

If therefore, you have any such letters, and have room towards the close of your second volume, it is my opinion, you would do well to insert them, or give them by way of Appendix. For, as I perceive, your *third* volume will contain matters of recent date, the letters, at which I hint, could not come into that with any degree of propriety, as they were written some years since.

I am,
Madam, your friend
and well-wisher,
C— L—

This friend's hint struck me very forcibly; and I have accordingly looked over my correspondence, and selected from it such letters as seem to me to come under the scope of his idea; and shall close this volume therewith – But my friend seems to have forgot, that I had no letter from Mr Lawless, while he was abroad.

Barbadoes, May 26, 1784
Dear Leeson,
We *arived* here yesterday, after a remarkable fine passage of about six weeks from the time we sailed from Cove: we had very fine weather, except two or three days; we had squally weather the 6th and 7th of May, where we parted with the rest of the transports, and do not expect *there arival* for seven or eight days.

Barbadoes is reckoned the most beautiful and healthful, of any of the Windward Islands; and I only regret we are not to remain here; we dine to-day with the Governor, and to go to a ball in the evening. I would wait to give you a description of it, but the packet sails at three o'clock to-day, and could not have an opportunity of *writeing* to you perhaps *wile* we remained here. For, as soon as the other transports *arive*, we go to *Anteaque* and St Christopher's.

I forgot to mention to you, that I put into Madeira the 18th, *were* we got a pipe of Madeira wine; but remained there only eight hours, and had not an opportunity of *writeing* to you.

My dear Leeson, from the time we parted with you, your heavenly person never left my sight, your image was *allways* before me, and thought of nothing but the blissful moments we spent together. And although you were fond of another man, and your showing me his letters made me jealous and *distracted* for a moment; but, when I again thought of the length of way you came to see me, made me love you in spite of myself. The instant I got to Cork, I got your dear *pickture* set in as elegant a manner as I possibly could: I constantly wear it on my finger, and kiss it an hundred times a day.

I can't say any more, as the man *is* called to take my letter on board.

Your's, sincerely,

S.L. C— M.

Don't write to me until you receive another letter from me, as perhaps I will never *ceive* it.'

Brimstone-hill, St. Christopher's,

Nov. 4, 1784.

My dearest Leeson,

The instant I received your long wished-for, and most *heavenly* letter, I seized it with rapture, and every line I read gave me fresh vigour, and animated my poor debilitated spirits. When you mentioned Circular Road, *Rotundo,* Plays, and all the public amusements, I sighed, and brought to my recollection the many times I have been with you, and the many blissful moments I spent in your company. I once flattered myself, my dear Leeson, we should some time or other, be compleatly happy. But when I came to the part of your letter, where you mentioned B O B, all my hopes were blasted; and every pleasing reflection my poor heart could possibly suggest, were *totoly* vanished! I stop'd – considered, and thought of the past pleasures, I never could repeat. – Your long wished-for lover will be at last happy. I saw a gentleman here, who informed me he was getting, or had got into some young regiment; and that they were going home immediately, and believed *the* were now on their passage home.

Since I have been so unfortunate as to give you my affection, while you were fond of another man: I am my own persecutor, and have no one to blame but myself. While I was connected with you, I loved you sincerely, and seriously thought of no other woman; you are in possession of my heart, and while I think of your being with another, who loves you as I do, is enough to distract me. I suppose this letter will make you one of the happiest women existing. For, as to Bob's going home, is as certain, as that I am in the island of St Kitt's, if he got a commission, for I know that all the troops that are in the East Indies, are to be relieved in Spring, if not already. And suppose, he only wanted to supprise you, when he mentioned two years; for, if he is in any regiment in the East Indies, you may expect to see him next Summer. And I – must content myself with this reflection! The woman I love is to be in the arms of another, to be in a broiling climate, which is subject to every calamity of the *climes,* and never to see my native country. My foreboding spirit, suggested some extraordinary event had happened: for, a few nights ago, after my usual custom of kissing your *pickture.* I *lef* it on the table, the window being up, it was blown of, and fell in a mug of water, that was by the bed-side, which disfigured it as you see: I send it to you, in hopes you will *replease* its former beauty; I expect it shortly, and will think it an age, until I have it once more in my possession. Ten thousand thanks for the *ribon* you sent me, and it must partly supply the place of the ring, and will *ware* it to my *wach,* until I get it.

I have been a witness to two earthquakes and a *hurrican,* since I came to this country; the *hurrican,* I suppose you must have heard of, in the news-papers. But it is impossible that pen can describe, or that your imagination, can form any con-ception of the *scen* of horror, that presented to our view in the morning. You would see fields of sugar-canes, whirled in the air, and scattered over the face of the coun-try; trees were torn up at a blast, and driven about at the mercy of the wind; wind-mills blown down; the fixtures, and stills of several hundred weight, were wrenched from the ground, and battered to pieces; even houses, were no protec-tion; you would see the roofs of some blown off at a blast, while others were totter-ing, imagining every moment, *the* would come down, and crush to death the unfortunate inhabitants.

I have nothing particular to tell you, there is no news of any sort, in this part of the world, only what I have mentioned; so must conclude, with giving my best wishes to P. Butler, and all friends. Hedges sends his respects to you, D. Butler, likewise. I believe I will be shortly removed to *Antique,* when I am I will let you know. Adieu, my dear Leeson; every blessing attend you. The next letter I receive from you, I suppose, will be the news of Bob's *arival* in England.

Your's, my dear Leeson,
very sincerely,
S.L. C— M.

The above two were the only letters I received from the West Indies. However, as I have some more of Bob's letters from the East, I insert the following.

Cape of Good Hope,
25th Dec., 1783.
I have the pleasure of informing my darling love, that I arrived safe this day, after a good passage so far; which is reckoned the longest half between England and India: I should have written on my passage from *Martinica,* had any thing hap-pened that could have afforded you the smallest entertainment. Indeed weather, and the heat of the ship, has been so great that it was almost impossible to stay below: there are twelve gentlemen passengers besides servants; the ship only a lit-tle larger than the one you dined in at Spithead; it is at sea where we are obliged to shut every air-hole, you will easily judge very disagreeable; the captain, who is a very fine spirited young man, is very fond of me, which makes every one in the ship very attentive; indeed I have the good fortune of pleasing almost every one, which is not very easy, as there are so many parties in almost every ship; but you know one of the last requests you made of me was, not to quarrel, which I shall

ever attend to in every occurrence where my honor is not called in question; indeed I shall attend to every thing I think could please you, if you were present, and live in hopes of our once more meeting to be happy, and never to part, which I do not despair of; and be assured, the farther I am from you, the more deeply is your image rivetted in my soul; all the little occurrences that ever happened between us come into my mind when awake, and when *asleepling,* I dream of you every moment; I one time think myself in Dublin, and you and me riding; at another, I fancy that I had returned, and you would not see me – that you preferred some one else; and I leave you to judge what my feelings must be when I dreamed, that at another time I thought I had got a fortune, and that you and I were driving in a phaeton; then indeed was I completely happy; but, alas! it was all but a dream. We shall remain here but a few days, and shall then, I believe, go to Madras, which we shall reach in two months, if we are *looky,* from whence I shall hire a two months passage to Bombay, where I hope I shall be well received. If I had a hope of seeing you at that time, how happy I could make myself, but shall exist on the idea of your being so, and endeavour to reconcile myself to fate. The climate of Bombay is remarkable healthy, almost as moderate as England, I'm told; – I think with myself if I had a little house there, and you with me, I should live content for ever, but that would be too much for me even to hope; how oft at night do I clasp you in my loving arms, and wake, and find it all a vain dream. I hope you are enjoying yourself with every diversion the town affords, from home. I dreamed once that my father was dead. I shall hope to hear from you shortly after my arrival at Bombay.

The ship that carries this is just ready to sail, but you may depend on hearing from me by every opportunity, which is all the comfort I can now afford you; may you be as happy as I shall be wretched, till we again meet; says.

Your own doting little

BOB

> The soul don't from the body part,
> With half the anguish or the smart,
> That I now tear thee from my heart,
> Which I so freely gave thee.

I embrace the present opportunity to tell you that I am well. I had a long letter written to you of, many sides, containing an account of every thing that occurred to me since I had the happiness of writing to you last; but unfortunately my servant has stolen it, with my pocket book. I have had many losses by the villainy of servants; at one time my watch, shoe, knee buckles, hat, and twenty-five pounds; at another, four guineas a great part of my linen, and pocket book: these were losses I could but ill afford; however, I am resolved to make the best of every misfortune or accident. But why do I tell you such things that I know will give you pain, and can afford me no pleasure to relate; but the satisfaction I have in communicating every thing to you that relates to myself, as I would know how affect-edly you would sigh for me, and say, *my Bob,* should I never have the happiness of returning, how eagerly shall I kneel before you till I hear from your lovely lips; come to me, my Bob, *for ever.* I have applied for a commission in the 36th; I believe my recommendation is gone home; should I have the good fortune to obtain it, I may hope to be in England in three years, perhaps two, an age, you'll say. But the fates have decreed it, and we must submit, and then my darling the pleasure I should have in telling you every thing about India, a place nineteen thousand miles from where you are; and perhaps never again to be called away. I have met with many here that I little suspected. Callage, who I have heard you mention; but I avoided him cautiously. He came out, I believe, in the navy. I remember a Mr Lawler at your house the night that M'Dermott cut his hand with the glass; he is now lieutenant and quarter master to the 102d regiment; he treated me with a great deal of attention, and we often drank your health in half pint bumpers. Should you see him in Dublin, he'll mention me to you; I dare say, he expects to be there in about a year. He has made some money, by bearing two posts, and seems to spend it freely, as most people do here. Would you believe it that Miss Scriven, who lived at the Green (you must have heard of her), arrived here this week, married to a writer. I never was more surprised in my life than when I saw her; but nothing is strange under the sun. I am now embarked on board the Defence, a 74 gun ship; we sail for Bombay to-morrow, where I hope to be blessed with a letter from my heavenly Peggy; with what rapture I shall gaze on it, and eagerness break the seal. May every blessing shower down upon thy head, my heavenly darling. It is now one year since I left England; if I could promise myself with any degree of certainty a sight of you, my delight, I could exist on the bare thought. I have been very unlucky in not finding the people I was recommended to. I mentioned to you that general Mathews, on whom I chiefly relied, was taken prisoner and poisoned. Mrs Dixon's son suffered the same fate; he was eldest captain and chief confidant to the general. I shall make every enquiry with respect to his affairs when I reach Bombay; I shall shew her letters to him, and will do every thing in my power to represent her situation in the most lively colours, that some thing may be done for her. I am told he died very rich, but what has, or will become of his property, is very uncertain. Mrs Pierson's son is very well, I am told by those who have seen him lately. He was in all the campaign until within a few days of the capture of general Mathews, and was fortunately left behind in a small fort. I have received more attention from one letter that Brown gave me than all the others I had to this place. His brother is now a captain in General Burgoyne's light dragoons, quartered near this. I have met with a Mr Gibbons since I came here, the very person I heard you and Sally speak of: he is an officer of this establishment, has been a long time a prisoner, and has got leave to go home for his health: he is indeed the most emaciated man I ever saw. Whether he goes to Dublin, or not I don't know with certainty, but suppose he will: I also met a Mr Baily, who knew your picture immediately. This place is amazingly stupid, and very inhospitable to strangers. I have scarcely been acquainted with a single family since I came here. I'm told Bombay is much better in that respect, but miserably poor: the heat here is excessive. I assure my love, I sleep generally in the open air, with no other covering than a pair of drawers. How different that, my love, from your charming bed and heavenly arms. But why do I intoxicate my brain with the idea of what, perhaps I may never enjoy; yet, yet, I will hope and live in anxious expectation. Did you but know the feelings that distract me at this moment, you would give a tear to your ever doting Bob, for my heavenly delight I may with truth say, I'll never change, nor time, nor place, *my* faith shall move. I dreamed last night I had got five hundred pounds a year, and was going home to purchase a company; would to heaven it were reality; I then might say I had a prospect of being really happy, which is not to be expected I fear in this unfortunate kind of world. I shall write to you on my arrival at Bombay. May I entreat you by every thing that is sacred, by every thing that is lovely, by your own darling self to take care of your health, as I know you have a constitution, if taken care of, is equal to any thing; therefore, my love, do it a little justice, that I may once again gaze on that lovely form, whose image is ever before my eyes. There is no entertainment in this stupid place; nothing like a public place, only a ball once a fortnight, and concert once a fortnight. This is very different from Dublin, you will say; where you have something pleasant every night. The amusement of this country is riding or driving phaetons. It is hardly possible to walk any distance until one is accustomed to the heat. I have had a gentleman's phaeton and horses generally to attend me for these last two months, a beautiful pair of grays. O God, if I had you in it with me; the horses are very handsome and amazingly sprightly; you judge I drove in stile, and astonished the natives. I can say but little about myself. I have been very near wanting money, but never absolutely, still got a supply in time. I have been obliged to live on my own bottom, which is very expensive. We cannot get the plainest dinner less than a pagado, which is eight shillings sterling. I hear that Brown is on his way coming out; so that I shall hope to see him on my arrival at Bombay; if I do not, I shall think you have forgot me; the very thought is worse than death, but that can never be the case, for my darling is too good. I shall write you particularly when I get to Bombay. I am distracted with dreams every night, which makes me imagine that some thing has happened at home since my departure. Should it be in my favour, you may expect me in England very soon. Let my fate be what it may, my prayers shall ever be for your happiness; which I think your own goodness of heart will ever ensure you. I shall conclude, with offering prayers for your happiness, let what will befall your doting,

BOB

end of Volume II.

Nothing extenuate, nor set down aught in malice.
SHAKESPEARE.

MEMOIRS

OF

MRS. MARGARET LEESON,

WRITTEN BY HERSELF;

IN WHICH ARE GIVEN ANECDOTES, SKETCHES OF THE
LIVES AND BON MOTS OF SOME OF THE
MOST CELEBRATED

CHARACTERS

IN

GREAT-BRITAIN AND IRELAND,

PARTICULARLY OF ALL THE

FILLES DES JOYS

AND

MEN OF PLEASURE AND GALLANTRY

WHICH HAVE USUALLY FREQUENTED HER CITHEREAN
TEMPLE FOR THESE THIRTY YEARS PAST.

IN THREE VOLUMES.

VOL. III.

REASON prescribes strict Laws for giddy Youth,
But the warm temper leaps o'er cold Decree ;
And when once past the bounds that should restrain,
Rambles at large, tho' conscious it should not.
Yet, let not Censure, with its brow austere,
Too heavy fall upon the erring Fair.
He is a CHOICE DIVINE, who practices
That which he teaches others.——'Tis by far
More easy to tell Twenty what to do,
Than be the One of Twenty who will do it.

A NEW EDITION, WITH CONSIDERABLE ADDITIONS.

DUBLIN:

PRINTED AND SOLD BY THE PRINCIPAL BOOKSELLERS.

1797.

Price, sewed, 10s. 10d.

Gent.Mag.May.1790.Pl.II.
p.396.

Fig.1. Front of the Building. used by Daly's Club.

Daly's Club House, designed by Francis
Johnston, opened in 1790. Scene of the hoax
perpetrated on William Alexander English.

Book One

CHAPTER ONE

[*Setting up in Pitt Street, the Ultimate Client, and Some Few Brief Lives*]
I SHALL NOW COMMENCE with the most memorable epoch of my unfortunate life, bidding adieu to *Bob* and *Bobbadil,* and all such paltry bagatelles. After I had elegantly fitted out my house in Pitt-street, which I had furnished in the most superb and luxuriant style, with lustres, gerandoles, branches, *elastic beds,* lascivious prints and paintings, and every matter that genius or fancy could suggest to the most heated and eccentric imagination, I, on or about the beginning of the year 1784, set up an elegant equipage, with a couple of smart footmen in embroidered liveries, an aldermanic ruby faced coachman, and not only a complete suite of servants, but a fresh importation of delicious *Filles-de-Joys,* chosen by myself from the purlieus of Covent Garden and Drury-Lane: being thus prepared for a smart winter's campaign, who dare vie with honest Peg? Now at the very zenith of my glory, the reigning vice queen of the Paphian Goddess, I could not have chosen a finer season for the Loves and Graces to sport in than the winter of 1784; 'twas the beginning of the administration of the gay, the witty, the gallant, the convivial Rutland, whose court outrivaled that of Comus himself. Shortly after I was compleatly and elegantly settled

in Pitt-street, as Mrs M'Clean, Miss Love, Mrs Stevenson alias Brooks, Mary Read, Kitty Netterville and I, were soberly drinking our tea, we were surprised with the trampling of horses at the door, and a monstrous tanta-rara, when behold to our amazement who should be announced but his Grace himself, attended by two of his Aid-de-Camps and a troop of horse, the latter of whom remained on horse-back armed cap-a-pee, with swords in hands, from one o'clock in the morning 'till five in the afternoon of the next day, sixteen hours!! to the no small surprise and amusement of the whole neighbourhood, and indeed of the entire city, who all flocked to behold the state, the exalted Peg was worshipped in by the Vice King of the realm. The Aid-de-Camps soon decamped with an *impure* each, but as for honest Charley, he and I, *tete-a-tete,* drank and spilled three or four flasks of sparkling Champaigne, after which we retired together, for his Grace would take no partner but myself, and in the morning he paid me a profusion of compliments on the happiness he enjoyed in my company; swearing he would give ten thousand pounds his beautiful, his diving Dutchess, was as much mistress of the art of pleasing, as I had the good fortune to be, and as a proof of the sincerity of his declaration, he had me immediately placed on the Pension List under a borrowed name, for three hundred pounds a year, assuring me, I deserved it much better than S—, though he had done much more for her.

Oh! how pleasing 'tis to please.

His Grace paid me afterwards frequent visits, but not in the same state, and indeed I must do his memory that justice, that 'twas never his intention, the troop should have followed him to *Pitt-street;* when he set out he was in a state of intoxication, nor did he ever know he was so powerfully attended 'till he was on his return to the Castle, when with great vexation he espied his valiant life guards all drawn up about my door; however I took care of the poor fellows, and had them properly plied all night, with the *pure native* and a large portion of Maddocks' Irish porter, than which, not Whitbread's boasted beverage ever excelled, though the produce of the *nasty Thames.* This adventure produced a number of *pasquinades,* and every news-paper teemed with anecdotes of Peg and Charley; and at the play house a few nights afterwards, when the reigning gods of the upper regions were sporting their witty talents, all upon *poor me,* they roared out – 'Peg who lay you with last?' on which I with the greatest *nonchalance,* replied, 'MANNERS you black-guards;' this repartee was received with universal plaudits, as the *bon mot* was astonishingly great, the Duke himself being in the royal box with his divine Dutchess, who was observed to laugh immoderately at the whimsical occurrence, for 'tis a known fact, that this most beautiful of woman kind that ever I beheld, never troubled herself about her husband's intrigues; she was the very reverse of poor Lady W—, who absolutely languished 'till she died, in consequence of the criminal intercourse between the Hon. Mrs S. and her noble stripling. About a week after this affair, which made no small racket, I found two of the ladies of the S—d family had taken possession of the front of my box, Lady F—H—t and Lady G—Q—, however, I took no sort of notice of them, and contrary to my usual custom, I suffered them to remain in quiet possession of their places, seating my good ladies in the row over them, and placing myself between the *honourable pair;* who not seeming to like their company, became extremely uneasy, and at last arose to begone; when I told them with a very audible voice, so as to be heard by the whole house, 'Ladies don't be ashamed to be seen in my company, no doubt half the house know I am a wh—e, and the other half are as well convinced that you are arrant t—s, and pray tell me now, who are so fit to go together as wh—s and th—s? Though you must confess the wh— is a much safer acquaintance than the th—f.' This you may be assured was received by my good friends the Gods, with their usual applause; for I must confess they have always been very partial to any of my *bon mots,* and though I can't help acknowledging, they sometimes gave me, to use a slang phrase, 'Great goose,' yet upon the *whole,* they received me with much kindness, and they had no right to do otherwise, as I was always humane and charitable to all who were distressed, and was besides a remarkable *good pay.*

In my account of the Duke's first visit to me, I made mention of a Mrs Brooks, then Mrs Stevenson, who had just come up from the North, with the pretty *Jenny Neilson,* Miss Polly Dalzell, and two or three other blooming northern lasses. This abbess, who was driven from Belfast, by the majesty of the mob, who would have taken away her life, on account of the cruel murder of a Mrs Donnelly, whose husband was the favoured *Ciscibeo* of this lady, who 'twas thought instigated him to the perpetration of the diabolical cruel deed, had it not been for the interference of the well known and unfortunate Mr A—s G—th, who on account of his being the principal person who set the prosecution on foot against D—y, was the only one the populace would listen to, and merely on his account they spared her life; I say this lady, when in Belfast, moved in the humble style of an apple and orange woman, sometimes sharing her favours (and an ill favored wench she was, though elegantly made and possessed of a good address) with any porter who could afford to give her a shilling; however she now moves in a much higher sphere, keeping an excellent house for the reception of her north country friends, the Rev. G— P—, the veteran Waddell C—, honest W—ls—y, &c. &c. in Darby-square, nor could any lady of the town cut a genteeler figure than Mrs Brooks, or shew a finer covey of birds; though a few years before I was told, she picked up a gentleman in the town of Belfast, who being intoxicated invited her home with him (his lady being in this city) and absolutely took her into his bed in the dark, but as soon as the day appeared the gentleman became tolerably sober (the very same who afterwards saved her from the fury of an incensed mob,) he was astonished at his own depraved taste, and giving her some trifle turned her out of, not only the bed, but the house, hardly giving her sufficient time to huddle on her rags; and notwithstanding all, this lady, now Mrs Brooks, has retired from business, after having made a very handsome fortune, and at present enjoys *otium cum dignitate,* with all the *sang-froid* of the most virtuous lady in the metropolis, keeping her gig and ponies, and her town and country house, why not? 'win gold and wear it.' For

> Gold makes a *Patrician* of a *slave,*
> A *dwarf* an *Atlas,* a Thersites brave;
> It guides the fancy and directs the mind,
> No *bankrupt* ever found a *fair one* kind.

Poor Brooks however notwithstanding all her good fortune, encountered many losses; Surgeon A—r particularly, who was her paramour, her constant bedfellow, her every thing, for he could enjoy no female with pleasure but Brooks, ran in her debt, and for wine, beds, —, &c. near an hundred pounds, which he never paid her, and at another time her house in Trinity-street was set in flames by the wanton gambols of a Mr T—s and a Miss Mary Russel, of Limerick, a dashing little girl, who in the height of their love feats, performed in the true Humphreys and Mendoza stile – *buff* to *buff,* forgetful of the candle, which was placed behind the arras, and regardless of the consequence, nearly perished like another *Semele* in love's flames; the bed, their wearing apparel, and all the furniture of the room, having been consumed to ashes, and they themselves, turned out of the house, like our first unhappy parents with not even a fig leaf to cover them, and who could attempt to censure *poor Brooks* when her entire property was at stake, through the lascivious whims of those capricious votaries of the *Cyprian Queen,* who must needs ape the Celestials, by making love *bare breeched* – not in clouds, but on *beds of down.*

> The first created male long wandered up and down,
> Forlorn and silent as his vassal beast,
> But when a heaven born maid like her appeared,
> Strange fancies fired his breast, untyed his tongue,
> And his first talk was love.

So by T—s and pretty *Russel,* they wished to enjoy their fill of love, as 'twas once practised in the Garden of Eden, but the angry Jove took umbrage at their presumption, and set fire to their elastic couch.

In the beginning of the year 1785, that memorable year, when tyranny and oppression first commenced their career in Ireland, when two of the first officers and best men in the kingdom, William Sharman and Amyas Griffith, Esqrs were dismissed from their employments, for their virtuous and independent principles, and struggles in the cause of liberty (but these were not the acts of my poor Charley, they were B—d's. Peace be ever to the *manes* of Rutland. A masquerade was publickly announced to be held at the Rotunda, for the benefit of my worthy friend *Hughes* of the gambling club house in College-green; immediately on this gratifying information (for the masquerade was to be patronized, matronized and sanctioned by the viceregal pair) I employed all my industry, to engage four of the prettiest *impures* I could select in all Dublin, whom I introduced as VENUS and the GRACES. Fanny Beresford appeared in the character of the Modern Venus, and Mary Read, Miss Love, the northern Mary Neilson, as the three Graces – as for myself I thought the character of the Goddess of Chastity, Diana huntress of the woods, would best suit me, as we were all in *masquerade,* for had I appeared in the character of *Cleopatra, Messalina,* the Ephesian matron or any such, it surely could not be deemed *masquerade;* as to be in masquerade is undoubtedly to be in an *assumed character;* thus I sported that of the goddess of *Chastity,* and kept it up as well as the famed Lady Arabella D— of charitable memory, would have done amidst her own *Magdalens. Beau Myrtle,* that unfortunate wight, appeared that night in the character of *Belzebub,* not a bad one for a young divine, and being inflamed by beauty and heated with Champaigne and Burgundy, of which he tippled too freely, he took most indecent liberties with the beautiful Vice Queen, by thrusting his nasty black hands into her fair bosom, and

attempting to do more; however he experienced the same fate of his proto-
type Lucifer of old, he was husled out of Paradise, admidst the execrations
of all the company, but more particularly of myself and fair group, who
seemed to be outrageous at the varlet's temerity; the drunken beau was
afterwards degraded, totally ruined and turned out of the university, in
consequence of which he eked out a scanty subsistence by writing for the
Man of Ireland, poor Jack Magee! and deliniating the characters of the sena-
tors of this nation, with some perspicuity and justice, for the *Dublin
Evening Post.*

At this masquerade I met with an officious young fellow in the character
of Lamb, a hair dresser, who stuck close to us, and paid us so great atten-
tion, that I was prevailed upon by the late Moll Hall of Johnson's-court
(who appeared in the character of the *Rosy God,* and a most incomparable
one she made) to invite him home with us to breakfast, for we all agreed to
adjourn to my house, 'the blissful seat of fun and revelry;' accordingly
young Mr C— (for that was my spark's name, and proud enough he was at
the invitation) accompanied us, and ever afterwards 'till I was obliged to
take very coercive measures to get rid of him, paid such amazing attention
to me and my girls, that he was scarce ever from our parties; he attended us
regularly at the play-house, as one of *my suite,* kept seats for us, ran of our
errands, picked up culls and would have turned bully for us, had he spirit
enough, and in fact would do any thing to oblige and please us; indeed
poor C— *had a very taking way with him,* which he soon convinced me of
to my cost, for he took the liberty of sending several suits of my *Dresden* as
well as a number of valuable lockets, rings, bracelets, pendants, watches,
pictures, and other trinkets, to Charles Aylmer Kelly's for sundry sums of
money; which on my discovering, and his refusing to restore me the dupli-
cates, that I might release my effects; together with his boasting of favours
from me, which he never obtained, for I always held such creatures in such
thorough contempt, I applied to my dear worthy friend – O'M—, who
immediately introduced me to an attorney of his acquaintance, who
marked a writ against my nimble fingered Mercury at my suit, and sent
him for his improvement to Ormsby's Seminary in Thomas-street, where
he remained swindling on his brother prisoners, till he got out in about two
years afterwards, on an insolvent act; I might have capitally prosecuted Mr
C— had I thought proper, however I concluded that the safest way of pro-
ceeding, especially as I had every assurance from Billy Jenkins my apothe-
cary, that his father the w— drawer, would pay his debts, and liberate him;

however I was in that respect deceived, his *papa and mama* allowed their *spem gregis* half-a-guinea a week and paid for his lodging, which with the young gentleman's adroitness at *Legerdemain,* in which art he was a great proficient, he lived very comfortably, and frequently had the honours of visits from several of my nuns, which was a great gratification to him, for the *name* of an amour was all this *genius* aimed at. How applicable are Rowe's lines, to these sort of butterflies, *mere maggots of the day.*

> Away, no woman cou'd descend so low,
> A skipping, dancing, worthless tribe you are,
> Fit only for yourselves, – ye herd together,
> And when the brisk glass warms your vain hearts,
> Ye talk of beauties that you never saw,
> And fancy raptures that ye never knew;
> Legends of saints, if saints had ever being,
> Are not so false, as the fond tales
> That ye relate of love.

Some time after my adventure with C—, I was visited by a most beautiful creature from Skibbereen in the county of Cork, she was indeed elegance itself.

> Just so among the trees superior shine,
> The hallowed cedar, and the stately pine.

This charming woman, wishing to become one of my boarders, told me she was the wife of a Mr A—, an estated gentleman of the county of Cork, who made so infamous a husband, that she had several years before obliged him to allow her a separate maintenance; that she afterwards formed a connection with a gentleman, under government, the cidevant Inspector General of the province of M—, who was married to a most amiable worthy woman, notwithstanding which, she had the pleasure of his company very frequently, as he continually contrived to spend as much of his time as possible in the town she chose for her residence, by which means he avoided giving any uneasiness to his lady, whom he passionately loved; that during this intercourse, she had three children by *her friend,* and 'never was a friend more dear;' that about eleven years ago, this gentleman in his opposition to government at a general election was ruined, by not only the loss of all his lucrative employments but of his effects, and finally his *liberty;* that lately hearing he was released from prison, but that his wife and only son were dead, and he himself in very embarrassed circumstances; she had come up to town on purpose to see him, and to render him any service in her power; that he received her affectionately, visited her after, and sometimes spent whole days and nights with her, but absolutely refused to live with her, at *her expence,* declaring that had he the means of supporting her in the stile he could wish, there was not a lady breathing (now he had lost his ever to be regretted Fanny) he'd rather spend the remainder of his life with, than with her; but as that was not the case, he must beg leave to decline her generous offer, as he was determined never to go into *keeping,* but at the same time, her happiness was his, and he'd esteem it as the highest blessing on earth to be permitted to visit her as often as possible, but that he never would be under any pecuniary obligations to her, and absolutely refused accepting of any part of her property, though she had made him an offer of her purse, which contained upwards of seven hundred guineas. This woman appeared so disinterested, and at the same time so lovely, and so accomplished, that I was fascinated with her, and made her an offer of my services, &c. as long as she thought proper to accept of them; she had a charming taste for *poetry* and the Belles Lettres in general, sung like a Syren, played inimitably well on the *piano forte,* and was in every respect one of the most accomplished and withal beautiful woman I was ever acquainted with. She told me her *seducer* had *ensnared* her with his rhymes, and repeated a number of beautiful poems and songs he had from time to time addressed to her, with many of her answers; during the time she remained with me, she admitted no male visitors but himself, and at last when she found she had not power to prevail with him to live with her, on her own *terms,* she took her farewell of me, and returned to the county of Cork, where shortly afterwards she married a Mr S—, a gentleman who had been long attached to her, who had buried his wife at the time A—e died, and who was in actual possession of near five hundred pounds estate a year exclusive of a lucrative and honourable appointment under government, which he acquired in a very *ungentlemanlike* manner. I have had several letters from her, expressive of her splendid way of living, but at the same time declaring, she would have been better pleased to have begged with her *friend,* than live in a palace with the little whiffler she had espoused: generous disinterested creature!! how few of the old sanctified puritannic tabbies of the present day can be compared to you, whose chief blemishes were *virtues.* She gave me the following account, which had been addressed to her by her friend, when in the hey day of his love.

Charming as angels in the realms above,
Heaven in her looks which prompt to instant love;
Resplendent graces, in her air appear,
In all her actions worthy and sincere;
Sweet as the violet or the vermile rose,
That in Elysium for love's goddess grows.
Innocence and truth, her actions ever grace,
Attractive smiles dwell always on her face,
Nor time her dear idea can erase.
Assist me every power to gain her heart,
To reign for ever there, in every part;
To spend my life in serving my sweet fair,
Eager to prove for her my every care;
Regardless of the world, for her I'll live,
In every act, her ever faithful slave;
Dearer to me than men to *doating hags,*
Gain to a miser, when he's crammed his bags,
Eager to hoard, tho' hungry and in rags.

CHAPTER TWO

[*Insulting the Earl of Westmoreland with Intent to Discourage,*
a 'Masonic' Masquerade at Pitt Street, and more Brief Lives]

SHORTLY AFTER THE DEPARTURE of this excellent lady, I had the
honour of a visit from the Earl of W—, then Lord L—t of I—, whose ami-
able Countess, as I said before, died of a broken heart in consequence of
his connection with that celebrated demy rep the honourable (heaven how
that word is prostituted!) Mrs —. On his Excellency's entrance I arose and
received him with much respect, blended with *hauteur and contempt,* but
on his attempting to be *too familiar,* I told him he must positively excuse
me, as in all my life I never admitted any freedoms from culinary *heroes,*
one of which description, he certainly could not deny himself to be, or he
never would have contracted with the brother of that celebrated *cock baud,*
Doctor Achmet, for his kitchen stuff, what the poorest huxter woman in
Dublin would blush to do; he denied the charge, – I insisted upon it, and

produced the *Phoenix,* a paper at that time in high esteem, in which his French cook had absolutely advertised him, – this was such damning proof, that W—d could not rebut my evidence, on which he and C—k, much chagrined, made a precipitate retreat, forgetting even to pay for the flask of Champaigne, the noble Vice-Roy had ordered upon his arrival. Pitiful! despicable! mean wretch! what a contrast to the excellent, generous, noble Rutland, whose like we never shall behold again. Monsieur *Le Conte* of worthy memory, was the head cook, who had the temerity to advertise his regal master, and 'tis rumoured that this very Le Conte, was in a few years afterwards extremely active in effecting a revolution and demolishing the odious Bastille. *Hughes's masquerade ball,* and my own mentioned in the former part of these memoirs, threw poor Moll Hall into the *masquerade mania;* she could speak of no other subject, and indeed to do her but common justice, the little fat pretty creature, who was (to use a French phrase) the very UN BON POINT, to hit the taste of even a prince; she was the life and soul of every festive party; she, I say consulted me on giving a masquerade ball, a *la Masonique,* as the gentlemen of that ancient and honourable fraternity in this city gave *sumptuous entertainments,* fandangoes and coteries, by inviting their friends and acquaintances to roast meat, and beating them with the spit; that is by clubbing them *sans ceremonie:* we accordingly agreed that every male creature, was to pay two guineas for his ticket, besides extra charges should he solicit to be admitted into conclave, or the *embrace delectable, i. e.* to the share of one of our fair guests beds. My house being the most roomy, convenient and fashionable, and furnished with the greatest variety of elastic beds (they being quite the *ton,* since poor Netterville's days,) *couches, paliasses,* &c. &c. was pitched upon for the *rendezvous* of all the *choice spirits,* the *bon vivants,* the *Loves,* the *Graces,* the comodites and momodites of the capital, to exhibit their charms, their wit, and their pleasantry in. No sooner said than done, *whip, fly, pass* and *begone;* Moll Hall, the proposer, *peace be to her gentle manes;* – Sturgeon, *Digges, Beresford,* the Ballyclear *Neilson; sweet Ballyclear, where there's no Sunday!* the Limerick *Russel,* and *Brooks,* were appointed matrons of the *splendid gala,* and Henry B— H—t, the old proprietor of the *Pretty Grove;* W— C— that ungrateful old letcher, who while his amiable wife lay barren by his side, for forty-five years and more, made a shift to knock triplets out of his kitchen maid; E— Rad— R— of convivial, cleanly and generous memory, John —S—, the identical little whiffling old gentleman, who is now wedded to the divine Kitty Attridge, one H— W— of Fethard in the county Tipperary, and M— K—, Esq; that civil pander, who rents *White Hall,* for the convenience of his friends, or second Achmet's Baths; – and a Mr B—, or M— of the B— Coat H—, were by us the female *coterie* appointed stewards, from whom all tickets of admission were to be issued, though some of us thought it would be rather hazardous, as W—l no doubt, would not forget his old gait of going, and consequently *smuggle* in a number of his northern *electors.*

All matters being thus adjusted, I threw five or six rooms into one, which I could always most conveniently do, by the help of sliding partitions, though indeed poor Surgeon B—r offered us the use of the Lock Hospital, near Donnybrook, for the occasion. At last the great, the important night arrived, big with the fate of the votaries of the *Cnidian Queen;* my rooms were crouded before eight o'clock, and many a fat sleek greasy alderman, sheriff's peer, common council man, and ruby faced parson honoured the entertainment with his presence; the late alderman W— of police and hated memory, and Moll Hall, led up in the characters of *Father Paul* and *Mother Cole;* B—h—set and Grove, in the characters of the Mayor of Coventry and Pretty Maud, both elegantly supported; – W—l C— and Brooks in Alderman Smuggler and Diana Trapes, the Rev. G— P— and *Mary Neilson,* in Tony Lumpkin and Miss Hardcastle; Mr Justice S—, the gauger (who endeavoured to fine me at the excise office for selling unlicensed liquors, and would have done it, had it not been for the interference of my old letcherous gallant Col— R—) and *Miss Pedero* of Bow Bridge, in the characters of the Fifing Girl and Drumming Boy, in the midst of a large recruiting party, headed by Mathews the bailiff, in the character of Serjeant Kite; but it would be endless to relate the different couples, and the characters they sustained; I shall only mention a few more of the most remarkable of the ladies, and give some little account of them:

[Mrs Robinson]

MRS ROBINSON, sported her sweet person in the character of the Blue Eyed Nun of St Catherine's, she was imported into this land of *Saints* by Lord F—tz-w—m, who kept her at Mother Grant's for some time; however Mrs Grant becoming rather disagreeable and austere, she left her, and took lodgings in Capel-street, where she unfortunately became acquainted with *Beau R—* the jeweller, from whom she purchased above five hundred pounds worth of plate and a pair of *set shoe buckles,* which he declared he'd give her a bargain of, and that he'd charge her but prime cost, *thirty-five guineas!!* and she foolish devil as she was, not doubting the supposed *brilliant gentleman's* honour or probity, paid him the money down; after which in a few days being discarded by her keeper, she was obliged to leave her lodgings, being no longer able to keep them in elegance; and return to *Grant's,* who not being satisfied, in depriving her of all the plate she had purchased from R——, robbed her of almost all her *wardrobe,* as a pretended compensation for former favours conferred on her!! Finding herself thus embarrassed, and reduced to her last guinea, she was obliged to have recourse to R——, to return him the paste buckles she had never worn; expecting at least to get half their value, but to her loss and astonishment *Beau Mordecai,* that blood sucking usurer, offered her no more than *five guineas!!!* which dire necessity obliged her reluctantly to accept of, in order to get as soon as possible to her own country; however as soon as I heard this poor woman's story, I made her a present of twenty guineas, and the honest creature, in two months after her arrival in London, sent me a package of callico, worth fifty pounds, and a beautiful edition of the *Woman of Pleasure,* with some of the finest cuts I ever beheld; would that all my debtors behaved in the same spirited principled manner, so that their names might be adorned with equal narratives, for I would much rather hold out the *wreath* than the *rod* – but alas! I found very few Mrs Robinson's among my acquaintances; upon the *whole,* I was plundered both by belles and beaux.

[Mrs Vallance]

MRS VALLANCE another of the fair votaries of the Paphian Queen, was born in Naas, her mother supported herself and beautiful daughter by spinning wool, and very properly sent her early to the *charity school,* but being naturally idle, she made no progress, and often, alas, have I heard her say, she repented she had not made a better use of her time. Almost as soon as Vallance got into her teens, Mr P——, with a few presents of *cloaths, baubles, money,* and *mellifluous speeches,* gained her affections, and whenever an opportunity served, even her mother (I often heard her tell it) encouraged her to gratify his passion, in *her own cabin;* however at length weary of a country life, she suggested the idea to her friend P——, who immediately took lodgings for her at Mr A——'s in Capel-street, where she resided for two years; by what she told me, P—— was very attentive and amorous for the first year, but finding herself at last neglected, she boldly at once ventured on the town; and on her first *entre* or *debut,* to use a theatrical phrase, she met with A— J—, who advised her to decamp with him to a Mrs Orde's, Great Britain-street, where he hired lodgings for her at a guinea a week, and he being at this time in Capel-street, within a few doors of her lodging, the pleasing moments passed unperceived away, for some little time, until one night at cards, Mrs Orde got jealous of her, as her husband, she imagined, made too free with her; and she intoxicated with pleasure and champaigne, spurned the gross idea, and in a pet, quit the house, and poor J— and she could find no place of reception, 'till at last they were through dire necessity, compelled to take refuge for the night in a cellar in West Arran-street; – next day however J— took lodgings for her at Mr U—r's in Dame-street, where they lived for a month; after which she became acquainted with the divine, the edifying Rector of Castle B—, a Mr C—, who adored her, though at the same time his wife was living, and often gave her presents, for what the poor *creature* could not enjoy, he has often insisted the poor girl to pull up her cloaths, and touching her – has exclaimed, oh! that I had you divine Vallance but thirty years ago. At length C—'s wife died, when he proposed marrying her, which proposal she unwillingly accepted, though not 'till he made her a present of *five hundred guineas,* after which he purchased an house on Ormond-quay, where they lived in every supposed harmony, he not in the least suspecting his friend J— enjoyed what he dearly paid for. J—s indeed has often given her a five guinea note, which she used to put in the old fumbler's pocket, and in exchange take a fifty pound note for it, as he was *near sighted,* and never suspected any loss, provided the number of notes were forthcoming. The old wretch at length growing jealous, made her life miserable, in consequence of which, she one night eloped, with all his property, besides many debts which she contracted, that C— was sued for, and obliged to make good, particularly one to my friend J—s P— for eighty pounds – Poor Jonas, who following the paths of his venerable namesake, with some variation, slipped into the belly of a BUCK – instead of a whale, and thereby hangs a tale! – The Rev. Divine attended his darling to this masquerade, and had the unspeakable pleasure of seeing himself made a cuckold of almost before his face, as she parted from him, and went into one of the recesses of the God of Love, at the end of the room, with her friend J—s, who did for her what C— never could.

[Mrs Grant]

Another of my fair masqueraders, who figured away that night, on the light *fantastic toe,* was a MRS GRANT, whose father's name, who was a dairy man, was Connor; she was born in *sweet Stony Batter,* and I have heard her myself confess, her father always supplied his *barn,* by cow stealing. Grant usually carried about the *ambrosial* beverage, morning and evening to her father's customers, and as we all know, a little pretty rosy cheeked milk girl attracts the attention of warm youths. J— H—, a gentleman whom she served in the Liberty, frequently plied her with cake and wine, and promised to make a Queen of her, or any thing she could mention, if she consented to become his mistress; being then of a virtuous cast, she despised his offers, and for a few nights sent a little girl, now the celebrated *Mrs Sinnott,* alias C—y, an acquaintance of hers, to deliver the milk.

Oh! the sweet lass with the milking pail.

At length thinking he had forgotten her, she went again to his house, where to her astonishment he opened the door himself, forced her into the parlour, and made her quaff potations to *Cupid and Bacchus:* As the trans- action happened in the Liberty, and the goddess was rather of a complying cast, he easily prevailed on her to suck in as much of the juice of the grape as threw her off her *center* of gravity, and entirely overpowered her senses, after which he took a coach, and brought her to Crown-Alley, to one Simp- son's; often have I heard her curse the *crooked mouthed rascal,* who on swearing falsely against a citizen, found in a few moments his mouth on his shoulder; here the fond couple had more wine, and concluded the scene, by every gratification. During the interval of a few days, spent in every lust and luxury, that College-green, or Simpson's neighbourhood could afford, she had the mortifying information, that her father was apprehended for cow stealing, and lodged in Trim gaol; however little con- cerned for the fate of the author of her being, she took no manner of notice of the intelligence, 'till unfortunately, it being assizes week in which he was arrested, he was tried, found guilty, and having snapped a pistol at the per- son whom he robbed, was hanged the second day but one after his convic- tion. By all accounts, and by her own confession, he had no fault in nature but one, he would deprive all the world, if he could, of their property, to aggrandize himself and his family. Are not there many dignified imperial royal robbers like him?

Poor H— bought her very genteel mourning, and took a house for her in Stafford-street, where they lived in amity 'till her extravagance con- tracted his income, when she, vicious abandoned woman, charged him on the police for robbery, since which time she has never heard of him: she then fortunately met with a Mr —, who hired another house for her in the same street, and he though a diminutive creature, as she often told me, pleased her much better than the *ascendancy* H—; she generally gives him a 10 *l.* note, going to the hazard table, and he seldom returns her less than one hundred, tolerable interest you'll say for her money; but her paramour is one of the luckiest little gamblers that frequents Daly's silver table.

[Nancy Hindes]

Another character worthy of notice was NANCY HINDES, who was born at Malhassey in the county of Meath; her father was cottier to Mr Hindes of that place; his young son *Allick* and she grew up together, and in their advancement to maturity laid aside all puerile play, and privately enjoyed every *venereal pleasure,* any loving couple possibly could on such occasions. Our sex being naturally fond of dress and show, she encouraged poor *Allick,* who was doatingly fond of her, to rob his brother Ralph, of every article he could convert into cash, besides ready money to a large amount, and all to gratify Jenny's ambition and vanity. At length being discovered, the fond pair were obliged to separate; Hindes, though poor, had a tolerable share of *beauty* and *spirits,* and consequently deserted the place of her nativity, and ventured up to town, where applying to Mrs C—, who kept a register office for servants, she was recommended to Mrs Orde of Great Britain-street, and accordingly not knowing what she was to encounter, hired with her for three guineas a year, and half what she made by defrauding the guests; and in this humiliating station she lived for three years, when, to her great happiness, a Lieutenant S—r took her into keeping, who having expended his own property, and much more, he being on the recruiting service, a Captain W— came to his lodgings, and seeing him much distressed, offered to lend him one hundred guineas, which being gratefully accepted, with sincere promises of returning it as soon as he could make a *lucky hit,* for he was a successful hazard player; he took accordingly an house in Great Britain-street for her, where she commenced business on her own account, made some money, and invited her poor distressed Allick to come to town, promising to share her last guinea with him. Allick accordingly agreed, and by what she told me there was not a woman in the kingdom better protected than she was by her two able bullies, who would beat and abuse every creature who would not spend money at her house, on what she called *Champaigne,* which, by the by, was merely *perry* – some time after this the unfortunate W— being called in haste to join his regiment, gave S— a letter of attorney to receive his rents in this kingdom; S— executed his commission, but alas! alas! not to his advantage, but to his lady's; in consequence of this new but illgotten acquisition Hindes and Sp— lived in every luxury the city afforded, whilst poor W— being disappointed in remittances, and that by his supposed *bosom friend,* in the moment of phrenzy put a period to his existence at Dunkirk, by shooting himself through the head.

[Mrs Wrixon]

Another of our masqueraders was the pretty WRIXON, she was born in Liverpool, her papa being a *chimney-sweeper,* who frequently during her childhood, whipped her in course with his other sweeps, as he termed it; poor Wrixon, if she was to be scourged to death, could not enter the funnel, and her mother being of a mild placid disposition, protected her as much as possible until grown to the age of maturity, thinking no doubt, when she became a *mistress sweep* (for her father intended to leave all his sootrican slaves under her protection and government) she might comfort her in her old age; but how greatly was the poor woman mistaken! poor Wrixon only waited to be seduced, and perfectly satisfied to gratify the first honest athletic fellow who might offer; walked into the fields near town, when observing two gentlemen with arms and without attendants, she followed at a distance, when in a few moments they exchanged shots, in consequence of which one fell, whose name was *Fox,* the other made a precipitate retreat; and the tender hearted Wrixon, went as it were to succour the distrest or dying hero, who after being supplied with some water, seemingly recovered, when Wrixon brought him to her sooty habitation, and finding he was likely to do well, stripped him of all his cash amounting to two hundred guineas, and some silver, his watch, a diamond ring and pin; and immediately consulted a butcher's boy her intimate acquaintance, one *Wrixon,* under whose name she ever afterwards went, who encouraged her to fly the kingdom, and he'd accompany her; no sooner said than done, they embarked in *Captain Harrison's packet,* and arrived in Dublin in August 1789; I can't forget it, as they spent the first night in my house, and in the morning purchased an house, that is, they fined down an house, in Great Britain-street. But Wrixon and his pretty female sweep, being both of an eccentric cast, frequently came to handycuffs, in which paroxisms of frenzy, they often discovered the depradations they had committed, not only on the poor duellist, but latterly on the unwary Irish, – in consequence of which, lest there might be any insurrection in the country, occasioned by these lawless band of ruffians called *defenders,* they determined to quit the kingdom, and more particularly so, fearing the man they had robbed might be in any way akin or connected to Mr Fox of Capel-street; indeed I always laugh when I think on't, but absolutely the sight or name of a *Fox,* would make poor Wrixon change an hundred colours.

Thus conscience does make cowards of us all.

[*Mrs Palmer*]

MRS PALMER, another of our tribe, was the daughter of John Kelly and Mary Slack; she was early bound to a milliner, with whom she lived for three years, and was seduced by a Captain Palmer, who brought her to town and hired lodgings for her at the Rev. Mr C—'s (Ormond-quay) rector of Castle B—, where she lived for some time; the Captain being called to his regiment, there was a Mr J— P—y, who by profuse presents and vast sums of money, prevailed upon her one night to go with him, as he said, to a friend's; but where should he bring her to, but Mrs Sterling's, Jervis-street, where, with the powerful assistance of some flasks of Champaigne, he prevailed on her to gratify his passion, which has been ever since repeated when opportunity and convenience offered. Disagreeing with Mrs C—, she took lodgings in King-street, where she unrestrained embraced her last lover, he being the second who enjoyed her. A woman once devirginated, will not stop at any other *faux paux.* A Mr C— was the next who proposed, and was admitted to live with her at intervals for three months; at length discovered by Pas—, an engagement took place, both being able bodied men, the contest was doubtful for some time, and at length J—s gave C— a chance blow, and levelled him with the ground, the unfortunate fair, thinking him dead, sent for the best advice in the neighbourhood, to a surgeon G—, who bled the vanquished C— and recovered him; for the authenticity of this narrative I refer my reader to Mr G— of Abbey-street. Mrs P— through this accident, was under the necessity of going after her Captain, and I am told they live perfectly reconciled, being since married.

[*Other Guests, and Would-be Guests*]

Besides these remarkable ladies, some of whose adventures I have sketched out, there were a number of the minor sort; as *Mary Read,* Poor *Rowe,* formerly *Ashmore, Miss Archbold,* who was then in high keeping with a Mr H—s *yclept* the S—, but for my own part I'll freely confess, I have never met with a more generous fellow. A Mr Le F—, son to a perfumer in Grafton-street, had the honour of my *fair hand* towards morning, for we kept it up from nine o'clock at night 'till five the next afternoon, when carriages being called we all separated; however I detained Le F—, who absolutely was the best woman's man, or as the gentlemen say of us, the best piece I ever met with, and that, I have been heard frequently to confess to my poor dear friend the late James W—n, who was undoubtedly the unrivalled *Christie* of this kingdom: the gentlemen who favoured us with their company were very numerous, senators from both houses, authors, &c. &c. &c. all flocked to this rare entertainment, which was, and has been unequalled; being an assemblage of all the choice spirits of the kingdom, *en mass;* Lewellen and Father Fay, both sent to the conductors for tickets, but as they had been so very recently and I might say wonderfully escaped the *fall of the leaf,* the ropes having been out for them for several hours before the arrival of their reprieves, I would by no means consent they should be accommodated; for I always had an aversion to any thing base or scandalous, and I challenge all *Ireland* this moment, to advance in any one instance, where a male or female received the slightest injury in my house or through my means, no, no.

> True conscious spotless honour knows no sin,
> She's doubly arm'd, who's innocent within.'

CHAPTER THREE

[Even More Brief Lives]

I SHALL NOW GIVE A farther account of a few more of my fair friends, whom to neglect would be unpardonable, and then proceed with the remainder of my chequered and whimsical memoirs: The following ladies, who should not be passed by, particularly graced this masquerade with their presence:

[Mary Fagan, alias Mary Crosbie]

MARY FAGAN, who was a foundling, was taken out of the hospital in the year 1775 by Mrs H—, who finding her a smart girl took her apprentice to herself (being a mantua maker) she behaved herself very well for some time, and got a tolerable knowledge of her business; Mary being red haired, and consequently prone to venery earlier than girls of a different colour, at the age of fifteen years, stole into the bed of Mrs H—'s youngest son, who was prevailed upon though unwillingly to gratify her passion; – time passed imperceptibly to the fond couple, who repeated their joys clandestinely for three years, 'till at length discovered by the mother, she was turned out of doors, when destitute and friendless she walked about the streets for some time, and at length fortunately met with a Mr Hone, son to the Creole who shot himself at Kitty Cut-a-Dash's House in Grafton-street, who prevailed on her to go with him to Mrs Orde's Great Britain-street, where they remained for three months, but at last his cash being spent, he was compelled to go to the country to shun his creditors; and in the interim, Mary remained at Orde's, but not getting remittances from her gallant, she prostituted herself to every honest fellow who offered: Fortune threw in her way a Mr C— of the College, who liking her, and having plenty of cash, took lodgings for her at a Mr H—. apothecary, in Capel-street, where they lived for three years in as much amity as man and wife; unfortunately for her, T— H—, who at this time was serving his apprenticeship to a druggist, visited her, and being discovered in her apartments by C—, he kicked him down stairs, and next morning reluctantly discarded his angel, though he passionately adored her; Mary Crosbie, for so we must now call her, again bereft of friends, went to board with a Mrs Moore, a celebrated b—d in Capel-street, where she exercised her natural powers with the best subjects that offered. Poor H—, considering himself the original cause of her misfortunes, *scraped up by every industry* a few guineas, and took lodgings for her in Aungier-street, where he visited her occasionally, and unable himself to support her extravagancies, brought her some good culls, particularly Mr R— H— of Capel-street, T— A—, Alex— Mc M—, Dan. M—, Mich. D—, J— U—, C— W—, &c. &c. in this way she procured *means delectable* for her lover and herself; but happiness alas! is seldom permanent – H—'s friends being acquainted with the proceedings, checked him severely and prevailed on him to swear he'd never see her more. Again destitute of a protector, she went and lodged with a Miss Boyd of Longford-street, of detested memory, who was the cause of a Mr Barlow's death, son of the widow Barlow; here she passed some miserable days, 'till she met with a Captain *Misset,* who took an house for her in Mecklenburgh-street, where they remained 'till she deprived him of the last guinea, and then gave his creditors information that they might arrest him with ease at her house; the unfortunate Misset was accordingly *pinned* and lodged in the Sheriffs Gaol, where he remained for two years in the greatest distress, after which he was removed to the Four Courts Marshalsea by Habeas Corpus, where he still continues.

Incautious youth beware of *Mary Crosbie!* who now rolls in every luxury, at the expence of the *distracted Misset.*

[*Elinor West*]

ELINOR WEST was a merry begotten, of R— A— of Capel-street, who when nine years old bound her to a ribbon-weaver, with whom she lived for three years, but being ill treated by her mistress, she went to her father, who, unnatural man, refused her every protection; upon which she repaired to a register-office and was employed by a Mrs West as children's maid, with whom she lived for two years and behaved remarkably well – Mrs West's eldest son, an attorney, by many presents and persuasions won her affections, and by repeated promises of marriage gained his *end.* Poor Nelly thus deprived of what virgins hold most dear, languished away, after reminding him of the vows he made, with a determined resolution never to perform; at length, the ungrateful West told her he was married – whereupon she, in a distracted fit quit the house, and went to a house of resort in Capel-street, where she met with a Mr N—, a grocer, who, captivated with her youth and smartness, supplied her with every necessary ornament of dress, &c. and then brought her to *Multifarnham* in the county Westmeath, where they lived in harmony for sixteen months; unfortunately a Mr James O'R— of Ba—s—na, visited at his lodgings, where he remained a few days, and seduced my poor Nelly, brought her with him to his country seat, where they remained until examinations at college, when he and she came to town and lodged at my house, where she behaved with the greatest candour and honour to her protector, until a Mr C— who sung remarkably well, paid a visit to Pitt-street during the absence of Mr O'R—, and having spent a few nights with her, she was so captivated with his music and *fine parts* that she eloped with him, though at that time 50 *l.* in my debt; however the honest girl in two months later, sent me inclosed a 60 *l.* note, with an account, that she was forsaken by C—, who on leaving her gave her debentures to the amount of 300 *l*. Mr West came to town shortly after, and though the cause of her mishap she doated on him, and passed some pleasant hours in his company, he being *engaged*. Elinor West, the name she had gone by ever since, having made away with the debentures given her by Mr C—, determined to get another protector, which she could not expect to find in private lodgings; she therefore went to Mrs Orde's, where she met with a Mr Eife, who ensnared by her agreeable manners and actions, offered to marry her and lay his whole property at her disposal; however she being naturally fond of liberty, and a volunteer in heart, declared she would rather be his mistress than wife, and as long as he behaved worthy her attachment, she would act with honour towards him; this candid declaration overwhelmed him with joy, and redoubled his love towards her; he accordingly took an house for her in Great Britain-street, where the reader may have an opportunity of hearing this narrative from her own delectable mouth.

[*Mary Atkinson, alias Mrs Mary Ottiwell*]

MRS OTTIWELL – was the daughter of William Atkinson of Belfast, flax-dresser, mathematician and wool-comber; her mother was a mantua-maker, in all which branches, she herself excelled; beautiful and good humoured, she behaved herself virtuously and modestly until that monster the Rev. Mr B—, under the specious veil of sanctity, invited her to his own house, where she remained as it were, to instruct his children, but he like a demon of darkness, despising the earthly functions he was ordained to discharge, and taking advantage of the innocent fair, when his family went abroad to spend the evening, committed a rape upon her body; horrid! horrid! in one of God's representatives!!! Mary – poor girl, reduced to the last extremity with shame (the transaction being discovered by an old woman who lay concealed in a cradle bed in the next closet;) and hearing that Mr Edward B—, afterwards Kingsmill, next morning was resolved to travel post to Dublin, solicited a seat in his carriage, which being granted, she packed up all her moveables (though small) they were her only treasure. I shall now leave the reader to judge what passed between the fair one and this old well-known *gallant;* suffice it to say, they arrived at the *Belfast Hotel,* at four o'clock in the morning, where the good old man ordered a bed for himself and his lady, and then finished what he had attempted to begin two days before, which though well-inclined, his age and infirmities prevented him to accomplish: The old gentleman being gratified, left poor

Mary in a strange house, without friends or money; unfortunate girl! what now to do was paradoxical; lamenting her situation, she was overheard by a gentleman in the next room, a Mr Henry O—, who offered his assistance, which being accepted by the unfortunate fair, he gave her a fifty pound note, and told her he'd take lodgings for her; – all his proposals being admitted, he hired apartments for her opposite the hotel, at a druggist's house, where they remained for some time. O— was profuse in his presents, until she had been discovered coming out of the druggist's room, one night as he returned home from the gaming table, where he had met with some hands as knowing as himself. Incensed at loosing his money, and the inconstancy of his mistress, he almost murdered her: Her shrieks being heard by K—y (that was the druggist's name;) he courageously broke open the door, which was bolted by the cowardly O—; and here a bout of boxing commenced; – Johnson and Mendoza could not take their ground with more skill or agility; the contest remained doubtful for some time; K—y taking courage being at home (a dunghill cock) tipped O— a Mendoza over the left eye, which levelled him with the ground, and left a mark on that part ever since. The unfortunate fair lay speechless during the contest, and Tom thinking himself victorious, took her in his arms, and swore by the Holy G— she should be his alone; and as soon as O— recovered the blow, coward like, he took his hat and run away, and never since paid K—y. Mary's misfortunes now commenced; Mrs K—, who was out on a visit, returning and finding a beautiful stranger in her apartments, ran distracted about the house; poor Ottiwell, now her name, knowing good manners, in imitation of Mrs K—y, ran mad also, and poor Tom, though master of his profession, was now more thunderstruck than ever on any like occasion; what was to be done was the question, he called for his man to bring him two streight waistcoats, which being fitted to the two unfortunate women, they were led in triumph, amidst the acclamations of the multitude, to the mad-house at Drumcondra – poor Tom no doubt must have been distracted, or he would have thought of a coach. Here Mrs Ottiwell, the subject of my story, lay for six months, during which time the infamous Harry never sent her any money. K—y thinking he had paid very well for his amour, sent deputies to Mr O— to request his interference on this trying occasion: O— *hardened to every delicate feeling,* desired he'd turn her out, and let her 'fish for herself'; both brutes alike, unfeeling and inhuman. The distracted Mrs Ottiwell was turned out on the town, without either guide or protector – fortunately for her, I in my carriage passing by, could not bear to see so much beauty unnoticed, and accordingly invited her to my house, which she gladly accepted: I brought her home, and during the course of eighteen months which she spent with me, I never in my life discovered better manners, more upright integrity, or more correct morals in any woman; at length she left me, through the influence of Ald— J—, and now I believe lives at Mrs M'Clean's, Eustace-street.

[*Bridget West, alias Bridget Featherstone, alias Bridget Orde*]

MRS BRIDGET ORDE, of whom I often made mention, with her father John West, kept an house of lodgers in Cook-street; she was the only person to attend the gentlemen and take care of every other domestic duty; at the age of fourteen she was seduced by a Mr Fetherstone of the county of Westmeath, who lived with her for three years at Mr W—'s, Bride-street, in the greatest love and harmony; at last she unfortunately bestowed some favours on honest Charley, which being discovered by her friend, she was dismissed with a present of 50 *l.* with which she purchased a small house in Queen-street, where she commenced procuress. Mr S— was a great friend to her, and who being fond of variety, frequently changed his miss once a week, and for every such purchase he paid her 101 *l.* Passing smoothly on in this line a few years, and thinking a more extensive trade more eligible; assisted by a Mr G—, she took a large house in Britain-street, where she commenced nocturnal plays and amusements of every sort; at this time she was called Biddy Fetherstone. A Mr Orde was the next who offered; a good natured man, but young and giddy, who in the course of a very short time spent his paternal property, and was compelled to go abroad to recover a fortune in the West Indies, which was left him by his uncle, which getting possession of, he returned, and still enjoys his loving though inconstant Biddy – now called Orde. During his absence she employed a Mr W— attorney, to settle her *affairs,* and allowed him a handsome salary, as she was this time in affluence; Mr W— was very attentive to his trust, and living always with her, obtained by every means foul and fair, large sums of money from every man who unfortunately became her debtor. Graham all this time in the country, at his mother's in the county Cavan, now resolved on returning to town, when he prevailed on the silly Biddy to call an auction, sell off her property, and convert every moveable (except two suits of clothes) into cash; he pretending to be afraid of bailiffs, took lodgings on George's-quay, where she visited him; the time drawing near for their departure, he took her trunk, which contained her *all,* on board the packet, telling her he would return in an hour, but alas! was never since heard of. Poor creature again distressed, applied to her friend Orde, who as usual, good natured fellow, purchased another house in Great Britain-street, where they live amicably until this day, and where she and her beautiful nymphs, may be inspected by the supposed *continent Priest* or *lecherous Archbishop;* she owes me 10 *l.* which I request she will give to the Friary of Denmark-street, for the purpose of masses for the salvation of my soul.

[Maria Ford]

MARIA FORD, another priestess of the little God, was the daughter of a respectable merchant of this city; being well educated and accomplished, she resorted every public place of amusement; one night at the Exhibition-house William-street, she danced with a Mr R— W— an handsome gallantman who sung very pleasingly; the innocent Maria was enamoured of him, and in a very little time became a sacrifice to his desires; being discovered by her mother, she was turned out of doors; however the constant Bob (this puts me in mind of my poor Bob) had neat lodgings furnished for her in Irish-town, and lived with her while his circumstances permitted; but cursed poverty, the inveterate enemy to many constant lovers, urged her to come to my house, where she behaved with every politeness to all who visited her; there was a B—y Y—n, who was very attentive to her and gave her large sums of money, with which she rigged herself to the best advantage, and without flattery, she was simply beautiful. In this manner a few years passed, 'till the luckless Ford, through some unforeseen mischance became much addicted to gin drinking, by which means she was neglected by her friends, – getting also into debt, she was compelled to go to Liverpool in defence of her liberty, where she lived for two years, saved some money, returned home, and honestly and generously paid me 100 *l.* which she owed me: – seeing her so well principled, I made her a present of the one-half; telling the circumstance to a Mr W—n, he became so captivated by her beauty and honest principles, that he took her into keeping, and now lives with her in the same lodgings Walsh originally hired for her. I dined with her a few days ago, and was much gratified on seeing the happy pair live in such excessive harmony. As some of the prime *characters and geniuses* in the kingdom were at this ball; my readers may judge it passed with great *eclat* and much celebrity, and as it was given in my house, the merit of the entire was bestowed to *Peg,* to *dashing Peg.* Amyas Griffith (who after he was ruined by a certain inveterate party, set up a paper called the *Phoenix,* of which he was sole *proprietor and editor*) gave a flourishing account of that whimsical entertainment, with all his own *hyperbolical* embellishments, and an addition of the late *Buck English's* (of murderous memory) impotent attempt, to enjoy me in one of the recesses, and my being heard to declare that, that infamous assassin was the SIXTH who had served me so:

> Eager to sin, though destitute of joy.

The late poor *Ned Nowlan,* author of, 'Sure thou wert born to please me,' editor and doer of the Freeman's Journal, was also there; and being much elevated, attempted to be happy with me, and served me in the same manner as the *Buck:* I was also honoured with the company of gimlet-eyed Andy A—, alias *Henry Harmless,* the wretched C—h, my late poor name-sake *Jack Plunket,* of innocent inoffensive memory; *Daly,* of the kingdom of *Kerry,* who came from the Devil's A—e-a-Peak; *Scot,* of *diabolical memory;* Mrs M—e the *authoress,* Captain K—y, Peter S—g—n, that unfortunate premature politician; the limping I— P— S—, of p—p—g memory; the over-reaching Captain R—ts, that African hero, who can play on all instruments of music, was master of languages, could cut anterchois [possibly *entrechats*] better than the *little devil* himself, was a much greater poet than *Milton,* a better orator than the renegado *K—,* a greater hero than the immortal *Wolfe,* and a finer gentleman than *Chesterfield;* this *great officer,* who pretended to every thing and knew nothing (the very counter-part of Mrs M—) must also crack of my favours; may B—lz—b carry off the impotent *quartetto:* these were the only men in the room who did not pay for their admission, except poor C—h, F—x, and A—g, not one of whom in all their lives, could ever say he was worth a crown, much less two guineas: poor John M—, the late worthy honest Bell of the Herald, of transmigrating memory; and my intimate friend Jack G—d were also there, as were indeed every man in the literary line in the metropolis, from Preston of tragedy memory, to poor blind Bartle Corcoran, the famous balad composer, on the Inn's-quay.

CHAPTER FOUR

[*Peg's marriage to Barry Yelverton, Jn, her election to the Freedom of the States of Castle Kelly, more Brief Lives, and an account of the death and burial of her friend and colleague, Moll Hall*]

IN A FEW DAYS AFTER this never to be forgotten masquerade, my old friend P— H—ll and Barry Y—, of whom I have made mention before, called to my house, when the latter gentleman, of whose abilities in every way I entertained a very poor opinion, 'popp'd the question' to me in form; for I had before from the detestation I held him in, absolutely refused to have any connection with him, or suffer him to take the smallest freedom; in consequence of which, the poor *lovelorn swain,* for he was absolutely enamoured, offered to marry me; this was a matter too serious to be refused, I knew to a certainty his father from his great legal abilities, would be very shortly created a peer, and the very sound of the Honourable Mrs Y—'s coach, the Honourable Mrs Y—'s chair, so tinkled in my ears, that I absolutely took him at his word, and a couple-beggar being sent for by my friend Phill, we were tacked together that very night, but not 'till the marriage articles were properly ratified, signed, sealed and delivered, in the presence of my friends H—tch—l, Le F—, and the late worthy James W—n, of whom I have already made honourable mention.

> Thus the happy knot is ty'd;
> Peg became a *virtuous* bride:
> Ring the bells and fill the bowl;
> Revel all without controul.
> Who so fair as lovely Peg,
> Who so blithe as Barry Beg.
> Who so blithe,' &c. &c.

All the *impures* in town (the noted ones I mean) came formally to congratulate me on my marriage, which was very handsomely announced in all the public prints, and many beautiful *epithalamiums* and songs were written on the joyful occasion; the very ballad singers caught the infection, and sung about the praises of 'the gallant B—y and his charming Peg', and blind *Charley O'Gallagher* in particular, and his little father-in-law *Mr Kinselagh,* were chaunting *madrigals* upon us, much longer than the honeymoon lasted; for alas! the *hard-hearted man,* no sooner was he surfeited of very imperfect enjoyment indeed, than he grew as cool as a cucumber, and had the impudence to say, 'he could not bear to *kiss my lips* they being always so plastered with *slave* or spermaceti ointment,' which I really must acknowledge I used every night to lay on, to prevent them from chipping; and you'll say my *poor lips,* so often smacked, had a right to be the worse for wear.

Our nuptials made such a noise, that at last the C— B— came to hear of them with astonishment and regret, and accordingly sent for me to demand an explanation; when I produced him my well authenticated certificate, at the same time assuring him, I looked upon the connection with such loathing, that for a very trifling consideration I was ready to relinquish every claim I had on *young hopeful;* whereupon the C— B— taking me at my word gave me five hundred guineas, and I gladly released his *pretty boy* from every conjugal tye, executing whatever papers he laid before me; which was very well for me, as in a few months afterwards he was arrested for a variety of pedling debts, and lodged in the *Sheriff's Prison,* where he remained in the most profligate course of life, 'till liberated by the benefit of an insolvent act; after which he called frequently to see me, but I was always denied to him.

[Freeman Peg, and the Fat Sappho of Drumcondra]

Some time after I got rid of my graceless spouse, I had the honour of being waited on by a deputation from the 'States of Castle-Kelly,' commonly called, the *Anecdote Club of Free Brothers,* with an able spokesman, the great and powerful Stony Batter king at arms, at their head, vulgarly *yclept* the Tomlinson; who in the name of that most respectable community, amounting to above five hundred members, presented the freedom of their commonwealth to *me and my nymphs and nymphlings,* elegantly engrossed on parchment inclosed in a beautiful silver box, with all the emblems of the beggars benison handsomely carved on it, and a delectable poem, called the Guide to Joy, or pleasures of imagination realised, written by the amiable Mrs H. now of Drumcondra; that once happy favourite of that prince of good fellows, whose birth-day was so elegantly celebrated, by the *La-bra Pleasura* of honest well meaning Magee, with his *racing-pigs, dancing-girls,* *grinning-hags, Cudgelling-blades,* &c. &c. &c. at the famous Fiat-hill, near this city. I accordingly received Stony Batter and the deputies with my usual affability, treating them with *cake* and *wine,* and returning a proper answer to their very polite and civil address; at the same time sending them their freedom of Pitt-street, and constituting and appointing that divine Sappho, so very fat and so very fair, to a seat in conclave, with all the *adults* of my *female menagerie.* Mrs H. is an authoress of much estimation, and as for a roguish poem of any kind I give her the BUSH, as no doubt her Guide to Joy, now in the possession of a friend of mine, and which I will give my readers in due course;* this charming effusion of fancy, beats any production for high colouring, brilliancy of style, and luxuriance of imagination, in that line now extant – *Rochester's Poems, Fanny Hill, the Cabinet of Love,* or *Kitty and Amynter,* being all mere trifles, when put into competition with that famous and unequalled poem.

Mrs H— was formerly a prodigious favourite of the P— of W—, her face was beautiful, her person rather too much in the *enbon point [embonpoint]* order, more than his own dear injured F—t; she was a lady of an amorous complexion, as will appear by her poem, and knew thee *outs and the ins* as well as any lady in Europe; when she came to this city, she advertised to read a poem of her own composition at the Exhibition-room in William-street, at opera price, half-a-guinea admission; however when the night appeared, and she had expended, in advertising, posting bills, puffs, &c. &c. five or six pounds, no person attended the curious exhibition, of seeing a *fat lady* with a parcel of tow under her jaws, read her own productions very *inelegantly* – but three or four printer's devils, whom their employers had given the lady's eleemosinary tickets to, as they could prevail on no other persons to accept of them. *'Sic transit Gloria Mundi:'* thus terminated mother H—'s exhibitions in this kingdom, since which, she has scarcely been heard of; but that my fair friends and I know she lives retired upon her princely pension, opposite *Broadhead's* in Drumcondra, where we have paid her frequent visits, and often had the pleasure of meeting with several literary characters both male and female.

A Mrs H—y in particular attracted my attention, she was the lady of an eminent attorney, was a pretty little *smart Brunette,* had a vast deal to say for herself, and had a pretty turn for poetry; *romantic girl!* 'twas that talent

---

* This very elegant Poem, (as we would not wish to offend the chastest ear, or tinge the cheek of blushing modesty with any indelicacy) will be printed by itself, and delivered *gratis* to such of the purchasers of these volumes, as would wish to be supplied with it.

and her propensity to novel writing brought her upon the town; were it not for that, she might have enjoyed much domestic felicity with poor Tom, who was passionately fond of her. In one of my visits here [*sic*], I also had the pleasure of meeting with the charming H—g—s, who after having squandered away near two thousand pounds a year, real estate, in debauchery and dissipation of every kind, was at length, to eke out a wretched existence, obliged to betake herself to the stage, where she cut but a very *la la* figure, 'till at length she went into keeping with H—l—n, who after having had three children by her, not only basely deserted her, but published her infamy in all the public prints of England, Ireland, and Scotland.

> Were you, you fair, but cautious whom ye trust;
> Did you but know how seldom fools prove just,
> So many of your sex would not in vain,
> Of broken vows and faithless men complain.

And again,

> Trust not to man, they are by nature false,
> *Dissembling, subtle, cruel* and *inconstant;*
> If a man talks of love, with caution hear him,
> But if he swears, – he'll certainly deceive you.

As H—n deceived poor H—s, – and *apropos,* now I have introduced that lady, I must inform my readers of a circumstance not generally known: – my heroine's father married her mother who was a beautiful woman, at a very advanced time of life, and during a term of eighteen years never had a child by her; 'till an unexpected visit from that celebrated genius *Buck English* (who remained at Mr H—'s hospitable mansion near Thurles, for upwards of two months) worked the happy effect; for in less than eight months after the departure of the Squire, who was also a senator of Ireland, Mrs H—s was safely delivered of that paragon of beauty, wit and bravery, Miss H—s, who as she grew up, gave strong intimations of her *real parent, lascivious, passionate, vindictive, aspiring, cruel, determined, and quarrelsome,* blended with a pusillanimity and meanness, which was better suited to the daughter of the Buck, who was merely foster-brother to poor Tom Cook of begging memory, than to the child of the poor innocent doating H—s; Cook having being nursed and suckled by the Buck's mother, who was the wife of a common unlettered *hind* near Tipperary, who fortunately found, when trenching potatoes, a large crock of money, on the

171

strength of which, he cunningly and gradually advanced himself in life, by taking cheap farms, &c. &c. &c. which enabled him to give his children good education, and leave the *sanguinary Buck* upwards of five thousand pounds a year!!! Such events as these happen frequently in the lottery of life, which put me in mind of those expressive lines:

> Thus equal crimes unequal fates have found,
> And whilst one villain swings, another's crown'ed.'

[*The death and burial of Moll Hall*]

So by poor Tom Cook, heir to Kiltinan, and a man of the first connections; whilst he is begging from door to door, his foster brother, the son of a Munster peasant, is rolling about in his gilt chariot, gambling at Daly's, or quaffing Champaign and Burgundy with some of the finest impures that Ireland or England can afford, either in Pitt-street or Johnson's-court; which brings forcibly and painfully to my feeling mind, the exit of my poor friend Moll Hall, in that court; a few days before she took ill, her word would go for any sum, nor was there a *wine-merchant,* a *grocer,* a *mercer,* a milliner, or an haberdasher in Dublin, who would refuse her any credit she desired; when lo! no sooner had the last breath quit the body of my friend, when citizen D—, as he calls himself, and every creature she was indebted to (following his infamous example) came down upon the house, and seized even upon the very bed she lay waking on – carrying all off without any legal authority whatever, leaving poor Hall upon the bare ground with three or four of her girls sitting weeping over her body, not knowing how to dispose of it; until at length this melancholy transaction reached my ears, when I sent a kitchen table and some oak chairs for the wake, as also *candles, cake, wine,* pipes and tobacco, together with cold meat and some of honest *Hutton's* good bottled porter; who would not have served any of God's creatures after such a barbarous manner: and in two days after her demise, I had her decently interred in St Anne's Church-yard, with this whimsical triplet engraved on her tombstone:

> Here lies honest MOLL HALL,
> Who once had *a great call,*
> And a fig for you all.

> She departed this Life the 22d of July, Anno Domini
> 1792, in the 49th year of her Age; and in remembr-
> ance of her many Virtues, for she was in the actual

Possession of all but ONE, and how many great Ones
retain that alone; her steadfast Friend and Compeer,
Margaret Leeson, of *Pitt-street Nunnery,* caused
this Stone, after being at the Expence of her Wake
and Funeral, and many Masses for her Soul's Repose,
to be placed over her.

Requiescent in Pacem.

I had this poor woman's funeral conducted with great taste, having hired six mourning coaches, in each of which sat four of the *sisterhood* as deep mourners, with scarfs, &c. &c. amounting in the whole to twenty-four, exclusive of which, my *own Carriage,* and several others belonging to very respectable people attended the funeral procession. Peace to her manes, she's no more; but in case of my own dissolution, and that I died as poor as *Hall,* would any human being do the like for my remains? indeed without vanity, I must say, there are very few possessed of a greater portion of the milk of human kindness, than I have ever been; and if charity covers a multitude of sins – honest Peg, thy only failing, of making use of what God gave, must be forgiven.

CHAPTER FIVE

[Peg's attempt to join the Abcderian Society, Magee's connubial problems, two mock marchionesses, and some more brief lives]

SOME TIME AFTER, the Abcderian Society for the relief of reduced and superannuated *teachers,* began to gain ground; I sent two guineas to Mr McC—e their secretary, desiring him to enroll me as the principal of Pitt street *boarding-school;* however the honest worthy *Puritan,* not chusing to be so taken in, sent the following note, and my money back.

John McC— presents his compliments to Mrs Leeson, cannot think of enrolling her with the several very respectable ladies who keep boarding-schools in this city, and who are an honor not only to all ladies in their line, but to human nature; if Mrs Leeson chuses a subject for ridicule, she has pitched upon a very improper person in McC—, and a very unfit one in the Abcderian Society, which is composed of some of the most respectable persons, of all descriptions in the community; however if Mrs Leeson persists in bestowing her charity, McC— has no objection to accept of her subscription as an *honorary member;* however she must excuse him from entering her as a *teacher,* as her *gaits* of *going,* would ill suit the pupils of the other professors; nor can McC— with propriety return her name among the subscribers, for insertion in Watson's Almanack, which would only subject the other boarding-school ladies to ridicule.

On the receipt of this note, I dispatched my messenger back with the money which McC— had returned, desiring him to enter me under what class he pleased, and assuring him, whatever degree of respectability he might please to place the other superintendants of boarding-schools in, I thought myself not inferior to any of them; *Nature* I told him was my *goddess* – and she, he could not deny as a classical man, had been worshipped from the earliest period; Eve herself took *nature* as her guide and tutoress, and all her children had travelled ever since in her divine foot-steps; I at the same time invited Mr McC— to my *academy,* where I told him, *stoic* as he was, I would hold him one hundred guineas, before he and I parted I would make him confess my *hypothesis* to be just. McC— returned no answer to this polite invitation, which made me believe he was afraid of encountering *me* and my *goddess.*

[Mrs Magee]

Just at this time the *woman of Ireland,* having come to an arbitration with poor Magee, who married her in one of his *paroxisms* of insanity, came to my house to spend some time; she was then in possession of about 300 *l.* which she made a shift to squeeze from honest Jack, on giving him a release; for she absolutely was married to him at a certain house in Great Britain-street, where also the nuptials were celebrated in great style; on her joining my *squad,* she told me in what elegance the printer had kept her for about two months, her own chariot, footmen, and coachmen in laced liveries, her house in College-green, and another at the Rock, confessing he had squandered away on her and *suite* upwards of three thousand pounds, and that he never would have discarded her, had it not been for her own overbearing conduct and tyranny; in consequence of which he swore 'he'd astonish her', and giving her a cruel (as she termed it) horse-whipping, turned her naked out of doors at about two o'clock in the morning; by this we see the instability of all sublunary matters, the *woman of Ireland* basely *flagellated,* and turned almost naked into the streets like any common prostitute, with a lacerated back; why be it so,

> *Priam* from fortune's lofty summit fell;
> Great Alexander, midst his conquests mourn'd:
> Heroes and Demi-gods, have known their sorrows;
> Caesar has wept, and she has had her fall.

At last Buck W—y (who had returned from a pilgrimage to Jerusalem, as an attonement for his sins, and to win some considerable wagers) for the honour of the thing, in order merely to have it to say, he had Mrs Magee, the *Woman of Ireland,* in keeping, took her from my house, after paying me for her board and lodging, and making me a very handsome present into the bargain; indeed I was not sorry to get rid of that exalted lady, as she became extremely troublesome, and was beside too fond of the native; and I often imagined she had imbibed part of the *mania* of her worthy spouse, and a worthier man, jesting apart, never existed; and I am happy to hear, at this present writing, that my poor honest friend, though still at Swift's, *by his own choice,* is perfectly in his reason; and now that his intellects are meliorated, and that he has lost all his eccentricities, is one of the best and most agreeable companions (by every account I could hear, for I never had the pleasure of his company since he became a ward of Chancery) in the kingdom. Indeed it would be a thousand pities any thing should go amiss with him, as he is one of the best of men, and kind for him, as there does not exist better characters than his worthy old father, his brother the worthy William Magee of Belfast, and indeed all his family.

[*Two Mock Marchionesses*]

In about a fortnight after I had got a good riddance of the *woman of Ireland,* Miss Mc Pherson from Banbridge called to see me; she looked wretchedly, and appeared in great distress and upon impatiently enquiring into her story, she told me, she and her unfortunate sister had been seduced by the late and present M— of D—, father and son; that the present man had cruelly disordered her wretched sister, and afterwards suffered her to languish under the disease, without affording her the smallest relief, or medical assistance, till she died; that for her part, her fate was milder, for her *hoary old letcher* was extremely fond of her; had her picture drawn by the late Jos. Wilson of Belfast, in various attitudes, dressed and naked; kept her in the most exalted stile, introduced her among his tenantry and

175

dependants, at all the *Hillsborough balls* and entertainments, and so thrust her down the throats of all the little country *squires,* squireens and squirts, and their ladies, in the vicinity of his residence; that she generally went by the title of the *Marchioness of* —; that at length, her most *noble antiquarian* beginning to tire of attempting what he was not by any means equal to, bestowed her fair hand upon a little inferior lowlived revenue officer, for whom he had procured an employment in the revenue; that she had willingly embraced the proposal, in order to get rid of her *old tormentor,* which was not the case, for by the permission and orders of her mean-spirited rascally husband, she was obliged to obey the mandates of her old teizing friend, who frequently sent for her to spend the night with him; that at last it pleased Providence to take her patron of fumbling memory from her, and shortly afterwards her *accommodating spouse;* in consequence of which the present M—s refusing to allow her the smallest support, and finding herself despised by those who in better days courted her acquaintance, she had ventured up to this city in quest of adventures, and begged my assistance to forward her in her amorous *career;* though I saw nothing in McP—n that could promise any emolument, yet as 'twas my constant study to alleviate the miseries of all the *woe-worn animals* who applied to me for relief, I heartily welcomed her to Pitt-street, lent her five guineas to get a change or two of linen, which she stood very much in want of, and pushed her into company by the title of the cidevant *M—ss,* which had the desired effect, and procured her a few gallants, who would never have noticed her as plain *Molly Mc Pherson.* While this lady was in the character of my *Protegee,* another sham Marchioness came to pay her a visit; she was a lady who had been in *high keeping* with the late worthy honest Marquis of A—, who had no fault on earth, but too great an attachment to the brandy bottle, in which he'd indulge with any of his own servants, from the hour he rose in the morning, till he'd get so drunk as not to be able to walk through the streets; and many and many a time, has this most noble peer visited me in that state – a state of utter stupefaction. Among other no less curious anecdotes which this lady amazed us with, was an assurance, that though the Marquis had kept her in her coach for several years, she had in all that time no sort of connection with him; with astonishment, we both asked her in a breath, for what purpose he had kept her? 'for merely the unspeakable pleasure' answered she archly, 'of picking, washing, and cleaning my pretty little toes, which he took great delight in, and in which pleasurable, innocent, and innofensive pastime he as often spent hours; 'twas the greatest gratification to him on earth, nor did he (said she) indulge in any other, as in all the time we spent together, he never was even rude enough to give me a kiss; however I amply made up for the time I lost with this poor drunken *peerless Peer,* as the instant he left me, I sent for my poor friend Frank Mc G—, and with him enjoyed every *luxury of love,* – both laughing heartily at —'s whimsical letch.' She told me, however, that her friend wh was a married man, and had at that time an excellent employment in La Touche's bank, was some time before the Marquis's death obliged to abscond, he having made too free with the cash, his connection with her, having given him too great a taste for *dissipation* and *debauchery* of all kinds. Observing that my two Marchionesses were extremely fond of each other, I invited my fair visitor, for she really was a charming creature, to spend some time in my house *en famille,* which she, nothing loth, gladly accepted of, in consequence of which I also introduced her as the titular Marchioness Dowager of A— to all my friends, and very shortly she became a great favourite, for she was a sprightly, gay, agreeable woman, sung an *arch song* with a great deal of humour, and often has set the table in a roar with whimsical accounts of her toe-picking Marquis of *harmless memory.*

My mock Marchionesses drew a great deal of company, for as I said before, they had much to say for themselves, and the very name of receiving civilities from ladies, who had been favourites of the first men in the kingdom, was such a stimulus to the gay, the unthinking and the giddy, that neither of my Marchionesses ever slept a night unoccupied while they remained in Pitt-street, which was near nine months, during which time they realized upwards of three hundred pounds each, besides paying me very genteely and honourably; and then took flight for England, accompanied with two *veteran officers,* one a Lieutenant Colonel, the other a Major, who took such a liking to them, that for the last three months, they were scarcely ever out of my house; and tho' the younger of them was past his grand climacteric, yet they both confessed they had never been better pleased in their lives – repeating the old adage, 'that old cocks tread sure', and so it really happened, for Mc Pherson left the kingdom *great with child* – so much for the nobility.

[Mrs Elizabeth Bennett, alias Betty Quigley, alias Mrs O'Falvey]
And now I shall descend to the lady of a celebrated itinerant pedlar, one BENNETT, well known in the Masonic world, by a humourous song that

was composed on him, on his applying to a most respectable lodge to be admitted one of their fraternity, with the reception he met with from them; a full, witty and whimsical account of which, with notes critical and explanatory, my readers will find in the edition of *Ahiman Rezon* (printed by my dear and worthy friend Tommy Wilkinson of Winetavern-street) dedicated to the *Master, Wardens,* and *Brethren* of the Orange Lodge of Belfast, beginning with

> How Bennett was made, a pedlar by trade,
> A Mason of whimsical order;
> We stript him quite bare, deprived him of hair,
> And painted his skin like a border, &c. &c.

MRS ELIZABETH BENNETT, ALIAS BETTY QUIGLEY, was as fine a woman as ever I beheld; a face like an angel, a complexion equal to the lily and the rose, bewitching eyes, and a bosom like hillocks of *driven snow,* which rose, as Chesterfield said, in his elegant song of 'Fanny blooming fair,' than which the English language can't possibly produce a better, 'suing to be pressed.' Mrs Bennett, when she came to my house, was about forty, quite in the *en bon point* order, which was the rage, and why not? when the *heir apparent* sighed for nothing less, than fat, fair, and forty, – with b—m and b—b—s in abundance, just such a woman was Mrs Bennet, with a luscious county of Kerry brogue which rendered her all captivating; on her introduction to me she accosted me with 'Arrah my dear Mrs Leeson, or Mrs Plunkit – but by my soule I know you better by the name of Plunkit, for I have been after hearing of you since I was dat high, you see I have come all the phay from Waterford, to be after spending a few days in your mighty agreeable company, and I have brought you a *prisant or two* to ensure my *whelcome;*' on which she drew from her pocket, a piece of the most beautiful embroidered muslin I ever beheld, which she told me she had smuggled, with a variety of other valuables, from the East India fleet, when they lay in the river Shannon, which was the first place she had been tempted to share her person with any man but her husband; that in the town of Tralee some revenue officers had seized a great parcel of goods from her, after she had returned from the fleet, and that in order to have them restored, her husband being then in Cork gaol, she had permitted one of the principal officers to take what liberties he pleased with her, in consequence of which, as she remained in sweet Tralee for upwards of eight months, she brought poor Bennett home all the contraband goods, with a chopping boy into the bargain, whom she was delivered of in about two months after her return. However Bennett could not relish the latter, though she honestly told him, she had prostituted herself for his sake, in order to regain his property; and this in some degree appeased him, especially when he was told the officer was the gentleman who officiated as master, when he was initiated into the mysteries of freemasonry in the county of Cork: she also informed me, that Bennett having been released from prison, by virtue of an *insolvent act,* they had taken up their abode in Waterford, where they kept a little shop since the year 1780; that however as her husband grew old he grew peevish, and at length became intolerable, continually upbraiding her with her *faux pas,* and beating and abusing her constantly, in consequence of which she had scraped all she could together, money and effects, and had come up to town, in order to make the most of her person she possibly could, and she had no doubt of success, as she'd be quite a new face on the town, and if her glass did not deceive her, she was still what the men call *a damn'd good piece,* and so she must have been, as in all my life I never saw, with all her vulgarity, a more dashing looking woman, nor with all, a more innocent or generous creature; indeed she fascinated all who conversed with her; her *open innocent, sweet countenance,* her broad county of Kerry brogue, 'haw dau you dau my sweet friend,' pronouncing the *i*'s and *u*'s so divinely broad, in short alltogether, that is, the *tout ensemble,* she was every thing a man could possibly wish; in fact she was what the French call a *'je ne scai quoi.'* This darling woman lived with me, esteemed by all who knew her, until a countryman of her own, a Mr O'Falvey, fell desperately in love with her, and by flattery, presents, and promises, prevailed on her to accompany him to that romantic earthly paradise Killarney, from whence I received a letter from her, not a month ago, expressive of her gratitude and the sense she entertained of the civilities I had shewn her, and promising when an opportunity offered, to send me various rarities which that country spontaneously abounded with; she also mentioned the happy state she was in; that *Bennett* was no more, and that her dear *Falvey,* by whom she was then with child, had made an honest woman of her, as the poor dear simpleton termed her marriage to us, which at once shewed my girls and I the *naivete* of the heart; but as blind Billy Jenkins often says, 'we were not angry with her', 'twas merely the effusions of an honest simple heart. In her letters she also informed me she kept her coach and was visited by all the neighbouring families, who paid her every respect she could possibly wish for.

[*Mrs Mary Roberts*]

Another of my visitors, was a fair lady of the name of Mrs Roberts – she was a foundling, whom the unnatural parent left at the door of a Mr Roberts, Batchelor's-walk; he caused her to be sent to nurse, and reared her at his own expence, until she was ten years old, when the spirit of infamy began to appear. -

Mr R— was very fond of her, and used to have her in his office, out of which she contrived to take a hundred pound bank note, which she gave to a John Cunningham, a cadet servant, who visited the girls of the house, and who was hanged a few months afterwards for the robbery of the North mail. Mr R. good natured enough, sent Mary to board and lodge with a woman in the county Wicklow, near the Dargle, when in a little time she became acquainted with a Mr N— B—, who prevailed on her to quit her lodgings and go home with him, where she did not long behave herself prudently. He came home one night intoxicated, with a large sum of money, fifty guineas of which she, though young (only twelve years old) found means to conceal in the folds of her petticoats, which being discovered by B—, he dismissed her, giving her but a solitary guinea for her past services. She immediately set off from the Cross-roads, and meeting a carman, who told her he was going to Dublin, she embraced the opportunity and went with him; he left her in a cellar in Mary's-lane, which we called a *preferrer's* for under servants; here she took lodgings at the moderate rate of sixpence a week. Not long after she was noticed by a Mr H— of the Custom House, who being amorously inclined, hired her; she lived with this gentleman some short time; though short, she found means to ease him of a great part of his property, which was considerable, but he, inclined to dissipation, did not discover his inamorata until reduced to the last extremity; she being young, and he being unwilling to expose himself, after getting the duplicates of clothes and some few articles of plate, turned her off: being now deprived of every friend, and money, except what trifle she had after leaving H—, she became troublesome to every passenger, by means of a notorious set of robbers who she became acquainted with – being smart and pretty, they employed her as a *decoy duck,* she picked up every unwary person, and brought them into lanes appointed by this *banditti,* by whom the unfortunate men were stripped of money and wearing apparel – the chief places for these depredations were a lane in Jervis-street, Boot-lane, Green-street and Marlborough-green; among these fellows was one Lynch, a robber, of infamous memory, who took her to himself, and prevented any more street walking; he took rooms for her in Grafton-lane, and lived with her until he finished his career at the end of a rope in front of the New Prison – Mary being left sole heiress of this man's plunder, took a house in Strand-street, where she employed a few of her former thieving acquaintances, to assist her in depriving her unfortunate guests of every moveable; and her ingenuity was such, that at night she appeared as a grey headed old woman, and by day as a smart girl; by this means she evaded justice, and having saved some money in this very profitable employment, she quit her retirement and purchased a house in Abbey-street, where she became so troublesome that the neighbours resented her as a nuisance, and she was expelled that street by the grand jury, whereupon she purchased a house in Camden-street, where she now lives: I beg leave to add, that this lady would never have had a place in my memoirs, but that she introduced herself to me as an innocent country girl, whose parents abandoned her, and wished to put herself under my protection; but a very short period indeed, discovered to me the very dangerous inmate I had, for she improved on my old acquaintance C—e, and probably would have plundered me of the whole of my property, had I not discovered her in time; I hope therefore the unwary will be on their guard against her, which indeed was my only motive for her introduction here.

[*Margaret Whittle, alias Margaret Porter*]

My next boarder was a MARGARET WHITTLE, alias P—rt—r; she was the daughter of a very respectable farmer in the county of Wicklow, she married the unfortunate and wretched P—r, when very young, he being the son of a much esteemed clergyman in Whittle's neighbourhood, and a magistrate of the county; soon after she was married to the besotted P—r, he set up an extensive shop in Dublin, where my unfortunate *heroine* first became acquainted with a Lieutenant W—ms, brother-in-law to the famous Mrs Sinnott, who procured through her influence with her *Rt. Hon. Paramour,* a commission for him in the army: for we all know,

> A beauteous sister, or convenient wife,
> Are prizes in the lottery of life.

After W—ms's appointment in the army, he and his sister-in-law frequently visited Mrs P—r, until poor P—r failed; after which W—ms entirely took up his residence there, and Mrs P—r in consequence, declined any longer intimacy with Sinnott; the fact was, she was well inclined to commence business in that *line herself;* else distress could not have occasioned her lapse from virtue, as she plundered her unfortunate husband on his failure, of near three hundred pounds in specie, and a vast quantity of clothes and jewels, which she was absolutely in possession of, when she became a *votary of the Paphian Queen of fond desires,* Mrs Sinnott has been often heard to declare, she would exert every nerve and sinew to serve Mrs P—r in her *new mode of life,* and wished of all things on earth to fix her in some situation in her own line, – a *demi rep* of some consequence, with her coach and *suite* of servants; but the depraved P—r was far from being discreet, if she was, no lady of the *ton* would have had a better chance;

With her stand by, clear the way.

In fact, before she was two months on the town, she became so common, that Mrs Sinnott broke off all connection with her; and yet notwithstanding her *abandonment,* the unfortunate P—r, is happy to share her favour with every ruffian who can 'a crown afford,' honestly confessing his own weakness, but declaring that it totally proceeds from his affection for her, exclaiming that,

Angels were painted fair to look like her.

He some time ago made some effort to get into the army, and applied by memorial to the commander in chief for that purpose: however, that great and good character, on hearing of P—'s conduct, declared he would not disgrace the military character, by recommending such a contented nymcompoop to any appointment in the service, lest,

Boys should hoot the cuckold as he passes.

P—'s conduct being too gross for my acquaintance, I gave her warning to quit Pitt-street,* and forgave her some trifle she owed me, in consequence of her speedy compliance; as I was apprehensive if she remained much longer with me, she'd bring a reflection on the credit of my house, which was always the resort of the most luxurious and licentious votaries of the little God, but never of the abandoned and depraved.

---

* Mrs Porter now figures away in a neat furnished house in Mark-street, where she has a resort of the best company; particularly a noble D— who is passionately fond of her; her chief delight, is boasting to her votaries of the presents she receives from her *'noble slave,'* as she terms him, particularly a DIAMOND RING, a late offering of his, to this frail beauty.

[*Mrs Dalzell and the Bantry Ginger*]

The evening of the day that Mrs P— took her departure, a MRS DALZELL from the county Down, begged leave to see me; she was a fine person of a woman, with a beautiful face and *gilt to the water edge,* a very *soleil royal;* she was accompanied by another pretty little woman of her own complexion, a Mrs B—, *yclept* the Bantry *Ginger;* these ladies told me, they had the misfortune both to be married to creatures whom they, from their souls despised, poor contented cuckolds, who would gladly make the most of them. Mrs D— told me she kept a tavern in the town of Belfast, where she had left her *cara sposa,* who was himself a butter-buyer of some eminence; and Mrs B— informed me her husband had been a carpenter of some repute in the county of Cork, had afterwards commenced pedlar, and latterly, after having made a good deal of money through her exertions, had set up a shop in this city, where he was doing well, but yet his ignorance and vulgarity were so conspicuous, she was ashamed to be seen in his company, or to acknowledge him for a husband: both the ladies indeed seemed to vie with each other who should abuse her dear partner most; and both, I do verily believe, had sufficient cause; Mrs Dalzell in particular, who was a charming agreeable woman, with a pleasing Scotch accent, whereas Mrs B— appeared to be a little termagant, a vulgar Munster broganier vixen, with nothing to recommend her but her complexion; they both honestly acknowledged, they had in their time formed many connexions; and the lively Dalzell laughing told me, she had frequently, when her husband had got inebriated in the forenoon (which had often been the case and gone to bed), invited her gallant up to his room, and obliged him to gratify his and her desires in the very bed with her *snoring hog,* and by his side, to the no small terror of her afrighted friend, who was apprehensive of Dalzell's waking and finding him in her arms; however she told me, she delighted in trying the constancy, bravery, and prowess of her paramour in this manner, and no doubt it was a tryal with a vengeance, as her poor lover stood a chance of being murdered, or if he escaped death, of being ruined by a suit, instituted against him for *crim. con.* but little did the volatile lascivious Dalzell care for the fate of either husband or gallant, so she had satisfied her own whims, and had her laugh; indeed she has declared to me, the wicked devil, she often sported in her amorous dalliances more than was necessary, on purpose if possible to waken her stupid somniferous brute, and make him sensible of the manner she returned his infamous and besotted treatment, and slight of her world of charms; and I must confess, she was wife fit for any man in Europe; she also sung charmingly; among many other compositions was the following, which she told me, was addressed to herself by a Mr F—ch—r, who first caused her to stray from the paths of *virtue and morality*.

When first I saw, then just eighteen,
My sweet Dalzell appear,
Methought 'twas love's majestic queen,
With her enchanting air;
I gaz'd! I wish'd! I lov'd! I sigh'd!
I doated on her charms;
Ye Gods what cruel fates deny'd,
This treasure to my arms?
And shall a stupid brute refuse,
Such bliss, by Heaven design'd,
When lovely, she might justly chuse
A sentimental mind.
Think not, my fair, on censuring crouds,
Who envy you, your worth;
Your spotless fame, above the clouds,
Shall daily blazon forth:
Then grant to him, who loves you well,
The greatest bliss above;
And free from torment worse than hell,
A soul who's chain'd to love:
Give to his arms your lovely self,
That he may boast that bliss,
Above parade or worldly pelf,
To die upon a kiss.

This sweet though eccentric woman lived with me very near a year, after which, having made some money, she took it into her head to go off to America, that glorious land of liberty, and where that was, it was her country, where she soon got married to a very wealthy planter, with whom she lives contented and happy. As for the *Bantry Ginger,* her husband was arrested for debts she had contracted to a large amount and thrown into prison; and she herself, by what I can understand, is contented now to *char* about the prison, and dispense her favours around, for a casual support: for my part I have always hated her, an *insignificant, vulgar, presuming* creature, of very dishonest principles, who has made shift to cheat and rob me, in the space of a very short time, of upwards of forty guineas – exclusive of which, she thought proper to pilfer from every man who had connection with her, who all complained of her base, mercenary disposition. I must here premise to my moral readers, and I hope I may have many, that I would not have admitted these last two *married ladies,* or any others in *that line,* to an asylum in my *nunnery,* had they not given me perfect assurances they had followed that course of life for a length of time; that their husbands were well apprized of their profligacy, and that they were determined to take their *own way;* no, no, 'tis well known I never consented to the deflowering of virgin innocence; the seduction of a married woman, nor did I ever with my will, wish to entertain a married man in my house; but if it should so happen, I always took care they should meddle with no lady, if I could help it, who was not perfectly safe; many married women have applied to me, in the absence of their husbands, for lodgings for a few nights, without success; I even refused a certain lady well known in the fashionable world, and her spirited admirer, an appointment in my house to carry on their intrigue, in consequence of which they were obliged to resort to other methods, which led to a discovery, and turned the parties into ridicule and contempt; even a Reverend Divine, and the seduced wife of his friend and patron, I treated in the same manner, reprimanding her in very severe terms, and telling him he was a scandal and disgrace to his cloth; but enough of this digression, I must not tire the reader with numberless applications of this kind that occurred every day, but proceed to my own story.

CHAPTER SIX

[A professional wager, and an expedition to Cork and Kerry]

ONE NIGHT AS Mrs M'Clean, Fanny Beresford, Miss Grove and myself were playing a sober game of whist, we were interrupted by four inebriated bloods, who swore we must leave off playing and retire with them to another *game:* They were very young handsome fellows, and so urgent, that we complied on certain conditions, that they should deposit with us ten guineas each, and we agreed on our part that for every *perfect enjoyment,* one should be returned; our sparks closed the agreement with a burning smack each, and thus coupled we retired to our respective apartments, under promise of a disclosure of particulars the next morning at breakfast; when lo! *my gallant,* was the *only person* who was able to draw a single guinea; the other girls retained ten guineas each, and I nine, and that, I must confess, was owing to my own wonderful exertions, as I wished to lose *a guinea or two* if possible; as our beaux were so deadly drunk, that they, as soon as they got into bed, dropped instantly into the arms of *Morpheus.* This whimsical affair caused great laughter, and poor a figure as my *hero* cut in the groves of Venus, yet he certainly was the conqueror by a *chalk,* in consequence of which, being part of the agreement the night before, he was exempted from any club or expence in my house, and came off *Scot free,* except the nine guineas; the three other gentlemen looked rather blue upon the occasion; however it all ended with a laugh, and placed to the score of immoderate intoxication, for we all know that *Bacchus* and *Venus* never yet agreed.

That morning two of our sparks, with Mrs M'Clean and I, agreed to take an excursion to the divine Lake of Killarney, and in our way to touch upon *Youghall, Mallow, Limerick,* &c. &c. and pass as married people; accordingly, the gentleman who drew the guinea the night before fell to my lot, and I was not sorry for it, as he was a fine dashing fellow, and was, and had the means to be as generous as a prince; he was well acquainted in the country, and knew almost every body; M'Clean's friend, whose name was O'Brien, was also well acquainted in many parts of the country we were to pass through, and accordingly on the very next morning, early, we set off in my coach, attended by two footmen in laced liveries (belonging to our beaux) very well mounted, and without meeting with any accident, or any extraordinary occurrence, Mr and Mrs Purcell, Mr and Mrs O'Brien, for these were the names we went by, and their *suite,* after remaining some days in *Limerick, Youghall, Mallow,* &c. &c. (in all which towns we went into public, and received the visits of some of the first people of consequence, for our characters escaped totally unknown) arrived in Killarney on the first day of June, 1789, and putting up at the best inn, and a remarkable good one it was, built for the accommodation of visitors, by Lord Kenmare; my friend sent to a Mr Walter Eager, an acquaintance of his, to request his company to sup, and with him every thing was settled for our next day's entertainment; Lord Kenmare's barge was bespoke, as was also her worthy *coxswain* Mr Barry; a band of music was also provided, with *patteraroes,* and every requisite to render the excursion as delightful as possible; and while these matters were adjusting, I privately stepped out, having first enquired for the house, to see my fair and amiable friend, Mrs O'Falvey, formerly Bennett, and have some chat with her; 'tis impossible for me to describe the extacy she was in at meeting me, she clasped me round the neck and perfectly cried on my bosom; at length, however, when she was a little calm, we both agreed to be totally secret, with respect to what we knew of each other, and resolved that after my return, Mrs Falvey should pay me a visit, and represent me to her Kerry friends, as a lady who had once been a great friend to her; and she was to give the same instructions to her husband, who was a gentleman of great worth and honour, and in whom any confidence might be reposed; however, upon due consideration, Mr Falvey was totally averse to the matter, 'My dear Peg,' said he, 'Mrs Falvey's reputation would be totally ruined, amidst a circle of respectable acquaintance with whom she must always reside, if your story should be blasted, which may be the case, considering the variety and extent of your connexions, and the number of people who visit this place at this season of the year; whereas, my dear woman, if you should be found out to-morrow, you can return to your own house at will, and the only consequence that might result from the discovery, would be a few tilting matches, which your supposed *cara sposa* might be engaged in, in consequence of his introducing a lady of your complexion, under the character of a wife, to the hospitable and genteel inhabitants of this village; – had Purcell been married to you, though a whole camp, pioneers and all, had tasted your sweet body, it would not have signified; Mrs S——e of Cork, was never thought the worse of, though a common prostitute, after S——e made her his wife; nor was Mrs D——e, who was visited by the Countess of S—— and the first people in the county, after she had become the wife of her fool; but your case is widely different – therefore I would humbly submit to your better judgement, whether it would not be better for you and my sweet Betsy, to appear as total strangers to each other, except what may arise from your intercourse here; especially as Betsy is looked upon as a girl who never made a slip in her life, except in her marriage with the *pedlar,* as any indiscretion she might have been guilty of, in order to recover her *India goods,* never came to light, her friend being more the man of honour, and *the man* every way, than to kiss and tell; no doubt suspicions went abroad, as his conduct on the trial was thought most extraordinary; but it never went farther than bare surmise'; Falvey's arguments were deemed so good, that every thing he advanced was thought unanswerable, and the ladies parted, to meet the next morning as utter strangers, of which I was to apprize M'Clean. On the morning following, we accordingly took boat at Ross Castle, M'Clean and I, and our two male friends; Falvey and his wife, who had been invited by O'Brien, *Mr and Mrs Eager, and Mrs C—ll,* the latter of whom I must recollect to give some account of (as her memoirs are most curious) *Mr and Mrs McIllicuddy, Mr and Mrs B—r—h—tt,* Sir *B— D— and his Lady,* a *Miss Chute,* the grand daughter of one *Paradine,* a slator, of Tralee, who was married to a Captain in the army, whose name I totally forget; a *Mr and Mrs S—al—y,* and a *Mr John Lewis Fitzmaurice, Beau coup de Tournack,* and our worthy coxswain Mr Barry. The morning was remarkably fine, and as we took boat at five o'clock, we sailed through the lower and upper lakes, shot the bridge, fired our patteraroes at the Eagle's Nest; purchased salmon of the *hawl;* bought filberts from pretty little naked wood nymphs of the several islands we passed; enjoyed the delight of the chase on the water, with the melodious notes of the stag hounds, re-echoed a thousand times over; and at about five o'clock dined in the beautiful and romantic island of Innisfallen, where I left my name, and the names of the whole company, on one of the windows of the banquetting room, with my diamond ring: Heavens! what a place was here for love!!! I heard a gentleman of my acquaintance declare, 'If he had enjoyed the pleasures of the Lake, for a day, with the ugliest old hag of four score, and that there was no other object near him, to satiate his desires, he could not possibly help being enamoured with her, nor could he avoid enjoying her, if enjoyment could be obtained by force or otherwise.' Our salmon were divided in large cuts, and roasted on wooden skewers, round a fire of wood, and so delectable a treat I never partook of in my life: When the fishermen hauled in their nets, they permitted the gentlemen to pick three of the largest for half a crown, and I was informed they would have been perfectly satisfied with a shilling; exclusive of the salmon we had ham and fowls, a cold sirloin of beef, cold neats tongue, a cold mutton pye, an apple pye, some cheesecakes, a parcel of the finest cack-a-gee cider I ever smacked, with porter, Madeira, perry, sherry, port, claret, and some very excellent Nants brandy, that never was contaminated by the odious dip of a revenue rule, as also a bottle of the real North Country *native,* got on purpose for my companion M'Clean, for which she had the most unconquerable partiality. After we had dined, we were regaled with some of the finest gun-powder tea I ever tasted; 'twas most delicious, and procured for us by Mr Eager, who was a revenue officer; he told me he bought a large parcel of it on board the *Lord*

Holland, a few years before, for about five shillings a pound, and generously gave M'Clean and I a couple of pounds each, at the same price. Towards dusk we rambled about the charming island of Innisfallen; and Purcel and I could not resist the temptation of enjoyment under a lofty oak, and miraculously escaped detection, as the instant we were missed the whole island resounded with the names of Mr and Mrs Purcell – stole away – stole away – hark away, &c. &c. When it became quite dark we returned to town, and ended the bewitching *regatto* with an elegant supper, and a dance at the inn. The next morning, early, the same party, with the addition of a Mr and Mrs Gunn, betook ourselves to our boat, and after visiting all the islands, a whimsical motion was made by MrGunn, *i.e.* that each married couple should be landed on different islands, and left there to amuse themselves in the best manner they could for three or four hours, after which our coxswain, Mr Barry, was to sail round the several islands with any of the company who would wish to remain in the boat, and pick the different couples up, at the same time smilingly saying, that each lady and gentleman might personate an Adam and Eve in the Garden of Eden; the motion was seconded, and almost unanimously agreed to; Mr and Mrs Gunn, Mr and Mrs M'Illicuddy, Mr and Mrs Fitzmaurice, Mr and Mrs B—tt, and Mrs O'Brien, alias M'Clean, and her admirer; Mr and Mrs Eager, Miss Chute, and a Mr Fitzgerald her admirer; Mr and Mrs Falvey, Mr and Mrs C—ll, my friend Purcell and I – were landed on ten separate islands; the most beautiful our coxswain could hit upon amidst the heavenly variety, was appropriated to me; indeed the only person who appeared a little squeamish on the occasion, and did not receive the proposal with pleasure, was Mrs C—ll, but more of this lady hereafter: Purcell and I were landed on *Miss Plummer's Island,* where the arbutus, the geranium, the jasmine, and all the evergreens that ever nature formed, grew majestically spontaneously from solid rocks; and here, just when the sun was in its highest meridian, did we refine upon extatic luxuries, like our first parents in the Garden of Eden; we sauntered through this beautiful paradise, where the charming Plummer, once left *her fragrant stream,* from whence it borrowed its name; we also took refreshments with us, as did every other couple; and with great regret, after spending upwards of three hours in this divine place, we left the island, but not until Purcell carved upon a venerable oak, with his pen-knife, the following inscription, being determined to leave Killarney the next morning.

> Be it remembered, that on the third day of June, 1789,
> the divine Margaret Leeson of Pitt-street, in the city
> of Dublin, with her lover, enjoyed every pleasure the
> most refined love could imagine, in this luxurious
> spot, with her own Purcell; her enraptured lover,
> humbly presumes to alter the name of this enchanting
> island from *Plummer* to that of *Leeson.*

After our return to our Inn, we all supped together, when Betsy Falvey took an opportunity of letting me know that C— notwithstanding her prudery was no better than she should be, that she was the daughter of one *Attwood,* a blind brogue-maker, of Tralee, and had when on a visit with an uncle of hers in Cork, one Anthony Gumble Croneen, given her fair hand to a married man, though warned of the consequences, and assured from the very best authority, that Mrs Maudsly was living, for Maudsly the man whom she espoused, gave out that his wife was dead; but notwithstanding all these warnings, and the many letters she received on the business, the guilty wretch married John Cavendish Maudsly; the consequence of which was, he was prosecuted for *bigamy* in about a month after his marriage, by his real wife's friends, who were people of the first respectability, and sentenced to transportation for life. A few years after which Mr C— took her for *better for worse,* without connexions, beauty, fortune, sentiment, wit or reputation: and now my dear Purcell, said my agreeable Betsy, don't you think my Falvey made a much better choice? on which I told her, he certainly had, that C— had not only been guilty of gross prostitution and adultery, but had been the cause of separating man and wife, and of ruining the wretch she had unlawfully married. After spending a most agreeable night, and taking leave of our Killarney friends, we separated, and the next morning at the first dawn began our journey to the *little village,* and breakfasting at *Shine's* before eight o'clock, we dined at Macromp, and lay that night at Cork, where we spent a week; and Daly's company of comedians being then there, we exhibited our charms every night in the boxes; however I was too well known in Cork not to be immediately recognized, in consequence of which, and the visits of some *buckeens* there, that became troublesome, we resolved to shift the scene, and return to Pitt-street as soon as possible, but not as *Mrs Purcell* and *Mrs O'Brien,* but in our own proper characters, – as the identical *Leeson* and *McClean;* this frolic had however like to turn out very serious, as our sparks were called out two or three times, by some spirited gentlemen in the county of Kerry, for presuming to introduce women of our description under the colour of their wives, into their families; and poor Purcell in particular, was wounded in the right shoulder very desperately, though I must do him the justice to say, he behaved as brave as any man in his situation possibly could; – indeed upon mature deliberation, I do not think we carried the joke too far, though at the same time, I solemnly declare I never spent my time more agreeably in my life, particularly the scenes in *Plummer's Island* shall never be forgotten, 'whilst memory holds a seat in this distracted globe.'

> Killarney Lake, how sweet its smiles,
> With verdant hills and stately isles,
> And buildings, many lofty piles,
> And ever blooming Berry.
> Of all the seats give me *Dunlow,*
> Where gaiety smiles, and bumpers flow,
> And heavenly scenes divinely shew,
> A paradise in Kerry.

While I was on this party, I by chance met with my old acquaintance, Mr Ned T—ns—d, who some years before made a noise in that part of the country, from the following circumstance. At the time of our glorious Volunteers, those real disinterested saviours of their country, when 'twas deemed dishonourable not to be accoutred *a la militare;* this gentleman, by way of jest, formed a corps of his own choice, consisting of a few *eccentric men* of fortune and fashion, who called themselves JOLLY DOGS, wearing white coats faced with green, with white waistcoats and breeches, all embroidered with silver, and most curious epaulets, extremely rich, of *black and silver,* each resembling the p-vi-s of a man, beautifully executed, and this passed so well that they went into every public place, and mixed with all companies with these *b—wd—y epaulets,* totally unnoticed, except by a few intimates in the *male line,* who to be sure, could not keep the joke from their wives; – for this curious corps were all married men of *avowed gallantry;* to make therefore some *eclat,* as they never appeared under arms, they gave a splendid regatta, to which all the quality in the neighbourhood were invited; and when the boat-race, and the amusements of the water were over, we were regaled in a beautiful island belonging to Mr Thomas Green, with every viand and beverage the East and West Indies, and Europe could produce, and in the midst of this hilarity, the ladies began to admire the uniforms of the JOLLY DOGS; one in particular, a Miss F—m—g, declared she'd purchase a uniform, and become a *Jolly Dog,* 'That you can't, Betty, by G—,' said Ned T—ns—d, 'but I'll tell you what will answer the same purpose and you'll be *up to it* to a shaving, you may purchase the uniform, and call yourself a proud b—tch.' The young lady, who was an innocent good creature, was so incensed that she burst into tears – but as for my part, I actually bought a riding dress, made up after the same fashion, epaulets and all, and on my return to town sported it at the play house, on the Circular Road, and every where I went, for the remainder of that summer, telling every one I had joined a corps of *proud b—tches* in the barony of *West Carberry*.

CHAPTER SEVEN

[*Problems at Pitt-street, Fanny Beresford, and
the strange tale of Dr Bell the magnetist*]

A DAY OR TWO AFTER my arrival from this pleasant and never to be forgotten excursion, I had discovered that during my absence, Miss Grove and Miss Philips, two ladies that I had as boarders, led such a life of riot and dissipation as really to be a nuisance to the neighbourhood; this circumstance gave me a considerable share of anxiety, as my house was ever known to be as quiet and regular as any one in town, and upon a more minute examination, I found the former of these ladies, had made free with a large quantity of my furniture, which she contrived to get out of the house, under pretence of exchanging them by my directions, for some of more new and fashionable patterns, she sure enough made the exchange, but it was for money, to Mr F— of Bride's-alley, who, Jew like, gave about the eighth of the value. This conduct determined me to lessen my family, and as God had assisted my industrious endeavours, with what a moderate person would call *independence,* I began to reflect that it was high time for me to think of retiring from business, I accordingly agreed with a gentleman in the building line, to compleat a house for me on a lot of ground I had taken on the Black Rock road, it was to be finished in a year in the most complete and comfortable manner, and for which I contracted to pay five hundred guineas. I determined to have one year or two more of pleasure, and then take my leave of public business, and get into the shade of retirement, to pass the remainder of my days in ease and independence. This resolution I was fully determined to carry into execution, and the first step I was induced to take was, to not only contract my family, but also to select my visitors, and by degrees to wean myself from the round of company and dissipation I was accustomed to move in; I therefore instantly discharged Miss Grove and her vicious companion Philips, and took into my house *Fanny Beresford,* of whom I made former mention; this young woman was of a sweet disposition, and in whose company I found real pleasure – she was of a most reputable family, who gave her an excellent education; she was my principal amanuensis, and who prepared these my adventures for the press. Just at this time, she was engaged in an amorous and whimsical adventure, the relation of which amused me very much, and as she was the principal actress in it, I shall beg leave to give it a place here.

She had been taken into keeping by a Lieutenant B—e, and lived very pleasant and happily with him at the barrack in Arklow, where he was quartered, 'till this adventure caused a temporary separation. I shall give it to the reader in her own words.

I was surprised with a visit from two of my old friends in Dublin, who came to Arklow on purpose to see me; one was a young printer, and the other the son of a very eminent tea-merchant, Mr H—n. It was in the Whitsun holidays that these young bloods, well mounted, made their appearance, assuming the character of *Peers,* with their stars and other symbols of nobility, and to do them but common justice, they acted their parts to admiration, as they were vastly more generous, and had more cash, than many of our sprigs of fashion and rank; these, I say, arrived about eleven o'clock in the morning, and as my gentleman had dined that day at Wicklow, insisted that I should dine with them at the inn, to which invitation I consented; they prevailed on me to take advantage of the absence of my friend and accompany them to Dublin, and I not much liking a secluded country life, and fond of variety, agreed to the proposal with pleasure; and while dinner was getting ready, every preparation was made, a horse hired, and I took an opportunity of equipping myself for the journey, which I had some difficulty of doing, as our movements were beginning to take wind; – however, after dinner, on pretence of taking a ride, we took to the road, caring little for what I left behind, and knowing my friend was too generous to withhold my clothes and trunks, we pursued our way to Wicklow: indeed a thousand times I was sorry for the precipitate step I had taken, for if we had met my gentleman coming home from Wicklow, I knew the consequence must have terminated very unpleasantly; however on we went, but to our very great amazement, after we were from Arklow about four miles, and on getting on a rising ground, we perceived a troop of horse after us; no doubt my flight being discovered, and the fear of the vengeance of the Lieutenant, was the cause of the pursuit; however my two friends were not at all dismayed, prevailed on me to quit the high road, and take refuge with them in a cabbin that lay at the end of a field near hand, and my friend Type, whose presence of mind never forsook him, gave half-a crown to a countryman, to tell, when enquiry was made from him by the troop, that he saw us return to Arklow through a bye-road (very fortunately one offered itself to his view) which he pointed out; this had the desired effect, and after our pursuers returned, and was out of sight, we set spurs to our horses, continued our journey, and arrived safe at Wicklow at ten o'clock that night; we immediately called for supper, and in the interim a quarrel arose between my conductors, relative to me, each insisting on the possession of me for the night; it was referred to myself, and as it would be unjust to give a preference to one, I recommended they should draw lots for the prize: this idea was immediately adopted, and my friend the Grocer was the happy man; this was no sooner settled, than we were surprized with the voice of the Lieutenant; we knew he had been in the house, as my two friends breakfasted there in the morning, and had seen him, and as they were intimately acquainted, the Lieutenant expressed his sorrow, that he could not be in Arklow to receive them at dinner; and on our arrival the first question we asked was, whether he was in the house, and was answered by the waiters, that he was, and in company with a club of gentlemen: this you may be sure made us more circumspect; however to put the best face on the matter, I went to my bed-chamber where I ordered my supper, after binding the waiters to secrecy; and the Lieutenant supped with my two friends, they assuring him, his fair mistress was quite inconsolable for his company at Arklow, and he was determined to set off at the first light, so as to surprise her at breakfast. You may be sure my dear friend, my situation was not of the pleasantest; but to compleat this chapter of accidents, my friend Type played a deep game; after getting his friend dead drunk, he slipped from table and took possession of my chamber, where he fortified himself by placing a chest of drawers and half a dozen chairs against the door, and then very soberly stripped himself and slipped into my bed, where I had been about an hour. I was not very sorry for this trick upon the grocer, but I was apprehensive in revenge he would *'peach,'* and so make terrible work; however he was so compleatly intoxicated he had not the power to stir, and he was left on the floor by the Lieutenant, who retired to his own room, and who at the peep of day set out for Arklow: about three o'clock in the morning, *Tea and sugar* came to my door and demanded admittance, but he was soon cooled by Type, who very deliberately got up, opened the door, and dragged him by the feet down two pair of stairs, and left him to ruminate on his adventures in a flagged hall. However at breakfast all animosity was forgot, and I reconciled the friends by assuring my Tea-selling spark, he should to a certainty have all his wishes gratified in Dublin; – we after breakfast continued our way to town through Bray, and arrived in town the same evening.

Here my friend Beresford concluded her story, and I was well pleased with the favourable issue of this adventure, as I was ever an enemy to quarrels of every kind, and I also had the satisfaction by my interference, of reconciling the Lieutenant to Fanny, with whom she lived 'till his regiment was ordered to his own country (Scotland), and my fair friend was too much attached to hers, to accept of his invitation to accompany him, after which she returned to my house.

At a large party one night at my house, we had the pleasure of the company of Colonel Mercer, who among a number of pleasant stories, related the following, which is not generally known. It happened in the 49th regiment, of which he was the Colonel. There was a private soldier, whose mother nursed the colonel; this man had several times deserted, but was by the good colonel got off from punishment; it happened that the corporal, another soldier and himself, not only had deserted but actually took away some articles belonging to the regiment; it was during the American war, where delinquents of this nature seldom escaped; they were soon apprehended, tried by a general court martial, and sentenced to be shot; this man as usual made application to the colonel, but he declared, that to save him was totally out of his power, and advised him to prepare for death; – the evening before the fatal day, he entreated the favour of seeing the colonel, who did accordingly attend him; he asked, was there no hope, no possibility of changing the punishment, but the colonel solemnly declared that his fate was fixed, and *die he must;* 'Then sir,' says the soldier, 'I am perfectly well reconciled to my fate, I have only one request to beg of you, which I cannot die in peace till you grant, and which you must *pledge your honor* to fulfill, it will not be attended with trouble, and the expence will not amount to a guinea.' The colonel imagining, it was some request he had to make relative to his body, and without hesitation gave his honor, his request should be complied with, 'well then,' says the man, 'you are a man of honor, and I shall die in peace, well knowing you will be equal to your promise, – my request is, that when I am *shot dead,* you will instantly in presence of the whole regiment, *turn up my body and kiss my a—e.*'

The colonel's promise was sacred and he could not be off; he however so effectually exerted himself, as to prevent so disagreeable an exhibition, and got a *free pardon* for the three soldiers: he added, that after so narrow an escape the soldier reformed, and turned out afterwards one of the best in the regiment.

My readers must have recollected the celebrated Doctor Bell, the magnetizer; among the rest of my visitors at that period he was one, and a libidinous little dog he was; he frequently gave me and my friends admission tickets, to hear his lectures and see his experiments on *somnambulism* and *sleep-walking;* it was really astonishing to see how the people (and the most sensible and best informed too) were *gulled* by this foreign *Chevalier d'Industrie;* he affected to shew his mighty powers on a Miss W—r and several others, and from his absolutely persuading them they were actually asleep, strange to tell, they affected to *nod.* A gentleman requested of the Doctor, to try his *magnetic powers* on him, and send him to the regions of *Morpheus,* his answer was, that the gentleman being in rude health, and having an *athletic* constitution and strong nerves, he could not grant him his wish immediately, but if he wished to be put in *contact* with a *MrGodsell* a *madman,* who was then in company, he should be instantly gratified with a *paroxism of madness,* or if it was more agreeable to him, he should have *a raging fit of the gout,* an *inveterate venereal complaint,* or a *burning fever,* 'which, sir, do you prefer, either shan't last more than an hour?' The gentleman, who was no other but Mr L—e, made a precipitate retreat, almost chilled with horror at the proposal, and left the doctor to exult in his success; indeed the doctors fame was so industriously spread about by his female disciples, Mrs Fitzm—, Lady G—, Mrs S—, and a few old tabbies, who imagined he was the *great Lama,* just come to diffuse universal knowledge and the cure of all distempers. I shall forbear to mention the names of a number of gentlemen who paid large premiums to this follower of *Mesmer,* to be initiated into the *occult sciences;* among a variety of the distempered who attracted my attention, round his wooden oval machine, filled with *coal ashes* and *dirt,* and having crooked bars of iron all round, opposite to each of which there was a chair, and a patient, conveying the *animal fluid,* with their hands into the *system;* I discovered a worthy old friend of mine, of whose worth and abilities in his line, I was long acquainted with, it was Mr Charles C—, a celebrated watch-maker, who came for advice for a complaint in his eyes, the Doctor after taking his guinea, sent for a glass of water, and made him *squat* down on the floor, and first opening the lash of the blind eye (he was then blind of one eye) and after stroking it over with his *magnet,* closed it again, he then opened the other, and dipping his *magnet in the water,* let *one drop* fall into the eye, and then with a *consequential look and voice,* pronounced 'rise up sir, *I pronounce you a cure:*' He then gave him the *magnetized water,* with strong injunctions to expose it to the rays of the sun every morning to retain its *magnetic powers,* and to use it as a *lotion* to strengthen the cure; however: this curious eye water had such an effect upon poor C—g, that a few weeks afterwards he was *stone blind,* in which melancholy situation he continues to this day. The Doctor soon after this *wonderful cure,* terminated his career in Dublin, being *detected in an amour* with one of his fair disciples, whom he had prevailed on to admit *his animal fluid* into the *proper* receiver, which he assured her, would give her all the knowledge she wished for, without the trouble of study; the discovery compelled him to make a precipitate retreat: he then shifted his quarters to Cork, where the novelty of his *amazing art,* gave him a kind reception into the families of some of the first people in that city, who immediately formed a club for propagating the rudiments of that *wonderful metaphysical science;* his particular intimates were, Doctors Longfield, Callanan, and Gibbings; Sir Henry Mannix, Mr Bousfield, Mr M.R. Westrop, Sir Robert Warren, Mr Leslie, Mr Morrison, Messrs Hearvey and Deaves, Edmond R. Kinselagh, Hickman and Grey, Sir R. Kellett, Mr Bonwell, and Father Synan, the celebrated *Protestant Priest,* &c. &c. &c. his disciples and followers in that very hospitable city, and who paid the Doctor largely for their initiation into the misteries of *somnambulism,* were very numerous; among which were Mr White, Mr J. Franklin, Mr Snowe, Mr Bastable, and the Roscius Mr Dan. Connell; – Mr Pope, Mr George Jack, and the facetious Tommy Howard; Messrs St Leger, Travers, T. Jones, Wassy, Durden, Haly, and Knapp, with numberless others whose names are not worth enumerating; – but notwithstanding the powerful encouragement he met with, from some fatality or other, he contracted debts he was unable to satisfy, in consequence of which he was thrust into gaol, where all his friends deserted him, which gave him an opportunity of studying the *occult sciences* at his leisure: He was afterwards liberated by the interference of the *Humane Cork Society,* and went back to France (his native country) where *Roberspierre's* [*sic*] *magnet* (i.e. the guillotine) soon terminated his career, and put him into a state of *somnambulism* from which he will never awake.

Mrs Leeson's Eccentricities

AS I FOUND IT IMPOSSIBLE to introduce every remarkable occurrence of my life, in the regular order it happened in; I appropriated a book which I called my *'Eccentricities;'* and to which I committed every little adventure, which I thought one day or other, would afford me some entertainment; tho' I little thought then of committing either them or any Memoirs of mine to the press. I am therefore determined the public shall have them without *variation* or *alteration*, – let them therefore speak for themselves.

One day in the month of July, 1791, Groves, O'Brien, Beresford, Burnet, old Mrs Sterling, Mrs Bennis, a few more of the first rate impures and I, attended by our Aid-de-Camp Squire C—e, took an excursion to Rath-farnham, to view the charming retreat of Captain Southwell, the *little Dargle,* and after very minutely examining all the beauties of that enchanting spot, adjourned to Laughlin's tavern, on the ponds, where we dined and spent the remainder of the day; by accident the company of Printers and Booksellers, amounting to upwards of fifty persons, happened to be there also. After we had finished our dinner and drank half a dozen of choice champaigne, we ordered wine, tea, &c. into the garden, and were regaling ourselves very merrily when we were waited upon by a deputation of six of that respectable body, who hearing we were there, sent to compliment us; in consequence of which I ordered more wine, and after finishing two or three coopers, the lads of the *Frisket* insisted on treating us, which I peremptorily refused, telling them, if they could drink an hogshead in my company on such an occasion, they should not pay a farthing, and accordingly more wine being brought in, my *Typographers* began to grow *fine* and *mellow,* particularly the son of my poor friend Bartle C—n the *Hibernian Poet laureat,* who made some amorous advances towards me, which fired the blood of my hero C—e between whom and young C—n, a battle royal ensued in presence of the whole company in the garden. In the course of the scuffle C— pulled off *Type's* wig and threw it to Fanny Beresford, who instantly went aside, and filled the *brown-bob* with the briny produce of her lucious fountain, after which she returned it to C—e, who not dreaming of its consecration, thrust it in its inundated state into his Nankeen breeches, which caused a vast deal of merriment, as notwithstanding the heat of Fanny's constitution, poor C— found his *privities* extremely chilled, which caused him in a paroxism of rage to throw the well sluced peruke into a running brook at the bottom of the garden, from whence it was carried off never to be recovered by the heir of *old Bartle;* who was obliged to return to town with an handkerchief tied about his bald pericranium, to the no small diversion of the company. A select party of these gentlemen did me the honor of supping at my house that evening, and generously laid down a guinea each for their entertainment, my friends Jack S—e and P—W— by their lively wit and *singularity of humour,* keeping the table in a roar the whole night.

One day that we spent at Drumcondra, *Broadhead,* our landlord, did not as I thought treat us with that deference we expected, and accordingly I left the following couplet, written with my diamond pencil on one of his parlour windows,

> Not *Broadhead* but *Flathead* you surely should be,
> As you're really a *Flat,* in the *highest* degree.
> M.L.

One evening as *Joe* the *game cock* and I, were talking upon the impossibility of the existence of such monsters as S—d—s and C—t—s in such a land of *beauty* as ours; a loud rap announced some person of consequence; when seeming terribly alarmed, lest it might be Buck *Lawless* with whom I lived at that time, I requested with tears in my eyes, his lordship would be kind enough to step into a *clothes-press* which stood in my dressing room, and on his lordship's politely complying, I turned the key on him, and amused myself with my favourite L—g for about half an hour, when I walked out with him, leaving his lordship a *close prisoner* till my return, when I had the honour of liberating him, almost stifled and pressed to death in the presence of eight or ten of my *laughter-loving wenches,* who absolutely were convulsed with laughing, at the ridiculous figure his lordship cut on being released from doing *Cupboard* duty.

A Gentleman of my acquaintance, who before his misfortunes was looked upon as a celebrated Wit, happened to meet me one morning on the road to Rathfarnham, and asking me very politely the way? I directed him to go *straight forward;* – 'Zounds madam,' exclaimed he, 'if that be the case I shan't be able to get there this night.' – 'Why so,' said I, 'Lord Loftus's house is not a quarter of a mile off.' 'Aye,' replied the *eccentric,* 'I'll allow that, but you have cruelly desired me to go *straight forward,* which is a thing impossible – as, if I was dismounted, you'd find me as *crooked* as the *line of beauty.'* – 'I'll charge you nothing for that,' said I laughing, and galloped off.

Another day as I was riding in the Park, with a little diminutive dwarf-looking servant trotting after me, Sir B— Balderdash bawled out, 'yarrow Piggy, what thing's that's behind you?' My A—e, Sir B.' said I, 'would you choose an introduction in the *old fashioned way?*

Another day as I was riding on the Rock road, a *Buckeen* accosted me with, 'By G— Peg, I wish I was st—g you.' – 'O Lord, sir!' exclaimed I, 'what good would that do me?' 'Why Peg, it would make you as lively and sprightly as possible.' 'Oh,' replied I, 'would it so? why then for heaven's sake st—e my Mare, for she's as lazy and dull as the devil.' My spark rode off like a cur who had lost his tail.

Once on the road to Cork, I stopped at the sign of the *Angel,* which was kept by two sisters whose christian names were Faith and Prudence; on my first stopping there I was treated with the greatest good manners, every thing the best in its kind with the most reasonable charges: however, on my return back in about six weeks, all was changed; the Angel was converted into a Shoulder of Mutton, and on enquiry I found the eldest sister *Miss Faithy* was dead, and that miss Prue was not a whit better than she should be. On which a Wit in my company left the following *Jeu d'Esprit* on one of the panes of the window:

When *Faith* and *Prudence* lived here,
An *Angel* kept the door:
But *Faith* is dead, the Angel fled,
And *Prudence* turned a wh—e.

Once in a large company of *Belles* and *Beaux* at my house, the tide of ridicule was turned against a gentleman in company well known in the literary world, who happened to have the misfortune of having *crooked legs,* on which he pleasantly said (holding out his right leg,) 'You may make what fun of me you please, but I'll hold you an unlimited rump and dozen; there is a worse leg than that in the company.' A gentleman present thinking that impossible, closed with the bet, on which he produced his left leg, which was much more deformed than the right) and won the wager, to the no small pleasure of all present. In *Edwin's eccentricities* Mr Williams takes notice of this excellent *Bon Mot,* but not with the justice it deserves. Williams says Mr G— produced *the fellow* to the leg the wager was held upon, when, in reality, he produced a *worse,* which made the jest more excellent; besides Mr Williams relates it as happening in Belfast, when it actually happened at my Table in a large mixed company of Munster gentlemen, and fashionable Impures and Demi-reps of the Ton.

On my being told that the late Stephen R. who was an active agent for the Ministerial party at the famous Carrickfergus election (when C—n the *Smuggler* was returned Member for that town against the united powers of *eleven Peers* of the realm) was arrested and thrown into prison at the suit of his democratic Baker, to whom he owed sixty pounds for bread; and that Amyas G—th, Esq. was dismissed from all his employments under the crown, on account of his opposition to the Court Candidate the late honorable Joseph H—. I heaved a heavy sigh and said, 'Alas! poor Stephen, you have lost your *Liberty* for your *Bread,* whilst my poor Amyas has lost his *Bread* for his *Liberty.*'

The tax upon Salt was long whispered about, before it was agitated in the house of Commons: I exclaimed (hoping however it would never take place) 'damnation to them! they have already taxed poor Paddy's *brogues,* and now they purpose not to give him *Salt* to his *Porridge.*'

When the famous companion and *Fides achates* [*sic*] of secretary P—, pretended Count R— the chimney doctor, was mentioned to be only a spy, sent here and also to England by the *French Directory,* to feel the pulses of the two kingdoms, I burst into an immoderate fit of laughter saying – 'By Jupiter, he has fairly *smoked us all,* peeped into our private recesses, and will shortly perhaps pay us another visit, and send us to his country seat Rum-ford to get our A—s new bottomed.'

One evening I had the pleasure of the company of my friend P—n immediately after the publication of that diabolical tragedy called *Democratic Rage,* which was cramm'd down the throats of all his Majesty's dutiful and loyal subjects, – in order to impress the *Canaille* with horror against the *Sans Coulottes* [*sic*], I took the liberty of sending to his lodging a very handsome drinking glass with the following epigram written on it with my diamond pencil:

> Alas poor Lewis, what a fate was thine,
> Untimely taken off by Guillotine;
> Which roused the folly of a P—n's pen,
> To have thy memory slaughter'd o'er again.

On going thro' part of the county Wexford on a pleasurable excursion, my party happened to stop just at dinner hour at *Taghmon,* a little village in that county, where we could not get a morsel to eat, or any kind of lodging; on which I left on one of the *widow Breen*'s windows the following lines:

> Tis surely a bore,
> That a favourite wh—e,
> Praised by wits for her humour and fun,
> Should with *cash* in her purse,
> As if God sent a curse;
> Want lodgings in hungry Taghmon.

One evening in a large party at my house in Pitt-street, Saunders's newspaper was handed about, which announced the marriage of a Mr and Mrs Brush, the witty and facetious counsellor Curran who was one of the party instantly produced the following:

> Now Brush with Mrs Brush, a Brush may take,
> And Brush her Brush, so little Brushes make.

One day just as our *Catholic Brethren* had obtained some relaxations from the Popery laws, which in themselves were a disgrace to any nation, that *brilliant orator* and senator Sir B— Balderdash happened to call to see me, – when the subject turning on politics, I happened to mention the advantages the Catholics had gained that session, when the obsequious Knight and Baronet replied, 'Yes Peg, what you say is very true, *we* should all be very much obliged to his lordship our good Lord Lieutenant, for this very great indulgence,' – pronouncing his I's and U's with the luscious brogue of his own sweet *kingdom of Kerry.* Once I had the pleasure of visiting the Baronies of *East* and *West Carbery,* Bere and Bantry, with a captain T— my then husband *pro tempore,* and being invited to spend the day with a musical party of *Amateurs* in the town of Skibbereen, when the Rev. Charles Tuckey in particular, was to entertain us with his *musical glasses,* a species of sound at that time quite nouvelle, except with *Cartwright* himself, whose harmony was never heard of by any of the sprightly hospitable inhabitants of that obscure village; a number of old Milesian chieftains graced the board, *O'Donovan, O'Driscoll, O'Donoughoe, O'Falvey, Leary, M'Carthy, &c. &c. &c.* together with a variety of other gentlemen and ladies of the first consequence, Colonel T—d and family of Castle T—d, Edward T—d of White-hall, John T—d of THORNHILL, together with a heterogneous mass of F—k—s, H—gf—ds, Bald—ns, who never once suspected me to be a *Fille de Joy,* a young gentleman of the O'Driscoll race, a Mr *Dennis O'Driscoll,* who had just been imported from Crook-haven or Ballydahab, and who had never seen a *tree growing* till a week before, called upon me *'to be kaind enough to help him to a bit of the cap of the pye.'* 'What is it you desire to have, Sir?' said I. *'Only a small bit of the cap of dat dere pye,* I mean madam, de *kiver.* Oh! Sir, you shall of the *kiver or cap,* said I, be helped plentifully, and knowing the dish to be merely a deception of *bran* and *paste,* I dexterously whipped the entire covering off, and clapping it on his head, proclaimed aloud, to the no small entertainment of the much diverted company: 'Dennis O'Driscoll of Ballydahab, I create you and your heirs for ever lawfully begotten, the renowned knoghts of the order of the *Cap of the pye;* so in the name of St Patrick take off your *Helmet* and devour a part of it,' – and from that hour to this, Dennis O'Driscoll of Skibbereen in the county of Cork, goes by no other name than *'Cap of the Pye'* – nor did I ever hear that I was even suspected of being any other person than the lady of captain T—, and as such became an universal toast in that country, where I spent four months of the pleasantest of my life.

A Mr S—t—y, a hungry looking dog, son of a Cabinet-maker, lived with me on the Rock road for a few months as my favourite Paramour; during which time he by degrees *pollocked* (to use a new phrase for cozening or tricking one), me out of considerable sums of money; and not satisfied with that, he absolutely pawned a number of my trinkets and moveables, which the unprincipaled villain found means to secret from me. 'Tis really very singular how I suffered myself to be so duped by a contemptible miscreant who came into my house more on the footing of a servant than any thing else, and who at the time was actually in rags – but the old proverb is verified frequently on such occasions,

> Clap a Beggar on horse-back and he'll ride to the devil.

> I'll hunt the hated varlet all his days,
> No hour shall bring the dirty reptile ease.

A Mr Fleet—d an attorney, gave me an annuity of thirty pounds a year during my life, for my elegant house on the Rock-road, the bare erection of which by contract cost me five hundred pounds, besides upwards of a hundred I laid out on it myself during my residence in it; and surely the interest of that sum would have brought me in six pounds a year more than the honourable attorney allowed me, exclusive of which my constitution was so broken and my speedy death so certain, that the concerns during my life, should at least have brought me one hundred pounds a year: but what cared honest F—d so he brought the grist to his mill, and so he certainly has done to some purpose, as I am well informed on his laying out about one hundred pounds on the premises they will let for upwards of sixty pounds a year for nine hundred and ninety nine years, and he pays but six pounds a year ground rent.

As my customers were very numerous, it was impossible for me to recollect each person in company, especially as in general they were in a state of intoxication, or at least so impregnated with generous wine as to lose their retentive faculties and consequently forget to pay for their *Viands, beverage,* or *Filles de joys,* in which case when I could not bring to mind their names, I generally had a reference to their employments, some defect in their persons, the colour of their clothes, their provincial accents, &c. &c. As a specimen the following is given, taken from the 126th folio of my private ledger:

> Mr *Blinker,* the old country man
> from Thurles, I found out his name
> afterwards to be B—k—
> For Money lent, Wine, and sundries   £34 – 6 – 0

> *Captain Longnose,* the whiskered
> heroe with the county Limerick brogue.
> For Wine and passing my word to Miss
> Groves and Fanny Beresford that he
> would not bilk them   £18 – 6 – 6

Brown Billy from Kerry, with the yellow spencer, a week's Board and Lodging	£5 – 13 – 9
Flat W—l—n, whose father lived with the Collector who hanged himself. This buck was snaffled by two Catchpoles, Mooney and Sheridan, and I not bearing to see a gentleman in such hands advanced 3 Guineas, which with 2 flasks of Champaign he drank at my expence to thank me, – amount to 4 Guineas, – which he handsomely never thought proper to pay for,	£4 – 11 – 0
The curly pated Squire from Limerick, one Night's Lodging, a girl and a bottle,	£2 – 16 – 9
The Broganier Fool, from Tralee, with the long ruffles and tremendous sword, A—R—l, Esq; – Politely took a fancy to a gold Seal I had, and for which he *promised* to pay	£4 – 11 – 0

But this volume would not hold the half, could I at this moment bring myself to publish the names and transactions at full length. In this curious whimsical way I generally kept my accounts, and have often recovered notes of hand, I o's and other securities without ever troubling my head to see if the parties had signed them: there is one that was contracted and terminated singular enough: – A gentleman-like looking man, in the sea-faring line, had been arrested for a debt of £18 passed for wine, and having no acquaintance in town, begged to be carried to my house; the shark who had him in custody, gratified him, – and though I never saw him but once and only in company with a friend of mine, I sent for the plaintiff (a Grocer in Grafton-street) who took my note as a discharge for the debt, – the gentleman passed me his note with thanks as follows:

> In twenty-one days I
> certainly will pay Mrs Peggy Leeson
> nineteen pounds ten shillings.
> Witness my hand.

He unfortunately omitted both date and name, but he had a remarkable token about him that I could not forget, namely a wooden leg. Upon producing it however after to a Captain L. of Belfast, he told me he knew the person by the writing and description I gave of him; and that the note must have been passed by one Heighl—d, who had formerly been a midshipman in the Navy, and who was then in the Revenue, and that if his profession did not pervert his principles, he was certain, as a *Sailor,* he'd scorn to take any advantage, after so distinguished a piece of service from me; and that certainly the date and omission of the name was an oversight of his own. I accordingly applied to Heighl—d, and found that the *brave honest Tar* was sunk in the occupation of a pitiful mate of a *Revenue Cruiser;* for the scoundrel positively denied he had ever been in my house, or had even passed me a Note of any kind whatever; however he paid dear for his assertion, for I commenced a suit against him and fully proved the transaction, and his ingratitude, to the great satisfaction of the court. The debt and cost amounted to upwards of sixty pounds, which he was obliged to discharge.

Once on a trip I took with a gentleman to Belfast, I went to a *Coterie* there. Tom G—g (who had been an old blacksmith, but was then a top Merchant and joined with his brother-in-law the famous C—n) was *King,* and a Mrs P. a diminutive deformed hobgoblin, *Queen.* Among a great number of beautiful, well behaved, affable, charming women, one who was by far the most disagreeable, ordinary and ill-behaved in the room, attracted my particular notice; she was made up of conceit, pride and impertinence. With an *hauteur* that could not strike *awe* or respect, whatever it might *disgust.* On enquiring who this *creature* was, a Capt. Tom B. of the 70th Regiment informed me she was Miss Jenny G. daughter to the king of the *Coterie,* whom he had known to have followed the trade of a *Horse-shoer* in that town, but that now the case was altered, he had by smuggling and other such *honourable* practices, amassed a princely fortune, in consequence of which, not only Vulcan himself, but the whole family had become vain, saucy, imperious and impertinent, particularly Jenny, who absolutely stunk with pride. Having got my *cue,* I made it my business the whole night to turn her into ridicule: I whispered my partner H. W—n (as we were next couple to Jenny and her partner Count J—n from Pill-lane) loud enough to be heard, 'Pray has not that tall aukward thing a great deal of the *Black* about her countenance?' 'Hold your tongue you rogue,' answered Hill, 'don't you know her Papa, the king there, was a blacksmith.' 'What care I whether he was a blacksmith or a whitesmith, if his daughter could learn to behave herself with propriety; but, as Gay says,

All upstarts insolent in place,
Remind us of their vulgar race.

Before we left the ball room, I publickly before the whole company, wrote the following lines on one of the windows of the *Coterie* room which was held at the Donegall arms.

> Jenny G—g they say has wit,
> And some, they add, have felt it;
> She *walks* as if she was besh—t,
> And *looks* as if she smelt it.

Some years before the *French Revolution,* when *Roman Catholics* were thought to have a greater respect for the *Grand Monarch* than for their own good king; than which, *by the by,* no opinion on earth could be more erroneous; the earl of B. and Col. V. did me the honor to take a *petite soupe* at my house: the noble Lord sat on one side of me, and the Colonel at the other; when B. (thinking me a bigoted papist, and consequently inimical in his mind to church and state) taking up his glass, drank, 'here's the king, Peg, but not your king by God', on which, with the greatest *nonchalance* I took up my glass, and addressing the Colonel with a thump on the knee said, 'Well Colonel, here's the king, but not your king by G—d.' 'What do you mean Peg?' said the great colonel most learned in Irish; 'Colonel, I drank the toast merely as I got it; it is not that I don't love my own king the great and good king George, better than any Monarch on the habitable globe.' 'Bravo! bravo! Peg,' exclaimed lord B. 'by the L—d I believe his Majesty has not a better subject on earth.' 'Not one my Lord, and who has *exerted* herself *more* for the purpose of manning his Fleets and Armies; I have *incessantly laboured* for him day and night, and *sometimes* without a *shift* to my back.'

I have often wondered at the similitude between the heroes of antient *Greece and Rome,* and our own *modern heroes* of the dear *kingdom of Kerry;* a part of the world I love in my very heart. In fact I really believe more gentlemen have committed *Suicide* in that county, nay, in the very town of *Tralee* (I'll confine myself to that charming spot, where I have spent some of the pleasantest days of my existence; though utterly unknown to the dear, the hospitable inhabitants; for I absolutely lived there with a gentleman in the army for one entire year without ever being discovered; long, long before my excursion to the divine Lake of Killarney). Imprimis then, to my own knowledge. My dear Edward D—y, the most accomplished gentleman of the name, shot himself at an obscure Inn in the north of Ireland. When an Ensign in the Army, he lived on his pay oeconomically [*sic*] and prudently like a gentleman, but when by his marriage and the bequest of his worthy brother Arthur, he came into the receipt of about eleven hundred pounds a year, he ran in debt, he was attacked by the clamours of unrelenting creditors, his nerves were unstrung, his feelings superlatively great; and he made at once with a loaded pistol his own *quietus.*

Francis C—l, Esq. brother to the husband of Miss A—n, who has been mentioned before, was tried in London for the commission of a *rape,* and condemned to be hanged, but by the interference of his countryman Lord Shelbourne, was pardoned; in consequence of which he returned home, with his last speech, confession, and dying words in his pocket, and deliberately shot himself. This line from Ovid was found in his pocket,

No body shall kill Ajax but Ajax himself.

Thomas H—k—n, Esq. an eminent physician and a gentleman of worth and honour, on his eldest brother's reforming, as they call it (*i.e.* turning Protestant and taking possession of the entire property of the whole family, consisting of himself and five brothers): (Glorious law! enacted by a band of merciless, sanguinary villains,) took a resolution to starve himself, and absolutely lived upon water alone for forty one days, refusing any other sustenance, though importuned by the first ladies in the town, who on their knees implored him to take nourishment, but in vain; he languished for forty one days and expired. And upon being asked whether he felt much pain in fasting, he declared that for the first three days he was in great agony, but for all the rest of the time he had not the smallest inclination to eat.

Samuel M—r—s, Esq. after inviting a very large company to spend the day with him, just as dinner was dishing, stepped into his carriage which happened to be at the hall door, and blew his brains out, to the no small mortification of the company, who thereby lost a splendid entertainment.

The Rev. Fitzm—e B—t, after having paid his addresses to an amiable young lady for a number of years, at last obtained her consent, and accordingly the writings having been compleated and every matter adjusted, and the day fixed for the celebration of the nuptials, the Rev. Divine (who was a worthy, a most excellent man, and in affluent circumstances) retired to the stable the evening before the completion of all his wishes were to have been ratified, and hung himself on one of the collar braces.

William B—h—t, Esq. collector of the county, a gentleman in possession of estated property, to the amount of near six thousand pounds a year besides his collection; he was also married to an amiable, sentimental and beautiful lady, by whom he had a number of fine children, and possessed a character in high estimation among all his numerous friends and acquaintances, notwithstanding all which (in short though in possession of all the good things in this world) he deliberately finished his existence by hanging himself in one of his stables, to the great grief of a virtuous affectionate wife, a large family of children and servants, and a multitude of friends and near relations.

Crosbie M——ll, Esq. an eminent attorney, hearing of the immersion of the late poor Baron Power near the Light House, notwithstanding he had been returned for the borough of Tralee, that he had given thirty thousand pounds with his daughter in marriage to the late Sir B. D——y who was afterwards fairly pistoled by C—— in a duel. In fact notwithstanding M——ll had risen to be the greatest man that ever was or will be in that *august* family, and had the cleverness to die *nine hundred thousand pounds* in debt, – yet upon mere speculation and chance, in order to obtain the place of the Barons Register in the regions of Tartarus, had the temerity to plunge after him and seek an asylum in that country from *whose bourne no traveller returns*. The following epitaph was written by me on the occasion.

> Here M——l lies whom not a soul bemoans,
> For whom we see no tears, nor hear no groans;
> Death and the devil snatched him quite away,
> The devil take death for suffering him to stay
> Among us longer than his natal day.
>
> M.L.

Besides these *suicides* which all happened in *my own memory,* there were many others if I could bring them to my recollection; and what is still more extraordinary, the gentlemen were all contemporaries and school-fellows, all educated in the town of Tralee at Young's school; all excellent scholars and accomplished gentlemen, and in general highly respected by all who had the pleasure of their acquaintance; and what is very singular, there was not one of them who had not one time or other basked in the sunshine of my bewitching smiles: They all in turn had been my devoted slaves and admirers, from whom I had received vast sums of money. Indeed I often think my poor friend Henry B——t will go the same road, and as little regretted as his compeer C——e M——ll.

AN EXCLAMATION,
Written by a gentleman on Mrs Margaret Leeson's
retiring to the country for the benefit of her health.

Why droops the head, why languishes the eye?
What means the flowing tear, the frequent sigh?
Where are the lenient med'cines to impart,
Their balmy virtues to a bleeding heart.
Fancy no sweet ideas can suggest,
To lull the raging tumult in my breast;
In vain, or Wit invites, or Friendship calls,
Wit dies a jest, and conversation palls.
No scenes amuse me that amused before,
Since what delighted once, delights no more;
The budding plants of variegated hue,
The blossoms opening with the morning dew,
The vernal breeze that gently fans the bowers,
The laughing meadows and enlivening flowers,
Th' enameled garden where the roses bloom,
And gaudy pinks so pregnant with perfume,
All, all in vain with charms united glow,
Since *Leeson's* gone, they but increase my woe.
'Twas she enliven'd Nature all around,
And made the heart with every joy abound:
'Twas she illumined all, with brightening rays,
The feathered *Choir* to her addressed their lays.
But stop, Oh man! thy plaintiff strains suppress,
Since they can never make thy griefs the less.
Perhaps some power divine may yet create,
Some beams to brighten up thy present state;
May yet restore unto thy longing arms,
Thy much loved Peg with renovated charms.
Then songs of gratitude, and joy, and praise,
As thankful tributes to that power raise.

TRUTH *and* FALSHOOD; *a Fable.*
Addressed to Mrs Margaret Leeson, who had been
given to understand the Author had written something
against her.

Soon as the *Iron Age* on Earth began,
And vice found easy entrance into Man;
Forth from her cave infernal *Falshood* came,
Falshood the hate of Gods, of Men the same.

A silken robe she wore of various hue,
The colour changing with each different view.
Studious to cheat, and eager to beguile,
She mimick'd Truth and ap'd her heav'nly smile.
At length she saw celestial Truth appear,
Serene her brow, and chearful was her air.
A lily robe was girt about her waist,
And o'er her arms a radiant mantle cast.
Thus Truth advanced unknowing of deceit,
And *Falshood* bowing low began to cheat.
'Hail charming maid, bright as the morning star,
'Daughter of Jove, and heaven's peculiar care.
'Why walk we thus regardless of our ease,
'Exposed beneath the sun's meridian blaze.
'Let us repair to yonder river's side,
'To bathe and sport our limbs within the tide.
Thus spoke the Phantom, and with friendly look
Supporting what she said, approach'd the brook,
Truth followed, artless unsuspicious Maid,
And in an evil hour the voice obeyed.
The Fiend upon the margin lingering stood,
The Goddess naked leaped into the flood.
Sporting she swam the liquid surface o'er,
Unmindful of the matchless robe she wore.
Not Falshood so – She hasty seized the vest,
And in the beauteous spoils herself she drest.
Hence Falshood cheats us in the fair disguise,
And seems Truth's self to all unwary eyes;
With safety dares to flatter, fawn and sooth,
For who knows falshood when array'd like truth?
Therefore dear *Leeson* let no slanders bias
Your honest heart against your friend *Amyas.*

N.B. The above produced the Author a guinea each for ten Tickets for his benefit
at the Theatre Royal.

A SONG,
Addressed to Mrs *Leeson,* when Miss *Plunket,* by her first Seducer.
Air, Nancy Dawson.

I.
Of all the last and beautious race,
Which Jove did give, this Earth to grace,
Not one has such an heavenly face

As charming Peggy Plunket.
The Sun is deadened by her eyes,
A swimming brightness from them flies,
Like constellations in the skies,
So bright is Peggy Plunket.

II.

Nature looks gay when she appears,
And *Winter* too refrains from tears;
A golden age the world shares,
When blessed with Peggy Plunket.
So chearful, affable and gay,
The gods take pleasure to array
This lovely Maid like fragrant May,
And call her Peggy Plunket.

III.

Blessed happy Man! doomed to untie
Her zone, and with transporting joy
In sweet extatic raptures die
On lovely Peggy Plunket.
And when from paradise he'll wake
A second blissful draught to take,
A heaven like this no one can make
On earth but Peggy Plunket.

The Town Major of Dublin, one N—n, who squints most horribly, called at my house in Pitt-street with an intent to treat Jenny Neilson and I with some excellent champaigne, that *Ferns* had then just imported, half a dozen cases of which he sent me. And after drinking a couple of flasks, he asked us could we hide another bottle? *undoubtedly* was the answer. 'Well then Peg, call for one.' 'Oh! by G—' said I, 'N—n I see a *cast* in your eye.' 'Then send for a cast,' cried N—n laughing very heartily, 'or two if you are equal to them.'

As my readers have often heard me mention the *Kingdom of Kerry,* it may not be incurious to know why that county was first called a kingdom. A great number of people from that county having been obliged to emigrate for bread to France, the late poor *Lewis* when he used to ask from whence that *General,* that *Admiral,* that *Bishop,* or that *Abbe* came, was generally answered; 'may it please your Majesty, from Kerry.' 'Pray then,' replied the ill-fated Lewis, 'What part of the Kingdom of Kerry is Ireland in?'

The following humorous ballad, was written by a friend of mine in consequence of a grand *Fandango,* which *Squire Crupper* gave us at his *Villa,* at which most of the *Filles des Joys* of the City were assembled.

The Crupper-making Squire
of Whitehall;
A new Ballad.
Tune – Galloping dreary Dun.

I.

A CRUPPER-MAKING SQUIRE, I certainly am,
Galloping dreary Mick,
A Crupper-making squire I certainly am,
With my old auctioneer called *slippery Sam.*
With my haily gaily, cheat away daily,
Jockeying, cantering, auctioning, mortaring,
Saddling, dreary Mick.

II.

I'm lord of White-hall, and drive my own gigg,
Galloping dreary Mick,
I'm lord of White-hall and drive my own gigg,
And for those I have cheated I care not a fig.
With my haily, gaily, &c. &c.

III.

A Brother I have, called poor Cockney Jack,
Galloping dreary Mick,
A brother I have, called poor Cockney Jack,
A swindler, a cheat, and a Munster crack,
With my haily, gaily, &c. &c.

IV.

I've converted Whitehall to a Mansion so fine,
Galloping dreary Mick,
I've converted Whitehall to a Mansion so fine,
Where Jockeys and Filleys drink, gamble and dine.
With my haily, gaily, &c. &c.

V.

Sure Achmet's famed baths to mine can't compare,
Galloping dreary Mick,
Sure Achmet's famed baths to mine can't compare,

Where there's such an assemblage of
   black, brown and fair,
With my haily, gaily, &c. &c.

VI.

The famed widow Shee, squire Walpole's own dear,
Galloping dreary Mick,
The famed widow Shee, squire Walpole's own dear,
And sweet Kitty Doran* shall also be there.
With my haily, gaily, &c. &c.

VII.

Peg Plunket shall honor my board at White-hall,
Galloping dreary Mick;
Peg Plunket shall honor my board at White-hall,
And Buxom Joan Driscoll, shall lead up the ball,
With my haily, gaily, &c. &c.

VIII.

'Squire Edgeworth is always at my *table D'Hote,*
Galloping dreary Mick,
'Squire Edgeworth is always at my *table D'Hote,*
And many adventurers not worth a groat,
With my haily, gaily, &c. &c.

IX.

The brave Colonel S—y, once of the Police,
Galloping dreary Mick,
The brave Colonel S—y, once of the Police,
And Lamprey the chandler, because we're not nice,
With my haily, &c. &c.

X.

You know I once kept a† capital ride,
Galloping dreary Mick:
You know I once kept a capital ride,
Where all kinds of Quadrupeds were duely tried,
With my haily, &c. &c.

XI.

To Bipeds I now have turn'd my mind,

---

* This lady was formerly kept by Henry Langley, of Lisnerock, and afterwards lawfully married to squire Walpole, Lord C—ll's cousin german.
† In Exchequer-street, it was called the *Menage.*

Galloping dreary Mick:
To Bipeds I now have turn'd my mind,
And at White-hall you'll find them gentle and kind,
With my haily, &c. &c.

XII.
The Cyprian Temples must go to decay,
Galloping dreary Mick:
The Cyprian Temples must go to decay,
As *White-hall* from them all will carry the sway,
With my haily, &c. &c.

XIII.
The Sentimental Mag. will inform you more,
Galloping dreary Mick:
The* Sentimental Mag. will inform you more,
Where I've got an engraving behind and before,
With my haily, gaily, cheat away daily,
Jockeying, cantering, auctioning, mortaring,
Galloping dreary Mick.

Taking a ride one day with a near relation of the late unfortunate Geo. Rob. F—tz-G—d, soon after his execution, and on passing by a luxuriant field of hemp, he enquired of me what that was, that looked so green and flourishing? 'Only you'd be angry,' said I, 'I'd tell you.' 'Angry, madam, 'tis impossible any thing you could say or do, would make me angry.' 'Then,' replied I, 'that's the very *Salad that choaked your cousin Fitz—G—d;*' he pretended to put it off with a laugh, but I am convinced he never forgave me, and certainly I was very much in error; for,

Who for the short delight of being smart,
Wou'd lodge a sting within a brother's heart.

When poor Mrs Jane E. M— of poetical memory, was waddling from shop to shop, and cellar to cellar, collecting subscriptions for her abominable trash, in which office she was indefatigable; she was frequently observed to sir for hours together in an eminent apothecary's shop in this city, as an *amicus curiae,* for that lady also dealt largely in *nostrums,* and took upon herself to cure every *scrophulous complaint, King's evil, Leprosy;*

---

* We by no means mean a Mag-pye, but a publication replete with wit and sentiment; printed by Jones, of *Grafton-street;* and conducted by the very ingenious Mr Lewis, corrector of the press, &c. In which the CRUPPER-MAKING 'SQUIRE has published a view of this Temple, dedicated to the PAPHIAN QUEEN.

and in fact all *incurable disorders;* that witty, that elegant authoress Mrs B—tti—r, being asked, if she ever met with Mrs M—e at Mr —'s shop, as she frequently called there to see her friend Mr Griff—th, replied that 'perhaps she might, but if so, she mistook her constantly for the great Mortar.' – 'But where was the pestle,' said Jonathan —, 'Oh as for that, you must ask Mr G—ff—th, I looked upon him as pestle to the great Mortar.'

When the *Dog in Office* abused a late eminent and worthy Printer in this city, I laughingly said – 'Well what need they be surprised, sure 'tis very natural for hungry dogs to lick *Pots* on all occasions, when they meet with any.'

Hearing that Gif—dini, as Mrs B—r calls him in her Gibbonaid, was honoured with above one hundred black beans, when he had the effrontery to be proposed a member of the Lawyers' Club, – I told him, on his calling to see me, that, 'all he had to do, to live well the winter, was to lay in a good stock of bacon, as his brethren the Lawyers had contributed to supply him with plenty of *beans.*' – The son of the Dog sneaked off, as if in reality he had *lost his tail,* and by all accounts, jesting apart, young H—y effectually made a singer of him, so that if one trade fails, he can't miss of bread among the *Castrate* of the Drama.

One morning meeting the celebrated Mr G—iff—th on the Circular-road, I asked him what the devil made his legs so diabolically crooked? – 'S—g one of my mother's maids standing,' answered he, with the greatest *sangfroid* imaginable. I could not be angry, my question deserved the answer.

One night at *Daly's Hell,* Buck English, that sanguinary hero, happened to fall fast asleep, when a thought came into the heads of some gentlemen engaged at silver hazard, to frighten the Buck out of his wits, and accordingly, without the smallest noise, had the fire removed, and all the candles extinguished, after which they began to make a horrid racket with the *dice,* 'Seven or eleven,' – 'Seven's the main,' – 'By G—d, Sir, that's not fair,' – 'I appeal to the groom porter,' – 'Rascal D—p—t, what did Lawler throw?' – 'You lie, you lie you villain,' – 'Damn your body, take that.' – Then swords were drawn, and a dreadful clashing and uproar ensued; all the while the dice rattling away. In the midst of all this *tremendous din,* the Buck awoke frightened out of his wits, fearing the Almighty to punish him for his *murderous deeds* had struck him blind, and falling on his knees, for the first time since his arrival to manhood, began to ejaculate in the most devout manner, all the prayers he could recollect, not omitting his old *ave maria,* for the Buck was reared a good Roman Catholic; and in this lamentable situation, he was removed quite in the dark, to a bed prepared for him in the house, where he remained in inconceivable agony, being certain he had lost his sight. A little before day light he was visited by most of his companions, who were determined to carry the joke a little farther; they pretended it was noon day, began to condole with him on his misfortune, and recommended Mr Rouviere the celebrated oculist to him; having no doubt but his ability would restore him to his sight. The Buck was assisted to dress by some of the servants (still in the dark) all the time bemoaning his misfortune and promising that if Heaven would be pleased to work a miracle in his favour, to immediately seclude himself from the world, and pass the remainder of his days in a convent in France: But as soon as Sol's gladsome rays had convinced him of the trick played on him, he started (forgetting all his sanctity), and full of sentiments of revenge he jumped from his chair, with the pious determination to blow poor Peter D—p—t's (the groom-porter) brains out, and to call L—r, D—y, O'B—, Charley S—l, Jack P—t, Major B—r, Jack L—y, Buck L—ss, and a number of other Dupes and Blacklegs to a severe account; in fact nothing but blood and slaughter was to be dealt around; however, by all accounts, the matter ended with poor D—t's being knocked down and kicked by the Buck.

> The Duke of Brunswick and his mighty men,
> Went up the hill, and then came down again.

I once by mere accident at an Inn in Cashel, happened to breakfast in company with three very remarkable ladies and their husbands, *Moll Roe, Ally Croker,* and *Kate of Aberdeen,* all celebrated beauties in their time, but then converted into old married ladies by the names, styles, and titles of Mrs Walsh, wife to a captain Walsh of the county Tipperary, a virtuous worthy woman, notwithstanding that highly obscene and ridiculous song, beginning with,

> I met Moll Roe in the morning,
> Her tail it was draggled with dew, &c.

which was composed on her out of mere fun by a Popish priest. Mrs Langley, wife to Charles Langley, Esq; of Lisnerock in the county of Tipperary, also, was the famous *Ally Croker,* and a Mrs Mercer the lady of Major Mercer, was the beautiful Kate of Aberdeen. To make up the peerless quartetto, I made bold to add the name of the celebrated Margaret Leeson, and I actually left the four names on a pane of glass in poor Bob Keating's parlour.

I recollect once I was in Belfast with my first love, at the time of *Thurot's* landing at Carrickfergus, a number of French officers were on their *parole* in that town, and were treated with the greatest attention, hospitality and politeness by the inhabitants. At a very large entertainment, given by the late worthy *Joe Wallace,* all the French gentlemen having been invited, one in particular (anxious to know as much of our language as he possibly could) went into the kitchen, and enquired of the surly cook the names of several dishes, and at length asking her the name of a *plate,* in *English,* the cook tired with his ridiculous interrogatories answered, – 'C— Monsieur,' – the Frenchman happy in being able to converse a little in English, happened to sit near a Miss T—y, an old maiden tabby, who had finished the leg of an hare she had been help'd to, which the officious attentive polite Frenchman observing, said to her, 'Mademoiselle T—y, you have got no *hare* upon your C—', meaning her plate, which occasioned Miss T—y's precipitate retreat, to the no small diversion of the company, who were highly entertained with the Frenchman's blunder, and the old maid's confusion, which was the greater, as Monsieur by all accounts happened to stumble on the *truth.* It is worthy of remark that the identical officer mentioned here, when the fire of musketry was going on in the principal street in Carrickfergus, between the English troops under major Jennings and the French, a child of about 6 years of age, ran out among them to see what was going on, and narrowly escaped being shot; with great presence of mind he quitted the battle, took up the child in his arms, and carried him back to the house, and then rejoined the ranks. A piece of humanity that a modern Frenchman would blush to own. This anecdote though very little known now, was in great measure the cause of the very handsome reception the French officers met with afterwards in Belfast.

I once had the pleasure of the company, for one night, of the facetious Ned Townsend of White-hall in the county Cork, who told me the following anecdote: A French gentleman, Monsieur Le Roque, happened to be on a visit with him for several days, and his custom was the instant the cloth was removed, he retired to the garden to smoke his pipe, in consequence of which always on his return the ladies used to teize him by their enquiries of, – 'Captain where have you been?' 'Where do you go always after dinner?' 'You're certainly courting some of the tenants' daughters,' &c. &c. &c. The poor Frenchman on these enquiries, not one of which he understood a syllable of, was always mute, and on his telling the distress he felt, on not being able to satisfy the ladies, to his hospitable entertainer, Mr Townsend replied, – 'Why Captain when those inquisitive girls ask you again, tell them the honest truth, that you were F—g.' – The Frenchman highly pleased, that he knew how to answer the ladies, was impatient till he put his newly acquired learning into practice, and accordingly on his return the next day after taking his whiff, all the ladies were open mouthed with, – 'O! Captain where were you? what were you doing? &c. &c.' – '*Me phas F—g;*' replied the innocent Captain. 'Oh! fye, Captain,' said one of the gentlemen, 'don't say so.' – 'Upon my *vord I tell de truth; me phas only F—g,* and Mr T—d here can vouch for me if he pleases.' This set the table in a roar, put La Roque into the greatest confusion, and obliged the ladies with a smothered laugh to withdraw; Ned T—d vociferously roaring out, – 'The devil mend you girls, the devil mend you.'

When in Tralee along with a gentleman, we happened to be at a horse race where was a most beautiful and charming young lady, Miss Eliza Paine, since married to a Mr F—r; this gentleman when courting her, among a variety of little *Jeu d'Esprit* that he addressed to her, and which he daily communicated to me (being on terms of great intimacy with my gentleman), was the following:

> Whilst some seek out for *glory,* others *gain,*
> My wish is somewhat *strange;* to be IN *Paine.*

And sure enough he soon was to his heart's content, for they were shortly after married, and in nine months after, she was brought to bed of *three children,* who were all healthy, and lived.

The unfortunate prodigal and spendthrift Sir Henry Echlin, who ran through an estate of four thousand pounds a year, besides about ten thousand pounds in ready cash, by *sheer eating and drinking,* and afterwards was reduced to the sad alternative of a subaltern revenue employment, with a salary of about forty pounds a year, once at my house compared himself to an *Earth-quake:* 'An *Earth-quake,* Sir Henry,' said I, 'how so?' – 'because, Peg,' replied he, 'I have *swallowed up* above *five thousand* acres of land – did you ever hear of any earth-quake doing much more?' If this was an extemporaneous thought, 'twas extremely witty; but were I to take notice of all the flashes of wit, and brilliant *bon mots* that passed in my presence, I could furnish my readers with a much larger, better and more genuine collection, than Joe Millar's and Edwin's Eccentricities, put together.

I had for a number of years a man and a maid servant, who were man and wife, and who served me very faithfully, but she happened to be so *prolific,* that regularly every year she was brought to bed in my house. I jocularly remonstrated with the man, why he brought such a continual expence and trouble on himself? When he answered with a true Cork brogue, – 'Yerrow why now my jewel now, how can we help it? I wish YOU, or some honest good natured Christian would *cut out of us both,* the *means* of getting any more, for 'pon my soul now I'm tired of the work, for it brings nothing but trouble and vexation, and runs away with all our earnings besides now.'

This brings to my recollection an anecdote, told me by the late Sir John C—t of Ardrum in the county of Cork; in presence of one of his tenants who came to pay him some rent, he desired his lady *pro tempore,* Miss C—t—es, to be exact in waking him early in the morning, to go on some very particular business; she protested it was not in her power, as she generally slept so sound, that 'twas late every day before she awoke; when they were interrupted by the well meaning countryman, who in the honest simplicity of his heart begged to be heard: 'Pon my soul my Lady, when *I wants* to get up at the first light, *I houlds my water over night,* and I never found it to fail, and if you will try yourself to night, I'll be bound for it you will wake Sir John early enough.'

For the honour of the lady's memory I cannot omit relating an anecdote heard of that suffering pattern of her sex, the late Mrs Francis Gr—ff—th; soon after her unfortunate husband was liberated from a long confinement, by a *nonsuit* he obtained against his infamous plaintiff, who was afterwards disrobed for malpractices; a *Doctor Kelso,* of harmless memory, a near relation of the late Jos – called upon them, just as they were sitting down to a frugal meal of bacon and peas soup; Mr Grif—th, though generally hospitable in the extreme, on eyeing what was for himself, his wife, son and maid, and not thinking it quite enough, did not even ask the doctor to sit down; however, it was not so with his highly respected and admired wife, she asked the doctor to partake of what they had? [*sic*] And he '*nothing loth,*' not having tasted a morsel for three successive days, sat down and greedily devoured, not only the bacon and soup, but all the bread, butter and cheese in the house, with two *potted herrings* into the bargain. With astonishment and hunger poor G—ff—th beheld the mighty havock and devastation, and as soon as the *learned doctor* had taken his leave, and as they sat down to tea and toast, to make up for the loss of dinner; he asked

Mrs G—th, – 'Why then my dearest Fanny (considering we had such very short commons,) why could you think of asking that *wretched hungry Doctor* to dine with us?' – 'For the very reason,' replied the angelic woman, 'that he was both *wretched and hungry.*' – Let this *answer of hers* be *enrolled in* the *registry* of *Heaven.* Did *Sterne,* the *immortal Sterne,* ever write or say any thing half so sentimental? But she really was as the poet says:

> The *best of mothers* and the *best of wives,*
> The best of *friends,* – she led the best of lives.

CHAPTER EIGHT

[*Peg retires, attempts suicide, fails, and finds religion*]

ONE EVENING I HAD the favour of a visit from two remarkable gentlemen, a Mr B— and a Mr T—lb—t; however, being in no very good humour, and having read an account in some of the public prints, of their having refused to pay an unfortunate gentleman (who had through necessity set up a paper) for their *Election Advertisements,* amounting to upwards of sixty pounds, I absolutely refused entertaining such unprincipled fellows, telling them freely my mind, and giving them as good a lecture on the heinousness of such gross dishonesty, as either *Wesley* or *Whitfield* could have done, nay, I doubt if the divine Kirwan's admonitions (whom I perfectly adore) would have struck so great a panic into the hearts of my depraved beaux, as my ex-tempore rhapsody did; indeed to use a vulgar expression, I sent them off with a flea in their ear; and in fact I preached so much to these gentlemen, that I absolutely wound myself into a fit of enthusiasm; I took an horrible retrospective view of the course I had run, and all of my past life; and falling on my knees, addressed myself most devoutly to the God of nature, – 'Omniscient Father of all,' cried I, 'does *Peg Leeson* (or rather Peg *Plunket,* for I could have no legal claim to *Leeson,* having never been really married but to Y—,) set up for a reformer of Men and Manners? – The depraved, the wretched, the prostituted, the polluted Peg; does she, I say, presume to preach up morality to *would-be senators* and *highborn men?* the wretch who has reduced herself below the dignity of almost any of the animals of thy numerous and wonderful creation; for there's not creatures of the four-footed tribe, would go indiscriminately from male to male, and suffer perhaps a score in four and twenty hours to enjoy their favours; and yet this, wretched abandoned Peg, thou hast done, oh! horrid! horrid! – what a sink of infamy, thou hast been all thy life in, – in vain you may solace yourself with the idea of your being charitable, humane, compassionate, tender hearted; of what avail are all those virtues to a blasphemous prostitute? Who shared her charms indiscriminately with every ruffian who could afford a price.' These reflections made a deep impression on my mind and spirits; I offered up my Orisons to an offended Deity, I contemplated in my mind the blessings I had let slip: Heavens, said I, what happiness had been my lot, had I observed my honoured parents! had I been married young to some worthy man, I might now have been blessed with a smiling happy progeny, whereas I shall leave nothing behind me but the traces of my infamy, to hand down my abandoned name to posterity; in all my life I have not secured a real friend; the prostitutes my associates, and the libertines whose caresses I submitted to, all despise me; to add to my distress, I felt an oppression, a load upon my spirits, that I could not shake off, and in a fit of delirium I drank four ounces of *thebiad tincture,* and thought I had at once made my own *quietus;* but how was I mistaken, the deceitful opium worked no such effect, I found myself extremely weak; grew sick in my stomach and threw up a deal of stuff, after which I lay in a state of stupefaction, without taking the least nourishment for upwards of eight and forty hours, when in a languid state I arose, utterly detesting my own existence, and regreting that the *opium* did not take the desired effect, and bring me to my *eternal rest.* M'Clean and Miss Sands, one of her lively *virgins,* called upon me almost as soon as I was dressed, not hearing of my indisposition, with an intent that I should take them to *Laughlinstown camp,* but I excused myself, and instead of trifling with them as usual, gave them a severe lecture on their past lives; which made them imagine I had lost my senses; but I persisting in my exhortations, they both burst into immoderate laughter, and ran out of the house, almost in convulsions. As soon as they had left me, I locked myself up, and rather devoutely praying for very near an hour, wrote the following ex-tempore verses addressed to the Deity:

I.
Where e'er, O God, I turn my eyes,
Thy wisdom is display'd;

E'en I myself – myself surprise,
So fearfully I'm made.

II.
If to the deep I bend my sight,
The long extended main
Bids me to tremble at his might,
Who can its force restrain.

III.
The nurse and *grave,* old mighty *earth,*
His power immense declare;
Who with a *Fiat,* gave thee birth,
And flung thee in the air.

IV.
Who made your mountains and your rocks,
'Tis he who daily fills,
With horn'd herds, and fleecy flocks,
Your islands and your hills.

V.
But what are herds and flocks to those,
His bounty doth supply,
The creatures of ten thousand globes,
Beyond the mortal eye.

VI.
And the creation over past,
Where night and silence reign;
The great interminable vast,
     Is all his wide domain.

VII.
In various wonders I am lost,
And yet the subjects fire;
For to applaud you – oh! thou know'st,
Is all my soul's desire.

VIII.
Till at thy nod, with great amaze,
We'll see this nether world,
Burst all at once into a blaze,
Again to Chaos hurled.

IX.
Lord fit us all for that dread day,
Oh! may we then appear;

223

(When all your glory you display,)
Fit objects of your care.

X.
Immortal placed in realms above,
We'll view all nature run,
Within due bounds, – nor *Venus* move,
Too near the *evening Sun.*

XI.
All sects, all kinds must own thy sway,
And each alike you'll bless;
Who at thy grand tribunal day,
Thy talent did increase.

XII.
The dreadful thunders when they roll,
Thro' clouds and air disturbed;
And storms of hail from pole to pole,
Intended for our good.

XIII.
The cattle bound about the land,
E'en four-foot creatures dread;
The thunder falling from the hand,
Of him, who all had made.

XIV.
To fright the tyrant on his throne,
To shew a power above;
    And wake the peasant when alone,
To praise his God with love.

Had lady Arabella Denny lived, a lady who has left but one like herself behind, *Mrs Latouche;* that paragon of *charity, piety* and *humanity,* I would have given all I possessed to the *Magdalen asylum,* and retired into it myself. In fact I did not know how to act, I was determined as I said before, to shake off my profligate acquaintance, both male and female, and gracious heaven! where was there to be found a reputable one, who would associate with the abandoned *Peg Plunket?* Oh! piteous case, that no penitence, no contrition for past levities can atone for a lapse from virtue – the wretched *Magdalen,* has no Saviour now to take her to his bosom; if she is poor she must continue so, for our ladies *of virtue* are *too delicate,* too *sentimental,* too refined, to succour or give bread, or encouragement to an honest W— who was in the possession of more good and amiable qualities, than ever fell to the lot of such made up Automatons of the day, – '*Sans face, sans teeth, sans shape, sans hair, sans principles, sans everything.*' – Being deserted now by all the world, I was resolved to take refuge in the sanctuary of religion; and being bred a *Catholic,* I immediately sent for the Rev. Dr *Leonard,* who administered every divine consolation to me in his power, and indeed I found all comfort in his spiritual advice; at the same time I must premise to my readers, that I was no bigot to sect or religion; I believed the honest *Indian,* or the wild *African,* who worshipped his God his own way, was as sure of salvation, provided he improved the talent God had endowed him with, in worthiness and charity, as his holiness the Pope of Rome. In fact all religions were alike to me, but as I had been brought up in the *Catholic persuasion,* and had never known a preacher of the word of that religion, to frequent my house – whereas it always swarmed with abandoned Abbies of the established church. I thought it safer to confide in them, than in men, most of whom had connections, if not with myself, with poor creatures in my house. As for my creed, I honestly declare I do not believe in any one I ever read or heard of. 'I religiously and devoutly believe in one true and only God, and no other; and I farther believe, that in deeds of charity, humanity, and benevolence, I go the readiest way to please and honor that all-seeing Being, who must delight in beholding the animals of his creation, made happy by the exertions of each other. In fact, I would wish to do unto all mankind as I would wish to be done by; I would also worship the God of nature, in spirit and in truth, no matter whether in a Mosque, a Meeting-house, Chapel, Church, Synagogue, bed or field; and THAT creed, in my opinion, will carry any poor sinner to the realms of bliss; – I hold good works, in great veneration, and can't agree with your Swaddling pretended devotees who exclaim: '*Only believe and yours is heaven.*' – At that rate, a person may rob and murder, and commit the greatest atrocities, no matter what, so they have Faith; but I say, 'Charity covers a multitude of sins,' – and faith, without good works, is like a garden without seed, which produces nothing but weeds and rubbish. I now kept entirely at home, and could have wished for the society of some amiable reduced gentlewoman, whom I might support in decency, and leave what I might die possessed of to. But what creature on earth, would become an intimate of mine? Oh! heavenly Virtue, how precious art thou, how much should you be valued, for when thou art gone, every place becomes an hell; conscience like a foul fiend, haunts the wretch who's deprived of thee, and hurries her from one extreme of wickedness to the other, till at last she's brought, like poor Vangable, of equestrian memory, to the very zenith of human misery!!!

VANGABLE, after leading a life of the greatest dissipation and debauchery, and after figuring away at Astley's Amphitheatre in Peter-street, and exhibiting her wonderful powers of horse-man-ship, to crouded and admiring audiences; she, I say, contracted every infamous disorder, and died not only rotten with venereal complaints, but to add to her misery, she was also afflicted with the Herodian distemper; and on the cold bed of death, requested I would give orders to have her put into a slit deal coffin, bor'd all over with holes, and have her taken about a league out to sea, and thrown into the ocean; such was her dying request, which I minutely complied with.

Alas poor Vangable.

Absent or dead, still let a friend be dear,
A sigh for absent claims, the dead a tear.

I wrote to my two friends, Mrs S— and Mrs Falvey, informing them of my reformation, and received very satisfactory letters from each, in which they extolled my resolution, and expatiated largely on their own domestic felicity; advising me to go off to England or Scotland, and that they had no doubt, from my agreeable manners and sweetness of temper, I would soon meet with a companion, who would render the remainder of my days happy: but alas! the idea of mankind became detestable to me;

I'd that within, which baffled human art,
A burning fever, – and a broken heart.

No, no, I was resolved never to venture on the shoals and quick-sands of matrimony; besides, in my opinion it would be baseness in the extreme, to go to a strange country, and palm myself upon any honest gentleman, as a woman of honor; who wretch like me, had trod in the paths of prostitution for upwards of thirty years, – Gracious Heaven!

The blackest ink of fate, was sure my lot,
And when she wrote my name, she made a blot.

CHAPTER NINE

[Peg's first companion in her retirement, Miss Eliza Edmonds,
debts owed to her, and some of her debtors, the success of the first
two volumes of the Memoirs, *and additional money trouble]*

IN MY ANSWER to Mrs Falvey, I requested she'd prevail on a Miss Eliza-
beth Edmonds, a poor young lady, whom I had got acquainted with at Kil-
larney, and who wished (thinking me a virtuous married lady) to be hired
as my waiting woman; however I then would not hear of it, as Pitt-street
house, at that time, would be a bad asylum for my sweet black-eyed senti-
mental girl; I now however thought she'd prove a great acquisition in my
retirement; and entreated my dear Betsy Falvey to send her to me without
delay, – and accordingly in about a month afterwards, I was made happy in
the agreeable society of my poor dear Betsy, who had, herself wrestled with
adversity for several years, 'a woe worn daughter of affliction.'

[Elizabeth Edmonds]

MISS EDMONDS was the illegitimate daughter of the famous Billy the
Beau, so celebrated in the annals of gallantry; her mother's name was V—
y, whom the Earl, her father, debauched at the age of fifteen. Miss V—y
was at that time, one of the most beautiful creatures under Heaven, with
all the loves and graces sporting in her train; but notwithstanding all her
charms and a most excellent education (for her connections were as good
as her seducer's), she fell a prey to the 'insidious wiles of faithless man.'
Billy the Beau, triumphed over her virtue, in consequence of which my
poor Betsy Edmonds, this child of sorrow from her infancy, made her
melancholy debut in this world; her mother died in consequence of her
birth: the blame entirely resting upon little L—hy an unskilful country
Accoucheur, than whom, nature herself had proved a better. The death of
Miss V—y was a source of affliction to the noble Earl of G—, my Betsy's
father, who took all imaginable care of the little darling; and when she
arrived at a proper age, put her to one of the best schools in the city of

Cork, where he sent her for her education; and where in the commence-
ment of her teens, she unfortunately became acquainted with one
Edmonds, the natural son of a gentleman of an immense fortune of that
name, – who thinking his fortune would be made by a connection with so
rare and choice a sprig of nobility, found means to carry her off, vi et armis,
to the county of Clare, where they were married by a Couple Beggar; as
Edmonds was really a pretty gentleman, poor Betsy in a very short time
became perfectly satisfied with her lot, and having often solicited her hus-
band for a legal marriage, as no licence could be obtained, the banns were
called publicly in church, three different times, when they were indissol-
ubly tied, with all the forms of the established church, before a crouded
congregation, in the parish church of Ennis in the county of Clare. In vain
did poor Betsy sue to her noble father for forgiveness; and as fruitless were
Edmond's applications to the author of his being: The miserable though
beautiful pair, were left to shift for themselves, and drag out a wretched
existence, in penury and want. Poor Mrs Edmonds had three children who
died almost as soon as born; and her husband at length, though doatingly
fond of her, yet as he could not support her equal to his wishes, he joined a
marching regiment just going off to America, to fight those sons of Free-
dom, who by their exertion in the glorious cause, obtained emancipation
from the mother country, and was killed at Bunkers Hill: where many a
gallant youth, as well as Edmonds, and the unfortunate Jonas Griffith
(whose head was shot off fighting at Edmonds's side) paid the great debt of
nature most prematurely. Poor Edmonds and Griffiths went off volunteers
together, obtained Ensigncies the same day; and lost their lives the day
after, fighting side by side; some of the fatal effects of that truly unfortunate
war, by which our country has irretrievably lost some of its most brave and
faithful inhabitants.

Some time after the death of Edmonds, his disconsolate relict, hired as
own woman to the late beautiful divine and elegant Mrs M—w, and went
with her to France: – where that stain to human nature, the parricidal
Orleans, whose will was absolute at that time, unfortunately grew enam-
oured with her incomparable mistress: which as soon as she became
acquainted with, in order to avoid his detested overtures and addresses, left
France, she and poor Betsy, in a cartel ship that was bound for England; –
and on the passage, oh! horrid to relate, the whole crew and prisoners,
amounting to upwards of sixty ruffians, mutinied against the captain and
officers of the vessel, whom they bound; and afterwards brutally ravished

the heavenly mistress, and her charming companion; every man of them alternately satisfying his infamous lust: in consequence of which, poor Mrs M—w languished in a melancholy situation for a few days, and died; leaving her fellow sufferer who survived her, her clothes, watch, a few trinkets, and a trifle of money; with which she retired to a farm-house near Killarney; where I luckily became acquainted with her, and from herself learned the mournful story, which was most dreadful, as several of the miscreants who had committed the foul crime, laboured under a certain disorder; in consequence of which Mrs Edmonds was obliged to have recourse to medical assistance: – as would be the case with her angel mistress, had not the great disposer of all things, in pity, taken her to himself.

> Sweet suffering faint, dear innocent, adieu,
> Angels were painted fair to look like you.

Soon after Mrs Edmonds's arrival, I found my affairs much embarrassed: – I certainly had in bonds, promissory notes, and I o's, upwards of two thousand pounds due to me; but what value could be set upon the obligations of unprincipled men of fashion, and a parcel of abandoned prostitutes; – in fact my affairs were so very much deranged, I was under the disagreeable necessity of disposing of my house and furniture in Pitt-street, and removing with my friend to my new house on the Black-rock road; which the produce of my Pitt-street house, &c. enabled me to fit up in a comfortable manner; and where we lived in a pleasing retirement, with only a little girl to attend us; as I would by no means suffer Mrs Edmonds (though she offered her services,) to undergo any more slavery than myself. In this place the thought first struck me, of publishing my chequered Memoirs, as my ready cash was fast diminishing imperceptably away; and all my bonds, and securities for money, could not procure me a shilling, many of which I placed in the hands of rascally vile attornies; in return for which, I was furnished with bills of costs, and insolent threatning letters. Thus circumstanced, my only source for profit and revenge was the publication of my unfortunate life; resolving to publish the names of several persons to whom I was indebted for my ruin, in the last volume: and so I certainly will, as 'tis rather cruel that my substance should be lavished among a parcel of people, whose ideas do not extend farther than the brute creation. H— B— after living upon me for years (he and his husseys), only sneers at me when I present his bond to him for payment; and such is the case with T— H—, W— T— G—, W— B—, Rich— W—, M— O'C—, Jack B— of Wexford, a simple gentleman, a surveyor of Excise at Tralee; the late self dubbed Knight, and the old B—, who returned the late worthy C— M— for a seat in his borough, for a certain valuable consideration, in favor of his shem gregis, Mr O'B—, another limb of the law; who thought it damn'd hard to be obliged to pay at my house, a guinea and a half for a bowl of Turtle soup and a flask of sparkling champaigne, which the unpolished boor called eel broth and perry; no bad substitute by the bye for these luxuries. Two wooden headed Aldermen who were scarcely ever out of my house. Squire B—, a sheriff's peer, and Mr B— an heel rubbing Catiff, who, under pretence of recovering debts for me, cheated me of upwards of fifty pounds; another celebrated gentleman, famous in story, who was disrobed in all the Courts, equal to an exhibition in the pillory, and thrown for life into Newgate. Mr K—, that precious pander, who not only robbed me of my profession by setting up in my line, but run a bill with me to a considerable amount, without the smallest notion of paying; and C—, who plundered me under cover of an Insolvent act; and one Coleman, who acted as my waiter for very near two years, carried off effects to a considerable amount; – with a number of others, who owe me among them very near three thousand pounds, for all which I have specialties to produce. Relative to my Memoirs, when I had the two first volumes ready I sent them about to my particular friends in trade, whom I had dealt with; and they all behaved extremely liberal on the occasion: and for which I shall ever retain the most grateful acknowledgements; in fact all the gentlemen in business were every thing I could wish. I merely sent the two volumes to them sealed up and directed without any card or letter, and I never got a smaller return from any one of them than a guinea; so that by the publication, after paying all expences, I found I had cleared upwards of *six hundred guineas,* but what signified that sum to a woman who knew not how to turn it to any sort of use; one of an extravagant turn, who never knew what oeconomy was; and who always as she got money very lightly (light come light go), threw it away as it came, like the amiable *Desdemona,* when in confinement in the Four-courts Marshalsea, who having received a benefaction of one guinea from the late worthy Robert Shaw, send the entire out for a *brace of woodcocks* and a *flask of champaigne,* though 'twas well known, neither she or her poor husband had tasted a morsel for two days before. Oh! the depravity of human nature; would it not have been much better for the pretty Desdemona, to have sent out for a leg of mutton, a loaf of bread, a quart of the *pure native,* or a pot or two of porter, and a little tea and sugar: – but there is no accounting for these things. As I said before, my resources for getting money were all dried up, in a very short time. I began for the first time in my life to feel accute distress; while my money lasted poor Edmonds and I lived luxuriously, though quite within ourselves; for except a few mendicants whom I always relieved, we scarcely admitted any others: – the virtuous and the good I could not expect, and the vicious I was determined to shun. By degrees all my finery, went to the Pawnbrokers; above a dozen miniature pictures, beautifully set, for which I scarce got the value of the gold; my repeater set round with brilliants, with a number of diamond rings of very great value, all went the same road merely to eke out a loathed existence. At length one morning when all was gone, and even the duplicates sold for what they would bring; Edmonds and I was sitting very melancholy over the dying embers of a wretched fire; when a woman I had often dealt with for *East India goods, teas, lawns, china, &c.* a Mrs *Deborah O'Dowd*, formerly *Debby Casey*, a very pretty little ginger, who had been seduced when very young by a Mr Y— of the county Kerry, by whom she had one son, now an eminent physician of great repute: and after marrying one Dowd a tobacco twister, a very uncouth brute of a fellow, poor Debby was in the habit of granting favours to such gentlemen, as she really had an esteem for, and who were her customers. I say this girl having found out where I lodged, and being also well acquainted with Mrs Edmonds, called to know if I wished for any thing in her way? And on my answering with tears glistening in my eyes, that I had not where-with-all to buy our breakfast, much less to purchase fineries of any kind: the good-natured creature insisted on her lending me half her stock of cash, amounting to ten guineas, and besides made me a present of a pound of Gunpowder-tea, and two beautiful India shawls, one to each of us; and though sorely distressed, we were sometime before we could be prevailed upon to receive such compliments from our pretty petty chapwoman; – however, at last like Romeo's apothecary, 'our necessities but not our wills complied.' Very shortly after that supply was nearly exhausted, a young fellow, a quandom [*sic*] footman of mine, brought me (prefacing his present with, 'I hear you are writing books Madam,') a quire of gilt paper, a bottle of ink, a pen-knife, a bundle of pens, and his *whole quarter's wages*, amounting to two guineas, at the same time blubbering like a child, after ejaculating, – 'Good Heaven did I ever think it would have come to this. You my ever honoured mistress, who were good and charitable to every creature who appeared distressed.' 'Twas in vain I urged the impossibility of my bringing myself capable of accepting the wages of the poor honest fellow's labour; all would not do; he declared he had no use for the money, and would take it much to heart if I refused his little mite; hinting that surely it would never lessen my consequence, in accepting a trifle from a *poor creature*, who had formerly owed so much to my bounty and humanity; for the poor lad took a bad fever when with me in Pitt-street, and I need not tell my readers I had every possible care taken of him; and he deserved nothing else from me, having been always an honest, faithful good servant. At last I accepted of his affectionate offering, which affected not only me, but Mrs Edmonds so much, that we both shed tears of gratitude; and I poured forth my acknowledgements to my party coloured friend with the greatest candour and sincerity; and little as his present was, it enabled us to dine and spend the day comfortably; which would not have been the case had not divine providence thrown him in my way; and I must confess, that the all-seeing Power was ever good to me, and that I never was in imminent distress, that some channel or another did not open for my relief; however I now found myself in the very abyss of misery, for having occasion to go to Fleet-street in order to settle for a debt I owed Mr O'B— a wine merchant: I was arrested for £15, at the suit of a Grocer in Grafton-street, by Matthews my quandom [*sic*] friend, who had once figured away at one of the masquerade balls, in the character of *Serjeant Kite*, he carried me to his spunging-house, without a shilling in my pocket, or any means left for subsistence; and my very bed in the hospitable purlieus of a Spunging-house, would be two shillings a night, with perhaps a bed-fellow or two if there was a necessity, forced upon me in the bargain.

CHAPTER TEN

*[At the spunging house in Angel Court: the charity of Captain
Mathews, meeting an old flame (Purcell, of Plummer's Island),
the death of Betsy Edmonds, and Peg's rescue by Mr Falvey]*

IN THIS *HOPELESS, HELPLESS* situation I remained 'till towards night, when my faithful friend, Mrs Edmonds came to me with a supply of cakes, wine, tea and sugar, which the honest soul procured by the impawnment of all the little remains of her *wearing apparel*. That evening a very pretty little woman was shewn into our apartment, who though a *married woman* and even a *femme couverte* (such is the glorious uncertainty of the law,) was arrested for about eleven pounds; and to aggravate her misfortune, she was arrested by a ruffian of the name of Mooney, who with the look of a hangman, and the manners of a Yahoo, took her into custody; and with the most dreadful imprecations threatened to drag her through the streets to his own villainous lock-up-house, if she did not immediately give him five guineas: this mode of extorting money, and which is his constant custom, she was well acquainted with; but knew it was contrary to law[*] ; and absolutely refused to go to his house, where she knew every imposition was put in practice against the unfortunate prisoners; however as this miscreant found she was firmly determined not to go to his infamous dirty and loathsome house, sooner than put her into the sheriff's goal, committed her to the care of one of his own tribe, Mr Matthews, who if it is possible to be respectable in such a profession, is so in a very high degree: and I am proud to pay a tribute of acknowledgment to his worth and humanity, as I had an opportunity of witnessing his, and his worthy familys' tenderness to a number of unfortunate prisoners.

This debt was incurred by obtaining necessaries for her infamous husband, in the Fourcourts-marshalsea. On our beginning to *cotton together*, to use a vulgar expression; for I could not help taking a liking to her, as she was a beautiful little woman: she told me her father was steward to the Right Hon. Mr C—, and a man of much wealth; that at the age of fourteen she was married to one Mulligan, who conducted business for an eminent brewer in this city; – that Mulligan (who was old enough to be her father,) by extravagance and dissipation of every kind, was thrown into the Fourcourts Marshalsea before they had been married two years, where they both got acquainted with a counsellor S—, who was married to an old lady, a Mrs E—, who in order to preserve her jointure (particularly circumstanced,) never acknowledged her marriage; the consequence of which was, she was also a prisoner as well as her spouse; both for very considerable sums. That as the counsellor and his lady, to save appearances, had separate apartments in the marshalsea, and never were known to sleep together; he, as a person will, 'kiss the child for sake of the nurse,' became seemingly very much attached to her husband, had him every day, and

---

*This despicable CATCHPOLE had been convicted for a practice of this kind, and suffered three months imprisonment besides a fine.

consequently herself to breakfast, dine and sleep; and at last for, and in consideration of his giving up all his right and title of her, and a house of her's near Mount Brown, S— gave him two hundred pounds, but not before Mulligan formally put the lawyer in full and ample possession of the premisses. She told me her nefarious husband had frequently put S— and her to bed together, tucked them in, and upon taking away the candle wished them – 'a pleasant night.' – She also informed me, that the cause of her present imprisonment, which certainly was illegal in the extreme, was for groceries, and other things which she had taken up to support her vile husband and self, before she had got under the patronage of S—. She also acknowledged she never loved or esteemed S—, no more than she did her husband; as she really might be the grand-daughter of either of them, being then but two-and-twenty; that revenge (what wont an injured woman do,) was the cause of her succumbing to the vile adulterous bargain. In fact she told me both her husband and Cicesbeo had been liberated by an Insolvent act; and her husband being applied to for payment of the goods she had procured for his use when in durance vile: and he not only refused payment, but denied her to be his wife; she was in consequence arrested by virtue of a writ marked against her, by an infamous fellow one J. B—, who had been a brother prisoner with her husband; and had also like him, been enlarged by virtue of the Insolvent act. I could not help pitying, and admiring this poor artless creature, who was plunged into every complicated misery by her base husband. Our society was farther enlivened by the company of an agreeable girl, Miss F—, who had been seduced and brought from England by a nobleman, who soon cast her off: when she was reduced to the necessity of turning common street-walker for subsistence; and having ran a bill with a Milliner to a considerable amount, at the time she was in keeping by his lordship. She was, poor creature, a stranger and desolate, – thrown into the very same Spunging-house with us. As was also a very fine gay fellow, an English lad, one Jessop, who held a genteel appointment in the castle, immediately under the secretary; – and he being much smitten with the charms of his country woman, married her in the prison; in consequence of which, she was at liberty to go where she pleased: and very shortly afterwards through the dexterity and influence of an amorous judge, obtained his liberty, and returned with him to England where I was told he was shortly afterwards executed, for swindling a merchant out of a considerable sum of money. Poor Mrs Mulligan, also, did not remain with us more than a week, when her honest father hearing of her distressed situation, procured bail for her, – with an intent to litigate the debt, and bring her husband if possible to condign punishment. During all these transactions, my poor friend (who never quit me but to bring me relief,) and I, spent our time in extreme misery; often times being obliged to our friendly keeper and his wife for a breakfast and dinner: a breakfast and dinner: – indeed, I must acknowledge Matthews's civility, who relaxed much from the severity of the character of the keeper of a lock-up-house with regard to me: suffering my poor friend to share my bed, without any extra charge, and inviting us to dine, sup or breakfast, whenever he observed us in want of cash. While I remained there, the widow of a captain P—d also joined our society, a beautiful sentimental woman, who soon connected herself with one of the first Portrait-painters in Europe, a Mr W— R—n, by whom she proved pregnant. It may not be incurious here, to inform my readers, of some anecdotes of this celebrated artist, who once kept his carriage and suite of servants, and lived in the greatest style. A Mrs M— a married lady, and one of the most beautiful of women, sat to him for her portrait; which when finished, he refused giving her, saying, – 'He could not think of parting with it, as like another Pygmalion he had absolutely fallen in love with the work of his own hands.' – 'That is something strange,' replied the lady, 'when you might so easily gain possession of the original.' – 'Why madam,' said the painter, 'I always understood you had been married to Mr M—?' 'So I was,' said she, 'but our marriage was never consummated, nor never will, for he is totally impotent; we have been married now upwards of five years, and he never had any more connection with me than you had.' – The painter took the lady at her word; a separation legally and immediately took place, and thy were indissolubly joined in Hymenial fetters, to both their satisfaction. She soon after the birth of her first child, shared her favors with a certain judge, long since defunct; to the no small grief of Mr R—n, who perfectly adored her: – during his confinement at Matthews's, his lady never paid him a visit, however he retaliated upon her, for her indifference, by his close attachment to the agreeable widow, who afterwards died in child-bed, in consequence of that amour; – and R—n and his wife, her paramour the judge, being dead, as I mentioned before, are gone to Philadelphia, where by what I can learn, they live in happiness and splendour. As Mrs R—n never had any connection with any person but her husband, save the *honourable judge*, with whom she appeared publicly about from place to place, and sometimes to the knowledge of poor R—n; sleeping with him at his lodgings, and entertaining him for days and nights together in R—n's own houses, both in town and country; for he had built many elegant houses, and was in the receipt of near two thousand pounds a year, when he married her.

I need not depict to my fair readers my dreadful situation; though at the same time I must premise that had I not reformed, I would not have been thus abandoned and distressed. While I led a vicious course of life I had friends in abundance, but the moment I turned my thoughts to virtue, I was deserted by all, except a few of the worthy citizens of Dublin, with whom I had honestly dealt for a number of years, and indeed I must own that Providence, in whom I put my entire confidence did not totally desert me: – One evening as Mrs Edmonds and I were drinking tea with our landlady, a prisoner was introduced, at first I took no sort of notice of him, not even lifting up my eyes at his approach; and as for my part, I was so entirely altered both in dress and appearance, that it was impossible for him to distinguish the gay, the volatile *Peg Leeson*, in wretchedness, misery and rags, in a lock-up-house: – at last upon Mrs Matthews pressing me to take another cup: I ventured to look up, and to my inexpressible astonishment, beheld in the person of the prisoner my friend Purcell, with whom I had spent so agreeable, so extatic a day on *Plummer's Island*; – the instant I recollected him our guilty commerce flashed on my senses like an electric shock, and I fainted away, when he running to my assistance, at last recollected the features of the woman, with whom not many years since he had spent such agreeable days; he also remembered Edmonds, whom he had often seen with me at Killarney; and fater recovering me from the fit, and kindly embracing me, and saluting Edmonds, he gave us to understand, how sorry he was to meet us in that situation: assuring me I should never want a shilling, while he had one, and that he would divide his last guinea with me. After making him a suitable return for his kind enquiries, good wishes and offers; I made him a low distant courtesy, and retired: but I was not long in my apartment, when he followed me and taking me aside, hoped I had no objection to give him part of my bed; which I peremptorily refused, but not with any degree of resentment; as how could I be displeased with such a request from a man who had so often enjoyed all my charms unrestrained? – A man whose caresses I met more than half way; no, I argued with him in a mild manner, I told him my resolution had been fixed as fate, and that for the remainder of my wretched life, no man should ever take the smallest liberties with me: – that I was really a thorough penitent, and should die so. When he found I was determined, he dropped his suit with the proviso, that as I would not share my bed with him, I must at least submit to suffer him to share his purse with me. With which proposal, with great reluctance I complied: – on which he reckoned the contents of his purse, which amounted to twenty-five guineas; thirteen of which he threw into my lap. The next morning I sent Edmonds out to redeem some necessaries of ours, that she had pawned since our incarceration, and which indeed we could very badly do without. The addition of Mr Purcell's company much enlivened our society, as he was a very agreeable entertaining man, who abounded with anecdotes; he also sung very pleasingly, and had a pretty taste for poetry; which he proved by the following impromptu; – which he sung upon receiving a visit from a Miss Dorathea A—g of the county Clare, – to the tune of the well known song, of the

PRISONER'S WELCOME

I.

Welcome, welcome sweet Dorinda,
 To this gloomy dismal place;
 You illumine more than window,
 By the bright'ning ray, your face.

II.

Grieve not at my situation,
 Nor repine at Heaven's decree;
 Providence, my preservation,
 Will me from this prison free.

III.

Breathe to him a fervent prayer,
 Innocence does claim regard;
 Heaven will grant your boon sincere,
 And your friendly aid reward.

IV.

I feel the aid, implored already,
 Comfort sent me from the skies;
 Such as charm'd my heart sweet lady,
 When I first beheld your eyes.

V.

Smile on charmer, since in smiling

You can happiness diffuse;
Stranger to the art beguiling,
Smile on Purcell and his muse.

And so she did, for in a few days the dear man was liberated, and finding me inexorable (as I am certain his attachment to me prevented him from entering into any matrimonial engagement,) he seriously paid his addresses to the divine Dora, as he called her, who had a large independent fortune, and led her to the alter [*sic*] of Hymen: – after which he went down with his charming bride to Ennis in the county Clare; where they are settled for life: but not before he made me another very liberal present with solemn assurances of future protection, and assistance; with an offer of an asylum in the county Clare, if I could be prevailed upon to accept of one; he also behaved very genteely to poor Edmonds, and promised her, she should not want a friend while he lived, on account of her fidelity to me and my ruined fortunes.

After his departure I employed one John F— a scoundrel, who had been several years a prisoner at Matthews's and else where, and had been indulged by Matthews to walk out, in consequence of becoming a setter for him, and upon occasion a bailiff: but this nefarious wretch, than whom a greater does not exist, served me as he did the unfortunate proprietor of the Phoenix, who unwittingly took him into his employment as a clerk, and in consequence was destroyed by his art and practices. This fellow after receiving several sums of my money, had himself removed by Habeas Corpus into the Four-courts Marshalsea; obtained the benefit of the late Insolvent act, and now with my property figures away as an eminent Pawn-broker, under pretence of having being left a fortune by a relation of his in the county of Kilkenny: worthless fellow, who was bred up a shoe-boy, and a pot-boy to a paltry ale-house; – and has lived upon rapine and plunder ever since.

An upstart miscreant fit for any job,
To tuck a felon, or to head a mob.

In vain was it that I sent about to all those who were indebted to me, and wrote melancholy letters to them descriptive of my deplorable situation; not one of them would deign to send even an answer to any of my supplicating epistles: – and I must have inevitably perished had it not been for (as I said before) the humanity of my keepers, and the benevolence of certain persons whom I had formerly dealt with; Mr Kennedy, of the

Waterford glass-house, Mr Tinkler paper-stainer, and Mr Corbet, of Great Britain-street: I also received some assistance from many of my old friends, Mr T. Swords, Mr Courtney and Mr Frank Higgins, Mr David Weir, the two Mr Marsh's, Mr Lefavre, Messrs Blackwoods, Mr Stanley, all the Beresfords, &c. &c. the humanity of these gentlemen to me was beyond praise, and which I acknowledge with heart felt gratitude, and I am sure I,

> Can plead no title to their favors past,
> And only wish for worth to make them last.

Mr Henegan of Mount Brown, Mr Manders of James's-street, the worthy captain Ormsby, governor of the Four-courts Marshalsea, the Rev. Mr K— and Doctor M'D— of the Meeting-house, Doctor T—, counsellors V— and M'N—, with those great luminaries of the law counsellors Egan and Curran: Mr John Magee of Swift's hospital; and all the principal gentlemen in the Printing and Bookselling trade, who not only encouraged the sale of my Memoirs, but greatly contributed by their exertion and recommendation to get the whole impression sold. These gentlemen also, were so kind as to set a subscription aflote[sic] for me, which produced a tolerable sum (great indeed,) in my present situation.

> *Qui nunc prescribere longum est.*

Some weeks after to add to my misfortune of imprisonment, which was with this blow advanced to the very zenith, my amiable friend, the good, the kind, the humane Betsy Edmonds, breathed her last in my arms; she died of a decline in the thirty fifth year of her age, in consequence of the severe usage she met with; and had it not been for the humanity of Captain Eyre, then a prisoner in the Four-courts marshalsea, I should not have known how to accomplish the interment, being again reduced to want: but I was determined this noble minded generous creature, should have every respect and attention paid to her remains; the kindness of the humane Captian enabled me to do so, and very handsomely.

> Sweet Betsy, 'whose like I never shall behold again –
> Peace to her gentle manes – She is gone to that
> country from whose bourne no traveller returns.'

After the loss of my Betsy, no human misery could equal mine, I gave myself up entirely to despair and often invoked the Almighty to take me to himself. My spiritual comforter frequently called to see me, and in his discourses I found my only consolation. In this situation I was meditating on my past life, when I was told a gentleman wished to see me in the parlour, and what was my surprise when on coming down I perceived my friend Falvey, who had kindly undertaken to settle my affairs without my knowledge and had compounded with all my creditors for about forty guineas, which he had collected, and above thirty more from the Whig-club. As he had undertaken my deliverance, he declared he would never quit me, till he brought me out, and accordingly, after settling with my kind keepers, who behaved very generously on the occasion, he called a coach, and ordering the driver to proceed to the Rock, where he had taken apartments for a month; to my inexpressable rapture; (for all was surprise to me, in fact like a dream,) he led me into an apartment where the first object that struck me, was his sweet, affectionate, affable, unassuming wife, who received me in the most friendly manner: – she informed me they had been in town (on law-business, which was happily terminated in their favor,) for near three months, that Mr Falvey had made many enquiries about me and poor Mrs Edmonds to no purpose, till at length he luckily called to see a friend of his, who was in the same sponging-house with me, where he heard of the death of Mrs Edmonds, of my melancholy situation and exemplary life; and immediately came to the resolution of having me liberated, though obliged to do it at his own expence: – and accordingly the next day after dining with a member of the Whig-club, he introduced my story, and immediately collected from these worthy characters upwards of sixty guineas: – his next object was to go among my creditors, and compound my debts, which was easily done, as they had given up all hopes of receiving any thing, thinking I must be shortly relieved by an Insolvent act, or by a wooden habeas, i.e. a coffin, as they were by no means unacquainted with my ill state of health. And here I must say that very few knew of my imprisonment, as it was generally rumoured and believed in the city, that I had paid the great debt of Nature; which circumstance was even mentioned in the public papers, this report I by no means contradicted, as it was more flattering to my pride (and I still possessed a share notwithstanding my misfortunes,) that the idea of my death got abroad, than that the public should be acquainted with the true cause of my sequestration from the world. My dear friend detained me at the Rock, but quite incog. for about three weeks, when they were obliged to set off in the Limerick stage, on their way to Kerry, but not before they had settled me in a comfortable lodging in Clarendon-street, and had taken care I had money sufficient, to serve me in a moderate manner for a month or two; at the same time advising me by all means to publish the third volume of my Memoirs without loss of time, assuring me they would use their endeavours to procure me a number of subscribers in the counties of Limerick, Cork, Kerry, Waterford, Tipperary and Clare; – and desired I would as soon as possible send them a number of my proposals, with proper receipts annexed.

CHAPTER ELEVEN

[Kindness from a former colleague, Peg pillaged by her servant Mary Neill, the Earl of Bristol to the rescue, an outing to Blackrock that went wrong, and a Crow Street benefit marred by cheats and spongers from Peg's past]

ON THEIR DEPARTURE I seriously set to work, and in less than three months had the materials for the volume ready for transcription; – living all the time quite retired, and seeing no creature except my priest and amanuensis, – the former of whom being of a liberal education, had the kindness to look over my manuscript and correct it: he told me the public were by no means well pleased with my former production, and that whoever my editor was, he did not avail himself of my hints and copy, as he should have done, and much regretted that he had not at that period the satisfaction of knowing me, as he should have endeavoured to render the work more worthy the public attention. There were a few more friends who had assisted me in my distress, and whom it would have been the highest ingratitude to be denied to: the only lady of my former acquaintance, who made any enquiries about me was Miss Love, who sent me several presents from time to time, and offered me (with the consent of her kind keeper,) an apartment in her house, if I thought proper to accept of it: But I was determined for the remainder of my life not to give the world the least handle to take hold of – I knew very well, That

> On eagles' wings immortal scandal fly,
> Whilst virtuous actions are but born and die.

And had I gone to lodge with the generous good-natured Miss Love, it would be immediately imagined that I had turned (like the dog to the vomit) to my old vicious course of life. I judged with Caesar, that 'it would not be sufficient for me to be honest, if all the world did not believe me to be so.' – Indeed I became so bashful, and had contracted within these few months past, so much of the *mouvaise honte,* [*sic*] as the French call it, that I absolutely was ashamed to be seen abroad; and I could not if I was offered a thousand pounds for it, sit one hour in my own *quandom* [*sic*] favourite box at the Theatre Royal: in fact from being a bold masculine ter-magant, I became one of the most timid mild creatures on earth, quite sen-timental, – without a sentence tending to lewdness or blasphemy. This will shew what custom can do: I, who had been in the habit of every vice for the space of thirty years and upwards, to be so reformed in the course of about a year and half: – Indeed I can attribute my wonderful reformation as supernatural, and an inspiration from the *God of nature himself;* only to conceive, that the whole *wonderful work* should originate, with my repri-manding two fashionable swindlers for dishonesty; and this puts me in mind of a story I heard at Bath, when I went there for an importation of *impures:* – A remarkable profligate, and a great blasphemer, was riding by a Catholic chapel, under very heavy thunder and lightning, and on seeing the poor people, on the road contiguous to the mass house, crossing and blessing themselves, he began to turn them into ridicule, by crossing his horse, cursing, swearing and gibing, when a flash of lightning struck him to the ground, and killed him on the spot; this caused a great alarm through the country, and every body concluded, – the *impious blasphemer* was overtaken by the vengeance of Heaven, and of course would *be damned.* But on the Sunday following, to the amazement of the gazing multitude, there was found growing on his grave (by the bye I believe it to be all fable,) a beautiful leaf, with the annexed exhortation and verse in let-ters of gold:

> *Don't judge, lest you should be judged.* For,

> 'Between the stirrup and the ground,
> 'I mercy craved, and mercy found.'

There can be no doubt of repentant sinners' finding mercy with their maker: – and I was determined not to trust in Chesterfield's wicked lines:

> Sin then, dear girl for Heaven's sake,
> Sin on, and be forgiven;

> Sin on, and by repentance make
> A holyday in Heaven.

As I could not with propriety make a personal application, I was determined to send my proposals every where; and accordingly thro' the medium of the Penny-post, enclosed them to every creature whose name I found in Wilson's Directory and Watson's Almanack; and from numbers received very handsome subscriptions: – I often wished I had as much *bronze* in my face, as Mrs J— E— M. the *English poetess,* who certainly is a credit to the *kingdom she came from;* then should I by my exertions, have realized a handsome fortune; but poor Mrs B-tt-r herself, that elegant charming sentimental writer, was never more timid or backward in forwarding a subscription than I was, I could certainly address any person by letter, but it was death to me to make a personal application. One evening in the dusk I muffled myself up, and ventured for the sake of the air, to take a walk in Stephen's-green, which was within a few yards of my lodging, and on my return, to my utter mortification and surprise, found a deserted unprotected girl I had hired to go of errands for me, had carried off all my clothes, with a small tea-chest, in which I had upwards of thirty guineas; being the full amount of the subscriptions I had received from friends, to whom I had enclosed my proposals, this was a severe blow I was by no means prepared for: Gracious God! exclaimed I, to what further miseries am I reserved! To have my all, I may say, taken from me, by an ungrateful wretch, whom I had taken in for charity; – the very identical *Mary Neill,* whom the unaccountable *Hamilton Rowan,* made such a ridiculous rout about. All I had left now was the two guineas, and a few shillings I had in my pocket, when I walked out, with the bare clothes on my back, which were the very worst I had, as I only wrapped an old plaid about me; the vile creature, who by what I learned afterwards was viciously inclined, did not even leave me a change of linen. Mrs T— indeed, my good-natured landlady, did all she could to comfort me, assuring me I should not want while she had it, bidding me trust still in a Divine Providence, who never diserts those who merit protection, and reminding me of my own expressions to herself, when I had so often been relieved: – and indeed the words were scarcely out out [*sic*] of her mouth, when I received a letter from the Earl of Bristol, – that patriotic, exentric, little prelate, – with an enclosure of fifty pounds: – My acquaintance with this noble and reverend Peer was short but singular – about sixteen years before, when I had been in London, he was introduced to me, and his lively manner made such an impression on me, that I consented to have him for a bed-fellow for one night: – The morning after, he made a thousand apologies for his want of cash, and solemnly promised I should not be a loser by indulging him; however I thought no more of it, nor possibly ever would, only the pressure of misfortunes fell heavy on me, in consequence of which he occurred to me, and I made enquiry for his address, and wrote to him a few months before, among a number of my old acquaintances, without ever expecting any answer, or that he even would recollect such a person as I ever existed; – the event proved I was mistaken, and shewed the generosity and gratitude of this worthy and honorable Peer. The *rara avis in terris.* Oh! Providence divine, exclaimed I (dropping on my knees,) thou wonder working God, how has the wretched Plunket merited this goodness? – After some little time in fervent prayer, I arose up and embracing my land-lady acknoweledged the truth of the observation she made, declaring I would never again, let what would befall me, distrust in a divine and watchful providence. The next morning as I was at breakfast, I was most agreeably surprised at a visit from Debby Dowd, my generous charitable *smuggler,* who so critically relieved Mrs Edmonds and I in the height of our distress. She came, she told me, to know if I wanted any thing in *her way,* and if I did I was extremely welcome to take what I pleased till I could pay her: and accordingly I bought a few yards of muslin from her, the making of a cloak, and two pounds of Gunpowder tea, at prime cost, as she would receive no more; and paid her the money she had lent me; but all I could do, I could not prevail on her to take payment for the tea and other matters, she had given poor Mrs Edmonds and I. She told me her situation was vastly improved since she had seen me last, that her husband whom she honestly owned, she never could endure was dead, and that she was then married to one *O'Connor,* a very eminent shop-keeper in Castle Island; and that in fact, she was under no necessity to travel, but that as she had for a long time been used to it, she could not avoid now and then taking an excursion; however, she said, she travelled then in a little capriolet, which she drove herself, with her goods under her, and only once or twice a year: – on her road to this city, when she came to purchase goods, stopped at such towns, as she thought might turn out to advantage; she also pressed me to take an airing with her and spend the day in some outlet or other, and accordingly to gratify my generous benefactress, who would take no denial, I complied, and we spent the day at the Three-tun-tavern at the

Black-rock, where the worthy landlord, Bishop, paid us every attention, and gave us every delicacy (and unquestionably his house, independent of his own civility and accommodating manners, is the best place of entertainment in that charming place) the season could afford, and at a very moderate price. On our return to town it was rather late, we were stopped near Bagatrot Castle by three armed villains, who were proceeding to riffle our pockets, when two gentlemen, who I had formerly known, a Mr P—l and Mr W—, hearing our cries, gallopped [*sic*] up to our assistance, and rescued us from our assailants, who took to their heels and made their escape, but not without loss of blood, as one of our deliverers fired at the most desperate of the rogues, on his snapping a pistol at him, and wounded him; as appeared by the tracts of his blood for a considerable length of way, and notwithstanding all our enquiries and endeavours, the three by some means or other escaped; this adventure appeared in the public prints the next day, in the most delicate manner, without mentioning any name; – indeed since my misfortunes thickened upon me, all the Printers in the city have treated me in the genteelest manner, never mentioning my name with disrespect, the account of the robbery was merely this:

Last night as two ladies were returning from the Rock rather late, their carriage was stopped by three armed foot-pads, who would have robbed them, had it not been for the timely interference of two gentlemen who happened luckily to ride up, just as the miscreants were proceeding to violence; one of whom was desperately wounded, notwithstanding which they all escaped, though closely pursued for a considerable way.

Though my name was not announced in the papers, yet it was generally believed I was one of the persons who had been stripped; and Mr Daly the generous manager of the *Theatre Royal,* who was not only my very great admirer once, but particular friend, hearing of my melancholy situation, intimated to me, that he would give me a benefit free of every expence; not in my own name, as that would damn the business among the ladies of the *ton;* but in that of a distressed lady, &c. &c. You may judge I accepted of this generous offer, and once more intruded on my particular friends, by written applications, and inclosing them bills and tickets, in consequence of which as both play and entertainments were got up with all the strength of the company, which was an excellent one, I cleared upwards of ninety pounds, and would have a good deal more, had I not been cheated by a number of buckeens and swindling blackguards, my former acquaintances, who actually forced their services on me, to stand, sell and receive tickets at the different doors; and to my cost, when it was too late, I was acquainted with the motive of their *disinterested* offers; humanity alone prevents me from giving these jockies' names at *full length:* – the most specious of these *friendly swindlers* were Mr M— of High-street, Tom C— of Francis-street, and Mr S— of Ormond-quay; there were many more who *kindly* interfered to sell tickets for me, and ungenerously pocketed the produce, and never accounted with me for one of them; particularly one C—, formerly a *Small-beer Brewer,* a quandom [*sic*] keeper of the Sheriff's prison, – the Rev. Mr K—, a valliant *priest,* who accompanied Colonel D— to the Continent as a priestly recruiting crimp, to annihilate the *French,* – the widow of poor N— of poetical memory, who insinuated herself into my good graces, and pretended to be my friend; – a Mr Johnny G—n a shoe-maker, and a great devotee; and a number of others who are not worth animadverting on.

CHAPTER TWELVE

[*Peg meets and engages her last companion Margaret Collins, the visit to Drumcondra, the assault and rape, the discovery that both ladies have been infected with venereal disease, a forced change in lodgings, poverty, and Peg's last attempts to finish her manuscript*]

I WAS NOW AS TO PECUNIARY matters tollerably easy, I had what would support me and my servant girl, with decency for some time; exclusive of which I was every day receiving subscriptions for my third volume, the first two having been bought up with the greatest avidity: – I now began to lead a life of some comfort, my circumstances were good, my health in some measure reinstated, and my mind in a perfect calm; I regularly attended to my devotions, and was constantly visited by my spiritual guide a Mr L—d, who was not only the good priest but the gentleman, and who spared no pains to bring me not only to a proper way of thinking, but to a good opinion of myself, and indeed to this gentleman I in a great measure owe my preservation; else I certainly should through desperation, have been guilty of the horrid sin of a second time attempting to make an end of my poor self. In this situation I happened accidentally to meet with a woman, in whom I placed much confidence, she came to me recommended very strongly, and I hired her on my own terms: – she was a very fine elegant woman, of about thirty years of age, though *perfectly grey;* she told me she was the daughter of a respectable Farmer in Roscrea, that she had very early privately married the *Valet de chambre* of M— B—, Esq; near Burrisakane, and that her husband having saved a little money in that *poor gentleman*'s service (whose wife a lovely woman, eloped from him with a *military Cornuter,*) brought her up to Dublin, and set up an alehouse in Essex-street, where they had not carried on business for above three years when her husband failed, was arrested and thrown into the Four-courts-marshalsea, where they both remained in great distress, until he was liberated by the benefit of the late Insolvent act; when the base villain, her husband, deserted her (under pretence of jealousy, insinuating that she had granted favors to a married gentleman then in prison) and entirely quit the kingdom; in consequence of which, she applied in her distress to the gentleman whom *Collins* her husband pretended to be jealous of, who told her it would be ridiculous in the extreme, not to give the miscreant *cause* for his unjust suspicions; and the gentleman having been very kind to her when in the prison, which gave rise to Collins's surmises, and having buried his own lady, she gave way to his desires, and proved pregnant by him; which he for some time could hardly give credit to, as from her *snowy head* he conceived she was an *old woman;* however at last he was thoroughly convinced, on her being brought to bed of a fine boy, as like himself as one egg to another: – however as his circumstances were greatly deranged, Mrs Collins was obliged to put her child into the *Poor-house,* and to go to a service herself, which he provided for her, by recommending her to his own sister; with whom she lived till about a month before that angelic woman died; when she gave her the discharge; on the strength of which I agreed to hire her. This poor pretty woman proved a great comfort to me, as I found her intelligent, faithful, sober, discreet and honest; indeed when my distresses became too severe for human nature to bear, I found every consolation in my poor dear *Peggy Collins,* who never forsook me; and very shortly after my hiring her, I had great occasion for a trusty, faithful friend, who would sympathize in my uncommon and unheard of misfortunes. Peggy and I continued together in tollerable tranquillity for several months, untill one evening I took it into my head to take a walk towards Drumcondra, to see my old poetical friend Mrs H—, and took poor Peggy with me as a safeguard; and on our return in the dusk of the evening, we were attacked by five ruffians, who dragged us into an adjoining field, and after stripping us to our shifts, and robbing us of what cash we had about us, actually compelled us by force to comply with their infamous desires, and otherwise used us most cruelly, as we made as much resistance as was in our power; particularly poor Mrs Collins, who in her rage thrust her scissars, into one of the villains belly's [sic] at the very moment he was enjoying her, after they severally satiated their brutal appetites, they left us as I said before, stripped to our shifts, carrying off even our shoes and stockings, and indeed was it not for one of them, who had less ferocity than the others, they would have taken away our *very shifts;* – in this wretched situation we were obliged to return to Mrs H—, who kindly procured for us from her friend Broadhead's, shoes and stockings, with two old plaid cloaks; and in this miserable plight we arrived at our lodgings, very much cut and bruised, at about two o'clock in the morning: Mrs T— was astonished when she saw us, and when we related the way we had been treated, she absolutely shed tears of compassion, and would not let us retire till she made us take some warm punch, at the same time giving us every consolation in her power. Poor Peggy and I went to bed, but not to rest, and what was a greater affliction to us than all, in a few days afterwards, we found we were infected with the most wretched of disorders; in fact we were injured by the nefarious villains in the most virulent degree, and this in all my round of pollution was what I never experienced before; – almost frantic, and not knowing what to do; I was at first resolved to lye under the foul disease till it should terminate my wretched existence, but then on reflection I considered my poor Peggy's case, and at last determined to send for either blind Billy J—ns or Surgeon B—r, but in sending a note to the former, I found he had been for a considerable time a *Sunday beau,* and the poor surgeon was to my great grief in durance vile, for large sums of money; – I therefore applied to my worthy friend Mr Brady, who was obliged, our diseases were so virulent and obstinate, to put us both in a salivation, – in which we were for near three months, at the end of which time, we found ourselves reduced to skeletons, all our money exhausted, deeply involved with Mrs T—, our landlady, and our clothes in pawn: – A glorious situation for two poor miserable repentent sinners, who had not by any crime of their own, in any shape contributed to bring on these unheard of misfortunes; what to do we knew not, and what was still worse (as misfortune seldom comes alone) Mrs T—, and who could blame her, gave us warning to quit her house, at the same time assuring me she never would ask me for what I owed her, which amounted to about ten pounds, but that her husband wanted the room, we occupied, and she hoped that I would not take it amiss, in requesting me to provide myself by that day week at the farthest. I told her I was far from being displeased; on the contrary, I should ever hold the many obligations I lay under to her in grateful remembrance, and that I would provide as soon as possible, though very unequal to the arduous task, as I was so dibilitated, as to be unable to stand, and was not worth

a ducat in the world.

Just as Mrs T— had left me, my apothecary Mr Brady called upon me, to whom I related the result of my interview with my landlady; a consultation upon this took place, upon which it was resolved Mr Brady should immediately call to Mrs W— of Temple-bar, who had lodgings to let, and who some few years before had received some favors from me; a very good-natured sort of woman, Brady also knew her, and that she had one or two furnished rooms vacant; he accordingly immediately went to her and settling every matter with her, Peggy and [sic] took possession of our new apartments; where we lived in extreme want and misery, enduring both cold and hunger, and entirely indebted to our hospitable landlady for our support: – poor Peggy Collins soon recovered strength, but as for my part, I became weaker and weaker every day, and from anxiety and uneasiness, I fear I have contracted a fever; as poor Brady who has just left me, on feeling my pulse and inspecting my tongue declared I was not in a condition to sit up. Though I found my head light, I had recollection enough to know my situation; and I candidly confess I had forebodings of my speedy decease, however by the proper use of doctor James's fever powders, I got rid of my disorder; but for a considerable time felt a languor on my spirits, and a weakness in all my limbs: – I deeply regretted my present situation, not for fear of death as I was perfectly well reconciled to meet it with fortitude, but to be taken away when I was on the eve of handsomely repaying all my friends for their trouble; my volume now being not only finished, but nearly transcribed for the press: and as the public had generously encouraged my former publication, beyond what I could hope or expect, I had sanguine hopes the present volume, being more interesting, would be very productive, – and thereby enable me to be not only *just,* but *generous;* I hoped at least it would bring me in five hundred pounds clear; – but while I write I feel a gradual decline, from a broken heart and a destroyed constitution! Destroyed alas! near the last moments of my life; and in the most shameful barbarous manner. Good Heaven! my fingers refuse to do their office: – Oh! I am sick at heart, – my very brain wonders, – I fear it is *dooms day* with me! The Lord God of mercy, take compassion on me, oh! oh! … !!!

*[Three letters from Margaret Collins to Edward J——, Esq.,
recording Peg's last moments, death and funeral, and
an Impromptu on the Death of Margaret Leeson]*

TO EDWARD J——, Esq.

My dear, dear friend,

I am now to inform you, that my poor dear companion Mrs Leeson, is in the last stage of a decline, and not expected to live: two or three of the most eminent of the faculty, who have attended her these three months past have all given her over, they said her strength was entirely exhausted, and she was in that state from a decay of nature, that all human art could not recover her, and desired I would prepare for her speedy dissolution. Poor dear woman! a greater penitent never left this world; she has this three weeks past never been easy except when the good and worthy Doctor L——d is by her side, and indeed the humane man pays her the greatest attention; – oh! my dear Mr J——, we have experienced the greatest distress, and had it not been for the humanity of the medical and clerical gentlemen, who attended; and the goodness of our kind hostess, she and I must have perished, – must have died for want! – But hark I am called; adieu for the present, Heaven preserve the poor dear penitent.

Margaret Collins.
Temple-bar,
March 18th 1797.

From the Same to the Same.

My dear friend,

THIS morning at about four o'clock, my poor friend paid the great debt of nature, she died without the smallest evident pain, nature being compleatly exhausted; – with a firm reliance (from her unfeigned penitence, great trials and resignation to the divine will,) of salvation, notwithstanding the irregularity of the last forty years of her life; her last words were taken from Rochester's Elegy, whose works, and works of the sort, no doubt in her time she made too great use of,

> All Nature's works, now from before me fly,
> Live not like *Leeson,* – but like *Leeson* die.

Poor creature, she made a will, leaving all her property, amounting to upwards of three thousand pounds in the bonds, notes and 10's of a parcel of *Black legs,* Wh—s, Swindlers, and unprincipled men (who shamefully borrowed money with an intention of never paying,) in legacies, among her particular friends, after paying all her just debts, giving me for my life sixty pounds a year; poor mistaken creature, all the effects she has left on earth would not be sufficient to bury her, exclusive of her apothecary's bill, the sum due to Mrs T—, and which she felt particularly uneasy about in her last moments, and her rent to poor Mrs W—, where she died; exclusive of a number of Grocers' and Huxters' bills, which I was obliged to contract on her account, or she might have perished; – Mr H— of St James's-street, the worthy man, gave me credit to a large amount, for teas, sugars, wines, &c. and yet he did not like citizen D—, with poor Moll Hall, place keepers on the house the moment the breath parted from her body; on the contrary, he generously offered his assistance towards her burial, as did many other friends, Mr T—r of Great George's-street, and little M—y the cheese-man, Billy W—n the facecious and luxurious printer, Miss Love the *protegee* of little Harry H—, with many other friends; in short though she has so much money due to her, I would not know how to accomplish her interment, but for the kind assistance of the above humane individuals.

I remain your ever faithful
Margaret Collins.
March 22d 1797.

From the Same to the Same.
My dearest friend,
ALL is over; poor Leeson was this morning genteely interred in St James's church-yard, – many respectable citizens attended the funeral obsequies, which was conducted in the most regular manner, and though quite private yet it was *simplex munditiis,* what the Romans called, 'plain and neat.' – As for my part I am thrown upon the world without a friend on earth, or even a recommendation; for you know to have lived with Mrs Leeson, would be but an indifferent introduction to a discreet family, and notwithstanding for the time I was in her service, I never met with a more exemplary, pious, worthy, charitable woman. Could I have the pleasure of seeing you at the *Old Kennel* in Thomas-street, I want much to consult you about my future hopes and pursuits, and am in every situation of life

Your very grateful
Margaret Collins.
March 25th 1797.

IMPROMPTU,

On the Death of Mrs MARGARET LEESON, who departed this mortal
Life the 22nd Day of *March* 1797, in the 70th Year of her Age.

COME all you vot'ries of the Cyprian queen,
In silent sadness, join the mournful train:
Your lady Paramount is now no more;
Untimely wafted to the Stygian shore.
Tho' to her share some grosser failings fall,
Read her sad life and you'll forgive them all:
Poor Peg, tho' *meritriciously* inclined,
Possess'd a noble and a generous mind;
Good-natured, friendly, affable and gay,
What pity 'twas she ever went a stray;
Tho' all must own Peg Plunket had her day.
If to relieve the mendicant distress'd,
If to *pour balm,* into a mind oppress'd,
If to act up to Nature's sacred laws,
If innate honesty, can gain applause,
If true repentance for your errors past,
And cruel hardships e'er you breath'd your last,
Can gain redemption, from great mercies God,
Leeson; you must acquire a bless'd abode.

Table of Identification

p.5   *Earl of Cavan*: either Charles Lambert, 3rd Earl of Cavan, d.1702, or Richard Lambert, 4th Earl of Cavan, d.1742 (*Complete Peerage*).

p.26   *Mr H— P—, of High St*: no directory of merchants and traders in Dublin survives for the late 1740s, and no merchant or trader answering to this description is listed in *Wilson's* for 1753. There is a 1783 posting for a Henry Plunket, woollen draper, of 20 High St, who might possibly be a descendent of the original Mr H— P—.

p.29   *Mr Droope*: William Drope, merchant, of Abbey St (*Wilson's*).

       Mr Moore: John Moore sen., goldsmith, of Christ Church Lane, off Inns' Quay (*Wilson's*).

p.35   *Countess of Clonmel*: Margaret Lawless, daughter of a Dublin banker, who married John Scott (*Complete Peerage*).

pp41-2 *an Englishman, named John Van Nost*: the sculptor of the equestrian statue of George II (Constantin Maxwell, *Dublin Under the Georges*, p.99).

p.47   *Captain Mathews*: Captain Benjamin Mathews, one of Mrs Leeson's friends and lovers, subsequently proprietor of a Spunging House in Angel Court (Kelly, David, 'The Conditions of Debtors & Insolvents in Eighteenth-century Dublin', *The Gorgeous Mask*, p.107).

p.49   *Surgeon Cleghorn*: actually a physician, George Cleghorn, of 6 Eustace St (*Wilson's*).

       Dr Cullum: a surgeon, William Collum, of 41 Moore St (*Wilson's*).

p.50   *Kitty Cut-a-Dash*: Mrs Katherine Netterville, d.1787, a well-known Dublin courtezan frequently mentioned in these *Memoirs*.

p.50   *Lord Boyne*: Frederick Hamilton, 3rd Viscount Boyne, d.1772 (*Complete Peerage*).

p.56   *Lord Cl—m*: Lord Clanwilliam, *i.e.* John Meade, 1st Earl Clanwilliam, (1744–1800), created Earl Clanwilliam in 1776 (*Complete Peerage*).

p.61   *Mr L—*: the Rev. Mr Lambert, a student at TCD (identification from the Introduction to the 1798 re-issue of the *Memoirs*). This could only be Thomas Lambert, who entered TCD as a sizar in 1763, became a Scholar in 1765, and took his BA in 1767 (*TCD Alumni*). Mrs Leeson's statement that Lambert was reading for a higher degree in divinity, if correct, indicates that her liaison with him began after the Spring Commencements of 1767, before the termination of his Scholarship in 1770.

p.65   *Mr Grogan*: Edward Grogan, mercer, of 7 Dame St (*Wilson's*).

       Mr Moore: John Moore, goldsmith. *See* above, note for p.29.

       Mr Kilpatrick: possibly Kirkpatrick, if so, Mrs Netterville's principal keeper would have been Alexander Kirkpatrick, merchant, subsequently Alderman and Sheriffs' Peer (*Wilson's*).

p.69   *a man … famous for contriving to mount nearer to Heaven*: Squire Baloon, *i.e* Richard Crosbie, brother to Sir Edward Crosbie, Bt. Born in 1755, Richard Crosbie was Ireland's first aeronaut, making a series of balloon flights, one an attempted crossing of the Irish Sea, in 1785 and 1786. He is thought to have died in 1800 (*DNB*).

p.70   *Moncrieffe*: Richard Moncrieffe, Sheriff of the County of the City of Dublin, 1779–80, subsequently Alderman, Mayor, and Sheriffs' Peer (*Wilson's; Watson's*).

       Worthington: William Worthington, Sheriff of the County of the City of Dublin, 1779–80, subsequently Alderman, Mayor, and Sheriffs' Peer, also subsequently knighted (*Wilson's, Watson's*).

       Surgeon Vance: William Vance, of College Green (*Wilson's*).

p.71   *Counsellor Wolfe*: Theobald Wolfe, of Aungier St (*Wilson's*).

       Judge Henn: William Henn, then (in 1779) Third Justice in the Court of King's Bench (*Wilson's*).

p.73   *Miss Catley*: Anne Catley, actress, singer and comedienne (?45–1789). Her liaison with Lascelles is hinted at in both Gilliland's *Dramatic Mirror*, and *DNB*.

       Colonel Lascelles: Colonel, and subsequently General Francis Lascelles, a long-serving member of the military establishment at Dublin Castle (*Watson's*).

p.86   *Wybrants's boat*: Liffey ferry service run by James Wybrants, of the Liverpool Packet House, George's Quay (*Wilson's*).

p.87   *Mr Georgi*: Signor St Giorgio, musician and impressario, promoting a season of Italian Opera at the Theatre Royal, Smock Alley, in the winter of

1781–2 (T.J. Walsh, *Opera in Dublin*, pp. 170–2).

Signor Carnavalli: Signor Carnevale, violinist and impressario, in partnership with St Giorgio, promoting the season of Italian Opera at the Theatre Royal. He was married to Signora Castini, who was allegedly Henry Grattan's mistress (T.J. Walsh, *Opera in Dublin*, pp. 170–2).

p.88 *Mrs Judge*: Mrs Anne Judge, one of Mrs Leeson's friends and colleagues, as opposed to rivals and colleagues. She appears as Katherine Netterville's main rival in the satire *An heroic epistle from Kitty-Cut-a-Dash to Orinooko*, and also named along with Mrs Leeson, Sally Hayes and Katherine Netterville in a Free Trade squib in the *Dublin Evening Post*, 24 December 1779, p.[1]C.

p.89 *Mr Roe*: George Roe, Keeper of Newgate Prison (Henry, Brian, *Dublin Hanged*, p.24). It is clear from Mrs Leeson's narrative that Carnevale was taken to Old Newgate in the Cornmarket, and not to the New Prison in Green St. Old Newgate was in the process of being demolished from 1780 to 1782 (B. Doorley, 'Newgate Prison', *The Gorgeous Mask*, pp.122–3).

four of the most desperate, ill-looking fellows of bailiffs: identified in the Introduction to the 1798 re-issue of these *Memoirs*, *Pref.*, p.17 as Sheridan, Moloney, Mooney and Broome.

p.93 *Mr Robinson*: Henry Robinson, High Constable of the City of Dublin (*Watson's*).

Mr Warren: Nathaniel Warren, subsequently Lord Mayor of Dublin (1782–3), and MP for the City of Dublin (*Watson's*; *Wilson's*).

Mr Crawford: possibly John Crawford, house painter, of 64 Townsend St (*Wilson's*).

Mr Meares: possibly George Meares, grocer, of 4 Little Britain St (*Wilson's*).

Lord St Lawrence: courtesy title of the heir to the Earldom of Howth, *i.e.* William St Lawrence, b.1752 and succeeding to the title as 2nd Earl of Howth in 1801 (*Complete Peerage*).

Lord Westport: courtesy title of the heir to the Earldom of Altamount. Mrs Leeson's recollection of titles in this instance is suspect. The 3rd Earl of Altamount, John Denis Browne, succeeded to the title in 1780. His heir, the Lord Westport, would hardly have been out of swaddling-clothes by 1 May 1782 (*Complete Peerage*).

Lord Headfort: courtesy title of the heir to the Earldom of Bective, *i.e.* Thomas Taylour (1757–1829), succeeded to the title in 1795, and created Marquis of Headfort in 1800 (*Complete Peerage*).

Lord Molesworth: Richard Nassau Molesworth, 4th Viscount Molesworth, (1748–93). Described in the *Complete Peerage* as a profligate who had been some years a lunatic and ward of Chancery prior to his death.

p.94 *The Duke of Leinster*: William Robert Fitzgerald, 3rd Duke of Leinster, b.1749, succeeded to the title in 1773 (*Complete Peerage*).

p.102 *Mr Maquay*: either George or John Leland Maquay, sugar-bakers, of 143 Thomas St (*Wilson's*).

p.107 *A noble Lord of my own name*: probably Joseph Leeson, 1st Earl of Milltown (1711–83), the son of Joseph Leeson, brewer, of Dublin. He was created Earl of Milltown in 1763. As Mrs Leeson did not move from Wood St to her new house in Pitt St until the beginning of 1784, there is an outside possibility that this was a gift from his son, Joseph Leeson, 2nd Earl of Milltown (1730–1801) (*Complete Peerage*).

Captain F——e: Captain Stephen Freemantle, aide-de-camp to the Lord Lieutenant in 1783 (*Watson's*).

Alderman Warren: Nathaniel Warren. *See* above, note for p.93.

p.108 *Counsellor B——y*: probably J.E. Batty, of 1 Chatham St, or possibly Peter Bayly, of College Green, or Richard Bayly, of South King St (*Wilson's*).

p.112 *Captain St Leger*: the Hon. Richard St Leger, Captain, and aide-de-camp to the Lord Lieutenant (*Watson's*)

J— W——: identification made more fully in the Introduction to the 1798 re-issue to these *Memoirs*, *Pref.* 1798, p.24, as John Wh——ly, possibly John Whaley, d.1849, Buck Whaley's younger brother (see *Buck Whaley's memoirs*, p.xxix).

p.113 *captains Boyle, Hanger, Freemantle, Monck, Cradock and M'Guire*: with the exception of 'Captains', Hanger and M'Guire, who proved untraceable, these officers were all aides-de-camp to the Lord Lieutenant in 1783: Lieutenant Boyle, Captain Stephen Freemantle, Major Henry Monck, and Captain Francis Craddock (*Watson's*). Mrs Leeson's connection with Captain Freemantle is alluded to in a squib published under the headline Notice, in the *Dublin Evening Post* of 3 May 1783, p.[3]A. He is referred to as 'Major Domo Friezemantle', and both Mrs Leeson and Moll Hall are named directly in the text of the squib.

p.123 *General Burgoyne*: Sir John Burgoyne, 7th Bt Sutton (1739–85). He raised a regiment of Light Dragoons for India in 1781, and was promoted to Major General in 1783 (*DNB*).

Captain Courtnay: Captain G.W.A. Courtnay, RN, commissioned in 1782, and officer commanding the *Eurydice*, an armed ship carrying twenty-four guns (*Exshaw*).

p.124 *General Mathews*: Brigadier General Richard Mathews, d.1784, conducting an unsuccessful campaign against Nabob Tippoo Sultan in Western Hindoostan (*British Library Gen. Cat.*).

p.125 *S.L. C——m*: S.L. Cunnynghame, Mrs Leeson's lover and keeper in succession to Robert Gorman.

p.128   *Lord G—d*: Lord Guilford, identification made in the Introduction to the 1798 re-issue of Vol. III of these *Memoirs, Pref.* 1798, p.22. Guilford or Gillford is the courtesy title of the heir to the Earldom of Clanwilliam, here Richard Meade (1766–1805), succeeded to the title in 1800 (*Complete Peerage*).

       a noble Earl: John Meade (1744–1800), 1st Earl of Clanwilliam. *See* above, note for p.56.

       a noted attorney… *M—l*: Crosbie Morgell, identified in the Introduction to the 1798 re-issue of Vol. III of these *Memoirs, Pref.* 1798, p.22. Crosbie Morgell committed suicide in 1794 (Barrington, *Personal sketches*, Vol. I, pp.457–8).

       Captain M—ws: Captain Benjamin Mathews. *See* above, note for p.47.

p.129   *D—d L—*: identified in the Introduction to the 1798 re-issue of these *Memoirs, Pref.* 1798, p.23 as David Latouche, Governor of the Bank of Ireland (see also *Watson's*).

       gentleman who lived not far from Linen Hall: possibly Alderman Henry Bevan, of Linen Hall St (*Wilson's*; Linen Hall *Dir.*).

       Mr B—r of Kilkenny: Walter Butler (1770–1820), subsequently Lord T—s and the 18th Earl of Ormond. When his father, John, succeeded to the Earldom in 1791, young Butler acquired the courtesy title of Viscount Thurles. He succeeded to the title in 1795 (*Complete Peerage*).

p.134   *C— L—*: possibly Christopher Lewis, bookseller, of 67 Grafton St (*Wilson's*) Throughout the 1770s Richard Lewis used to advertise his services as Corrector of the Press, and as a potential editor for first-time authors. It is possible that both men are related.

p.136   *S. L. C—m*: S.L. Cunnynghame. *See* above, note for p. 125.

p.139   *General Mathews*: Brigadier-General Richard Mathews. *See* above, note for p.125.

       General Burgoyne's light dragoons: see above, note for p.123.

p.143   *Bob*: Robert J. Gorman, Mrs Leeson's lover and keeper, 1782–3.

       Bobbadil: S.L. Cunnynghame, Mrs Leeson's lover and keeper in succession to Gorman. 'Bobbadil' is a a two-edged joke: Cunnynghame imitated Gorman in writing sentimental letters, hence little Bob, but he also shared a surname with General Robert Cunninghame, a member of the General Staff attached to Dublin Castle throughout much of this period (*Watson's*).

p.144   *Honest Charley*: Charles Manners, 4th Duke of Rutland, and Lord Lieutenant from 1784 to his death in 1787 (*Complete Peerage*).

p.145   *his divine Dutchess*: Mary Isabella Manners (*née* Somerset), daughter of the Duke of Beaufort (*Complete Peerage*).

       poor lady W—: Sarah Anne Fane (*née* Childe), first wife of the Earl of

Westmorland (*Complete Peerage*).

the Hon. Mrs S—: The Hon. Mrs Sinnott, identified later in the text as a demi-rep and lover of the Earl of Westmorland.

S—d family: identified by the contemporary annotator of Vol. III as the Stratford family.

Lady F— H—t: identified by the contemporary annotator of Vol. III as a Lady Fitz Herbert.

Lady G— Q—: identified by the contemporary annotator of Vol. III as a Lady Queade.

A—s G—th: Amyas Griffith, a Dublin radical printer, originally from Belfast (*Wilson's*; *vide* Bigger, Francis Joseph, *Amyas Griffith, Surveyor of Belfast 1780–1785*, [Belfast 1916]).

D—y: Donnelly (identification from text).

p.146   *the Rev. G— P—*: possibly George Phillips, born Kileen, county Tyrone, in 1708 or 9, who took his BA from TCD in 1734, and his MA in 1738. This appears to be the only G— P—in orders from the right part of Ireland (*TCD Alumni*).

p.146   *Waddell C—*: Waddell Cunningham, elected as MP for Carrickfergus in controversial circumstances in 1784 (*H of C Journ.*)

p.146   *honest W—ls—y*: Richard Wellesley, Earl of Mornington, the Duke of Wellington's father (*Complete Peerage*).

p.146   *Humphries*: Richard Humphries, prizefighter (*DNB*).

p.146   *Mendoza*: Daniel Mendoza, pugilist. His book, *The Art of Boxing*, was published in Dublin in 1792 (*DNB*; *ESTC*). He visited Dublin in October 1788, *Dublin Evening Post*, 14 October 1788, p.[3]A.

p.147   *B—d*: identified by the contemporary annotator of Vol. III as the Duke of Bedford, *i.e.* Francis Russell, 8th Duke of Bedford (*Complete Peerage*).

p.147   *Lady Arabella D—*: Lady Arabella Denny, a Dublin philanthropist, deeply involved in the management of, and fund-raising for the Magdalen Asylum in Leeson St (*Watson's*).

p.148   *Mr C—*: Possibly the Mr C—e, whose father was referred to slightingly as a wire-drawer, *i.e.* an inferior copyist, by Mrs Leeson. *See* below, note for p.180. If so, the father could only have been John Clare, painter, of 14 Dorset St (*Wilson's*).

O'M—: Brian O'Meagher (barrister), of Mabbot St (*Wilson's*).

Ormsby's Seminary: a private Spunging House. Captain William Ormsby was also Governor of the Four Courts Marshalsea (*Wilson's*).

p.149   *Billy Jenkins*: William Jenkins, apothecary, of 45 Dame St (*Wilson's*).

Mr A—: identified by the contemporary annotator of Vol. III as a Mr Attridge.

the cidevant Inspector of Munster: John Gahan, the Surveyor General of

Munster (Revenue) (*Watson's*).

p.150 *Earl of W—*: John Fane, Earl of Westmorland, and Lord Lieutenant (*Complete Peerage*).

p.151 *Mrs —*: the Hon. Mrs Sinnott. *See* above, note for p.145.

Doctor Achmet: Achmet Boromborad, *i.e.* Patrick Joyce, the Kilkenny Turk, proprietor of the Dublin Baths, Bachelor's Walk (Barrington, *Personal Sketches*, Vol. I., pp230–41).

p.152 *C—k*: Edward Cooke, Under Secretary at Dublin Castle (*Watson's*).

W— C—: Waddell Cunningham. *See* above, note for p.146.

E— Rad— R—: Ebeneezer Radford Roe, a first cousin of Frances Griffith, Amyas Griffith's wife. He is mentioned in her obituary in the *Dublin Evening Post*, 6 June 1793, p.[3]D.

p.153 *M— K—*: Michael Kelly, Manager of the Ménage in Capel St, and subsequently of a pleasure garden and brothel in Whitehall, County Dublin, also known as 'the Crupper-Making Squire'. *See* below, note for p.213.

Mr B—, M— of the B— Coat H—: Mrs Leeson's recollection of this particular guest is somewhat confused. The Blue Coat Hospital had a Board of Governors and a Schoolmaster, but no Master as such. None of the Schoolmasters has a surname beginning with 'B', and only one of the Governors, Sir Samuel Bradstreet, Bt, could remotely fit her description (*Watson's*).

W—l: Waddell Cunningham. *See* above, note for p.146.

Surgeon B—r: identified by the contemporary annotator of Vol. III as a Surgeon Bolger. This is Charles Bolger, of 13 Suffolk St, who had a long association with the Lock Hospital (*Wilson's*; *Watson's*).

alderman W—: Sir William Worthington. *See* above, note for p.70.

B—h—set: identified by the contemporary annotator of Vol. III as a Henry Blennerhasset. See also below, note for p.208.

W—l C—: Waddell Cunningham. *See* above, note for p.146.

the Rev. G— P—: possibly George Phillips. *See* above, note for p.146.

Mathews the bailiff: Captain Benjamin Mathews. *See* above, note for p.47.

Beau R—: Edward Rice, jeweller and goldsmith, of 13 Capel St (*Wilson's*).

p.155 *A—J—*: possibly Alderman Caleb Jenkins, bookseller (*Wilson's*).

Mr U—r: John Usher, apothecary, of 62 Dame St (*Wilson's*).

Mr C—, Rector of Castle B—: possibly a reference to a member of the Cruise family, of Castle Blakeney [Caslteblakeney], Taiquin, County Galway (*Lewis*). However, no member of that family appears to have passed through TCD, Oxford or Cambridge, or to have been ordained. What is more, the church there was ruinous, and had to be rebuilt in 1812, so Mrs Leeson may well have been referring to the family's rights as Rectors providing vicars for that Parish.

p.159 *Mr Fox*: Mr George Fox, merchant, of 46 Capel St (*Wilson's*).

C——: possibly an allusion to the Cruise family. *See* above, note for p.155.

Surgeon G——: possibly Alexander Graydon, surgeon, of 7 Jervis St (*Wilson's*). Jervis St runs from Upper Abbey St to the Liffey.

p.160 *Mr Le F——*: the son of Peter Le Favre, perfumer, of 54 Grafton St (*Wilson's*).

Lewellen: Margaret Lewellen or Llewellyn, the procuress implicated in the rape of Mary Neill in May 1788, who was pardoned and released from Newgate, sometime in April 1789. There are numerous references to her in pieces of campaigning satire (both verse and prose) directed against Francis Higgins, and published in the *Dublin Evening Post* during the summer of 1789. *See* also Rowan, Archibald Hamilton, *Sufferings*, for a more detailed account of the original incident.

Father Fay: Father Patrick Fay, a forger, also under sentence of death, released from Newgate at the same time as Mrs Lewellen, and referred to in the anti-Higgins satires published by the *Dublin Evening Post*.

p.161 *Mrs H——*: possibly Mrs Jane Hamilton, of Jane Hamilton & Co., milliners and haberdashers, of 140 Capel St (*Wilson's*).

Mr C——: William Crosbie, son of Maurice Crosbie, Dean of Limerick. Despite his entanglement with Mary Fagan, he took his BA from TCD in 1796, and was called to the Irish Bar in 1794, subsequently succeeding to the Barony of Brandon (*TCD Alumni*).

Mr H——: Joshua Holmes, apothecary, of 76 Capel St, and prior to that, of Pill Lane (*Wilson's*).

Mr R—— H—— of Capel-street: either Robert Hallam, house-painter of 57 Capel St, or Robert Hovenden, merchant, of 23 Capel St (*Wilson's*).

R——A——: Robert Armstrong, apothecary, of Capel St (*Wilson's*).

p.162 *West, attorney*: John West (who was actually a barrister), called to the Irish Bar in Trinity Term 1788 (*Wilson's*).

Mr N——: Michael Nugent, grocer, of 37 South Great George's St (*Wilson's*).

James O'R—— of Ba—s—na: James O'Reilly, entered TCD on 1 October 1790, was elected to Scholarship in 1792, and took his BA in 1794 (*TCD Alumni*).

p.163 *Mr Edward B——, afterwards Kingsmill*: Edward Bruce or Brice, Surveyor of the Port of Belfast (Revenue), who assumed the arms and name of Kingsmill in 1787, d.1796 (*Watson's*; *Landed Gentry*, entry under Kingsmill).

p.164 *Henry O——*: identified by the contemporary annotator of Vol. III as a Henry Ottiwell.

K——, druggist: identified by the contemporary annotator of Vol. III, as one

Kinsey. The text gives his forename as Thomas, *i.e.* Thomas Kinsey, of Kinsey and Farrell, druggists, 107 Capel St (*Wilson's*).

Mendoza: Daniel Mendoza, pugilist. *See* above, note for p.146.

p.165   *Ald. J—*: Alderman Caleb Jenkins, bookseller (*Wilson's*).

honest Charley: Charles Manners, 4th Duke of Rutland. *See* above, note for p.144.

Mr G—: Mr Graham, identified from a subsequent reference in the text.

p.166   *R—W—*: Robert Walsh, identified from a subsequent reference in the text.

p.167   *Buck English*: William Alexander English, of Ranelagh Road, obituary published in the *Dublin Evening Post*, 8 May 1794, p.[3]C: '… His early days were marked by a dissipation, and a profusion so lavish, as to procure him the name of *Buck English*. The middle part of his life was spent in the Four-Courts-Marshalsea, … and years previous to his death were spent in suing for recovery of his estate.'

Mrs M—e: Jane Elizabeth Moore, poet and autobiographer (*Todd*).

Captain K—y: identified by the contemporary annotator of Vol. III as a Captain Kelly.

Peter S—g—n: identified by the contemporary annotator of Vol. III as Peter Seguin.

Preston: William Preston, playwright, author of *Democratic Rage* (*DNB*).

Bartle Corcoran: Bartholomew Corcoran, Dublin printer specializing in chap books, cheap school texts, ballads, &c. (*ESTC*; *Wilson's*).

p.168   *P— H—*: Philip Hatchell. The surname is identified by the contemporary annotator of Vol. III, *i.e.* Philip Hatchell, apothecary, of 45 Grafton St (*Wilson's*).

Barry Y—: Barry Yelverton, junior, second son of Barry Yelverton, Chief Baron of the Court of Exchequer, and subsequently created Earl of Avonmore (*DNB*). Barry junior is described fairly baldly in Sir Jonah Barrington (*Personal Sketches*, Vol. II, pp37–9) as a profligate who came to an unspecified and unpleasant end.

Le F—: Possibly Le Favre. *See* above, note for p.160.

p.169   *C— B—*: Chief Baron, *i.e.* Barry Yelverton, senior.

Mrs H. now of Drumcondra: Possibly the Mrs Robert Hill, Drumcondra, who died in December 1796, The family tombstone recording her death and burial is still extant in Drumcondra Churchyard.

p.170   *P— of W—*: the Prince of Wales, subsequently George IV. For a brief account of his liaison with Mrs Fitzherbert, *see* his entry in *DNB*.

F—t: Maria Fitzherbert. For a brief account of her life, *see DNB*. p. 10

p.172   *citizen D—*: Miles or Myles Duignan, grocer, of 68 Grafton St (*Wilson's*).

p.173   *Mr McC—e*: John McCrae or M'Crae, Secretary to the Abcderian Society (*Watson's*).

p.175   *Buck W—y*: Thomas, known as Buck or Jerusalem Whaley (*DNB*), and see also *Buck Whaley's memoirs*.

M— of D—: identified by the contemporary annotator of Vol. III as the Marquis of Downshire. This rather unedifying father and son double-act would therefore be Wills Hill, created Marquis of Downshire in 1789, d.1793, and his son Arthur Hill (1753–1801), succeeded as 2nd Marquis in 1793 (*Complete Peerage*).

p.176   *Marquis of —*: identified by the contemporary annotator of Vol. III as the Marquis of Abercorn, *i.e.* John James Hamilton, created Marquis in 1790, d.1818 (*Complete Peerage*).

p.180   *Lynch*: Larry Lynch, Dublin felon executed in 1792 (Henry, Brian, *Dublin Hanged*, p.23).

C—e: possibly the son of John Clare, of Dorset St. *See* above, note for p.148.

p.181   *P—rt—r*: Porter, identification from subsequent text.

Rt. Hon. Paramour: the Earl of Westmorland. *See* above, note for p.151.

p.182   *a noble D—*: the Duke of Leinster, if so this would be the 3rd Duke, William Robert Fitzgerald. *See* above, note for p.94.

p.188   *Sir B— D—*: Sir Barry Denny, MP for Tralee (*Watson's*).

p.191   *Mr Ned T—ns—d*: Edward Mansel Townshend, of St Kames Island and Whitehall, County Cork (*Landed Gentry*).

p.192   *Mr F—of Bride's Alley*: Robert Fannin, cabinet-maker and auctioneer, of 15 Bride's Alley (*Wilson's*).

p.193   *Mr H—*: the son of Philip Higginson, tea merchant, of 26 College Green (*Wilson's*).

p.195   *Colonel Mercer*: Lieutenant Colonel John Mercier (*Watson's*).

p.196   *Charles C—*: Charles Craig, watchmaker of Fishamble St and subsequently of Capel St (*Wilson's*).

p.198   *C—*: possibly the son of John Clare, of Dorset St. *See* above, note for p.148.

Captain Southwell, of little Dargle: Captain William Southwell (Richard Lewis, *A Guide to the City and County of Dublin*, Dublin 1787, p. 283).

p.199   *Bartle Corcoran*: Bartholomew Corcoran, printer. *See* above, note for p.167.

Joe the Game Cock: Joseph Leeson, 1st Earl of Milltown. *See* above, note for p.107.

Buck Lawless: John Lawless, Mrs Leeson's lover and keeper during the 1760s and 1770s.

p.200   *Lord Loftus*: Henry Loftus, Earl of Ely (*Complete Peerage*).

Sir B— Balderdash: Sir Boyle Roche, MP for various constituencies during his long career in the Irish House of Commons, notorious for his often colourful and inappropriate expressions (*DNB*).

p.201   *C— the Smuggler*: Waddell Cunningham. *See* above, note for p.146.

the democratic Baker: possibly Miles Duignan. *See* above, note for p.172.

Amyas G—th: Amyas Griffith, printer. *See* above, note for p.145.

Joseph H—: Joseph Hewitt or Hewett, the unsuccessful candidate in the Carrickfergus election of 1784 (*H of C Journ.*).

secretary P—: Thomas Pelham, Chief Secretary at Dublin Castle (*DNB*).

Count R—, the chimney doctor: Sir Benjamin Thompson, Count Rumford (*DNB*).

p.202 *P—n*: William Preston, playwright. *See* above, note for p.167.

Curran: John Philpot Curran (*DNB*).

p.203 *Sir B— Balderdash*: Sir Boyle Roche. *See* above, note for p.200.

Colonel Townshend: Richard Townshend, of Castletownshend, MP for Cork, High Sheriff of Cork, and Colonel in the Cork Militia (*Landed Gentry*).

Mr S—t—y: Mr George Stacy, cabinet-maker of 20 Whitefriars St. A Richard Stacy, following this profession in the 1780s at 18 Duke St, is also listed in *Wilson's*.

Mr Fleet—d: Mr Charles Fleetwood, of 13 Whitefriar St (*Wilson's*).

p.205 *Heigh—d*: the only logical expansion would seem to be Heighland.

p.206 *Tom G—g*: Thomas Greg, Belfast merchant (Benn, *History of Belfast*, Vol. II, p.182).

C—n: possibly Eldred Curwen, Belfast merchant (Benn, *History of Belfast*, Vol. II, p.182).

Mrs P.: Mrs Ann Pottinger, Belfast merchant's wife, and sister-in-law to Greg (Benn, *History of Belfast*, Vol. II, p.182).

Capt. Tom B.: Captain Thomas Batt (Benn, *History of Belfast*, Vol. II, p.21).

Count J—: either Thomas Jordan, hosier, of 40 Pill Lane, or Henry Jackson, ironmonger, of 87 Pill Lane (*Wilson's*).

earl of B.: possibly the Earl of Bective, in which case, this would be Thomas Taylour, the 1st Earl, b.1724 created Earl of Bective in 1766, d.1795 (*Complete Peerage*).

p.207 *Col. V.*: Colonel John Vaughan (*Watson's*).

p.208 *Lord Shelbourne*: William Petty, 3rd Earl of Shelbourne, and subsequently 1st Marquis of Landsdowne (*Complete Peerage*).

the Rev. Fitzm—e B—t: the Rev. Fitzmaurice Botet, son of John, *medicus*, of County Kerry, entered TCD as a sizar in 1755, elected Scholar in 1757, and took his BA in 1759 (*TCD Alumni*).

William B—h—t: William Blennerhasset, Collector of Revenue at Tralee, who died sometime after December 1794 (*Watson's*).

p.209 *Crosbie M—ll*: Crosbie Morgell. *See* above, note for p.128.

Baron Power: Richard Power, Baron of the Court of Exchequer (Ireland), who committed suicide in the spring of 1794 (Sir Jonah Barrington, *Personal sketches*, Vol. I, pp.450–7).

Sir B. D—y: Sir Barry Denny, MP. *See* above, note for p.188.

Henry B—t: Henry Blennerhasset. *See* above, note for p.208.

p.210   *N—n, Town Major of Dublin*: possibly Nathan, Mayor of Dublin, *i.e.* Nathaniel Warren (Mayor 1782–3), and subsequently MP for the City of Dublin. *See* above, note for p.93.

p.212   *Ferns*: John Ferns, wine merchant, of 10 Mitre Alley, and subsequently of 44 Abbey St (*Wilson's*).

p.213   *Squire Crupper*: Michael Kelly. *See* above, note for p.153.

Achmet's famed baths: the Dublin Baths, Bachelor's Walk, run by Patrick Joyce, *alias* Dr Achmet Borumborad. *See* above, note for p.157.

p.214   *Squire Edgeworth*: possibly Robert Edgeworth, the brothel bully implicated with Margaret Lewellen in the Mary Neill rape case (Archibald Hamilton Rowan, *Sufferings*, p.8).

Colonel S—y: Colonel the Hon. Stephen Digby Strangeway (*Watson's*).

Lamprey the chandler: Edward Lamprey, chandler, of 12 South Great George's St (*Wilson's*).

p.215   *Sentimental Mag.*: a magazine published by John Jones, of 111 Grafton St, between 1792 and 1795 (British Library, *General Cat.*).

Geo. Rob. F—tz-G—d: George Robert 'Fire-eater' Fitz-Gerald, duellist and proprietor of a private army in counties Galway and May, executed in 1786 (O'Higgins, *Trials*, and Sir Jonah Barrington, *Personal Sketches*, Vol. III, pp. 133 *et passim.*).

Jane E. M—: Jane Elizabeth Moore. *See* above, note for p.167.

Mrs B—tti—r: Henrietta Battier, journalist and satirist, d.1813, author of *The Gibbonade* (*Todd*).

Jones, of Grafton-street: John J., printer, of 111 Grafton St (*ESTC*; *Wilson's*).

p.216   *Mr Lewis, corrector of the Press*: Richard Lewis. *See* above, note for p.134.

Griff—th: Amyas Griffith. *See* above, note for p.145.

the Dog in Office: John Giffard, Sheriff of Dublin 1793–4, mentioned in Battier's *The Gibbonade*, and the subject of satirical pieces published in the *Dublin Evening Post* in the summer of 1794. Giffard also had close links with the Orange Order in Dublin (Sir Jonah Barrington, *Personal sketches*, Vol. I, pp291–4).

Giffardini: Harding, son of John Giffard, subsequently identified in Mrs Leeson's text as Harry.

Mrs B—r: Henrietta Battier. *See* above, note for p.216.

Buck English: William Alexander English. *See* above, note for p.216.

Rascal D—p—t: Peter Davenport, groom-porter at Daly's Club, identification from the text.

p.217 *Mr Rouviere*: Joseph Rouviere, occulist, of 24 Great Ship St (*Wilson's*).

Peter D—p—t: Peter Davenport. *See* above, note for p.216.

Major Mercer: possibly John Mercier, promoted to Lieutenant Colonel in 1789. *See* above, note for p.195.

p.218 *Thurot*: Francois Thurot, Captain in the French Navy, who landed at Carrickfergus in 1759, d.1760 (British Library, *General Cat.*).

Ned Townshend: Edward Mansel Townshend, of Whitehall and St Kames Island, County Cork. *See* above, note for p.191.

Monsieur Le Roque: possibly John Rocque, cartographer (British Library, *General Cat.*).

p.219 *Sir John C—t*: Sir John Colthurst, Bt, of Ardrum, County Cork (*Watson's*).

Mrs Frances Gr—ff—th: Frances Griffith, wife of Amyas Griffith, printer, for whom, *see* above, note for p.145.

Doctor Kelso: Hamilton Kelso, physician, of 9 Bull Lane (*Wilson's*).

p.220 *Mr Gri—th*: Amyas Griffith, printer. *See* above, note for p.145.

p.221 *Mr B.*: Charles Brenan, a journalist previously with the *Dublin Evening Post*, who acted as election agent for Richard Wogan Talbot, and was, in Mrs Leeson's opinion, in part responsible for the collapse of *The Phoenix* (see also Brian Inglis, *Freedom of the Press in Ireland*, p.58).

Mr T—lb—t: Richard Wogan Talbot, who sat as MP for Dublin county from 1791 to 1792, until ejected from Parliament on the proving of a petition for Undue Election, filed by a rival candidate, John Finlay (*H of C Journ.*).

an unfortunate gentleman: Amyas Griffith, proprietor of *The Phoenix* (Brian Inglis, *Freedom of the Press in Ireland*, p.58. *See also* above, note for p.145.

Wesley: John & Charles Wesley, founders of Methodism (*DNB*).

Whitfield: George Whitfield, prominent Methodist preacher, and close associate of the Wesleys (*DNB*).

the divine Kirwan: William Blake Kirwan, Dean of Kilalla, and noted charity Dublin preacher throughout the 1780s (British Library, *General Cat.*).

p.227 *Billy the Beau, Earl*: William Crosbie, 1st Earl of of Glandore: created Earl in 1776, d.1781 (*Complete Peerage*).

p.228 *Duc d'Orleans*: Louis Philippe Joseph de Bourbon-Orléans, better known as Philippe Égalité. He renounced his title and stood successfully for election to the National Convention. He voted for the execution of Louis XVI in January 1793, and was himself executed during Robespierre's Terror, in the following November (*Encyc. Brit.*).

p.232 *Mr O'B—*: Cornelius O'Brien, merchant, of 2 Fleet St (*Wilson's*).

a Grocer in Grafton-street: Miles 'Citizen' Duignan. *See* above, note for p.172.

p.233 *a ruffian of the name of Mooney*: Lawrence Mooney, proprietor of a Spunging House in Angel Alley (David Kelly, 'The Conditions of Debtors and Insolvents', *The Gorgeous Mask*, p.107).

p.238 *John F——*: possibly Joseph Fenton, pawnbroker, of 48 Fleet St, is the only new pawnbroker with the right initial letter in his surname to appear in *Wilson's*. His name first occurs in the *Directory* for 1796.

unfortunate proprietor of the Phoenix: Amyas Griffith, printer. *See* above, note for p.145.

p.239 *Mr Kennedy*: John Kennedy, Waterford glass merchant, 50 Stephen St (*Wilson's*).

Mr Tinkler: George Tinkler, paper-stainer, 42 South Great George's St (*Wilson's*).

Mr Corbet: William Corbet, bookseller and printer, 57 Great Britain St (*Wilson's*).

Mr T. Swords: Thomas Swords, bricklayer, Leeson St (*Wilson's*).

Mr Frank Higgins: Francis Higgins, proprietor of the *Freeman's Journal*, better known as the Sham Squire. For a brief account of his career *see DNB*.

Mr David Weir: David Weir, master builder, 5 Denziel St (*Wilson's*).

the two Mr Marsh's: James Marsh, ironmonger, of 28 Kennedy's Lane, and Patrick Marsh, upholder & auctioneer, of 33 Brides Alley (*Wilson's*).

Mr Lefavre: possibly Peter Le Favre. *See* above, note for p.160.

Messrs Blackwoods: Hans & Price Blackwood, merchants, 4 Harcourt St (*Wilson's*).

Mr Stanley: Arthur Stanley, merchant, Bride St (*Wilson's*).

all the Beresfords: possibly the Beresfords of Beresford, Lighton, Woodmason & Needham, bankers, Beresford Place (*Wilson's*).

Mr Henegan: Peter Henegan, grocer, of 55 Fleet St (*Wilson's*).

Mr Manders: Richard Manders, of 113 James's St (*Wilson's*).

Captain Ormsby: William Ormsby, Governor of the Four Courts, Marshalsea. *See* above, note for p.148.

Counsellor M'N: Leo M'Nally, of 57 Dominick St (*Wilson's*).

Counsellor Egan: John Eagan, KC, of 13 Ely Place (*Wilson's*).

Counsellor Curran: John Philpot Curran (*DNB*).

p.243 *Mrs J— E— M.*: Jane Elizabeth Moore. *See* above, note for p.167.

Mrs B—tt—r: Henrietta Battier. *See* above, note for p.215.

Mary Neil: Mary Neill, allegedly the victim of a double rape by the Earl of Carhampton and Francis Higgins, which occurred in May 1788, in a brothel run by Margaret Lewellen and Robert Edgeworth. Archibald Hamilton Rowan, the eccentric radical barrister, championed her cause (Archibald Hamilton Rowan, *Sufferings*).

Earl of Bristol: Frederick Augustus Hervey, Earl of Bristol from 1779, and Bishop of Derry from 1768, d.1803 (*Complete Peerage*).

p.246   *Mr S— of Ormond Quay*: possibly George Simpson of 16 Upper Quay (*Wilson's*).

widow of poor N—: Mrs Newburgh, widow of Colonel Thomas Newburgh (*née* Blacker) (1689–1779). Considerably younger than Newburgh at the time of her marriage, she subsequently married Dr Craddock, Dean of St Patrick's Cathedral (J.D. O'Donoghue, *The Poets of Ireland*).

John G—n, shoemaker: possibly a phonetic rendering of John Ging, shoemaker, of 25 Castle St (*Wilson's*).

p.248   *Mr L—d*: Dr Leonard, Mrs Leeson's RC confessor, identified from the text.

Mrs H.: possibly Mrs Robert Hill. *See* above, note for p.169

Billy J—ns: William Lionel Jenkins. *See* above, note for p.149.

Surgeon B—: Charles Bolger. *See* above, note for p.153.

p.250   *Edward J—*: possibly Edward Jones, apothecary, of 7 Fleet St (*Wilson's*). The proximity of Fleet St to Temple Bar, combined with Mrs Leeson's need for some form of medical attention, seems to point to Mr Jones.

p.251   *Doctor L—d*: Dr Leonard. *See* above, note for p.248.

citizen D—: Myles Duignan. *See* above, note for p.172.

Mr T—r of Great George's-street: George Tinkler. *See* above, note for p.239.

little M—y the cheeseman: Bernard Murray, cheesemonger, of 3 South Great George's St (*Wilson's*).

Billy W—n the facetious and luxurious printer: William Watson, printer & bookseller, of 7 Capel St (*Wilson's*).

Select Bibliography

NEWSPAPERS
The Dublin Evening Post, 1779–97
The Freeman's Journal, 1763–97

OTHER PRINTED SOURCES
Abstracts from the Companion to the Grave; or Every Man his own Undertaker (Dublin 1778).

Alumni Cantabrigensis ..., J. & J.A. Venn (eds), 4 vols & 6 vols (Cambridge 1922–54).

Alumni Dublinenses ..., G.D. Burtchell & T.U. Sadleir (eds) (Dublin 1935).

Alumni Oxoniensis ..., J. Foster (ed.), 8 vols (Oxford 1888–92).

Ball, F. Elrington, *The Judges in Ireland 1221–1921*, 2 vols (London 1926).

Barrington, Sir Jonah, *Historical Memoirs of Ireland*, 2 vols (London 1809–33). *Personal Sketches of his own times*, 3 vols (London 1827–32).

Battier, Henrietta, *Gibbonade. First number* (Dublin 1793); *The Gibbonade: or, the Political Reviewer. First number. The second edition* (Dublin 1794); *The Gibbonade: or Political Reviewer. Second number* (Dublin 1794); *The Gibbonade: or Political Reviewer. Third number* (Dublin); *The Kirwanade: or Political Epistle. Humbly addressed to the modern apostle! ... No. I* (Dublin 1791); *The Lemon, ... in answer to a scandalous Libel entitled The Orange* (Dublin 1798).

Bell, John, *The General and Particular Principles of Animal Electricity and Magnetism* (London 1792).

Benn, George, *A history of the Town of Belfast*, 2 vols (London 1877–88).

Bigger, Francis Joseph, *Amyas Griffith, Surveyor of Belfast, 1780–1785* (Belfast

1916); *The Magees of Belfast and Dublin, printers: with some notes on the Willson, Callwell, and other families* (Belfast 1916).

Black, Frank Gees, *The epistolary novel in the Eighteenth Century a Descriptive and Bibliographical Study* (Eugene 1940).

Block, Andrew, *The English Novel 1740–1850 a Catalogue including Prose Romances, short stories, and translations of Foreign Fiction...*, (intr. by John Crowe & Ernest A. Baker) (London 1961).

The British Library, *General Catalogue of Printed Books*, 360 vols & 6 suppl. vols (London 1975). *The Eighteenth Century Short-Title Catalogue.*

Burke, Ashworth P., *Family Records* (London 1897).

Burke, Sir John Bernard, *A Genealogical and Heraldic History of the Landed Gentry of Great Britain and Ireland*, 2 vols (9th edn, London 1898).

Cleland, John, *Memoirs of a Woman of Pleasure*, 2 vols (London 1749); *Memoirs of a Coxcomb* (London 1751).

Cokayne, George Edward & the Hon. Vicary Gibbs, *The Complete Peerage of England, Scotland, Ireland, Great Britain and the United Kingdom*, 12 vols (London 1910–54).

Dickson, David (ed.), *The Gorgeous Mask: Dublin 1700–1850* (Dublin 1987).

Dickson, David & Richard English, 'The La Touche dynasty', *The Gorgeous Mask: Dublin 1700–1850* (Dublin 1987), pp17–39.

Dictionary of national biography, Sir Leslie Stephen & Sir Sidney Lee (eds), 22 vols (reprint, Oxford 1921–2).

Doorly, Bernadette, 'Newgate Prison', *The Gorgeous Mask: Dublin 1700–1850* (Dublin 1987), pp121–31.

Dublin: a Satirical Essay in Five Books. By a Young Author (Dublin 1788).

Encyclopaedia Britannica, 23 vols & index and atlas vol. (Chicago, London, Toronto, Geneva, Sydney, Tokyo & Manila 1970).

Exshaw, John, and successor publishers, *The English Registry or, a Collection of Lists fitted to be bound up with Watson's Almanack* (annual publication, Dublin 1750–97).

Fitzpatrick, William John, *Ireland before the Union; with Revelations from the Unpublished Diary of Lord Clonmell* (Dublin 1867); *Irish Wits and Worthies; ...* (Dublin 1873); *The Sham Squire and the Informers of 1798* (3rd edn, Dublin 1867).

Gilbert, Sir John Thomas, *A History of the City of Dublin* (3 vols, Dublin 1861).

Gilliland, Thomas, *The Dramatic Mirror; containing the History of the Stage from the Earliest Period, to the Present Time...*, 2 vols (London 1808)

Henry, Brian, *Dublin Hanged. Crime, Law Enforcement and Punishment in late eighteenth-century Dublin* (Dublin 1994).

An heroic epistle from, Kitty Cut-a-Dash to Oroonokon (2nd edn, Dublin 1778).

Huish, Robert, *Memoirs of George the Fourth*, 2 vols (London 1830).

Inchbald, Elizabeth, *The Farce of Animal Magnetism. In three acts. As performed at the Theatre Royal* (Dublin [false imprint – probably London] 1792).

Inglis, Brian, *The Freedom of the Press in Ireland, 1704–1814* (London 1954).

Ireland–House of Commons, *Commons Journals of Ireland 1613–1800*, 19 vols & 3 index vols (Dublin 1795–1802).

Kelly, David, 'The Conditions of Debtors and Insolvents in Eighteenth-century Dublin', *The Gorgeous Mask*, pp98–120.

Kelly, Michael, *Reniniscences of M.K. of the King's Theatre with Original Anecdotes of Many Distinguished Persons*, 2 vols (London 1826).

King's Inns Admission Papers, E. Keane, P.B. Phair & T.U. Sadleir (eds) (Dublin 1982).

Lewis, Richard, *A Guide to the City and County of Dublin* (Dublin 1787).

Lewis, S., *A Topographical Dictionary of Ireland*, 2 vols (London 1837).

Lloyd, Hannibal Evans, *George IV. Memoirs of his Life ... with Numerous Personal Anecdotes* (Treuttel 1830).

McDowell, Robert Brendan, *Irish Public Opinion, 1750–1800* (London 1944); *Land & Learning: Two Irish Clubs* (Dublin 1993).

Maxwell, Constantia Elizabeth, *Dublin under the Georges 1714–1830.* (rev. edn London 1956); *Country and Town in Ireland under the Georges* (rev. edn Dundalk 1949).

Mayo, Robert D., *The English Novel in the Magazines 1741–1815 with a catalogue of 1375 Magazine Novels and Novelettes* (Evanton and London 1962).

Memoirs of a Demi-rep of Fashion; or, the private history of Miss Amelia Gunnersbury, 2 vols (Dublin 1776).

Mendoza, Daniel, *The Art of Boxing* (Dublin 1792).

Mooney, Tighernan & White, Fiona, 'The Gentry's Winter Season', *The Gorgeous Mask: Dublin 1700–1850* (Dublin 1987), pp1–16.

Moore, Jane Elizabeth *Miscellaneous poems, on Various Subjects* (Dublin 1796).

O'Donoghue, J.D., *The Poets of Ireland* (Dublin 1912).

O'Higgind, Paul, *A Bibliography of Irish State Trials and other Legal Proceedings* (Abingdon 1986).

O'Keeffe, John, *Recollections of the Life of John O'Keeffe, written by Himself*, 2 vols (London 1826).

Oulton, Walley Chamberlain, *The History of the Theatres of London*, 2 vols (London 1796).

Phillips, Teresa Constantia, *An Apology for the Conduct of Mrs T.C. Phillips, more particularly that part of it which relates to her Marriage with an eminent Dutch Merchant*, 3 vols (London 1748–9).

Pilkington, Letitia, *Memoirs of Mrs Letitia Pilkington, written by herself, ...*, 2 vols (Dublin; London reprint 1749); *Memoirs of Mrs Letitia Pilkington*, Iris Barry (ed.) (London 1928).

Plomer, Henry Robert, *A Dictionary of the Printers and Booksellers who were at work in England, Scotland and Ireland from 1726 to 1775* (London 1932).

Raven, James, *British Fiction 1750–1770, a Chronological Check-list of Prose Fiction printed in Britain and Ireland* (Newark 1987).

Read, Charles, *The Cabinet of Irish Literature*, revised by Katherine Tynan Hinkson, 4 vols (London 1904).

Rowan, Archibald Hamilton, *A brief investigation of the sufferings of John, Anne, and Mary Neal* (Dublin 1788); *The trial of R. Edgeworth, for subornation of perjury* (Dublin 1788).

Summers, Montague, *A Gothic Bibliography* (London 1941).

Todd, Janet, *A Dictionary of British and American Women Writers* (London 1984).

Walsh, John Edward, *Ireland Sixty Years Ago* (Dublin 1851).

Wlash, Thomas Joseph, *Opera in Dublin, 1705–1797; the social scene* (Dublin 1973).

Watson, John, and successor publishers, *The Gentleman's and Citizen's Almanack* (annual publication, Dublin 1750–97).

Whaley, Thomas, *Buck Whaley's memoirs including his journey to Jerusalem, writted by himself in 1797 and now first published from the recently discovered manuscript*. Edited, with an introduction and notes, by Sir Edward Sullivan, Bart (London 1906).

Wilson, Peter, and successor publishers, *Wilson's Dublin directory … containing list of the names, occupations, and places of abode, of the merchants and eminent traders of the city of Dublin* (annual publication, Dublin 1753 and 1762–97).

Acknowledgments

My debts in the editing and preparation of Mrs Leeson's *Memoirs* for publication are many and varied. The arduous task of proofreading the main text was undertaken by Norma Jessop, Special Collections Librarian in UCD, and Peter Kenny, of the NLI. This involved line by line comparison of my text with hard copy generated from microfilm of the late eighteenth-century original, an extremely tedious and time-consuming operation.

Veronica Morrow, Keeper of Technical Services in the Library at TCD, Herbert H. Kilcloyne, and Bell and Howell, of Pearse Street, Dublin, provided invaluable logistical support, both in converting the microfilm to hard copy, and in preparing the raw text for publication.

Dr David Dickson, of the School of Modern History, TCD, Professor R.B. McDowell, SFTCD, and Dr Andrew Carpenter, of the Department of English, UCD, were generous with both time and advice. Eugene Hogan, of the NLI, produced the frontispiece and textual illustrations, and the National Gallery permitted the use of Milltown 703 as a cover illustration. Mary Paul Pollard kindly gave me access to portions of the text of her forthcoming *Directory of Dublin Printers and Booksellers*, soon to be published by the Bibliographical Society.

However, my deepest debt is to my friend Tim Lehane, of Radio 1, RTE. Had he not commissioned the original series, 'Georgian Graft', in 1993, Mrs Leeson and all her works and pomps might have remained safely tucked away in the catalogue and stack of the National Library of Ireland, and the measured text of an early twentieth-century footnote.

Index of Place-names

All entries for individual streets and buildings in London, Dublin, Paris, Cork and Belfast will be found in the directory entries for these cities. Place-names in County Dublin appear listed in directory format under the heading Dublin, County.

Aberdeen, 217

America, 47, 53, 54, 56, 57, 66, 69, 79, 135

Angel Tavern (subsequently The Shoulder of Mutton), 200–1

Antigua, 135, 137

Ardrum, County Cork, 220

Arklow, County Wicklow, 193, 194

Ballyclare, County Antrim, 152

Ballydehob, County Cork, 203

Banbridge, County Down, 175

Bantry, County Cork, 203

Barbados, British West Indies, 111, 135, 136

Bath, 114, 242

Bay of Biscay, *see* Biscay

Belfast, 145, 163, 204, 205; Donegal Arms, 205

Bengal, 124

Bere, County Cork, 203

Biscay, Bay of, 120

Blackrock, County Cork, 68

Bombay, 123, 124, 138, 139, 140

Borrisokane, County Tipperary, 247

Bray, County Wicklow, 194

Brimstone Hill, St Kitt's, British West Indies, *see* St Kitt's

British West Indies, *see* West Indies

Bunker Hill, Charlestown, Mass. (Battle of), 228

Burchell's Inn, Nineteen Mile House, County Kildare, *see* Nineteen Mile House

Cape of Good Hope, *see* Good Hope

Carrickfergus, County Antrim, 218

Carton, County Kildare, 113

Cashel, County Tipperary, 217

Castleblakeney, County Galway, 155

Castletownshend, County Cork, 208

Cavan, County of, 6

Clare, County of, 228, 237, 238, 241

Clarecastle, County Clare, 108

Cobh, County Cork, 68

Corbetstown, County Westmeath, 5, 6

Cork, 66, 67, 111, 178, 179, 187, 190, 197; Glanmire, 68; Hammond's Marsh, 67; Sunday's Well, 68

Cork, County of, 150, 179, 183, 227, 241; brogue and speech patterns, 202, 203, 220

Cove, County Cork, *see* Cobh

Crookhaven, County Cork, 203

Curragh (The), County Kildare, 50, 52, 66
Dardistown, County Westmeath, 9, 15
Dargle (Valley), County Wicklow, 113, 180
Down, County of, 183
Downs, Glen of the, *see* Glen of the Downs
Drogheda, County Louth, 23, 25
Dublin, 6, 7, 8, 13, 14, 15, 17, 24, 43, 80, 86,
87, 98, 114, 115, 118, 126, 139, 163, 197;
Abbey St, 33, 159; Angel Court (Math-
ews' Spunging House), 232–9; Arran
St, 5, 16; Aungier St, 108, 161; Bache-
lors' Walk, 180; Barracks (now
Collins's Barracks), 100, 108; Belfast
Hotel, 163; Blue Coat Hospital, 158;
Boot Lane, 180; Bow Bridge, 153;
Bride St, 49, 165; Bride's Alley, 192;
Camden St, 181; Capel St, 153, 154,
155, 159, 161, 162; Channel Row
(Nunnery), 20; Circular Road (South),
36, 136, 192; Clarendon St, 21, 238;
College Green, 86, 147, 156, 175; Cook
St, 165; Cope St, 100; Crow St (The-
atre Royal), 242, 245; Crown Alley,
155; Custom House, 86; Daly's Coffee-
house, 47; Dame St, 52, 73; Dame St
(Rose and Bottle Tavern), 61; Darby
Square, 146; Drogheda St, 66, 69, 80;
Dublin Castle, 47, 144; Essex St, 247;
Eustace St, 165; Exchequer St (The
Menage), 214; Fishamble St, 132; Fleet
St, 232; Four Courts' Marshalsea
(Prison), 132, 230, 233, 238, 247;
Fowne's St, 52, 73; Francis St, 246;
French St, 108; George's Quay, 85, 86,
165; Grafton Lane, 180; Grafton St, 63,
160, 161, 215, 232; Great Britain St,
155, 157, 158, 161, 163, 166, 175, 238;
Great George's St (South), 251; Green
St, 180; High St, 26, 246; Inns Quay,
29; James's St, 238, 251; Jervis St, 132,
159, 180; Johnson's Court, 108, 172;
King St, 159; Leeson St (Magdalen
Asylum), 224; Liberties, 156; Linen
Hall, 129; Lock Hospital, 153; Long-
ford St, 132, 161; Mark St, 182; Marl-
borough Green, 180; Mary's Lane, 180;
Mecklenburgh St, 86, 162; Newgate
Prison (Old Newgate, the Cornmarket),
71, 89, 100; New Prison (New New-
gate, Green St), 108, 181; New
Rotunda Gardens, 113, 136, 147; New
St (Nunnery), 105, 106; North Wall,
22; Ormond Quay, 155, 159, 146; Park
St, 37, 38; Parliament St, 73; Peter St
(Astley's Amphitheatre), 226; Phoenix
Park, 200; Pill Lane, 206; Pitt St, 94,
108, 143, 144, 162, 172, 176, 177, 182,
202, 228; Queen's St, 165; Ranelagh
Gardens, 71; Ranelagh Road, 36, 38,
55; St Anne's Churchyard, 172; St
James's Churchyard, 251; Smithfield,
29; Smock Alley, 34; Smock Alley
(Theatre Royal), 87–91; South Wall
(Light House), 209; Stafford St, 155;
Stephen's Green, 139, 243; Stoney-
batter, 156; Strand St, 29, 30, 181;
Summerhill, 130, 132; Swift's Hospital,
175, 238; Temple Bar, 249–51; Thomas
St, 100, 148; Thomas St (Old Kennel
Inn), 251; Trinity College, 70–71, 161;
Trinity St, 146; Whitefriar St, 131;
Williams St (Exhibition Rooms), 166;
170; Wine Tavern St, 178; Wood St,
47, 55, 56, 57, 87, 94
Dublin, County: Bagatrot Castle, 245;
Blackrock, 95, 175, 238; Blackrock
(Fiat Hill), 170; Blackrock Road, 192,
200, 203, 204, 228; Blackrock (Three
Tun Tavern), 244–5; Donnybrook,
153; Drumcondra, 164, 169, 247;
Drumcondra (Asylum), 164; Drum-
condra (Broadhead's Inn), 170, 199;
Laughlinstown Camp, 222; Mount
Brown, 234; Rathfarnham, 100, 200;
Rathfarnham (Laughlin's Tavern),
198; Rathfarnham (Little Dargle), 198;
Whitehall, 153, 213–15
Dunkirk, 158
Dunleer, County Louth, 23, 24
Eagle's Nest, Killarney, County Kerry, 188
East Carberry, County Cork, 208
East Indies (India), *see* India
Ennis, County Clare, 228, 238
Eyrecourt, County Galway (Heathlawn),
127
Fethard, County Tipperary, 152, 153

France, 197, 228
Glen of the Downs, County Wicklow, 113
Good Hope, Cape of, 120, 121, 122, 123
Gosport, 120
Heathlawn, Eyrecourt, County Galway, *see* Eyrecourt
Hillsborough, County Down, 175, 176
Holyhead, 85, 96
India (East Indies), 118–24, 136
Inisfallen Island, Killarney, County Kerry, 189
Keating's Inn, Cashel, County Tipperary, 217
Kerry, County of, 203, 209, 240, 241; brogue and patterns of speech, 178, 179
Kilbeggan, County Westmeath, 12
Kildare Town, 50, 51, 52, 126
Kildare, County of (Mr Leeson's estates), 36
Kilkenny, County of, 238
Killarney, County Kerry, 179, 186–190, 227, 236
Killough, County Westmeath (Mrs Leeson's birthplace), 5, 12, 13, 15, 17
Kiltinan, County Tipperary, 172
Kinnegad, County Westmeath, 5, 27
Leixlip, County Kildare, 113
Limerick, 146, 152
Lisnarock, County Tipperary, 214, 217
Little Village, Killarney, County Kerry, 190
Liverpool, 156
London, 79, 80, 96, 97, 111, 114, 116; Cleveland Row, 83; Covent Garden, 143; Drury Lane, 143; Ranelagh Gardens, 83; Regent's Park, 84; Richmond, 85; Strand (The), 84; Temple Bar, 84; Tothill Fields (The Bridewell), 85; Vauxhall Gardens, 83
Macroom, County Cork, 190
Madeira, 118, 120, 121, 122, 135
Madras, 121, 123, 138
Malhassey, County Meath, 157
Mallow, County Cork, 186
Manchester, 98
Martinique, 136
Maryborough (Portlaoise), County Leix, *see* Portlaoise
Miss Plummer's Island, Killarney, County Kerry, *see* Plummer's Island

Mullingar, County Westmeath, 12
Multifarnham, County Westmeath, 162
Naas, County Kildare, 126, 154
New York, 53
Nineteen Mile House, County Kildare (Burchell's Inn), 50, 52, 66
Paris; Bastille, 152
Plummer's Island, Killarney, County Kerry, 189, 191, 236
Portlaoise (Maryborough), County Leix, 126
Portsmouth, 97; common, 122
Rock (The), County Dublin, *see* Blackrock *in* Dublin, County
Rock Road (The), County Dublin, *see* Blackrock Road *in* Dublin, County
Roscrea, County Tipperary, 126, 247
Ross Castle, Killarney, County Kerry, 187
Rotunda Gardens, Dublin, *see* New Rotunda Gardens *in* Dublin
St Kitt's (St Christopher's), British West Indies, 111, 135, 136; Brimstone Hill, 136
Scotland, 122, 195
Shannon (River), 178
Shine's Inn, Killarney, County Kerry, 190
Shoulder of Mutton Inn (formerly The Angel Tavern), *see* Angel Tavern
Spithead, 120, 136
Taghmon, County Wexford, 202
Thornhill, County Cork, 203
Thurles, County Tipperary, 171
Tipperary, County of, 171, 241
Tralee, County Kerry, 111, 178, 179, 190, 209, 218; (Young's School), 209
Trim, County Meath, 156
Tullamore, County Offaly, 5, 6, 10, 11, 16, 111
Waterford, 179
Waterford, County of, 241
West Carberry, County Cork, 192, 203
West Indies, British, 135, 136
Whitehall, County Cork, 203, 218
Wicklow, 193, 194
Wicklow, County of, 193
Windward Islands, British West Indies, 135
Youghal, County Cork, 186
Young's School, Tralee, County Kerry, *see* Tralee

Index of Persons

A—, Andrew (Andy), guest at the 'Masonic Masquerade', 167

A—, Mr, of Capel St, Dublin, 154

A—, T—, keeper of Mary Crosbie, 161

A—g, Mr, father of Miss Dorothea A—g,

A—g, Mr, guest at the 'Masonic Masquerade', 167

A—g, Miss Dorothea, of County Clare, subsequently Mrs Purcell, 237–8

A—r, Mr, surgeon, 146

Abcderian Society (The), 173–4

Abercorn, Marquis of, see Hamilton, John James

Abercorn, 'Mock Marchioness of', former mistress of John James Hamilton, briefly employed by Mrs Leeson in Pitt St, 176–7

Anecdote Club of Free Brothers (The), see States of Castle-Kelly (The)

Archbold, Miss, prostitute and kept woman, 160

Armstrong, Robert, apothecary, of Capel St, Dublin, 162

Ashmore, Miss, friend of Mrs Leeson, 124

Atkinson, Captain, officer of the watch (St Anne's Parish, Dublin), 108

Atkinson, Mary, prostitute, calling herself Mrs Ottiwell, 163

Atkinson, William, mathematician, of Belfast, father of Mary Atkinson, 163

Attridge, Mrs Catherine (Kitty), prostitute, 149–150, 248

Attridge, Mr, husband to Kitty Attridge, 149

Attwood, Miss, of Tralee, see C—ll, Mrs

Attwood, Mr, brogue maker, of Tralee, father to Miss Attwood, 190

B—, alderman of the City of Dublin, client and defrauder of Mrs Leeson, 230

B—, Sheriffs' Peer of the County of the City of Dublin, client and defrauder of Mrs Leeson, 230

B—, Mrs, 'the Bantry Ginger', prostitute briefly employed by Mrs Leeson at Pitt St, 183–4

B—, H—, client and defrauder of Mrs Leeson, 229

B—, John (Jack), client and defrauder of Mrs Leeson, 229

B—, M—, of Borrisokane, Mr Collins's employer, 246

B—, N—, keeper of Mary Roberts, 180

B—, W—, client and defrauder of Mrs Leeson, 229

B—e, Lieutenant, keeper of Fanny Beresford, 193

B—r, Major, gambler present at Daly's Club during the hoax on Buck English, 217

Balderdash, Sir B., see Roche, Sir Boyle, MP

Bantry Ginger (The), see B—, Mrs, 'the Bantry Ginger'

Barlow, Mr, Guest at the 'Masonic Masquerade', client and victim of Miss Boyd, 161–2, 167

Barret, Mr, client of Mrs Leeson, and rival of her lover, S.L. Cunynghame, 125

Barry, Mr, coxswain of Lord Kenmare's barge (1789), 186, 187, 189

Bastable, Mr, of Cork, dupe of Dr John Bell, 197

Batt, Captain Thomas (Tommy), of Belfast, 206

Battier, Mrs Henrietta, journalist and satirist, 215–16, 243

Batty, J.E., barrister, of Chatham St, Dublin, 110–11

Beatty, Mr, brother-in-law to Mrs Leeson, 5

Beatty, Mrs, elder sister to Mrs Leeson, 5, 6, 12

Bective, Earl of, see Taylour, Thomas

Bedford, Duke of, see Russel, Francis

Beg, Mr, London confidant and go-between of John Lawless, 82

Bell, Mr, of The Herald, journalist and guest at the 'Masonic Masquerade', 167

Bell, Dr John, mesmerist, magnetizer, quack, and fraudster, 195–7

Bennet, Mr, itinerant pedlar, first husband of Elizabeth O' Falvey, 177–8

Bennet, Mrs Elizabeth, prostitute, see O'Falvey, Mrs Elizabeth

Bennis, Mrs, brothel-keeper and procuress, 198

Beresford, France (Fanny), prostitute employed by Mrs Leeson at Pitt St, probable amanuensis working on Volumes I. & II. of the Memoirs, 147, 152, 185, 193–5, 198

Beresford, Lighton, Woodman and Needham, Dublin Merchant Bank and corporate benefactor to Mrs Leeson during her imprisonment, 239

Billy the Beau, see Crosbie, William

Bishop, Mr, innkeeper (The Three Tuns, Blackrock, County Dublin), 244–5

Blackwood, Hans, Dublin merchant, benefactor to Mrs Leeson during her imprisonment, 239

Blackwood, Price, Dublin merchant, benefactor to Mrs Leeson during her imprisonment, 239

Blennerhasset, Mr (holiday acquaintance, Killarney, June 1789), 188

Blennerhasset, Mrs (holiday acquaintance, Killarney, June 1789), 188, 189

Blennerhasset, Henry, probably of Tralee, friend of Mrs Leeson, and client at Pitt St, also keeper of Miss Grove, 152, 153, 210

Blennerhasset, William, collector of revenue at Tralee, Kerry suicide, 208–9

'Blinker', client of Mrs Leeson, at Pitt St, 203

Bolger, Charles, surgeon, of Suffolk St, Dublin, 153, 248

Bonsfield, Mr, of Cork, dupe of Dr John Bell, 197

Borumborad, Dr Achmet (The Kilkenny Turk, i.e. Patrick Joyce of Kilkenny), 151, 213

Botet, the Rev. Fiztmaurice, Kerry suicide, 208

Bourbon-Orleans, Louis Philippe Joseph de, Duc d'Orleans, 228

Boyd, Miss, prostitute, of Longford St, Dublin, 161–2

Boyle, Lieutenant, aide-de-camp to the Lord Lieutenant (1783), 113, 114

Boyne, Lord, see Hamilton, Frederick

Brady, Mr, apothecary attending Mrs Leeson during her last illness, 249

Brady, Mr, brother-in-law to Mrs Leeson, 7, 8, 26

Brady, Mrs, elder sister to Mrs Leeson, 7, 22, 26

Breen, the Widow, innkeeper (of Taghmon,

County Wexford), 202

Brenan, Charles, journalist and petty criminal, 221

Bristol, Earl of, *see* Hervey, Frederick Augustus

Broadhead, Mr, innkeeper (Broadhead's, Drumcondra, County Dublin), 199

Broganier Fool (The), *see* R—L, A—

Brooks, Mrs, brothel-keeper and procuress, of Trinity St and Darby Square, Dublin, originally Mrs Stevenson, and formerly of Belfast, 143, 145–7

Brown Billy, client of Mrs Leeson, at Pitt St, 205

Browne, John Denis, Earl of Altamont, 93

Bruce, Edward Kingswill, surveyor of the Port of Belfast, seducer of Mary Atkinson, 163–4

Brush marriage, punning comparison of a genuine marriage, involving a Mr Brush, with the more informal ceremony of leaping over a broom to solemnize a common-law union, 202

Buck English, *see* English, William Alexander

Burchell, Mr, innkeeper (Nineteen Mile House, County Kildare), 50, 52, 66

Burnett, Mrs, brothel-keeper and procuress, of Whitefriar St, Dublin, 131, 132, 198

Burgoyne, Major-General Sir John, 123, 139

Burroughs, John, 124

Butler, Mrs, procuress, of Clarendon St, Dublin, mother to Michael Kelly, 'the crupper-making squire of Whitehall', 21, 152

Butler, Walter, Viscount Thurles and subsequently Earl of Ormond, client of Mrs Leeson at Wood St, 129–30

C—, Mr, client and defrauder of Mrs Leeson, 230

C—, Mr, Dublin confidant of John Lawless, 59, 60

C—, Mr, Dublin brewer, and defrauder of Mrs Leeson, 246

C—, Mr, defrauder of Mrs Leeson, of Francis St, Dublin, 246

C—, Mr, keeper of Mrs Palmer, the prostitute, 159

C—, Mr, singer, 162, 163

C—, Mrs, keeper of a register office for Servants, 157

C—, Mrs, wife to the keeper of Mrs Palmer, 159

C—e, Mr, pimp and bully employed by Mrs Leeson, 181

C—h, Mr, guest at the 'Masonic Masquerade', 167

C—ll, Mr, (holiday acquaintance, Killarney, June 1789), 188

C—ll, Mrs, (holiday acquaintance, Killarney, June 1789), also bigamously married to John Cavendish Maudsley, 188, 189, 190

C—ll, Francis, Kerry suicide, 208

C—t—es, Miss, kept woman of Sir John Colthurst, of Ardrum, County Cork, 220

Callanan, Dr, of Cork, dupe of Dr John Bell, 197

Callage, Mr, officer, RN, 139

Carleton, Captain, officer of the watch (St Anne's Parish, Dublin), 108

Carnavalli, Signor, Italian violinist, conductor and impresario, 87–91

Casey, Deborah (Debbie), prostitute, subsequently Mrs Dowd, 231, 244–5

Cashel, Mr, client of Mrs Leeson at Wood St, 93

Cashel, Mr, early client and lover of Mrs Leeson, 62–2, 64

Catley, Miss Ann, actress and singer, 73–4

Caulfield, James, Earl of Charlemont, cousin of Mrs Leeson's first keeper, Thomas Caulfield, 30, 33

Caulfield, Thomas, wine merchant, of Abbey St, Dublin, Mrs Leeson's first keeper, 30–3, 34

Cavan, Earl of, *see* either Lambert, Charles, or Lambert, Richard

Cavendish, James, client of Mrs Netterville, 50, 51

Charlemont, Earl of, *see* Caulfield, James

Chute, Miss (holiday acquaintance, Killarney, 1789), 188, 189

Clanwilliam, Earl of, *see* Meade, John

Clare, Mr, petty fraudster, son of the copyist

John Clare, 148

Clare, John, wire drawer and copyist, 148

Cleghorn, George, physician, of Eustace St, Dublin, 49, 55

Clonmel, Countess of, *see* Scott, Margaret

Coleman, Mr, waiter, and defrauder of Mrs Leeson, 230

Collins, Mr, husband who deserted Margaret Collins prior to her employment by Mrs Leeson, 246

Collins, Mrs Margaret, paid companion to Mrs Leeson at the time of her death, 246–51

Colthurst, Sir John, of Ardrum, County Cork, keeper of Miss C—t—es, 220

Company of Printers and Booksellers, 198

Connell, Daniel, of Cork, actor, dupe of Dr John Bell, 197

Connor, Mr, cattle thief and father of Miss Groves, the prostitute, 155

Cook, Edward, Under Secretary and subsequent Chief Secretary of State in Ireland, 152

Cook, Thomas, 'the beggar of Kiltinan', 171–2

Corbet, William, printer and bookseller, benefactor to Mrs Leeson during her imprisonment, 239

Corcoran, Bartholomew (Bartle), printer, bookseller, and balladeer, 167, 168–9, 198

Cork Humane Society, 197

Courtney, Captain G.W.A., RN, commander of the *Eurydice*, 123

Courtney, Mr, benefactor to Mrs Leeson during her imprisonment, 239

Craddock, Captain Francis, aide-de-camp to the Lord Lieutenant in 1783, and client of Mrs Leeson at Wood St, 113

Craig, Charles, Dublin watchmaker, dupe and victim of Dr John Bell, 196–7

Crawford, John, house painter, of Townshend St, Dublin, guest at the 'May Day Masquerade', 93

Croker, Ally, courtezan and beauty, subsequently Mrs Langley, 217

Croneen, Anthony Grumble, uncle to the bigamously married Mrs C—, ll, 190

Crosbie, Mary, prostitute and kept woman, 161–2

Crosbie, Richard, balloonist, aeronaut, and leader of the Pinking-dindies, 69–71

Crosbie, William, 'Billy the Beau', Earl of Glandore, 227–8

Crosbie, William, keeper of Mary Crosbie, and son of Maurice Crosbie, Dean of Limerick, 161

Cruise, family holding lands at Castle Blakney, County Galway, 155, 159

Crupper-making squire (The), *see* Kelly, Michael

Cullum, William, surgeon, of Moor St, Dublin, 49, 55

Cunningham, John, cadet servant and petty thief, 180

Cunningham, Waddell, MP (the Smuggler), 146, 153, 201

Cunymghame, S.L. (Bobbadil), client and lover of Mrs Leeson, 99, 110, 111, 114, 125–7, 135–7, 143

'Curly Pated Squire' (the), client of Mrs Leeson, at Pitt St, 205

Curran, John Philpot, barrister and wit, 202

D—, Colonel, 246

D—, Michael, keeper of Mary Crosbie, 161

D—e, Mrs, respectably married ex-prostitute, 187

D—n, Richard (Dicky), client and friend of Mrs Leeson, 107

D—y, Mr, gambler present at Daly's Club during the hoax on Buck English, 217

Daly, Mr, of Kerry, guest at the 'Masonic Masquerade', 167

Daly, Richard, 'the Irish Roscius', actor-manager, patentee of the Theatre Royal, Dublin (both Smock Alley and Crow St), friend and former client of Mrs Leeson, 90, 156, 157, 216, 245

Dalzell, Miss Polly, prostitute, 145, 183–4

Darcy, family holding lands at Dardistown, County Westmeath, 9

Darcy, Mrs, of Corbetstown, County Westmeath, 5

Dardis, Mr, seducer of Mrs Leeson, 18–27; verses addressed by him to Mrs Leeson, 211–2

Davenport, Peter, groom-porter at Daly's
Club, present during the hoax on Buck
English, 216–17

Deaves, Mr, of Cork, dupe of Dr John Bell,
197

Denny, Lady Arabella, philanthropist asso-
ciated with the Dublin Magdalen Asy-
lum, 147, 224

D[?enn]y, Arthur, brother to Edward
D[?enn]y, the Kerry suicide, 207–8

Denny, Sir Barry, MP, 188, 209

D[?enn]y, Edward, Kerry suicide, 207–8

Digges, Mrs, prostitute, guest at the
'Masonic Masquerade', 152

Dillon, Mrs, brothel-keeper and procuress,
of Fishamble St, Dublin, 132

Dixon, Mrs, mutual friend of Mrs Leeson
and Robert Gorman, 118, 124, 139

Dog in Office (The), see Giffard, John, Sher-
iff of the County of the City of Dublin

Donegal Arms coterie, Belfast, 205–6

Donnelly, Mr, of Belfast, alleged murderer,
lover of Mrs Brooks, 145

Donnelly, Mrs, of Belfast, murder victim,
145

Doran, Catherine (Kitty), prostitute and
beauty, subsequently Mrs Walpole, 214

Dowd, Mr, tobacco twister and first husband
of Deborah Casey, 231

Dowd, Mrs Deborah, see Casey, Deborah

Downshire, Marquis of, see Hill, Wills and
Hill, Arthur

Driscoll, Joan, prostitute and procuress, 214

Droope, William, merchant, of Abbey St,
Dublin, early potential client of Mrs
Leeson, 29

Drumgoold, Mrs, of Drogheda, disapprov-
ing female relative of Mrs Leeson, 23,
25, 26

Duignan, Myles, 'Citizen Duignan', grocer,
money-lender, and radical politician,
172, 250

Durdan, Mr, of Cork, dupe of Dr John Bell,
197

Eagan, John, barrister, and benefactor to Mrs
Leeson during her imprisonment, 239

Eager, Mrs (holiday acquaintance, Killar-
ney, June 1789), 186

Eager, William (holiday acquaintance, Kil-
larney, June, 1789), 186

Eanes, Captain, son of Mrs Dixon, 124, 139

East India Company, 118

Echlin, Sir Harry, 219

Edgeworth, Robert, 'Squire Edgeworth',
pimp to Margaret Llewellyn, and
rapist, 214

Edmonds, Mr, husband to Eliza Edmonds,
228

Edmonds, Mrs Eliza, illegitimate daughter
to the Earl of Glandore, and compan-
ion to Mrs Leeson, 227–9, 231, 232,
233, 236, 237, 238, 239

Eife, Mr, keeper of Mary Atkinson, 163

Ely, Earl of, see Loftus, Henry, Earl of Ely

English, William Alexander (Buck English),
rake-hell, and bully, 167, 216–17

Eyre, Captain, benefactor to Mrs Leeson
during her imprisonment, 239

F—, Miss, prisoner in Mathews's Spunging
House, 235

F—ch—r, Mr, keeper of Miss Dalzell, 184

F—k—s, Mr, 202

F—m—g, Miss Elizabeth (Betty), guest at
Castletownshend, 191–192

F—r, Mr, fiancé of Miss Eliza Paine, 219

F—x, Mr, guest at the 'Masonic Masquer-
ade', 167

Faith, sister of Prudence, innkeeper (The
Angel Tavern), 200–1

Fane, John, Earl of Westmorland, and Lord
Lieutenant of Ireland, 151–2, 181

Fane, Sarah Anne (née Childe), Countess
Westmorland, first wife of John Fane,
145

Fannin, Robert, cabinet maker and auction-
eer of Bride Alley, Dublin, 192

Fay, Father Patrick, RC priest and convicted
forger, 160

Featherstone, family holding lands at Dard-
istown, County Westmeath, 9

Featherstone, Mr, of Westmeath, Bridget
Orde's first client, 165

Featherstone, Mrs, of Dardistown, County
Westmeath, 14

Fenton, Joseph, bailiff, pawnbroker, and
defrauder of Mrs Leeson, 238

Ferns, John, wine merchant, of Mitre Alley and Abbey St, Dublin, 212

Finlay, Mr, guest at the 'May Day Masquerade', 94

Fitzgerald, Mr (holiday acquaintance, Killarney, June 1789), admirer of Miss Chute, 189

Fitzgerald, George Robert, 'Fire-Eater Fitzgerald', 215

Fitzgerald, William Robert, Duke of Leinster, 94, 182

Fitz Herbert, Lady (née Stratford), accused of theft by Mrs Leeson, 145

Fitzherbert, Maria, morganatic wife of the Prince Regent, 170

Fitzm—, Mrs, of Dublin, dupe of Dr John Bell, 196

Fitzmaurice, Mrs, (holiday acquaintance, Killarney, June 1789), 189

Fitzmaurice, John Lewis (holiday acquaintance, Killarney, June 1789), 188, 189

Fleetwood, Miss, prostitute and kept woman, 56, 57

Fleetwood, Charles, of Whitefriar St, Dublin, 203

Ford, Maria, prostitute, 166–167

Fox, Mr, of Capel St, Dublin, 159

Fox, Mr, of Liverpool, victim of robbery by the Wrixons, 158, 159

Franklin, J., of Cork, dupe of Dr John Bell, 197

Freemantle, Captain Stephen, aide-de-camp to the Lord Lieutenant, 1783, and client of Mrs Leeson at Wood St, 107, 108, 113

G—, Lady, of Dublin, dupe of Dr John Bell, 196

G—, Mr, of Abbey St, Dublin, 159

G—, Mr, 'the bandy-legged writer', 201

G—d, John (Jack), guest at the 'Masonic Masquerade', 167

G—, W— T—, client and defrauder of Mrs Leeson, 229

George III, 207

George IV, 84, 169

Georgi, Signor, see St Giorgio, Signor

Gibbings, Mr, of Cork, dupe of Dr John Bell, 197

Gibbons, Mr (Junior), forger and admirer of Sally Hayes, 101–2, 139

Gibbons, Mr (Senior), father of Gibbons the forger, 101–2

Gibton, Mr, guest at the 'May Day Masquerade', 93

Giffard, Harding (Harry), son of John Giffard, 216

Giffard, John, sheriff of the County of the City of Dublin, satirized in the Dublin Evening Post as 'The Dog in Office', 216

Ging, John (Johnny) Dublin shoemaker, defrauder of Mrs Leeson, 246

Glandore, Earl of, see Crosbie, William

Godsell, Mr, of Dublin, lunatic and victim of Dr John Bell, 196

Gore, Mrs, extortioner, blackmailer, and mother of Kitty Gore, 131, 132

Gore, Catherine (Kitty), prostitute briefly employed by Mrs Leeson, 131–3

Gorman, Robert (Bob), of Blackrock, County Dublin, lover and friend of Mrs Leeson, 95–7, 98, 114, 118–24, 135, 137–40, 143

Graham, Mr, keeper of Bridget Orde, 165–6

Grant, Mrs (née Connor), prostitute and procuress, 153–4, 155–7

Gray, Mr, of Cork, dupe of Dr John Bell, 197

Graydon, Alexander, surgeon, of Jervis St, Dublin, 159

Green, Mrs, thief, and Mrs Leeson's London housekeeper, 83, 85

Green, Thomas, of Cork, merchant, 191

Greg, Miss Jenny, of Belfast, daughter of Thomas Greg, 206

Greg, Thomas, of Belfast, merchant, 206

Griffith, Amyas, printer, bookseller, and probable lover of Mrs Leeson, 145, 147, 166, 201, 219–20; author of Truth and Falsehood, a Fable, addressed to Mrs Leeson, 210–11

Griffith, Mrs Frances, wife of Amyas Griffith, 219–20

Griffith, Jonas, 228

Grove, Miss, prostitute employed by Mrs Leeson at Pitt St, discharged for rowdy behaviour and theft, 152, 153, 185, 192–2, 198

Guilford, Lord, courtesy title of heir of Earldom of Clanwilliam, *see* Meade, Richard

Gunn, Mr (holiday acquaintance, Killarney, June 1789), 189

Gunn, Mrs (holiday acquaintance, Killarney, June 1789), 189

H—, Captain, keeper and lover of Sally Hayes, 99

H—, Mr, of the Custom House, Dublin, keeper of Mary Roberts, 180

H—, Mr, of James's St, Dublin, 251

H—, Mr, keeper of Miss Archbold, 160

H—, Henry (Harry), keeper of Betsy Love (1796–7), 251

H—, J—, first seducer of Mrs Grant, 155, 157

H—, T—, client and defrauder of Mrs Leeson, 229

H—, Mrs, 'the fat Sappho of Drumcondra' *see* Hill, Mrs Robert

H—gf—ds, Mr, 171, 203

H—g—s, Mrs, actress and kept woman, 171

H—k—n, Thomas, RC physician and Kerry suicide, 208

H—l—n, Mr, keeper of Mrs H—g—s, 171

H—n, Mr, keeper and lover of Fanny Beresford, 193

H—y, Mrs, novelist, 170–1

Hall, Mrs Mary (Moll), brothel-keeper and procuress, of Mecklenburgh St and Johnson's Court, close friend to Mrs Leeson, 86, 87, 88, 93, 121, 129, 148, 152, 153, 172–3

Hallam, Robert, house painter, of Capel St, Dublin, 161

Haly, Mr, of Cork, dupe of Dr John Bell, 197

Hamilton, Captain, guest at the 'May Day Masquerade', 93

Hamilton, Frederick, Viscount Boyne, 50, 51

Hamilton, Mrs James, mantua maker, of Capel St, Dublin, 161

Hamilton, John James, Marquis of Abercorn, 176

Hangar, 'Captain', officer in the Viceregal guard (1783), 113

Hatchell, Philip, apothecary, of Grafton St,

Dublin, 168

Hawkesworth, Miss, fiancée, and subsequently wife of Thomas Caulfield, 33

Hayes, Sally, prostitute, close friend and occasional partner to both Mrs Leeson and Moll Hall, 66, 67, 74, 75, 80, 86, 87, 93, 94, 99, 101, 107, 110, 111, 113, 114, 121, 129

Headfort, Lord, courtesy title of the heir to the Earldom of Bective, *see* Taylour, Thomas

Healy, Mrs, prostitute, guest at the 'May Day Masquerade', 93

Hearvy, Mr, of Cork, dupe of Dr John Bell, 197

Heighland, Mr, 205–6

Heneghan, Peter, grocer, benefactor to Mrs Leeson during her imprisonment, 239

Henn, William, third justice of the Court of King's Bench (1779), 71

Hervey, Frederick Augustus, Earl of Bristol and Bishop of Derry, 243–4

Hewitt, Joseph, unsuccessful candidate to the Carrickfergus election (1784), 201

Higgins, Francis, 'the Sham Squire', fraudster, proprietor of the *Freeman's Journal*, and benefactor to Mrs Leeson during her imprisonment, 239

Higginson, Mr, son of Philip Higginson, tea merchant, of College Green, 193–4

Hill, Arthur, 2nd Marquis of Downshire, 175–6

Hill, Mrs Robert, of Drumcondra, County Dublin, possibly 'the fat Sappho of Drumcondra', 169–70, 248

Hill, Wills, 1st Marquis of Downshire, 175–6

Hinds, Allick, 157

Hinds, Nancy, prostitute, 157–8

Hinds, Ralph, 157

Hinkman, Mr, of Cork, dupe of Dr John Bell, 197

Holmes, Joshua, apothecary, of Capel St, Dublin, 161

Hovenden, Robert, merchant, of Capel St, Dublin, 161

Hughes, James William, proprietor of Hughes's Club, 147

Howard, Thomas (Tommy), of Cork, dupe of Dr John Bell, 197

Humane Society, Cork, *see* Cork Humane Society

Humphries, Richard, prize-fighter, 147

Hunt, Mr, minor officer in the Viceregal guard, 1783, 113

Isaacs, Mr, dulcimer player and singer, 66, 113

Jack, George, of Cork, dupe of Dr John Bell, 197

Jackson, Mr, box-keeper at the Theatre Royal (Smock Alley), 88, 89

Jackson, Mr, early client and friend of Mrs Leeson, 35, 36, 37, 38

Jenkins, Caleb, alderman of the City of Dublin, keeper of Mrs Vallance, 155, 164–5

Jenkins, William Lionel (Billy), apothecary, of Dame St, Dublin, 114, 248

Jessop, Mr, prisoner in Mathews's Spunging House, 235

Johnston, Mrs, brothel-keeper and procuress of Fowne's St, Dublin, 52–3

Jolly Dogs (The), mock Volunteer company formed in West Carberry, County Cork, under the leadership of Edward Townshend, 191–2

Jones, Mr, guset at the 'May Day Masquerade', 93

Jones, Mr, purser of *The Race Horse*, plying between Spithead and Madeira in 1783, 120, 121

Jones, Edward, apothecary, of Fleet St, Dublin, friend of Margaret Collins, 250–1

Jones, John, printer and bookseller, of Grafton St, Dublin, publisher of the *Sentimental Magazine*, 215

Jones, T., of Cork, dupe of Dr John Bell, 197

Jordan, Thomas, hosier, of Pill Lane, Dublin, 206

Joyce, Patrick, of Kilkenny, *see* Borumborad, Dr Achmet

Joyce, Mr, victualler, and brother of Dr Achmet Borumborad, 151

Judge, Mrs Ann, prostitute, friend of Mrs Leeson, direct contemporary and rival

of Katherine Netterville, 88

K—, Mr, pimp and defrauder of Mrs Leeson, 230

K—, the Rev. Mr, defrauder of Mrs Leeson, 246

K—, the Rev. Mr, of the Meeting House, benefactor to Mrs Leeson during her imprisonment, 239

Kate of Aberdeen, courtezan and beauty, subsequently Mrs Mercer, 217

Keating, Robert (Bob), innkeeper, of Cashel, County Tipperary, 218

Kellett, Sir R., of Cork, dupe of Dr John Bell, 197

Kelly, Captain, guest at the 'Masonic Masquerade', 167

Kelly, Mr, dulcimer player, 105–6

Kelly, Charles Aylmer, Dublin money-lender, 148

Kelly, John, 'Cockney Jack', brother to Michael Kelly, 'the Crupper-Making Squire', 212

Kelly, John, father to Mrs Palmer, the prostitute, 159

Kelly, Michael, 'the Crupper-Making Squire of Whitehall', 152, 213–15

Kelso, Dr Hamilton, physician and radical politician, 219–20

Kennedy, John, Waterford glass merchant, of Dublin, benefactor to Mrs Leeson during her imprisonment, 238–9

Kerry Suicides (The), a named group of alumni of Young's School, Tralee, who all committed suicide (1792–4), 207–10

Kirkpatrick, Alexander, alderman and sheriffs' peer of the City of Dublin, known as 'the Nabob', probable keeper of Mrs Katherine Netterville, 65

Kinselagh, Mr of Dublin, ballad singer, and son-in-law to Charley O'Gallagher, 169

Kinselagh, Edmond R., of Cork, dupe of Dr John Bell, 197

Kinsey, Thomas, druggist, of Kinsey and Farrell, druggists, Capel St, Dublin, 164

Kirwan, the Rev. William Blake, renowned Dublin charity preacher, satirized in

Mrs Battier's *The Kirwanade*, subsequently Dean of Kilalla, 221

Kitty Cut-a-Dash, *see* Netterville, Mrs Katherine

Knapp, Mr, of Cork, dupe of Dr John Bell, 197

L——, Captain, of Belfast, 205–6

L——e, Mr, of Dublin, potential dupe of Dr John Bell, 196

L——y, Mr, Mrs Leeson's second suitor, 9

L——y, John (Jack), gambler present at Daly's Club, during the hoax on Buck English, 217

Lambert, Richard, Earl of Cavan, kinsman of Mrs Leeson, 5

Lambert, Thomas, Earl of Cavan, kinsman of Mrs Leeson, 5

Lambert, the Rev. Thomas, keeper of Mrs Leeson, in succession to John Lawless, 61–3, 64, 65, 70

Lamprey, Edward, chandler, of South Great George's St, Dublin, 214

Langley, Mrs, *see* Croker, Ally

Langley, Charles, of Lisnarock, County Tipperary, 217

Langley, Henry, of Lisnarock, County Tipperary, keeper of Kitty Doran, 214

Lascelles, Colonel and subsequently General, Francis, keeper and protector of the actress, Ann Catley, 73, 74

La Touche's Bank, employer of Frank McG——, lover of Molly McPherson, 177

La Touche, Mrs, one of many philanthropic wives in the banking family, who died prior to Mrs Leeson's retirement, 224

La Touche, David (III), Governor of the Bank of Ireland, and client of Mrs Leeson at Wood St, 128

Lawler, Mr, former client of Mrs Leeson, 139

Lawless, John (Jack), *alias* Buck Lawless, Mrs Leeson's keeper and lover in succession to the original Mr Leeson, 35, 36, 37, 38, 41, 42, 43–55, 56, 57, 58, 59, 60, 67, 68, 69, 79, 80, 81, 82, 95, 114–18, 135, 199

Le Conte, M., cook to the Earl of Westmor-

land, allegedly involved in the storming of the Bastille, 152

Leeson, Mr, English merchant holding lands in County Kildare, the keeper from whom Mrs Leeson took her 'professional name', 35–42, 47

Leeson, Joseph, first Earl of Milltown and client of Mrs Leeson at Wood St, 'Game Cock Joe', 107, 199

Le Favre, Mr, son of Peter Le Favre, perfumer, of Grafton St, Dublin, 160, 168

Le Favre, Peter, perfumer, of Grafton St, Dublin, benefactor to Mrs Leeson during her imprisonment, 239

Leinster, Duke of, *see* Fitzgerald, William Robert, Duke of Leinster

Leonard, the Rev. Dr, RC priest, and confessor to Mrs Leeson during her last illness, 225, 250

Leslie, Mr, of Cork, dupe of Dr John Bell, 197

Lewis, Christopher, printer and bookseller, possible advisor on the production of the *Memoirs*, 134–5

Linen Hall Dangler, an aging admirer of Mrs Leeson, 128

Llewellyn, Mrs Margaret, the brothel-keeper and procuress, accomplice in the rape of Mary Neill, 160

Loftus, Henry, Earl of Ely, 200

Longfield, Dr, of Cork, dupe of Dr John Bell, 197

'Longnose', of Limerick, client of Mrs Leeson at Pitt St, 203

Love, Elizabeth (Betty), prostitute and friend of Mrs Leeson, 121, 124, 143, 241, 251

Louis XVI, 202, 212

Lynch, Larry, footpad, lover of Mary Roberts, and subject of the ballad 'The Night before Larry was Hanged', 180

M——, Mr, of High St, Dublin, defrauder of Mrs Leeson, 246

M——, Mrs, sitter for the artist W—— R——n, 235

M——, Daniel (Dan), keeper of Mary Crosbie, 161

M——r——s, Samuel, Kerry suicide, 208

M—w, Mrs, original employer of Eliza Edmonds, 228

M'Clean, Mrs, brothel-keeper and procuress, of Eustace St, Dublin, 143, 165, 185, 186, 222

M'Crae, John, secretary of the Abcderian Society, 173–4

M'D—, Dr, of the Meeting House, benefactor to Mrs Leeson during her imprisonment, 239

M'G—, Francis, lover of Molly McPherson, 177

M'Illicudy, Mr (holiday acquaintance, Killarney, June 1789), 189

M'Illicudy, Mrs (holiday acquaintance, Killarney, June 1789), 189

M'M—, Alex, keeper of Mary Crosbie, 161

M'Nally, Leo, barrister, of Dominick St, Dublin, benefactor to Mrs Leeson during her imprisonment, 239

Mc Neill, Mr, guest at the 'May Day Masquerade', 93

Mc Pherson, Miss Mary (Molly) of Banbridge, County Down, prostitute, kept woman serving both the first and second Marquis of Downshire, briefly employed by Mrs Leeson at Pitt St, 175–6

Magee, Mrs, wife of John Magee, a troublesome prostitute, briefly employed by Mrs Leeson at Pitt St, 174–5

Magee, John, proprietor of the *Dublin Evening Post*, the 'Man of Ireland', 148, 169, 174, 239

Magee, William, of Belfast, brother to John Magee, 175

Manders, Richard, of James's St, Dublin, benefactor to Mrs Leeson during her imprisonment, 239

Manners, Charles, Duke of Rutland and Lord Lieutenant of Ireland, client of Mrs Leeson at Pitt St, 143, 144–5, 147

Manners, Mary Isabella (*née* Somerset), Duchess of Rutland, 144, 145, 147

Mannix, Sir Henry, of Cork, dupe of Dr John Bell, 197

Maquay, George, sugar baker, of Thomas St, Dublin, 101, 102

Maquay, John Leland, sugar baker, of Thomas St, Dublin, 101, 102

Marsh, James, ironmonger, of Kennedy Lane, Dublin, benefactor to Mrs Leeson during her imprisonment, 239

Marsh, Patrick, upholder and auctioneer, of Bride's Alley, benefactor to Mrs Leeson during her imprisonment, 239

Mathews, Mrs, wife of Captain Benjamin Mathews, 236

Mathews, Captain Benjamin, veteran of the American wars, former client and lover of Mrs Leeson, and proprietor of the Spunging House at Angel Court, Dublin, 47, 48, 57, 58, 60, 128, 153, 232, 233

Mathews, Brigadier-General Richard, 124, 139

Maudsley, John Cavendish, bigamous husband of Mrs C—ll, 190

Maudsley, Mrs, first wife of Maudsley the bigamist, 190

Meade, John, Earl of Clanwilliam, 128

Meade, Richard, Lord Guilford, succeeded as Earl of Clanwilliam (1800), 128

Mears, Mr, guest at the 'May Day Masquerade', 93

Mendoza, Daniel, prize-fighter, 146

Mercer, Mrs, *see* Kate of Aberdeen

Mercer, Lieutenant-Colonel John, probable husband of Kate of Aberdeen, 195, 217

Milltown, Earl of, *see* Leeson, Joseph

Misset, Captain, keeper and victim of Mary Crosbie, 162

Molesworth, Richard Nassau, Viscount Molesworth, guest at the 'May Day Masquerade', 93–4

Monck, Captain, and subsequently Major, Henry, aide-de-camp to the Lord Lieutenant (1783), 113

Moncrieffe, Richard, sheriff of the County of the City of Dublin (1779–80), and subsequently Lord Mayor of Dublin, 70, 71

Mooney, Lawrence, catchpole and bailiff, proprietor of a Spunging House in Angel Alley, Dublin, 205, 233

Moore, Mrs, Procuress, of Capel St, Dublin, 161

Moore, Mrs, wife of John Moore, jeweller, of Inns Quay and Christ Church Lane, 29, 30

Moore, Mrs Jane Elizabeth, writer of verse, 215–16, 243

Moore, John, jeweller, of Inns Quay and Christ Church Lane, Dublin, 29

Morgell, Crosbie, attorney, and Kerry suicide, 128, 209

Morrison, Mr, of Cork, dupe of Dr John Bell, 197

Mulligan, Mr, husband of Mrs Mulligan, and would-be pimp, 233

Mulligan, Mrs, prisoner at Mathews's Spunging House, 233, 234–5

Murray, Bernard, cheesemonger, of South Great George's St, Dublin, attendant at Mrs Leeson's funeral, 251

'Nathan', Lord Mayor of Dublin, see Warren, Nathaniel

Neill, Mary, prostitute, petty thief, victim of a double rape allegedly by the Earl of Carhampton and Francis Higgins assisted by Robert Edgeworth and Margaret Llewellyn, briefly employed by Mrs Leeson as companion, 243

Neilson, Jenny, prostitute, 145, 212

Neilson, Mary, of Ballyclear, prostitute, 152

Netterville, Mrs Katherine (Kitty Cut-a-Dash), courtezan and beauty, professional rival of Mrs Leeson (1770s), 50, 51, 52, 63, 93, 117, 118, 143, 152, 161

Newburgh, Mrs, widow of the minor poet Colonel Thomas Newburgh, defrauder of Mrs Leeson, 246

Nost, John Van, see Van Nost, John

Nowlan, Edward, editor of the *Freeman's Journal*, guest at the 'Masonic Masquerade', 167

Nugent, Michael, grocer, of South Great George's St, Dublin, 162

O'B—, Mr, attorney and defrauder of Mrs Leeson, 230

O'B—, Mr, gambler present at Daly's Club during the hoax on Buck English, 217

O'Brien, Mr, client, and then squire of Mrs M'Clean, during the Killarney holiday, 186, 187

O'Brien, Mrs, brothel-keeper and procuress, of Longford St, Dublin, 132, 198

O'Brien, Cornelius, merchant, of Fleet St, Dublin, 232

O'C—, M—, client and defrauder of Mrs Leeson, 229

O'Connor, Mr, shopkeeper of Castleisland, second husband of Deborah Casey, the prostitute, 244

O'Driscoll, Denis, 'Cap of the Pye', of Ballydehob, County Cork, 203

O'Falvey, Mr, husband of Elizabeth O'Falvey, friend and benefactor to Mrs Leeson, 179, 186, 187, 240–1

O'Falvey, Mrs Elizabeth (*alias* Betty Quigley, *alias* Elizabeth Bennet), reformed prostitute and friend of Mrs Leeson, 177–9, 186–8, 190, 226, 227, 240–1

O'Gallagher, Charles (Blind Charley), of Dublin, ballad hawker and singer, 169

O'Meagher, Brian, barrister, of Mabbot St, Dublin, 148

O'R—, James, 162

Orde, Mr, Keeper, pimp, and subsequently husband of Bridget Orde, 165–6

Orde, Mrs Bridget, prostitute, brothel-keeper and procuress, of Great Britain St, Dublin, 161, 163, 165–6

O'Reilly, Mr, Mrs Leeson's first suitor, 8, 9

Orange Lodge, Belfast, verses dedicated to, printed by Thomas Wilkinson, 178

O'Reilly, Miss A. Mrs Leeson's mother, wife of Mathew Plunket, of Killough, County Westmeath, 5, 19

Orleans, Duc d', see Bourbon-Orleans, Louis Philippe Joseph de

Ormsby, Captain William, governor of the Four Courts Marshalsea, 148, 239

Ottiwell, Henry, alleged husband of Mary Atkinson, 164

Ottiwell, Mrs Mary, see Atkinson, Mary

P—, Mr, keeper of Mrs Vallance, 154

P—d, Mrs, widow, and mistress of the artist W— R—n, 235

P—l, Mr, rescuer of Mrs Leeson and Deborah Casey from highwaymen, 245

P—t, John (Jack), gambler present in Daly's Club during hoax on Buck English, 217

P—y, Jonas, 155, 159

Packenham, Captain, 123

Paine, Miss Eliza, of Tralee, 219

Palliser, Nelly, prostitute, 124

Palmer, Mr, admirer of Kitty Gore, 132

Palmer, Captain, husband to Mrs Palmer, the prostitute, 159

Palmer, Mrs, prostitute, 159

Pearson, Mr, guest at the 'May Day Masquerade', 93

Pearson, Mrs, mutual friend of Mrs Leeson and Robert Gorman, 121, 124

Pedero, Miss, of Bow Bridge, Dublin, prostitute, guest at 'Masonic Masquerade', 153

Pelham, Thomas, Chief Secretary of State for Ireland, 201

Petty, William, Earl of Shelbourne, and subsequently Marquis of Landsdowne, 208

Phillips, Miss, Rowd, prostitute discharged by Mrs Leeson from Pitt St, 191–2

Phillips, the Rev. George, client and friend of Mrs Brooks, 146, 153

Pinking-dindies, street gang composed mainly of students from Trinity College, under the leadership of Richard Crosbie, 69–71, 79

Plunket, Christopher, of Killough, Mrs Leeson's brutal elder brother, 6–10, 13, 15, 16, 27

Plunket, Garret, of Killough, Mrs Leeson's younger brother, 13, 14, 27

Plunket, H—, of High St, Dublin, one of Mrs Leeson's disapproving relations, 26

Plunket, John (Jack), guest at the 'Masonic Masquerade', 167

Plunket, Mathew, of Killough, Mrs Leeson's father, 5, 6, 13, 14, 18, 20, 21, 27

Pope, Mr, of Cork, dupe of Dr John Bell, 197

Porter, Mr, husband and pimp to Margaret Porter, 181–2

Porter, Margaret (née Whittle), of Mark St, Dublin, probably the kept woman of the Duke of Leinster, 181–2

Pottinger, Mrs Ann, Belfast socialite (1770s & 1780s), 206

Power, Richard, Baron of the Exchequer and suicide, 209

Preston, William, playwright (author of Democratic Rage), 167, 202

Printers and Booksellers, Company of, see Company of Printers and Booksellers

Prudence, sister of Faith, innkeeper (the Angel tavern), 200–1

Purcell, Mr, client of Mrs Leeeson at Pitt St, her squire during the holiday in the Ring of Kerry in June 1789, and her co-prisoner in Mathew's Spunging House, 186, 197, 188, 189, 236–8

Queade, Lady G— (of the Stratford family), accused by Mrs Leeson of theft, 145

Quigley, Elizabeth (Betty), prostitute, see O'Falvey, Mrs Elizabeth

R—, Colonel, guest at the 'Masonic Masquerade', 153

R—, Stephen, ministerial agent at the Carrickfergus election of 1784, 201

R—l, A—, 'the Broganier Fool', client of Mrs Leeson at Pitt St, 205

R—n, W—, artist and portrait painter, 235, 236

Ramage, Mr, of Smith & Ramage, Merchant Bankers, New York, 53

Read, Mary, prostitute, guest at the 'Masonic Masquerade, 143, 159

Redding, Mrs, procuress and friend of Mrs Leeson, guest at the 'May Day Masquerade', 93

Rice, Edward (Beau), jeweller and money lender, of Capel St, Dublin, 153, 154

Roberts, Captain, guest at the 'Masonic Masquerade', 167

Roberts, Mr, of Bachelors' Walk, Dublin, keeper of Mary Roberts, 180

Roberts, Mary, prostitute, 180–1

Robinson, Mrs, prostitute, guest at the 'Masonic Masquerade', 153

Robinson, Henry, high constable of the City of Dublin, chief of security at the 'May Day Masquerade', 93

Robespierre, Maximilien Marie Isadore, 197

Roche, Sir Boyle, MP (Sir B. Balderdash), 200, 203

Roe, Ebeneezer Radford, 152

Roe, George, keeper of Newgate Prison, 89

Roe, Mary (Moll), courtezan and beauty,

subsequently Mrs Walsh, 218

Roque, John, cartographer, 218

Ross, Mrs, procuress, 130, 131

Rouviere, Joseph, oculist, of Great Ship St, Dublin, 217

Rowan, Archibald Hamilton, United Irishman, eccentric, and champion of Mary Neill, 243

Rumford, Count, *see* Thompson, Sir Benjamin, Count Rumford, experimental physicist

Russel, Francis, Duke of Bedford, 147

Russel, Miss Mary, of Limerick, prostitute employed by Mrs Brooks at Trinity St, arsonist, 146, 147, 152

Rutland, Duchess of, *see* Manners, Mary Isabella (*née* Somerset), Duchess of Rutland

Rutland, Duke of, *see* Manners, Charles

S—, Countess of, 187

S—, Mr, barrister to whom Mr Mulligan attempted to sell his wife's sexual services, 233, 234

S—, Mr, early client of Bridget Orde, 165

S—, Mr, justice and guager, 153

S—, Mr, of Ormond Quay, Dublin, defrauder of Mrs Leeson, 246

S—, Mrs, of Dublin, dupe of Dr John Bell, 196

S—, Mrs, friend and correspondent of Mrs Leeson following her retirement, 226

S—, John, 150

S—, I— P—, guest at the 'Masonic Masquerade', 167

S—al—y, Mr (holiday acquaintance, Killarney, June 1789), 188

S—al—y, Mrs (holiday acquaintance, Killarney, June 1789), 188

S—e, Mr, husband of Mrs S—e, the Cork prostitute, 187

S—e, Mrs, of Cork, prostitute, 187

S—l, Charles, gambler present at Daly's Club during hoax on Buck English, 217

S—t—y, Mr, petty thief, 203

S—y, Colonel, 214

St Giorgio, Signor, Italian musician and impressario, 87

St Lawrence, William, Lord St Lawrence,

succeeded as Earl of Howth in 1801, guest at the 'May Day Masquerade', 93

St Leger, Mr, of Cork, dupe of Dr John Bell, 197

St Leger, the Hon. Richard, captain, and aide-de-camp to the Lord Lieutenant in 1783, 112

Sands, Miss, prostitute working with Mrs M'Clean in 1793, 222

Scott, Mr, guest at the 'Masonic Masquerade', 167

Scott, Margaret (*née* Lawless), Countess of Clonmel, 35

Scriven, Miss, friend of Mrs Leeson, of Stephen's Green, Dublin, and subesquently Bombay, 139

Seguin, Peter, guest at the 'Masonic Masquerade', 167

Shannon, Mrs, of Tullamore, County Offaly, 11, 12

Sharman, Miss, John Lawless's London mistress, 81, 82

Sharman, William, 147

Shaw, Robert, Dublin philanthropist renowned for his relief work in debtors' prisons, 230

Shee, the widow, mistress of Squire Walpole, 214

Shelbourne, Earl of, *see* Petty, William

Sheridan, Mr, catchpole and bailiff, associate of Lawrence Mooney, 205

Simpson, Mr, innkeeper and lodging house proprietor, Crown Alley, Dublin, 152

Sinnot, the Hon. Mrs, courtezan and mistress to the Earl of Westmorland, 145, 156, 181, 182

Slack, Mary, mother of Mrs Palmer the prostitute, 159

Smith, Mr, Dublin merchant and door keeper at 'May Day Masquerade', 93

Smith, Mr, brother-in-law to Mrs Leeson, 5, 9, 10, 11, 12, 13

Smith, Mr, of Smith & Ramage, merchant bankers, New York, 53

Smith, Mrs, elder sister to Mrs Leeson, 5, 6, 16, 26

Snowe, Mr, of Cork, dupe of Dr John Bell, 197

Southwell, Captain William, of Little Dargle, Rathfarnham, County Dublin, 198

Sp—r, Lieutenant, keeper of Nancy Hinds, 157, 158

Stanley, Arthur, merchant, of Bride St, benefactor to Mrs Leeson during her imprisonment, 239

States of Castle-Kelly (The), also known as Anecdote Club of Free Brothers, 169

Sterling, Mrs, brothel-keeper and procuress, of Jervis St, Dublin, 132, 159, 198

Stevenson, Mrs, of Belfast, prostitute, *see* Brooks

Strange, Mr, early potential client of Mrs Leeson, 29

Stratford, family to which Lady Fitz Herbert and Lady G— Queade both belonged, 145

Sturgeon, Mrs, prostitute and procuress, 152

Swords, Thomas, bricklayer, of Leeson St, Dublin, benefactor to Mrs Leeson during her imprisonment, 239

Synan, Father, 'the Protestant priest' of Cork, dupe of Dr John Bell, 197

T—, Dr, benefactor to Mrs Leeson during her imprisonment, 239

T—, Mrs, Mrs Leeson's landlady in Clarendon St, Dublin, 243, 248, 249

T—my, Captain, 203

T—s, Mr, client of Miss Mary Russel during the brothel fire in Trinity St, 146, 147

T—y, Miss, of Carrickfergus, 218

Talbot, Richard Wogan, briefly MP for the County of Dublin (1791–2), 221

Taylour, Thomas, Earl of Bective, and subsequently Marquis of Headfort, guest at the 'May Day Masquerade', 93, 207

Thompson, Sir Benjamin, Count Rumford, experimental physicist, 201–2

Thurot, François, captain in the French navy (d.1760), 218

Tinkler, George, paper stainer, of South Great George's St, Dublin, benefactor to Mrs Leeson during her imprisonment, and attendant at her funeral, 239, 251

Townly, Miss, prostitute, friend of Moll Hall, 88

Townshend, Colonel, 203

Townshend, Edward (Ned), of Whitehall, County Cork, officer in 'the Jolly Dogs', 191, 192, 203

Townshend, John, of Thornhill, County Cork, 203

Travers, Mr, of Cork, dupe of Dr John Bell, 197

Tresham, Mr, Richard Daly's box keeper at the Theatre Royal (Smock Alley), 90, 91

Trotter, Mr, friend of James Cavendish, 50, 51

Tuckey, the Rev. Charles, of Skibbereen, County Cork. 203

U—, J—, keeper of Mary Crosbie, 161

Ussher, John, apothecary, of Dame St, Dublin, 155

V—, attorney or barrister, benefactor to Mrs Leeson during her imprisonment, 239

V—y, Miss, Eliza Edmond's Mother, 227

Vallance, Mrs, prostitute and kept woman, 154–5

Vance, William, surgeon, of College Green, Dublin, 70, 71

Vangable, horsewoman, and performer at Astley's Amphitheatre, 226

Van Nost, John, sculptor, and part-time private eye, 41–2

Vaughan, Colonel John, 207

W—, Lieutenant in the RN, petty thief, 109–10

W—, Mr, rescuer of Mrs Leeson and Deborah Casey from highwaymen, 245

W—, Mrs, of Temple Bar, Dublin, Mrs Leeson's landlady at the time of her death, 249, 251

W—, C—, keeper of Mary Crosbie, 161

W—, H—, of Fethard, County Tipperary, guest at the 'Masonic Masquerade', 152, 206

W—l—n, Mr, 'the Flat', client of Mrs Leeson at Pitt St, 205

W—ms, Lieutenant, lover of Margaret Porter, 181

W—n, James, keeper of Mary Ford, 160, 166

W—r, Miss, of Dublin, dupe of Dr John Bell, 196

Wallace, Mr, surgeon on *The Race Horse*, 120, 121

Wallace, Joseph, of Carrickfergus, 218

Walpole, 'Squire', the Widow Shee's lover, and Kitty Doran's husband, 214

Walsh, Captain, husband of Moll Roe, 217

Walsh, Robert, singer and lover of Maria Ford, 166

Walsh, Mrs *see* Roe, Mary

Warren, Nathaniel, Lord Mayor of Dublin, and subsequently MP for the City of Dublin, guest at the 'May Day Masquerade', 93, 124

Warren, Sir Robert, of Cork, dupe of Dr John Bell, 197

Wassey, Mr, of Cork, dupe of Dr John Bell, 197

Watson, William (Billy), printer and bookseller, attendant at Mrs Leeson's funeral, 251

Watson's Almanack, used by Mrs Leeson as a mailing list in the distribution and sale of her *Memoirs*, 243

Weems, Nancy, prostitute, guest at the 'May Day Masquerade', 93, 124

Weir, David, master-builder of Denziel St, Dublin, benefactor to Mrs Leeson, during her imprisonment, 239

Wellesley, Richard, Earl of Mornington, father to the Duke of Wellington, client and friend of Mrs Brooks, 146

Wesley, the Rev. Charles, preacher, and co-founder of the Methodist Church, 221

Wesley, the Rev. John, preacher, and co-founder of the Methodist Church 221

West, Mrs Elinore, prostitute, 162

West, John, barrister, keeper of Bridget Orde, 165

West, John, father of Bridget Orde, 165

Westmorland, Countess of, *see* Fane, Sarah Ann

Westmorland, Earl of, *see* Fane, John

Westport, Lord, courtesy title of the heir to the Earldom of Altamount, *see* Browne

Westrop, Mr, of Cork, dupe of Dr John Bell, 197

Whaley, John, brother of Thomas (Buck)

Whaley, and troublesome client of Mrs Leeson, 112

Whaley, Thomas (Buck Whaley), probable keeper of Mrs John Magee, 175

White, Mr, of Cork, dupe of Dr John Bell, 197

Whitfield, the Rev. George, prominent Methodist preacher, 221

Whittle, Margaret, prostitute, *see* Porter, Mrs Margaret, prostitute

'Wiggy', Tullamore Grocer and third Suitor of Mrs Leeson, 10, 11

Wilkinson, Thomas (Tommy), printer and bookseller, of Winetavern St, Dublin, 178

Wilson, Joseph, of Belfast, portraitist, 175

Wilson's Directory, used by Mrs Leeson as a mailing list in the distribution and sale of her *Memoirs*, 243

Wilton, Mr, box keeper at the Theatre Royal (Smock Alley), 88, 89

Wolfe, James, 167

Wolfe, Theobald, barrister, of Aungier St, Dublin, 71

Worthington, William, sheriff of the County of the City of Dublin (1779), subsequently Lord Mayor of Dublin, and also knighted, 70, 71, 153

Wrixon, Mr, husband and pimp to Mrs Wrixon, the prostitute, formerly a butcher's boy, of Liverpool, 158–9

Wrixon, Mrs, prostitute, formerly of Liverpool, 158–9

Wybrants, James, proprietor of the Liffey Ferry, 86

Wynne, Mrs brothel-keeper and procuress, of Summerhill, Dublin, 130, 131, 132

Y—, Mr, seducer of Deborah Casey, 221

Yelverton, Barry, Chief Baron of the Exchequer, and subsequently Earl of Avonmore, briefly Mrs Leeson's father in law, 169

Yelverton, Barry (Junior), second son of Barry Yelverton, Chief Baron of the Exchequer, briefly married to Mrs Leeson, 166, 168–9, 221

THE

L I F E

OF

Mrs. MARGARET LEESON

ALIAS

PEG PLUNKET.

WRITTEN BY HERSELF:

In which are given *Anecdotes* and *Sketches* of the LIVES and
BON MOTS of fome of the moſt CELEBRATED CHARACTERS

IN

GREAT-BRITAIN AND IRELAND,

PARTICULARLY OF ALL THE

FILLES DES JOYS

AND

MEN OF PLEASURE AND GALLANTRY,

*Who usually frequented her CITHEREAN TEMPLE for theſe
Thirty Years past.*

THREE VOLUMES COMPLETE IN ONE.
A NEW EDITION WITH CONSIDERABLE ADDITIONS.

" She was 'tis true MOST FRAIL, and yet so JUST,
" That NATURE when ſhe form'd her knew not where——
" To claſs her."——
" A Dame of higheſt VIRTUE and of TRUTH,
" Or the POOR WRETCH that ſhe has chànc'd to be."
ANONYMOUS.

D U B L I N:
PRINTED AND SOLD BY THE PRINCIPAL BOOKSELLERS
1798.

Price ſewed, 5s. 5d.

Richard Crosbie (1755-1800), aeronaut and duellist, who led the gang of Pinking-dindies that wrecked Mrs Leeson's first brothel in Drogheda Street in November 1779.

David La Touche (1729-1817), Bank of Ireland Governor and regular client at Mrs Leeson's second brothel in Wood Street.

Charles Duke of Rutland appointed LORD LIEUTENANT and Governor General of the Kingdom of Ireland Feb.y 1784 Died there Oct.r 24th 1787 Universally Lamented

Her Grace The DUTCHESS of RUTLAND.

rles Manners (1754-87), Duke of and and Lord Lieutenant of Ireland. nest Charley' was Mrs Leeson's most ortant client when she opened her third hel in Pitt Street.

Mary Isabella Manners (1756-1831), Duchess of Rutland, as much a mistress of the art of pleasing as Mrs Leeson herself.

John Magee (d. 1809), proprietor of the *Dublin Evening Post*. 'The Man of Ireland', bitter opponent of Francis Higgins— a crusading journalist liked and respected by Mrs Leeson.

Francis Higgins (?1746-1802), proprietor of the *Freeman's Journal*. 'The Sham Squire', fraudster and spymaster, he proved an unexpected friend to Mrs Leeson when imprisoned in Mathew's Spunging House.

Barry Yelverton (1736-1805), Chief Baron of the Exchequer, subsequently Earl of Avonmore, briefly Mrs Leeson's father-in-law.

Frederick Augustus Hervey (1730-1803), Earl of Bristol and Bishop of Derry. A former client, he sent Mrs Leeson a timely fifty guineas after she had been robbed of her possessions by Mary Neill.

John Fane (1759-1841), Earl of Westmorland and Lord Lieutenant of Ireland. He was so cruel to his first wife that Mrs Leeson refused to accept him as a client.

Blackrock, County Dublin, in 1744 (from an engraving by Giles King, based on a painting by William Jones), where Mrs Leeson had hoped to enjoy her retirement.